Principles and Practice of Structural Equation Modeling
Second Edition

Methodology in the Social Sciences
David A. Kenny, *Series Editor*

This series provides applied researchers and students with analysis and research design books that emphasize the use of methods to answer research questions. Rather than emphasizing statistical theory, each volume in the series illustrates when a technique should (and should not) be used and how the output from available software programs should (and should not) be interpreted. Common pitfalls as well as areas of further development are clearly articulated.

PRINCIPLES AND PRACTICE OF
STRUCTURAL EQUATION MODELING

SECOND EDITION

Rex B. Kline

Series Editor's Note by David A. Kenny

THE GUILFORD PRESS
New York   London

© 2005 The Guilford Press
A Division of Guilford Publications, Inc.
72 Spring Street, New York, NY 10012
www.guilford.com

Printed in the United States of America

This book is printed on acid-free paper.

Last digit is print number: 9   8   7   6   5

Library of Congress Cataloging-in-Publication Data

Kline, Rex B.
  Principles and practice of structural equation modeling /
  Rex B. Kline.— 2nd ed.
    p.   cm. — (Methodology in the social sciences)
  Includes bibliographical references and index.
  ISBN-13 978-1-57230-690-5 (pbk.)
  ISBN-10 1-57230-690-4 (pbk.)
  ISBN-13 978-1-59385-075-3 (hardcover)
  ISBN-10 1-59385-075-1 (hardcover)
    1. Multivariate analysis.   2. Social sciences—Statistical
methods—Data processing.   3. Statistics—Mathematical
models.   I. Title.   II. Series.
QA278.K585 2005
519.5′35—dc22
                                                2004019784

For William C. Kline (1934–2003)

Beauty is a function of truth, truth a function of beauty. They can be separated by analysis but in the lived experience of the creative act—and of its re-creative echo in the beholder—they are as inseparable as thought is inseparable from emotion.

—ARTHUR KOESTLER (1964/1989, p. 331)

About the Author

Rex B. Kline, PhD, is an associate professor of Psychology at Concordia University in Montréal. Since earning a PhD in psychology, his areas of research and writing have included the psychometric evaluation of cognitive abilities, child clinical assessment, structural equation modeling, and usability engineering in computer science. Dr. Kline has published three books and more than 40 articles in research journals and is the coauthor of a teacher-informant rating scale for referred children. He lives with his wife and two children in Montréal.

Series Editor's Note

Second editions, like movie sequels, are usually not as good as the originals, except in unique cases. This is one of them. Just as the field of structural equation modeling (SEM) has evolved, so has Kline's book.

SEM is an analytic tool that is entering into middle adulthood. Its parentage is clear: Sewall Wright is the father, but Otis Dudley Duncan served as an able stepparent during its early years. As a young child it wondered about, but never really knew, the pleasures of latent variables. It had an awkward adolescent period in which it clung to the computer program LISREL as an identity marker. It owes a great deal to Peter Bentler and Ken Bollen, who guided it through its late adolescence. It is now mature, but new features are still being explored.

Kline's book has matured, too. Certainly, there was much to like in Rex Kline's first edition of *Principles and Practice of Structural Equation Modeling*. For consumers of structural equations rather than experts, it was replete with practical advice and explained complicated topics in simple and direct language. Another strength was that it included examples from a broad range of social and behavioral sciences—clinical psychology, education, cognitive science, behavioral medicine, and developmental psychology. Most of all, I think what made the first edition such a great book was Kline's contagious enthusiasm for the topic. He believed that the method, when properly applied, could answer important research questions. His intellectual passion for the topic was clearly evident.

So why, then, a second edition? There are several reasons. First, the field has new software and new versions of the old software. Many of these programs have added a graphical interface, which enables one to estimate a model in minutes. The difference is great: it used to be when I taught the subject in class, I lectured for 3 hours to explain how to estimate a model using the computer program LISREL. Now I show students how to do it in minutes. The second edition incorporates these new programs; plus the data and program syntax files on the accompanying Web page (www.guilford.com/pr/kline.htm) will give readers a strong sense of computer-based SEM.

A second feature of the new edition is its recognition of new topics: where we used to discard sample means in the statistical garbage heap, they are in fact ripe with information. So the book now discusses how they are included in a model. Kline has added a chapter on growth curve analysis, and he has added coverage of multilevel SEM and expanded the coverage of the relation between measurement models and structural models

These new and expanded topics relate to the third reason for a new edition. The book now has much more technical detail. Quite honestly, though I loved the first edition for its accessible explanation of SEM, I felt I didn't necessarily learn that much about SEM I didn't know. With the second edition, however, I learned a great deal, and much of what I learned, I thought I already knew! Kline has explained old topics in a way that sheds light on their fundamental meaning. He has managed to explain difficult concepts in a way that both novices can understand and experts can still learn something new.

There are many ways to measure SEM's importance as a method. Many universities have courses on the topic, there are over 10 computer programs that estimate such models, and there is extensive discussion of the methods on the Internet. By far the best measure, though, is that researchers actually use it. It is virtually impossible these days to pick up an issue of an empirical journal in the social sciences and not find at least one paper that uses SEM. Researchers love SEM because it addresses the questions they want answered. Perhaps more than any other technique, SEM "thinks" about research the way researchers do.

The first edition of this book was the inaugural volume in The Guilford Press series Methodology in the Social Sciences. I described it as "an intelligent, practical, and detailed introduction of a method that has become essential in the social and behavioral sciences." This second edition is its worthy successor.

DAVID A. KENNY

Preface and Acknowledgments

That the first edition of this book was so positively received by researchers, instructors, students, and reviewers (e.g., Beaubien, 2000; Glaser, 2000, 2002; Millman, 1998; Santor, 1999; Steiger, 2001) was very gratifying. Like the first edition, this second edition is intended as an accessible work about the principles and practice of structural equation modeling (SEM) for readers without extensive quantitative backgrounds. Accordingly, fundamental concepts of SEM are presented here in words and figures and not matrix algebra. Matrix algebra can convey a lot of information in a relatively small amount of space, but one must already be familiar with linear algebra to decode the message. Other works that better explain the mathematical foundations of SEM are cited throughout this book, and these works should be consulted by those interested in such presentations. Also, as in the first edition, many examples from various disciplines illustrate the application of SEM to actual research problems. Some of these examples were selected because there were technical problems in the analysis, such as when a computer program terminates its run with error messages. These examples give a context for discussing how to handle various problems that can crop up in SEM analyses.

Differences between the first and second editions are outlined next. The review of basic statistical concepts is now presented over two chapters. The first of these, Chapter 2, deals mainly with fundamental concepts of correlation, regression, and statistical tests. Readers with relatively strong backgrounds in these areas may be able to skim or skip this chapter. However, all readers should pay close attention to the material presented in Chapter 3, which concerns the preparation and screening of the data and basic principles of score reliability and validity (i.e., measurement theory). A total of eight different SEM computer programs are described in this edition (Chapter 4), compared with only three in the previous edition. Most researchers who apply SEM use one of these computer programs. There is a clearer separation of the coverage of core SEM techniques, such as confirmatory factor analysis, versus that of more advanced techniques, such as multiple-sample SEM. Specifically, Part II of this book deals with core SEM techniques only, and more advanced kinds of analyses are covered in Part III. Chapter 10 is a new chapter about the analysis of means in general and latent growth models for longitudinal data in particular. The presentations in all chapters have been updated to reflect changes in the state of the art and practice in SEM. Finally, there is also a home page on the Internet for this edition. From this home page, readers can download data summaries and computer program syntax files for many of the research examples discussed in this book. There are also other resources for instructors and students on this book's home page.

It was a pleasure again to work with the series editor, David A. Kenny, who is also one of my role models as a writer and thinker. C. Deborah Laughton, the Methodology and Statistics Publisher at The Guilford Press, arranged for several reviews of an earlier version of Parts I and II that were very helpful in producing the final version. Thanks, too, to these reviewers: Alexander von Eye, Department of Psychology, Michigan State University; Larry Price, Department of Education, Texas State University–San Marcos; Xitao Fan, Department of Education, University of Virginia; and Fred E. Markowitz, Department of Sociology, Northern Illinois University. The Guilford production editor, William Meyer, did a fine job with the technically challenging manuscript. I also received many constructive comments from members of SEMNET, an electronic discussion group for SEM, about an earlier version of Chapter 12, which deals with avoiding mistakes in SEM. (Information about SEMNET is presented in Chapter 1.) Also thanks to Werner Wothke of SmallWaters (Amos), Linda Muthén of Muthén and Muthén (Mplus), Peter Bentler of Multivariate Software

(EQS), Jim Steiger of Vanderbilt University (SEPATH), Leo Stam of Scientific Software (LISREL), and Michael Neale of Virginia Commonwealth University (Mx) for their comments on earlier drafts of descriptions of SEM computer programs. And the biggest thanks of all to my wife, Joanna, daughter, Julia Anne, and son, Luke Christopher.

Web address for *Principles and Practice of Structural Equation Modeling*, Second Edition: www.guilford.com/pr/kline.htm

Contents

 **Part I**

Fundamental Concepts

1

Introduction

This book is intended to serve as a guide to the principles, assumptions, strengths, limitations, and application of structural equation modeling (SEM) for researchers and students who do not have extensive quantitative backgrounds. Some familiarity with basic concepts such as correlation is assumed, but higher levels of statistical knowledge are not required before reading this book. Accordingly, the presentation is conceptually rather than mathematically oriented, the use of formulas and symbols is kept to a minimum, and many examples are offered of the application of SEM to a wide variety of research problems in psychology, education, and health sciences, among other areas. This book also has a home page on the Internet.[1] From the home page, readers can freely access support materials for this book, including data and program syntax files for many of the research examples, resources for instructors and students, and links to related Web pages. It is hoped that readers who complete this book will have acquired the skills necessary to begin to use SEM in their own research in a reasoned, disciplined way.

1.1 PLAN OF THE BOOK

The topic of SEM is very broad and every aspect of it cannot be covered comprehensively in a single volume. With this reality in mind, the main goals of this book are to introduce the fundamental concepts that underlie most facets of SEM and some more advanced techniques that

[1]www.guilford.com/pr/kline.htm

allow additional kinds of hypotheses to be tested. A learning-by-doing approach is strongly encouraged and is facilitated by two things. First, the data for every example reviewed in this book are summarized in tables, which allows the reader to reproduce any of the analyses discussed here. Many of these data summaries can also be downloaded from this book's Web site. Second, several widely used SEM computer programs are described in Chapter 4, including Amos, EQS, and LISREL, among others, and student versions of some of these programs are freely available over the Internet. (Links to these sites are provided in later chapters.) Readers who at present have no experience using an SEM computer program are not at any disadvantage, however. This is because the presentation in this book of fundamental concepts in SEM is not based on a particular software package. (More about this point later.)

Part I introduces ideas and vocabulary that are essential to understanding the general rationale of SEM. The latter part of the present chapter is about characteristics that all facets of SEM have in common. The main goal of Chapters 2 and 3 is to review basic statistical principles that form the foundation for learning more about SEM. Topics such as bivariate and multivariate correlation and regression, the rationale of statistical significance testing, and other fundamental statistical concepts are covered in Chapter 2. Readers already quite familiar with these topics may be able to skip this chapter. However, all readers should pay close attention to Chapter 3, which deals with the screening and preparation of data for SEM, a topic so important that it is considered before any specific techniques are described in detail. Ways to identify and rectify potential problems, such as severely nonnormal distributions, missing data, and outliers, are covered in this chapter. Chapter 4 builds a conceptual context for SEM relative to other, more conventional kinds of statistical methods such as multiple regression. Assumptions and examples of the types of research questions that can (and cannot) be evaluated with different types of analytical methods are considered. Chapter 4 also describes a total of eight different SEM computer programs. All of these programs can estimate a wide range of structural equation models, and most researchers use one of them to conduct SEM analyses.

Part II consists of four chapters devoted to basic SEM techniques. The majority of SEM analyses described in the research literature involve these core techniques. Chapters 5 and 6 are about path analysis. Path analysis is the original SEM technique, and path models concern effects among observed variables. The conceptual foundations of path analysis are introduced in Chapter 5, and Chapter 6 deals with the specifics of analyzing path models and testing hypotheses. Most of the issues considered in these chapters generalize to the analysis of models where hypothetical constructs are represented as latent variables. Their introduction in chapters that deal with path analysis reflects a pedagogical goal of ensuring that readers understand fundamental issues in SEM concerning observed variables before dealing with the added complexities of analyzing latent variables. The next two chapters are about standard kinds of latent variable models in SEM. Chapter 7 deals with the technique of confirmatory factor analysis (CFA) of measurement models. Chapter 8 extends these ideas to structural regression (SR or "hybrid") models that have features of both path models and factor analysis models. It is possible to evaluate a wide variety of hypotheses with these core SEM techniques, as is demonstrated with numerous examples.

Part III is concerned with advanced methods and avoiding common mistakes in SEM. Chapter 9 is concerned with the analysis of models with feedback loops, which reflect the presumption of mutual causal effects among two or more variables measured at the same time. These kinds of models require some special considerations in their analysis compared with more standard models where causal effects are represented as unidirectional (i.e., from presumed cause to effect but not in the reverse direction). Chapter 10 deals with the analysis of means in SEM, including latent growth models, and Chapter 11 is about the analysis of structural equation models across multiple samples. The latter type of analysis is concerned with whether a model has generalizability across more than one population. Chapter 12 is written as a "how-not-to" manual that summarizes ways that researchers can mislead themselves with SEM. Although most of these points are mentioned in earlier chapters in the book in the context of particular SEM techniques, they are all considered together in this chapter. Chapter 13 provides an overview of two additional advanced methods in SEM. These include the estimation of interaction or curvilinear effects of latent variables and the analysis of multilevel structural equation models for hierarchical data sets where some units are clustered under other units, such as students within classrooms. Although these methods cannot be covered in detail in a single chapter, this review is intended to at least make the reader aware of even more possibilities in SEM and provide pertinent references.

1.2 NOTATION

As with other statistical techniques, there is no "gold standard" for notation in SEM. Although the symbol set associated with the LISREL program is probably the most widely used in books and journal articles about SEM, it features a profusion of subscripted Greek letters (e.g., Φ_{11} or Λ_{31}) and matrix algebra that can be confusing to follow unless the reader has memorized the entire system. Instead, a minimum number of alphabetic characters are used to represent various aspects of SEM such as observed variables versus latent variables. Also, to avoid double notation, a distinction is not usually made between population values and sample statistics. It is assumed that readers are already aware of this difference and know that sample data can only be considered as estimates of population values.

1.3 COMPUTER PROGRAMS FOR SEM

Computer programs are important tools for the conduct of SEM. About 30 years ago, LISREL was essentially the only widely available SEM program. The situation is now very different, however, as there are many other choices of SEM computer programs including Amos, CALIS, EQS, Mplus, Mx Graph, RAMONA, and SEPATH, among others. *For this reason, the presentation of concepts in this book is not linked to a particular SEM computer program.* Instead, essential principles of SEM that users of *any* computer tool must understand are emphasized. In other words, the book is more like a guide to writing style and composition than a guide to how to use a particular word processing program. Nevertheless, the aforementioned chapter (4) about features of the SEM computer programs just listed should be helpful to readers who intend to use one of them for their own analyses.

Two further comments about SEM computer programs are warranted. First, it used to be that these types of programs were difficult to use, for two reasons. They required users to generate a lot of rather arcane code for each analysis, which was a time-consuming, tedious, and error-prone process. They also tended to be available only on mainframe computers, which required batch-file-type programming with stark command-line user interfaces. The increasing availability of powerful microprocessors and large amounts of memory and storage on affordable personal computers has dramatically changed both of these situations, however. Specifically, statistical software programs for personal computers with graphical user interfaces are much easier to use than their character-based predecessors. "User friendliness" in contemporary SEM computer programs is a near-revolution compared with older programs.

As an example of the issues just mentioned, consider a feature of the most recent versions of Amos, EQS, LISREL, and Mx Graph for personal computers. Users of any of these packages can still choose to write code in the applications' matrix algebra- or equations-based syntax. As an alternative, however, they can use a graphical editor to draw the model on the screen with boxes, circles, arrows, and so on. The programs then translate the figure into lines of code, which are then used to generate the output. Thus, the user need not know very much about how to write program code in order to conduct a very sophisticated type of statistical analysis. And this means that the importance of highly technical programming skills for the conduct of SEM is likely to diminish even further. For researchers who have a good understanding of the fundamental concepts of SEM, this development can only be a boon—anything that reduces the drudgery and gets one to the results quicker is a benefit.

The second comment is to point out that "push-button modeling" has potential drawbacks. For example, no- or low-effort programming could encourage the use of SEM in an uninformed or careless way. It is thus more important than ever to be familiar with the conceptual bases of SEM. Computer programs, however easy to use, should be only the tools of your knowledge and not its master. Steiger (2001) makes the related point that the emphasis on the ease of use of computer tools can give beginners the false impression that SEM itself is easy. That is, to beginners it may appear that all one has to do is draw the model on the screen and let the computer take care of everything else. However, the reality is that things often can and do go wrong in SEM. Specifically, beginners often quickly discover that analyses fail because of technical problems, including a computer system crash or a terminated program run with many error messages or uninterpretable output (Steiger, 2001). This type of thing happens because actual research problems can be very technical, and the availability of user-friendly SEM computer programs does not change this fact. Accordingly, one of the goals of this book is to point out the kinds of things that can go wrong in SEM and, I hope, provide readers with the conceptual knowledge to deal with problems in the analysis (i.e., to understand what went wrong and why). For the same reason, not all examples of SEM analyses described in later chapters are problem-free. Ways to deal with these problems are suggested in such cases, however.

1.4 STATISTICAL JOURNEYS

Learning to use and understand a new set of statistical procedures is like making a long journey through a strange land. Such a journey requires a substantial commitment of time, patience, and a willingness to tolerate the frustration of some initial uncertainty and inevitable trial and error. But this is one journey that you do not have to make alone. Think of this book as a travel atlas or even as someone to talk to about language and customs, what to see and what to avoid, and what is coming over the horizon. I hope that the combination of a conceptually based approach, numerous examples, and the occasional bit of useful advice presented in this book will help to make this journey a little easier, maybe even enjoyable.

Kühnel (2001) reminds us that learning about SEM has the by-product that students must deal with many fundamental issues of methods and general statistical concepts. One of these issues is measurement: It is impossible to analyze a structural equation model with latent variables that represent hypothetical constructs without thinking about how those constructs are to be measured. Measurement theory is too often neglected nowadays in undergraduate and graduate degree programs in psychology (Frederich, Buday, & Kerr, 2000) and related areas, but SEM requires strong knowledge in this area. The technique of SEM is a priori, which means that the researcher must specify a model in order to conduct the analysis. The model's specification must have some basis, whether it be theory, results of previous studies, or an educated guess that reflects the researcher's domain knowledge and experience. The emphasis SEM places on testing a whole model may be a kind of antidote to overreliance on statistical tests of *individual* hypotheses. Data analysis methods in the behavioral sciences need reform (Kline, 2004), and increased use of model-fitting techniques, including SEM, should be part of that. SEM techniques require that researchers consider alternative models that may explain the same data equally well. Use of SEM (and related techniques) should also foster a better awareness of the difference between a statistical model of reality and reality itself.

Let us begin our journey with an overview of properties common to almost all SEM techniques.

1.5 FAMILY VALUES

The term **structural equation modeling** (SEM) does not designate a single statistical technique but instead refers to a family of related procedures. Other terms such as **covariance structure analysis**, **covariance structure modeling**, or **analysis of covariance structures** are also used in the literature to classify these various techniques together under a single label. These terms are essentially interchangeable but—for clarity's sake—only the first will be used throughout this book. Another term that readers may have encountered is **causal modeling**, which is used mainly in association with the technique of path analysis. This expression may be somewhat dated, however, as it seems to appear less often in the literature nowadays. Although much of the next few chapters concerns various kinds of basic SEM methods, summarized below are some things that most of them have in common. These shared characteristics are first enumerated and then discussed in detail in the following paragraphs:

1. As mentioned, SEM is a priori and requires researchers to think in terms of models. But being a priori does not mean that it is exclusively confirmatory. Many applications of SEM are a blend of exploratory and confirmatory analyses.

2. The explicit representation of the distinction between observed and latent variables is characteristic of many structural equation models. This distinction makes it possible for researchers to test a wide variety of hypotheses.
3. The basic statistic in SEM is the covariance. It is possible, however, to analyze other types of data, such as means.
4. The technique of SEM is not just for nonexperimental (correlational) data. Instead, it is a very flexible analytical tool that can be applied to data from experiments, too.
5. Many standard statistical procedures, including multiple regression, canonical correlation, and the analysis of variance (ANOVA), can be viewed as special cases of SEM.
6. SEM is a *still* a large-sample technique. That is, although there are some recent suggestions in the literature about the analysis of structural equation models in smaller samples (described in later chapters), most applications of SEM still require large samples.
7. It is possible to test many different types of effects for statistical significance in SEM, but the role of statistical tests in the overall analysis is often less important compared with more traditional techniques.

1. *SEM is a priori.* Computer programs used for SEM require researchers to provide a lot of information about things such as which variables are assumed to affect other variables and the directionalities of these effects. These a priori specifications reflect the researcher's hypotheses, and in total they make up the model to be evaluated in the analysis. In this sense, SEM could be viewed as confirmatory. That is, the model is a given at the beginning of the analysis, and one of the main questions to be answered is whether it is supported by the data. But as often happens in SEM, the data may be inconsistent with the model, which means that the researcher must either abandon the model or modify the hypotheses on which it is based. The former option is rather drastic. In practice, researchers more often opt for the second choice, which means the analysis now has a more exploratory tenor as revised models are tested with the same data. A related point concerns the adjective "exploratory," which is often associated with

procedures like multiple regression or exploratory factor analysis. So-called exploratory techniques can also be used to test a priori hypotheses. For example, researchers can specify the order in which predictor variables are entered into a regression equation; they can also instruct a computer program that performs exploratory factor analysis to extract a specified number of factors. Thus, readers should not interpret the terms "confirmatory" and "exploratory" as applied to statistical techniques—SEM or otherwise—in an absolute way.

Jöreskog (1993) expressed the aforementioned ideas more formally by distinguishing among (1) **strictly confirmatory**, (2) **alternative models**, and (3) **model-generating** applications of SEM. The first refers to when the researcher has a single model that is accepted or rejected based on its correspondence to the data. There are few occasions, however, when the scope of model testing is so narrow. The second context may be more frequent than the first but is still restricted to situations where more than one a priori model is available. The last context, model generating, is probably the most common and occurs when an initial model does not fit the data and is modified by the researcher. The altered model is then tested again with the same data. The goal of this process is more to "discover" a model with two properties: It makes theoretical sense, and its statistical correspondence to the data is reasonable.

2. *Observed and latent variables.* Some standard statistical procedures do not offer a convenient way to differentiate between observed and latent variables. For example, ANOVA and multiple regression are concerned with (respectively) means and intercorrelations among observed variables, but neither procedure offers a straightforward way to test hypotheses at a higher level of abstraction. For example, a researcher may believe that dependent variables Y_1, Y_2, and Y_3 tap some common domain that is distinct from the one assessed by Y_4 and Y_5. There is no simple, direct way to represent this specific hypothesis in multiple regression or ANOVA. On the other hand, factor analysis programs, such as those available in widely used general statistical packages, such as SPSS or SAS, seem at first glance to address this issue. After all, a factor is something akin to a hypothetical, latent variable, isn't it? Well, not really—at least not as represented by some widely used exploratory factor analysis algorithms in those general statistical

packages. Although the distinction between observed and latent variables will be discussed in more detail later in the book, an overview is offered below:

a. Models do not necessarily have to have hypothesized latent variables. The evaluation of models that concern effects only among observed variables is certainly possible in SEM.
b. There is more than one type of latent variable, each of which reflects different assumptions about the relation between observed and unobserved variables.
c. Latent variables in SEM can represent a wide range of phenomena. For example, theoretical constructs about characteristics of persons (e.g., phonological processing, verbal reasoning), of higher-level units of analysis (e.g., characteristics of geographic regions), or of measures, such as method effects (e.g., parent vs. teacher informants), can all be represented as latent variables in SEM.
d. The observed-latent distinction also provides a way to take account of imperfect score reliability. This is not to say that SEM can be used as a way to compensate for gross psychometric flaws. It cannot—no technique can—but this aspect of SEM can lend a more realistic quality to an analysis.

3. *Covariances at center stage, but means, too.* Although basic principles of correlations and covariances are covered in more detail in the next chapter, a covariance is briefly defined here. The covariance between two variables, X and Y, is as follows:

$$cov_{XY} = r_{XY} \, SD_X \, SD_Y \qquad (1.1)$$

where r_{XY} is the Pearson correlation between X and Y and where SD_X and SD_Y are their standard deviations. A covariance thus represents the strength of the association between X and Y and their variabilities. Sometimes a covariance is referred to as an unstandardized correlation because it has no bounds on its upper and lower values. For example, covariance values of, say, −1,003.26 or 1,562.71 are possible. In contrast, the value of a correlation can range only from −1 to +1. Although this characteristic of correlations makes for easy interpretation, a covariance conveys more information as a single-number statistic than a correlation.

To say that the covariance is the basic statistic of SEM means that there are two main goals of the analysis: to understand patterns of correlations among a set of variables, and to explain as much of their variance as possible with the model specified by the researcher. The next several chapters are devoted to outlining the rationale behind these goals, but at this point it can be said that essentially all applications of SEM concern these ends. But some researchers, especially those who use ANOVA as their main analytical tool, have the impression that SEM is concerned *solely* with covariances. Although this perception is understandable because so much of the SEM literature is devoted to the analysis of covariances instead of means, it is in fact too narrow. The technique of SEM is actually a very flexible analytical approach that can incorporate the types of effects traditionally associated with ANOVA, including between-group and within-group (e.g., repeated measures) mean comparisons. It is also possible in SEM to test for group mean differences on latent variables, something that is not really feasible in standard ANOVA.

4. *The technique of SEM can be applied to nonexperimental and experimental data.* Another common view of SEM is that it is appropriate only for nonexperimental data. The heavy emphasis on covariances in the SEM literature may be related to this perception, but the foregoing discussion should suggest that this belief is without foundation. For example, between-group comparisons conducted within an SEM framework could involve experimental conditions to which cases are randomly assigned. Suppose that all participants in a study are asked to perform a challenging visual–motor task, such as mirror drawing. Some of these participants are randomly assigned to a condition in which they are told that their task performance reflects their intelligence; the rest of the participants are assigned to a condition in which they are instructed that the task is of trivial importance. Also suppose that the researcher uses four self-report measures of anxiety, two of which are believed to assess state anxiety and the other two trait anxiety. Techniques in SEM might be used to compare the means of the two groups of participants across the anxiety questionnaires and test the hypothesis that the four questionnaires measure two underlying constructs, state and trait anxiety. The technique of ANOVA might be used

to compare group means, but it lacks a direct way to distinguish between observed measures and underlying constructs. Techniques in SEM can also be used in studies that have a mix of experimental and nonexperimental features, as would occur, say, if cases with various psychiatric diagnoses were randomly selected to receive particular types of medications.

5. *The SEM family also includes many standard statistical procedures.* About 35 or so years ago, researchers started to realize that multiple regression and ANOVA are actually the same technique. More specifically, ANOVA is a special case of multiple regression, and both of these procedures are members of what is known as the **general linear model** (GLM). The GLM also includes the multivariate extensions of multiple regression and ANOVA—canonical correlation and multivariate analysis of variance (MANOVA), respectively—as well as exploratory factor analysis. All of these techniques—the whole of the GLM, in fact—are in turn special instances of SEM. Thus, the generality of SEM hinted at in the preceding paragraphs is very broad. In fact, many of the labels we have in our statistical vocabularies are merely conveniences that allow us to quickly associate something with the analysis (e.g., ANOVA, means from one dependent variable are analyzed; MANOVA, means from two or more dependent variables are analyzed; multiple regression, there are two or more predictors of a criterion variable). They may not, however, designate real differences in the underlying conceptual or quantitative framework. Although the theme of connections between techniques is elaborated in Chapter 4, it is safe to say here that the SEM family is one of the most inclusive statistical procedures used within the behavioral sciences.

6. *SEM is still a large-sample technique.* It is generally understood among statisticians that SEM requires large sample sizes. Because several factors affect sample size requirements in SEM, however, it is difficult to give a simple answer to the question of how large a sample needs to be. For example, the analysis of a complex model generally requires more cases than does the analysis of a simpler model. More complex models may require the estimation of more statistical effects, and thus larger samples are necessary in order for the results to be reasonably stable. The type of estimation algorithm used in the analysis also affects sample size requirements. There is more than one type of estimation method in SEM, and some of these may need very large

samples because of assumptions they make (or do not make) about the data.

Because sample size is such an important issue in research, however, some very rough guidelines are offered now. With less than 100 cases, almost any type of SEM analysis may be untenable unless a very simple model is evaluated. Such simple models may be so bare-bones as to be uninteresting, however. For descriptive purposes, sample sizes less than 100 would be considered "small." Between 100 and 200 subjects—a "medium" sample size—is a better minimum, but again this is not absolute because things such as the model's complexity must also be considered. Sample sizes that exceed 200 cases could be considered "large." Another, more empirical guideline about sample size is from Breckler (1990), who surveyed 72 studies published in personality and social psychology journals in which some type of SEM was conducted. The median sample size across these studies was 198, approximately "medium" according to the guidelines just mentioned. The range of sample sizes reported by Breckler was from 40 to 8,650 cases; a total of 18 studies (25%) had sample sizes greater than 500, but 16 studies (22%) had fewer than 100 subjects, or "small" sample sizes. A more recent survey by MacCallum and Austin (2000) of about 500 applications of SEM published in 16 different research journals from 1993 to 1997 found that about 20% of studies used samples of fewer than 100 cases. As is discussed in later chapters, though, the likelihood of encountering a technical problem in the analysis is more likely in SEM if the sample size is small. A small sample size also means that the power of statistical tests may be very limited. How to estimate power in SEM is considered later in the book.

7. *Statistical tests.* Statistical significance testing is a central part of many standard data analysis techniques. In ANOVA, for example, there are many methods for testing the statistical significance of mean contrasts, including post hoc tests, planned comparisons, and trend tests, among others. A great many effects can also be tested for statistical significance in SEM, ranging from things such as the variance of a single variable up to entire models evaluated across multiple samples. There are two reasons, however, why the results of statistical tests may be less relevant in SEM than for other types of techniques.

First, SEM allows the evaluation of entire models, which brings a higher-level perspective to the analysis. That is, although statistical tests of individual effects represented in a model may be of interest, at some point the researcher must make a decision about the whole model: should it be rejected?—modified?—if so, how? Thus, there is some sense in SEM that the view of the entire landscape (the whole model) has precedence over that of specific details (individual effects). The second reason why statistical tests may play a smaller role in SEM concerns the general requirement for large samples discussed earlier. With most types of statistical tests, it is possible to have results that are "highly" statistically significant (e.g., $p < .0001$) but trivial in absolute magnitude when the sample size is large. By the same token, virtually all effects that are not nil will be statistically significant in a sufficiently large sample. Indeed, if the sample size is actually large, a statistically significant result just basically confirms a large sample, which is a tautology (B. Thompson, 1992). For example, a Pearson correlation of .03 does not differ statistically from zero at the .01 level for $N = 100$, but the same near-zero correlation (.03) is statistically significant for $N = 10,000$. Although most researchers do not work with samples so large, it is still possible that some quite small effects could be statistically significant in SEM analyses even with only moderate sample sizes. Suggestions for the conduct of statistical significance testing in SEM that address the issues mentioned here will be discussed at various points throughout the book.

1.6 EXTENDED LATENT VARIABLE FAMILIES

Latent variables analyzed in SEM are generally assumed to be continuous. There are other techniques that specialize in the analysis of models with categorical latent variables. The levels of a categorical latent variable are called **classes**, and they represent a mixture of subpopulations where membership is not known but is inferred from the data (i.e., the observed variables). In other words, a goal of the analysis is to identify the nature and number of latent classes. The technique of **latent class analysis** is a type of factor analysis but for categorical observed and latent variables (e.g., Hagenaars & McCutcheon, 2002). A special type of latent class factor model that represents the shift from one of two different states, such as from nonmastery to mastery of a skill, is a **latent transition model**. There are analogs of techniques, such as multiple regression, for the analysis of categorical latent variables. In **latent class regression**, for example, a criterion is predicted by estimated class membership and other variables that covary with class membership. In contrast to standard regression techniques for continuous variables, the predictors in latent class regression can be a mix of continuous, discrete, or count variables[2] and the criterion can be continuous, discrete, or a repeated measures variable. It is also not assumed in latent class regression that the same predictor model holds for all cases.

Until recently, SEM techniques for analyzing continuous latent variables were generally viewed as relatively distinct families of techniques from those just mentioned for analyzing categorical latent variables. However, this view is changing because of recent attempts to express all latent variable models within a common mathematical framework (Bartholomew, 2002). For example, B. Muthén (2001) describes the analysis of **mixture models** with latent variables that may be continuous or categorical. When both are present in the same model, the analysis is basically SEM conducted across different inferred subpopulations. One of the computer programs for SEM described in Chapter 4, Mplus, can analyze all basic kinds of SEM models and mixture models, too. Computer tools like Mplus blur the distinction between SEM and techniques such as latent class analysis and latent class regression. Unfortunately, it is beyond the scope of this book to describe in detail the analysis of latent categorical variables. Instead, these issues are mentioned here to encourage readers to see SEM itself as a member of an extended family of techniques for latent variable modeling.

1.7 FAMILY HISTORY

No discussion of family values would be complete without some history. Do not worry, though—the home movies and slide projector are not coming out of the closet, as this overview is brief. Because SEM is a collection of related techniques, it does not have a single source. Part of its origins date to the early years of the 20th century with the develop-

---

[2]A count variable is the number of times an event happens over a particular time period such as the number of previous treatments for an illness in the past 2 years.

ment of what we now call exploratory factor analysis, usually credited to Charles Spearman (1904). Several years later, Sewall Wright, a geneticist, developed the basics of path analysis (1921, 1934), which was subsequently introduced by various authors to researchers in other disciplines such as sociology, economics, and later psychology. An annotated bibliography by Wolfle (2003) traces the introduction of path analysis to the social sciences. These measurement (factor analysis) and structural (path analysis) approaches were integrated in the early 1970s in the work of basically three authors, K. G. Jöreskog, J. W. Keesling, and D. E. Wiley, into a framework that Bentler (1980) called the JKW model. One of the first widely available computer programs able to analyze models based on the JKW framework (now called SEM) was LISREL, developed by K. G. Jöreskog and D. Sörbom in the 1970s and subsequently updated by them (e.g., 1981, 2003).

The 1980s and 1990s witnessed the development of many more computer programs and a rapid expansion of the use of SEM techniques in areas such as developmental psychology, behavioral genetics, sports medicine, education, and public health, to name just a few (e.g., Herschberger, 2003). The increase in the use of SEM during this time could be described as exponential. For example, it is difficult to pick up almost any issue of an empirical journal in the behavioral sciences and not find at least one article in which SEM was used. More and more students and experienced researchers alike are interested in learning about SEM. This interest is not likely a fad. This is because, as noted by David A. Kenny in the series editor's note in the previous edition of this book, researchers like SEM because it addresses questions they want answered and it "thinks" about research as researchers do. However, there are some troubling aspects about the way SEM is often applied that limit its potential. These shortcomings in the way SEM is used in practice are addressed throughout this book. Indeed, it is a major goal of this book to steer readers away from these poor practices and toward more sound ones.

1.8 INTERNET RESOURCES

There are many resources for SEM available over the Internet. One of these is an electronic mailing list called SEMNET that serves as a discussion forum for subscribed participants. There are about 1,500 members worldwide, and it can be a place for lively discussion among experts and nonexperts alike. Information about SEMNET can be found at the Website address presented in the footnote below.[3] There are also numerous SEM-related sites on the Web. You can find many of them using standard Internet search engines such as Yahoo!, Google, and AltaVista, among many others. There are student versions of some commercial SEM computer programs that can be downloaded for free over the Internet. These students versions do not have all the capabilities of the full versions, but they can be good learning tools. There is also a full-featured shareware (noncommercial) program for latent variable analyses (Mx Graph) that can be downloaded for free over the Internet. The Web site addresses for all computer tools just mentioned are given in Chapter 4.

1.9 SUMMARY

Characteristics essential to the SEM family were considered in this chapter, including its a priori nature, the potential to differentiate between observed and latent variables, the ability to analyze covariances as well as means, and the requirement for large samples. The SEM family is an extremely flexible set of techniques, applicable to both experimental and nonexperimental data. The ideas introduced in this chapter set the stage for reviewing basic statistical principles that underlie SEM, the subject of the next two chapters. Let us continue with our journey.

---

[3]www.gsu.edu/~mkteer/semnet.html

Basic Statistical Concepts

I. Correlation and Regression

One should bring to a journey of learning about SEM prerequisite knowledge about two major topics: (1) correlation and regression and (2) data preparation and screening. However, these are very broad topics to which entire books are devoted, so it is not possible to cover them in detail here. The goal is instead to review fundamental concepts that are especially relevant to SEM. This chapter reviews bivariate and multiple correlation and regression. It also deals with the logic of statistical tests and introduces the technique of bootstrapping. It is assumed that the reader has had at least one undergraduate-level course in statistics. For readers with this background, some parts of the discussions about bivariate correlation and regression and statistical tests should be a review. Although the topic of multiple correlation and regression may be new for some readers, its similarities to bivariate correlation and regression are emphasized.

2.1 STANDARDIZED AND UNSTANDARDIZED VARIABLES

A **standardized variable** has been transformed so that its mean is 0 and its standard deviation is 1.0. The most common way to standardize a variable is to convert its raw scores to z scores (normal deviates). A raw score X is converted to a normal deviate with the formula $z = (X - M)/SD$, where M and SD are, respectively, the sample mean and standard deviation. The latter is the square root of the sample variance $s^2 = SS/df$, where the numerator is the sum of squares, or $SS = \Sigma(X - M)^2$, and the denominator is the degrees of freedom, or $df = N - 1$. The statistic s^2 is an unbiased estimator of σ^2, the population variance. Note that some methods in SEM calculate sample variances as $S^2 = SS/N$, which estimates σ^2 with negative bias; that is, it is typically true that $S^2 < \sigma^2$. In large samples, however, the values of s^2 and S^2 are very similar, but s^2 is generally preferred in conventional statistical methods for smaller sample sizes, say, $N < 100$.

Statistical results computed with standardized variables are called **standardized estimates**, and they are interpreted in the same way for all variables. For example, the Pearson correlation r (defined next) is a standardized estimate of the degree of linear association between two variables. It is calculated with pairs of standardized variables, and a correlation between X and Y of, say, .60, means the same thing as a correlation of .60 between X and any other variable. In contrast, **unstandardized estimates** are derived with unstandardized variables, that is, with variables in their original units (metrics, scales) rather than expressed as z scores. The values of unstandardized variables are not all limited to the same range. Instead, their ranges are determined by the original metrics of the unstandardized variables. Thus, unstandardized estimates cannot be directly compared across variables with different scales. A covariance is an example of an unstandardized estimate. It is, in fact, an unstandardized form of r. As defined earlier, the covariance between X and Y, cov_{XY}, equals the product $r_{XY}\, SD_X\, SD_Y$. If variables Y and W have different scales, the values of cov_{XY} and cov_{XW} are not directly comparable. Suppose that $SD_X = 5.00$, $SD_Y = 10.00$, $SD_W = 20.00$, and $r_{XY} = r_{XW} = .60$. This implies that

$$cov_{XY} = .60\ (5.00)\ (10.00) = 30.00 \text{ and}$$
$$cov_{XW} = .60\ (5.00)\ (20.00) = 60.00$$

In words, even though the Pearson correlations between X and Y and between X and W are identical (.60), cov_{XY} and cov_{XW} are unequal because Y and W have different standard deviations.

Although researchers generally prefer standardized estimates, there is a strong preference in the SEM literature for unstandardized estimates. One reason is that the most widely used estimation methods in SEM assume the analysis of unstandardized variables. These same methods may not yield correct results if applied to standardized variables. There are also situations where standardized estimates may be inappropriate. These include (1) the analysis of a structural equation model across multiple samples that differ in their variabilities; (2) longitudinal measurement of variables that show increasing (or decreasing) variability over time; and (3) instances where the original metrics of the variables are meaningful rather than arbitrary (e.g., survival in years, salaries in dollars). In all three cases, important information may be lost when variables are standardized. In examples of SEM presented in later chapters, both standardized and unstandardized estimates are reported whenever it makes sense to do so. Although interpretation of standardized estimates is easier to master, for the reasons just cited readers should not rely exclusively on them.

2.2 BIVARIATE CORRELATION AND REGRESSION

Basic principles of bivariate correlation and regression are reviewed in this section. These ideas generalize to multiple correlation and regression, which are considered later.

Pearson Correlation *r*

The Pearson correlation r estimates the degree of linear association between two continuous variables X and Y. Its equation is

$$r_{XY} = \frac{\sum z_X z_Y}{df} \tag{2.1}$$

In words, r_{XY} is the total cross-product of z scores across X and Y averaged over the sample degrees of freedom. Its theoretical range is from -1.00 to $+1.00$. The endpoints of this range indicate, respectively, a perfect negative versus a positive linear association. If $r_{XY} = 0$, then there is no linear relation, but there could still be a curvilinear association between X and Y. (This point is elaborated later.) The squared correlation r_{XY}^2 indicates the proportion of explained (shared) variance. If $r_{XY} = .60$, for example, then X accounts for $.60^2 = .36$, or 36% of the variance in Y and vice versa.

Although the theoretical range of r is from -1.00 to $+1.00$, its actual range can be narrowed closer to zero under certain conditions. Specifically, r_{XY} could be about zero if (1) the relation between X and Y is nonlinear (more about linearity next); (2) the variance of either X or Y is relatively narrow (restricted); (3) the shapes of the frequency distributions of X and Y are very different (e.g., one distribution is positively skewed and the other is negatively skewed); or (4) the reliability of the scores on either X or Y is about zero. Score reliability, as well as score validity, are considered in the next chapter. It is also important to be aware of factors that do *not* affect the magnitude of r_{XY}. The means of X and Y (respectively, M_X and M_Y) have no bearing on r_{XY} (or on cov_{XY}). For example, if a constant of 10 points is added to the scores of X for every case, the mean of X is increased by 10 points but the value of r_{XY} is not affected. Thus, a statistical analysis that involves only covariances is insensitive to changes in means. In many data analyses, however, it is of utmost importance to take means into account. For example, when groups are compared or when a variable is measured on more than one occasion, information about means may be critical. Fortunately, there is a way in SEM to analyze means in addition to covariances; this topic is introduced in Chapter 10.

Statistical tests of correlations assume that the residuals (defined later) have a mean of zero and are independent, normally distributed, and have variances that are uniform across all levels of X. The last of these is known as **homoscedasticity**. Among the requirements just listed, the assumption of independence is probably the most crucial. Independence means that error in predicting Y from X for one case is unrelated to that of another case. For example, the independence assumption may be violated if two respondents complete a questionnaire together. This assumption is also likely violated if Y is measured on more than one occasion. The residuals of repeated measures variables tend to be **autocorrelated**, which means that unpredictability on one occasion is related to the next or previous occasion. A special strength of SEM is that it offers much flexibility for modeling error variances and covariances in repeated measures designs.

Linear, Curvilinear, and Interactive Relations

Presented in Figure 2.1 are examples of linear and other kinds of relations between X and Y. Figure 2.1(a) shows a positive linear relation: as

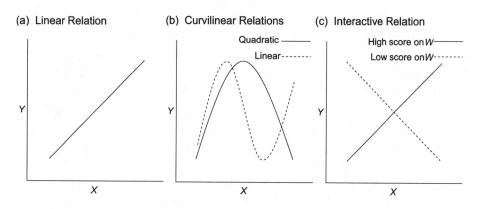

FIGURE 2.1. Examples of linear, curvilinear, and interactive relations.

X increases, so does *Y*. Furthermore, the rate of the increase is uniform across *X*. Two examples of **curvilinear relations** between *X* and *Y* are presented in Figure 2.1(b). The one plotted with the solid line is a quadratic relation in which scores on *Y* first increase then decrease as scores on *X* increase. If *X* is anxiety and *Y* is performance, for example, then this quadratic relation would indicate that only moderate levels of anxiety facilitate performance. The curvilinear relation plotted with the dashed line in Figure 2.1(b) is cubic because it changes direction twice: first scores on *Y* increase, then decrease, then increase again as the level of *X* increases. An **interactive relation** (also called an **interaction effect**) is illustrated in Figure 2.1(c). Interactive relations involve at least three variables. If the relation of *X* to *Y* changes as a function of a third variable *W*, then an interaction effect is indicated. Figure 2.1(c) shows the relations between *X* and *Y* for cases with high versus low scores on *W*. (Variable *W* could also be a dichotomous variable that represents group membership, such as gender.) Although the relation between *X* and *Y* is linear at both levels of *W*, its direction changes from positive at high levels on *W* to negative at low levels. Variable W in this example can be called a **moderator variable** because it moderates (predicts) the relation between *X* and *Y*. The term **moderator effect** refers to an interaction effect.

If one were to compute r_{XY} for graphs (b) or (c) of Figure 2.1, the values would be about zero. These results are potentially misleading because both graphs (b) and (c) show strong relations between *X* and *Y* but not of the type (linear) that can be estimated with r_{XY}. Although correlations (and thus covariances) do not reflect curvilinear or interactive relations, it is nevertheless possible to represent either type of relation in a regression equation. The technique of multiple regression (reviewed later) is required to do so, however. It is also necessary to create special variables known as product terms that represent curvilinear or interactive effects and include them in the regression equation. The same basic method used in multiple regression to analyze curvilinear or interactive effects is also used in SEM. Unlike multiple regression, though, SEM allows the analysis of curvilinear or interactive relations of both observed and latent variables. This topic is considered in Chapter 13.

Other Bivariate Correlations

There are other forms of the Pearson correlation for observed variables that are either categorical or ordinal. For example, the **point-biserial correlation** (r_{pb}) is a special case of r that estimates the association between a dichotomous variable and a continuous one (e.g., gender, weight); the **phi coefficient** ($\hat{\phi}$) is a special case for two dichotomous variables (e.g., treatment–control, relapsed–not relapsed); and the **Spearman's rank order correlation** (also called **Spearman's rho**) is for two ranked (ordinal) variables.

There are also some non-Pearson correlations that assume that the underlying data are continuous and normally distributed instead of discrete. For example, the **biserial correlation** is for a continuous variable and a dichotomy (e.g., agree–disagree), and it estimates what the Pearson r would be if both variables were continuous and normally distributed. A **polyserial correlation** is the generalization of the biserial correlation that does basically the same thing for a continuous variable and a categorical variable with three or more levels. Likewise, a **tetrachoric correlation** for two dichotomous variables estimates what r would be if both variables were continuous and normally distributed, and the **polychoric correlation**—the generalization of the tetrachoric correlation—does so for two categorical variables with two or more levels (Nunnally & Bernstein, 1994). Computing polyserial or polychoric correlations is relatively complicated and requires specialized software like PRELIS of LISREL 8 (Jöreskog & Sörbom, 2003), which estimates the appropriate correlations depending on the types of variables in the data set. The analysis of non-Pearson correlations in SEM for measurement models where the observed variables are not continuous is discussed in Chapter 7.

Regression

This presentation concerns only the case for two continuous variables. In bivariate regression, one variable is designated as the predictor (X) and the other as the criterion (Y). Based on their association, the computer constructs a regression equation that generates a predicted score on the criterion, $\hat{Y}$, given a score on the predictor. This process is also described as regressing Y on X. (If X is the criterion, then the description "regressing X on Y" applies.) The linear regression equation for unstandardized variables is

$$\hat{Y} = B X + A \tag{2.2}$$

which defines a straight line. The slope of this regression line is indicated by B, and its Y-intercept is A. The term B is called the **unstandardized regression coefficient** (weight). Its value indicates the predicted difference on Y given a 1-point increase on X. The intercept A is the value of $\hat{Y}$ when X equals zero. In the output of regression computer programs, the intercept may be labeled as the "constant." For example, the unstandardized regression equation

$$\hat{Y} = 2.30\, X + 10.00$$

says that a 1-point increase in X is associated with an increase of 2.30 points in Y and that $\hat{Y} = 10.00$, given $X = 0$.

The values of B and A in Equation 2.2 are those that satisfy the **least squares criterion**, which means that the sum of squared residuals, $\Sigma(Y - \hat{Y})^2$, is as small as possible for the sample. A **residual** is the difference between an observed score on the criterion and a predicted score from the unstandardized regression equation. If $r_{XY} = 1.00$ (or -1.00; i.e., the linear relation is perfect), then the residual equals zero for every case. If the association between X and Y is not perfect—with real data, the absolute value of r_{XY} is almost always less than 1.00—then some of the residuals differ from zero but their mean is zero. Residuals reflect the part of Y that cannot be explained by X, which implies that they are uncorrelated with X (i.e., $r_{X(Y-\hat{Y})} = 0$). Because the values of B and A are those that maximize the predictive power in a particular sample, they **capitalize on chance variation** in that sample. This implies that (1) the value of r_{XY}^2 tends to overestimate the population proportion of explained variance ρ^2 and (2) it is possible that similar values of B and A may not be found in a replication sample. This is a greater problem when the sample size is small. Ways to correct squared sample correlations for positive bias in the estimation of ρ^2 are discussed later.

The coefficient B of Equation 2.2 is related to r_{XY} and the standard deviations of X and Y as follows:

$$B = r_{XY}\left(\frac{SD_Y}{SD_X}\right) \qquad (2.3)$$

The value of B thus reflects the original metrics of both X and Y, which means that B will change if the scale of either variable is changed (e.g., X is measured in centimeters instead of inches). Also note that because B is an unstandardized statistic, its values are not limited to a particular range. For example, it may be possible to derive values of B such as –13.58 or 1,546.79. Consequently, a large numerical value of B does not necessarily mean that X is an "important" or "strong" predictor of Y.

The intercept A of Equation 2.2 is related both to B and the means of X and Y as follows:

$$A = M_Y - B\, M_X \qquad (2.4)$$

When X and Y are standardized, their means equal zero and their standard deviations are 1.0, which simplifies the regression equation for generating a predicted z score on Y, given an observed z score on X, to $\hat{z}_Y = r_{XY}\, z_X$. This formula describes a straight line but one with a slope equal to r_{XY} and an intercept of zero. For two standardized variables, the correlation between them is also the **standardized regression coefficient**. For example, given $z_X = 1.00$ and $r_{XY} = .60$, then $\hat{z}_Y = .60\,(1.00)$ = .60; that is, a score one standard deviation above the mean on X predicts a score six-tenths of a standard deviation above the mean on Y. A standardized regression coefficient thus indicates the expected difference on Y in standard deviation units, given an increase on X of one full standard deviation. Unlike the unstandardized regression coefficient B, the value of the standardized regression coefficient (r_{XY}) is unaffected by the scale of either X or Y.

Presented in Table 2.1 is a small data set with scores on X, a measure of working memory, and Y, a reading test where higher scores on both variables are a better result. The sum of the cross-products of the standardized scores across the five cases is $\Sigma z_X z_Y = 2.405$, so $r_{XY} = 2.405/4 = .601$, and the squared correlation is $.601^2 = .361$. That is, higher scores on the memory test are associated with higher scores on the reading test (and vice versa), and the two variables share 36.1% of their variance in common. The unstandardized regression coefficient and intercept for these data are calculated as follows:

$$B = .601 \ (4.690/6.205) = .455 \text{ and}$$
$$A = 25.000 - .455 \ (11.000) = 20.000$$

The unstandardized and standardized regression equations are

$$\hat{Y} = .455X + 20.000 \text{ and } \hat{z}_Y = .601 \ (z_X)$$

which say that (1) a 1-point difference on the memory test (X) is associated with an increase of almost half a point (.455) on the reading

TABLE 2.1. Example Data Set for Bivariate Correlation and Regression

| Case | Unstandardized | | Standardized | | |
	X	Y	z_X	z_Y	$z_X z_Y$
A	3	24	−1.289	−.213	.275
B	8	20	−.483	−1.066	.515
C	10	22	−.161	−.640	.103
D	15	32	.645	1.492	.962
E	19	27	1.289	.426	.550
M	11.000	25.000	0	0	—
SD	6.205	4.690	1.000	1.000	—
s^2	38.500	22.000	1.000	1.000	—

measure (Y); (2) the predicted reading test score is 20, given a memory test score of zero; and (3) cases with memory test scores one standard deviation above the mean are expected to have reading test scores about .60 standard deviations above the mean.

2.3 PARTIAL CORRELATION

The concept of an interaction introduces the idea that a third variable W can influence the observed correlation between X and Y. The technique of **partial correlation** also takes a third variable into account, but it concerns a different kind of phenomenon, **spuriousness**. If the observed relation between X and Y is due to one or more common causes, their association is said to be spurious. To illustrate the concept of spuriousness, consider the hypothetical correlations presented in Table 2.2 for three variables measured among children of different ages. Although the correlation between shoe size and vocabulary breadth is fairly substantial ($r_{XY} = .50$), it is hardly surprising because both are caused by a third variable, age (i.e., maturation).

The partial correlation $r_{XY \cdot W}$ removes the effect of a third variable W from both X and Y and reestimates their association. The expressions "controlling for W" and "holding W constant" describe partial correlation. These same expressions are sometimes used in experimental studies, but note that partial correlation is based on statistical correction. The formula is

$$r_{XY \cdot W} = \frac{r_{XY} - r_{XW} r_{YW}}{\sqrt{(1 - r_{XW}^2)(1 - r_{YW}^2)}} \tag{2.5}$$

The numerator reflects one aspect of holding W constant: the product of the bivariate correlations with W is literally subtracted out of r_{XY}. The denominator adjusts the total standardized variance of X and Y by subtracting out the proportions of each explained by W (e.g., $1 - r_{XW}^2$). Applied to the correlations in Table 2.2, the partial correlation between shoe size (X) and vocabulary breadth (Y) controlling for age (W) is calculated as follows:

$$r_{XY \cdot W} = \frac{.50 - .80(.60)}{\sqrt{(1 - .80^2)(1 - .60^2)}} = .04$$

TABLE 2.2. Hypothetical Correlations for Example of Spuriousness

Variable	X	Y	W
X Shoe size	—		
Y Vocabulary breadth	.50	—	
W Age	.80	.60	—

Because the association between X and Y essentially disappears when W is controlled, their observed relation as indicated by $r_{XY} = .50$ may be a spurious one.

Equation 2.5 for partial correlation can be extended to control for two or more external variables. For example, the higher-order partial correlation $r_{XY \cdot UW}$ estimates the association between X and Y controlling for both U and W. There is a related coefficient called a **part correlation** or **semipartial correlation** that partials external variables out of either X or Y but not both. An example of part correlation is not presented here, but it works on the same basic principle as partial correlation. Also, SEM readily allows the representation and estimation of possible spurious associations because of common causes.

2.4 MULTIPLE CORRELATION AND REGRESSION

Bivariate correlation and regression are actually special cases of multiple correlation and regression (from this point described simply as multiple regression), which allows for more than one predictor of the criterion. Considered next is the basic logic of multiple regression for the case of two predictors, but the same ideas apply when there are three or more predictors.

Basic Concepts

The basic results of a multiple regression analysis indicate (1) the total proportion of criterion variance explained by all predictors and (2) the relative importance of each predictor. Both types of estimates are adjusted for correlations among the predictors. The multiple correlation between predictors X_1 and X_2 and the criterion is represented here by the symbol $R_{Y \cdot 12}$. A multiple correlation is actually a Pearson correlation between observed and predicted criterion scores; that is, $R_{Y\cdot12} = r_{Y\hat{Y}}$. Unlike Pearson correlations, though, multiple correlations theoretically range from 0 to 1.00. The squared multiple correlation $R_{Y\cdot12}^2$ indicates the proportion of criterion variance explained by both predictors together. Note that the same factors that can restrict the observed values of Pearson correlations also affect $R_{Y\cdot12}$.

When there are two predictors, the unstandardized regression equation takes the form

$$\hat{Y} = B_1 X_1 + B_2 X_2 + A \tag{2.6}$$

where B_1 and B_2 are the unstandardized regression coefficients and A is the intercept. As in bivariate regression, the values of the coefficients and intercept in multiple regression are those that satisfy the least squares criterion in a particular sample (i.e., $\Sigma(Y - \hat{Y})^2$ is as small as possible). The unstandardized regression coefficients B_1 and B_2 of Equation 2.6 indicate the expected raw score difference in Y given a difference of a single point in one predictor while we are controlling for the other. For example, if $B_1 = 5.40$ and $B_2 = 3.65$, then the expected difference on Y is 5.40 points given a difference on X_1 of 1 point, with X_2 held constant; likewise, a 1-point difference on X_2 predicts a 3.65 point difference in Y while we are controlling for X_1. Because unstandardized regression coefficients reflect the scales of their respective predictors, the values of Bs from predictors with different raw score metrics are not directly comparable. The intercept A of Equation 2.6 equals the value of $\hat{Y}$ when the scores on both predictors are zero (i.e., $X_1 = X_2 = 0$). It can be expressed as a function of the unstandardized coefficients and the means of all variables as follows:

$$A = M_Y - B_1 M_1 - B_2 M_2 \tag{2.7}$$

The multiple regression equation for standardized variables is

$$\hat{z}_Y = \beta_1 z_1 + \beta_2 z_2 \tag{2.8}$$

where z_1 and z_2 are, respectively, standardized scores on X_1 and X_2, and β_1 and β_2 are, respectively, the standardized regression coefficients, also called **beta weights**. Note that some books use the symbol "β" to refer to a population parameter, but here it refers to a sample statistic. Beta weights indicate the expected difference in Y in standard deviation units controlling for the other predictors, and their values can be directly compared across the predictors. For example, if $\beta_1 = .40$, it means that the difference on Y is expected to be .40 standard deviations large given a difference on X_1 of one full standard deviation controlling for X_2; the term β_2 has an analogous meaning except that X_1 is held constant. Because beta weights are adjusted for intercorrelations among the predictors, their absolute values are usually less than those of the corresponding bivariate correlations of the predictors with the criterion. This is not always true though. Absolute values of beta weights can exceed those of the corresponding bivariate correlations. It is also possible for the absolute values of beta weights to exceed 1.0. When either occurs, a **suppression** effect is usually indicated. Suppression is described later.

Given two predictors, the formulas for the beta weights are as follows:

$$\beta_1 = \frac{r_{Y1} - r_{Y2}r_{12}}{1 - r_{12}^2} \text{ and } \beta_2 = \frac{r_{Y2} - r_{Y1}r_{12}}{1 - r_{12}^2} \qquad (2.9)$$

where r_{Y1}, r_{Y2}, and r_{12} are the bivariate correlations among the criterion and predictors. Beta weights are analogous to partial correlations in that both correct for a third variable (see Equation 2.5), but beta weights are not correlations. (Recall that the absolute values of beta weights can exceed 1.00.) Note that if the predictors are independent ($r_{12} = 0$), then each beta weight equals the corresponding bivariate correlation (i.e., there is no adjustment for correlated predictors). When there are more than two predictors, the formulas for beta weights are more complicated but follow the same basic principles. The relation between unstandardized and standardized regression coefficients in multiple regression is analogous to that in bivariate regression. For the case of two predictors,

$$B_1 = \beta_1 \left(\frac{SD_Y}{SD_1} \right) \text{ and } B_2 = \beta_2 \left(\frac{SD_Y}{SD_2} \right) \qquad (2.10)$$

The squared multiple correlation can be expressed as a function of the beta weights and the bivariate correlations of the predictors with the criterion. With two predictors,

$$R^2_{Y \cdot 12} = \beta_1 r_{Y1} + \beta_2 r_{Y2} \qquad (2.11)$$

The role of beta weights as corrections for the other predictor is apparent in this equation. Specifically, if $r_{12} = 0$ (i.e., the predictors are independent), then $\beta_1 = r_{Y1}$ and $\beta_1 = r_{Y2}$ and $R^2_{Y \cdot 12}$ is just the sum of r^2_{Y1} and r^2_{Y2}. However, if $r_{12} \neq 0$ (i.e., the predictors are correlated), then β_1 and β_2 do not equal the corresponding bivariate correlations and $R^2_{Y \cdot 12}$ is not the simple sum of r^2_{Y1} and r^2_{Y2} (it is less).

Because of capitalization on chance, squared sample correlations such as R^2 are positively biased estimators of ρ^2, the population proportion of explained variance. There are several different corrections that downward-adjust R^2 as a function of sample size and the number of predictors. Perhaps the most common form of this correction is

$$\hat{R}^2 = 1 - (1 - R^2)\left(\frac{df}{N-k}\right) \qquad (2.12)$$

where $\hat{R}^2$ is the adjusted estimate of ρ^2 and k is the number of predictors. In small samples, the value of $\hat{R}^2$ can be quite a bit less than that of R^2. The former can even be negative; in this case, $\hat{R}^2$ is interpreted as though its value were zero. As the sample size increases for a given number of predictors, the values of $\hat{R}^2$ and R^2 are increasingly similar, and in very large samples they are essentially equal. That is, it is unnecessary to correct for positive bias in a very large sample. See Snyder and Lawson (1993) for more information about corrected estimates of ρ^2.

Presented in Table 2.3 is a small data set with scores on X_1, X_2, and Y. Assume that scores on X_1, X_2, and Y are from, respectively, a measure of working memory, phonics skill, and reading achievement. Given $r_{Y1} = .601$, $r_{Y2} = .750$, and $r_{12} = .470$ for these data, the beta weights are calculated as follows:

$$\beta_1 = \frac{.601 - .750(.470)}{1 - .470^2} = .320 \text{ and } \beta_2 = \frac{.750 - .601(.470)}{1 - .470^2} = .599$$

The standardized regression equation for the data in Table 2.3 is

$$\hat{z}_Y = .320\, z_1 + .599\, z_2$$

and the squared multiple correlation is calculated as follows:

TABLE 2.3. Example Data Set for Multiple Correlation and Regression

Case	Unstandardized			Standardized		
	X_1	X_2	Y	z_1	z_2	z_Y
A	3	65	24	−1.289	.343	−.213
B	8	50	20	−.483	−.686	−1.066
C	10	40	22	−.161	−1.372	−.640
D	15	70	32	.645	.686	1.492
E	19	75	27	1.289	1.029	.426
M	11.000	60.000	25.000	0	0	0
SD	6.205	14.577	4.690	1.000	1.000	1.000
s^2	38.500	212.500	22.000	1.000	1.000	1.000

Note. $r_{Y1} = .601$, $r_{Y2} = .750$, and $r_{12} = .470$.

$$R^2_{Y \cdot 12} = .320 \, (.601) + .599 \, (.750) = .642$$

The memory and phonics variables together explain about 64.2% of the total variance in reading, and the overall correlation is $R_{Y \cdot 12} = .642^{1/2} = .801$. The adjusted estimate of ρ^2 is

$$R^2_{Y \cdot 12} = 1 - (1 - .642) \, (4/2) = .284$$

which is quite lower than $R^2_{Y \cdot 12}$ for these data (.642) because of the small sample size ($N = 5$).

The slopes and intercept of the unstandardized regression equation for the data in Table 2.3 are calculated as follows:

$$B_1 = .320 \, (4.690/6.205) = .242 \text{ and } B_2 = .599 \, (4.690/14.577) = .193$$
$$A = 25.000 - .242 \, (11.000) - .193 \, (60.000) = 10.771$$

The unstandardized regression is thus

$$\hat{Y} = .242 \, X_1 + .193 \, X_2 + 10.771$$

A difference of 1 point on the memory test (X_1) predicts a difference on the reading test (Y) of about .242 points controlling for phonics skill. Likewise, the difference on the reading test is expected to be .193 points for every 1-point difference on the phonics skill variable (X_2), with memory held constant. Because the memory and phonics variables have different scales, the values of their unstandardized weights are not directly comparable. However, we can directly compare the beta weights for the predictors, which are $\beta_1 = .320$ and $\beta_2 = .599$. These values indicate that the predictive power of the phonics test is about twice that of the memory test. That is, a difference on the phonics variable of a full standard deviation predicts a difference on the reading measure of about .60 standard deviations controlling for memory. In contrast, a difference of the same magnitude on the memory variable, but with phonics held constant, is associated with a smaller difference on the reading measure, about .32 standard deviations.

Specification Error

In probably most applications of multiple regression there ought to be concern about **specification error**, which refers to the problem of omitted predictor variables. An omitted predictor accounts for some unique proportion of total criterion variance but is not included in the analysis. Suppose that $r_{Y1} = .40$ and $r_{Y2} = .60$ for, respectively, predictors X_1 and X_2. A researcher measures only X_1 and uses it as the sole predictor in a bivariate regression analysis. The standardized regression coefficient for the *included predictor* in this analysis, X_1, is $r_{Y1} = .40$. If the researcher had the foresight to also measure X_2, the *omitted predictor*, and enter it along with X_1 as a predictor in the same equation, the beta weight for X_1 in this multiple regression analysis, β_1, may not equal .40. If not, then r_{Y1} as a standardized regression coefficient with X_1 as the sole predictor of Y does not reflect the predictive power of X_1 compared with β_1 derived with both X_1 and X_2 in the equation. However, the amount of the difference between r_{Y1} and β_1 varies with r_{12}, the correlation between the included predictor and the omitted predictor. Specifically, if the included and omitted predictors are unrelated ($r_{12} = 0$), there is no difference ($r_{Y1} = \beta_1$) because there is no correction for correlated predictors. But as the absolute value of their correlation increases

($r_{12} \neq 0$), the amount of the difference between r_{Y1} and β_1 due to the omission of X_2 becomes greater.

Presented in Table 2.4 are the results of three regression analyses. In all cases, X_2 is considered the omitted predictor. (The same principles hold if X_1 is the omitted predictor and X_2 is the included predictor.) Also constant across all three analyses are the bivariate correlations between the predictors and the criterion ($r_{Y1} = .40$, $r_{Y2} = .60$). The only thing that varies is the value of r_{12}, the correlation between the included and omitted predictors. Reported for each analysis are the overall multiple correlation and the beta weights (β_1, β_2) for the regression of Y on X_1 and X_2 together. For each case, compare the value of β_1 in boldface with that of r_{Y1} in Table 2.4. The difference between these values (if any) indicates the amount by which the bivariate standardized regression coefficient for X_1 does not accurately measure its predictive power compared to when X_2 is also in the equation. Note that when the omitted predictor X_2 is uncorrelated with the included predictor X_1 (case 1, $r_{12} = 0$), the standardized regression coefficient for X_1 is the same regardless of whether X_2 is in the equation or not ($r_{Y1} = \beta_1 = .40$). However, when $r_{12} = .20$ (case 2), β_1 is lower than r_{Y1}, respectively, .29 versus .40. This happens because β_1 controls for the correlation between X_1 and X_2 whereas r_{12} does not. Thus, r_{Y1} here *overestimates* the association between X_1 and Y relative to β_1. In case 3 in the table, the correlation between the included and omitted predictors is even higher

TABLE 2.4. Example of the Omitted Variable Problem

		Regression with both predictors	
Case	Predictor	β	$R_{Y \cdot 12}$
1. $r_{12} = 0$	X_1	.40	.72
	X_2	.60	
2. $r_{12} = .20$	X_1	.29	.66
	X_2	.54	
3. $r_{12} = .40$	X_1	.19	.62
	X_2	.52	

Note. For all cases, X_2 is considered the omitted variable; $r_{Y1} = .40$ and $r_{Y2} = .60$.

(r_{12} = .40), which for these data results in even a greater discrepancy between r_{Y1} and β_1 (respectively, .40 vs. .19).

Omitting a predictor correlated with others in the equation does not always result in overestimation of the predictive power of an included predictor. For example, if X_1 is the included predictor and X_2 is the omitted predictor, it is also possible for the absolute value of r_{Y1} to be *less than* that of β_1 (i.e., r_{Y1} *underestimates* the relation indicated by β_1) or even for r_{Y1} and β_1 to have different signs. Both of these situations indicate a suppression effect, which is described next. It should be noted, though, that overestimation due to omission of a predictor probably occurs more often than underestimation (suppression). Also, the pattern of misestimation may be more complicated when there are multiple included and omitted variables (e.g., overestimation for some included predictors; underestimation for others).

Predictors are typically excluded because they are not measured by the researcher. Thus, it is difficult to know by how much and in what direction the regression coefficients of included predictors may be "wrong" relative to what their values would be if all relevant predictors were included. However, it is unrealistic to expect the researcher to know and be able to measure all the relevant predictors of a criterion. In this sense, all regression equations are probably misspecified to some degree. If omitted predictors are essentially uncorrelated with included predictors, the consequences of a specification error may be slight. If not, the consequences of a specification error are more serious. The main way to avoid a serious specification error is through a careful review of existing theory and research, which may decrease the potential number of omitted predictors.

Suppression

Although there is more than one definition, perhaps the most general is that suppression occurs when either the absolute value of a predictor's beta weight is greater than its bivariate correlation with the criterion (e.g., β_1 = .60, r_{Y1} = .40) or when the two have different signs (e.g., β_1 = .10, r_{Y1} = −.30). So defined, suppression implies that the estimated relation between a predictor and the criterion while controlling for other predictors is a "surprise" given the bivariate correlation between that predictor and the criterion. Suppose that X_1 is amount of psychotherapy, X_2 is degree of depression, and Y is the number of previous suicide attempts. The bivariate correlations in a hypothetical sample are

$$r_{Y1} = .19, \ r_{Y2} = .49, \text{ and } r_{12} = .70$$

Based on these results, it may seem that the effects of psychotherapy are actually harmful because of its positive bivariate association with the criterion (i.e., more therapy is associated with more suicide attempts). When both predictors (depression, psychotherapy) are entered as predictors in the same regression equation, however, the results are

$$R_{Y \cdot 12} = .54, \ \beta_1 = -.30, \text{ and } \beta_2 = .70$$

Note that the beta weight for psychotherapy (–.30) has the opposite sign of its bivariate correlation with the criterion (.19). Also, the beta weight for depression (.70) is greater than its bivariate correlation with the criterion (.49).

The results just described are due to controlling for the other predictor. Here, people who are more depressed are also more likely to be in therapy ($r_{12} = .70$). Depressed people are also more likely to attempt to harm themselves ($r_{Y2} = .49$). Corrections for these associations in the multiple regression analysis reveal that the relation of psychotherapy to suicide attempts is actually negative once depression is controlled. It is also true that the relation of depression to suicide attempts is even stronger once the variable of the amount of psychotherapy is held constant. Omit either psychotherapy or depression as a predictor and the regression results with the remaining predictor are potentially misleading. This is an example of **negative suppression**, where the predictors have positive correlations with the criterion and each other, but one receives a negative regression weight. A second type of suppression is **classical suppression**, where one predictor is uncorrelated with the criterion but receives a nonzero regression weight controlling for another predictor. For example, given the following correlations in a hypothetical sample,

$$r_{Y1} = 0, \ r_{Y2} = .60, \text{ and } r_{12} = .50$$

the results of the multiple regression analysis are

$$R_{Y \cdot 12} = .69, \beta_1 = -.40, \text{ and } \beta_2 = .80$$

This example of classical suppression (i.e., $r_{Y1} = 0$, $\beta_1 = -.40$) demonstrates that bivariate correlations of zero can mask true predictive relations once other variables are controlled. A third type of suppression is **reciprocal suppression**, which can occur when two predictors correlate positively with the criterion but negatively with each other. See Smith, Ager, and Williams (1992) for more information about suppression.

Multiple Regression in SEM

Multiple regression is a widely used data-analytic method that is enormously flexible. As mentioned, it is possible with multiple regression to analyze curvilinear or interactive effects. This property in combination with the capability to represent categorical variables (e.g., the control group vs. all treatment groups) as predictors implies that essentially any type of analysis of variance (ANOVA) can be performed with multiple regression. Thus, multiple regression, which is sometimes viewed as a "correlational" technique for nonexperimental data, can also be applied to the analysis of means in experimental or nonexperimental studies. A similar overly narrow perception of SEM was mentioned in Chapter 1.

However, the role of multiple regression in SEM is actually rather limited. Multiple regression is very useful in data screening, which is discussed in Chapter 3. It can also be used in the technique of path analysis to estimate some, but not all, kinds of path models. If a structural equation model either has latent variables that represent hypothetical constructs or assumes that certain residuals are correlated, then multiple regression cannot be used to estimate the model. Other kinds of statistical methods described later in this book—especially maximum likelihood estimation—are used much more often in SEM. Understanding the basic ideas of multiple regression discussed in this section, though, will provide readers with a useful cognitive "bridge" with which to cross over to other methods that are used more often in SEM.

2.5 STATISTICAL TESTS

Many types of data analysis including SEM have an inferential as well as a descriptive focus. Inferential analyses concern the testing of hypotheses about **population parameters**, characteristics of a whole population, such as a mean (μ) or correlation (ρ). On the other hand, sample statistics, such as means (M) or multiple correlations (R), only estimate population parameters. What is perhaps the most basic form of a statistical test is the ratio of a sample statistic over its **standard error**. The latter is the standard deviation of a **sampling distribution**, which is a probability distribution of a statistic based on all possible random samples each based on the same number of cases. A standard error also estimates **sampling error**, the difference between sample statistics and the corresponding parameters. Given constant variability among population cases, standard error varies inversely with sample size. That is, distributions of statistics from larger samples are generally narrower than distributions of the same statistic from smaller samples.

There are "textbook" formulas for the standard errors of sample statistics with simple distributions. By "simple" it is meant that (1) the statistic estimates a single parameter and (2) the shape of the distribution is not a function of the value of that parameter. Sample means have simple distributions as just defined. For example, the formula for the standard error of a single mean is $s_M = s/N^{1/2}$. However, it is often more difficult to estimate standard errors for statistics that do not have simple distributions. There are approximate methods amenable to hand calculation for some statistics, such as sample proportions, where distribution shape and variability depend on the value of the population proportion (π). Such methods may generate **asymptotic standard errors** that assume a large sample. However, if the researcher's sample is not large, such estimated standard errors may not be very accurate. Finally, some statistics, such as R, have distributions so complex that there may be no approximate standard error formula that is amenable to hand calculation. Estimation of standard error in such cases may require special software (e.g., Kline, 2004, chap. 4).

In large samples under the assumption of normality, the ratio of an estimator over its standard error is interpreted as a z statistic in a normal curve with a mean of zero and a standard deviation that equals the standard error. A rule of thumb for large samples is that if the absolute value of this ratio exceeds 2.00, the null hypothesis (H_0) that the corresponding parameter is zero—also called a **nil hypothesis**—is rejected at the .05 level of statistical significance (i.e., $p < .05$) for a two-tailed test (H_1). The precise absolute value of z for the .05 level is 1.96 and for the .01 level is 2.58. Within small samples, the ratio of a statistic over its standard error approximates a t distribution instead of a z distribution, which necessitates the use of special tables to determine critical values of t for the .05 or .01 levels. Within large samples, t and z for the same estimator are essentially equal.

It is critical not to misinterpret the outcome of a statistical test. Suppose in a large sample that $p < .05$ for the z test of a nil hypothesis. This result says that the probability of observing in a random sample the value of an estimator as extreme as that actually found is less than 5%, assuming the parameter is zero. The outcome $p < .05$ does *not* mean that the probability is less than 5% that (1) the result is due to sampling error, (2) H_0 is true, or (3) the decision taken to reject H_0 is incorrect (i.e., a Type I error). The complement of p, or $1 - p$, does *not* mean that the probability is greater than 95% that (1) H_1 is true or (2) H_0 will be rejected in a future replication. These are common misunderstandings, and they generally involve the overinterpretation of a statistically significant result (e.g., Kline, 2004, chap. 3). It is also important to remember that p values reflect both sample size and effect size (which for the purposes of this discussion is the value of the estimator). This means that p could be low because of either a large sample size or a large effect size. This explains how a small effect can be statistically significant in a large sample or how a large effect can fail to be statistically significant in a small sample.

The failure to reject some null hypothesis is a meaningful outcome only if the power of the test is adequate. Here **power** means the probability of rejecting the null hypothesis when there is a real effect in the population (i.e., H_1 is true). Power varies directly with the magnitude of the real population effect and the sample size. Other factors that affect power include the level of statistical significance (e.g., .05 vs. .01), the directionality of H_1 (i.e., a one- or two-tailed test), whether the samples are independent or dependent (i.e., a between- or within-subjects design), the particular test statistic used, and the reliability of the scores. The following combination generally leads to the greatest power: a large sample, the .05 level of statistical significance, a one-tailed (directional) H_1, a within-subjects design, a parametric test statistic (e.g., t) rather than a nonparametric statistic (e.g., Mann–Whitney U), and scores that are very reliable.

The power of a study should be estimated when the study is planned but *before* the data are collected (Wilkinson & the Task Force on Statistical Inference, 1999). This is because it is too late to rectify a low-power test by doing things like adding more cases after the study has been conducted. Ideally, power should be as high as possible, such as >.85. If power is only about .50, then the odds of rejecting a false null hypothesis are no greater than guessing the outcome of a coin toss. In fact, tossing a coin instead of conducting the study would be just as likely to give the correct decision and would save time and money, too (Schmidt & Hunter, 1997). Unfortunately, the typical level of power in the behavioral sciences seems to be only about .50 (e.g., Rossi, 1997). Increasing sample size is one way to increase power. However, if the magnitude of the population effect is not large, the number of additional cases necessary to reach even a power level of .80 can be so great as to be practically impossible (Schmidt, 1996). This is a critical limitation of statistical tests in the behavioral sciences. Statistical tests in SEM, their proper interpretation, and the estimation of their power are discussed in later chapters.

2.6 BOOTSTRAPPING

Bootstrapping is a statistical resampling method developed by B. Efron in the late 1970s (e.g., see Diaconis & Efron, 1983; also Efron & Tibshirani, 1993). There are two general kinds. In **nonparametric bootstrapping**, the researcher's sample is treated as a pseudopopulation. Cases from the original data file are randomly selected with replacement to generate other data sets, usually with the same number of cases as the original. Because of sampling with replacement, (1) the same case can appear more than once in a generated data set and (2) the composition of cases will vary somewhat across the generated samples. When repeated many times with a computer (e.g., >1,000), bootstrapping simulates the drawing of numerous samples from a population. Standard errors are generally estimated in this method as the standard deviation in the empirical sampling distribution of the same estimator across all generated samples. Nonparametric bootstrapping generally assumes only that the sample distribution has the same basic shape as that of the population distribution. In contrast, the distributional assumptions of many standard statistical tests, such as the *t* test for means, are more demanding (e.g., normal and equally variable population distributions). A raw data file is necessary for nonparametric bootstrapping. This is not true in **parametric bootstrapping**, where the computer draws random samples from a probability density function with parameters specified by the researcher. This is a kind of Monte Carlo method that is used in computer simulation studies of the properties of particular estimators including those of many used in SEM that measure the fit of models to the data.

It is important to realize that bootstrapping is not some kind of magical technique that can somehow compensate for small or unrepresentative samples, distributions that are severely nonnormal, or the absence of independent samples for replication. In fact, bootstrapping can potentially magnify the effects of unusual features in a data set, which may compromise external validity (Rodgers, 1999). However, more and more SEM computer programs feature optional bootstrap methods for calculating the standard errors of model parameter estimates or fit indexes, which tend to have complex distributions. There are also bootstrap methods to evaluate whole structural equation models (e.g., Bollen & Stine, 1993; Yung & Bentler, 1996) that are not discussed in this book. An example of the use of bootstrapping to estimate the standard errors of estimated indirect and total causal effects is presented in Chapter 6.

2.7 SUMMARY

This chapter has reviewed fundamental concepts of correlation and regression that underlie many aspects of SEM. One of these is the idea of statistical control—the partialing out of one or more variables from other variables, a standard feature of most models analyzed in SEM. A related idea is that of spuriousness, which happens when an observed association between two variables disappears when the analyst is controlling for their common causes. Another is that of suppression, which occurs in some cases when the sign of the adjusted estimate of the relation between two variables differs from that of their bivariate correlation. One lesson of the concepts just mentioned is that the values of observed correlations may mask true relations between variables once intercorrelations with other variables are controlled. Another is the importance of including all relevant predictors in the analysis. Specifically, the omission of predictors that are correlated with those included in the model is a type of specification error that may result in misleading results. The magnitude of this problem is greater as correlations between included and excluded predictors increase.

2.8 RECOMMENDED READINGS

Cohen, J., Cohen, P., West, S. G., & Aiken, L. S. (2003). *Applied multiple regression/correlation analysis for the behavioral sciences* (3rd ed.). Mahwah, NJ: Erlbaum.

Kline, R. B. (2004). *Beyond significance tests: Reforming data analysis methods in behavioral research*. Washington, DC: American Psychological Association. (Chaps. 1–3, 9)

3

Basic Statistical Concepts

II. Data Preparation and Screening

The topic of data preparation and screening is crucial for two reasons. First, the most widely used estimation methods for SEM require certain assumptions about the distributional characteristics of the data. Unlike similar requirements of other statistical techniques that can be violated with relative impunity—the normality assumption of the *t* test, for instance—the same is not generally true in SEM. Second, data-related problems can make SEM computer programs fail to yield a logical solution, or "crash." A researcher who has not carefully prepared and screened the data may mistakenly believe that the model is at fault. Also reviewed in this chapter are basic concepts from measurement theory about score reliability and validity. Readers should note that it is not possible to thoroughly cover all aspects of data preparation–screening and score reliability–validity in a single chapter. Instead, this presentation is intended as a brief introduction, one that points out some of the basic options for approaching data- and measurement-related problems. More advanced works are cited throughout, and these should be consulted for additional information.

3.1 DATA PREPARATION

It is probably true that most primary researchers (those who conduct original studies) input raw data files for analysis with SEM computer programs. These same researchers may be surprised to learn that the raw data themselves are not necessary for many types of SEM. This is also true, however, for other statistical techniques. For example, it is possible to conduct a one-way analysis of variance (ANOVA) using only group means, standard deviations, and sizes, and a computer can conduct an exploratory factor analysis given just a correlation matrix. For reasons given below, it is important for researchers who use SEM computer programs to be aware of input options other than raw data files.

Basically all contemporary SEM computer programs accept either a raw data file or a matrix summary of the data. If a raw data file is submitted, the program will create its own matrix, which is then analyzed. The following issues should be considered in choosing between a raw data file and a matrix summary as program input:

1. It is necessary to submit a raw data file when (a) nonnormal data are analyzed with an estimation method that assumes normality but test statistics are calculated that correct for nonnormality or (b) a special estimation method is used that does *not* assume normal distributions or accommodates cases with missing observations. For analyses that do not involve any of these applications—and many do not—either the raw data or a matrix summary of them can be analyzed.

2. Matrix input offers a potential economy over raw data files, especially for large samples. Suppose that 1,000 cases are measured on 10 variables. The raw data file may be 1,000 lines (or more) in length, but the covariance matrix for the same data might be only 10 lines long.

3. Many journal articles about the results of SEM procedures contain enough information, such as correlations and standard deviations, to create a matrix summary of the data, which can then be submitted to an SEM computer program for secondary analysis. Thus, readers of these works can, without having access to the raw data, either replicate the original analyses or estimate alternative models not considered in the original work. See MacCallum, Wegener, Uchino, and Fabrigar (1993) for examples of this capability. Also, readers can replicate analyses described in this book using the matrix summaries that accompany each example.

4. Sometimes one might "make up" a correlation (or covariance) matrix using theory or results from a meta-analysis, so there are no raw data, only a data matrix. A made-up data matrix can be submitted to an SEM computer program for analysis. This is also a way to diagnosis certain kinds of technical problems that can crop up in SEM analyses. The idea just mentioned is discussed in later chapters.

If means are not analyzed (more about means momentarily), there are two basic types of summaries of the raw data—correlation matrices with standard deviations and covariance matrices. For example, presented in the top part of Table 3.1 are the correlation matrix with standard deviations (left) and the covariance matrix (right) for the raw data in Table 2.3 on three variables. Both of these matrices are in **lower diagonal form** where only unique values of correlations or covariances are

TABLE 3.1. Matrix Summaries of the Data in Table 2.3

Variables			Variables		
X_1	X_2	Y	X_1	X_2	Y
		Summaries without means			
Correlations, standard deviations			Covariances		
1.000			38.500		
.470	1.000		42.500	212.500	
.601	.750	1.000	17.500	51.250	22.000
6.204	14.577	4.690			
		Summaries with means			
Correlations, standard deviations, means			Covariances, means		
1.000			38.500		
.470	1.000		42.500	212.500	
.601	.750	1.000	17.500	51.250	22.000
6.204	14.577	4.690	11.000	60.000	25.000
11.000	60.000	25.000			

reported in the lower-left-hand side of the matrix. Most SEM computer programs accept lower diagonal matrices as an alternative to full ones with (redundant) entries above and below the diagonal, and can "assemble" a covariance matrix given the correlations and standard deviations.

It may be problematic to submit for analysis just a correlation matrix without standard deviations (or specify that all standard deviations equal 1.0). As mentioned, the most frequently used estimation methods in SEM assume that the variables are unstandardized. In fact, some SEM computer programs give error messages if the user requests the analysis of a correlation matrix. It is generally safer to analyze a covariance matrix or a correlation matrix with standard deviations. Accordingly, covariance matrices are analyzed for most of the examples presented in this book. The only exceptions are when the authors of the original works did not report standard deviations, which means that it was impossible to analyze a covariance matrix. In these cases, SEM computer programs with special methods that correctly analyze standardized variables are used.

Matrix summaries of raw data must consist of the covariances *and* means of the observed variables whenever means are analyzed in SEM. Presented in the lower part of Table 3.1 are matrix summaries of the data in Table 2.3 that include the correlations, standard deviations, and means (left) and the covariances and means (right). Both of these matrices convey the same information. Note that even if your structural equation model does not concern means, you should nevertheless report the means of all observed variables in written summaries. You may not be interested in analyzing the means, but someone else may be.

3.2 DATA SCREENING

Before either a raw data file or a matrix summary of the data is created for any type of SEM, the original data should be carefully screened for the problems considered next.

Multivariate Normality

The most widely used estimation methods in SEM assume **multivariate normality**, which means that (1) all the univariate distributions are normal, (2) the joint distribution of any pair of the variables is bivariate normal, and (3) all bivariate scatterplots are linear and homoscedastic. Because it is often impractical to examine all joint frequency distributions, it can be difficult to assess all aspects of multivariate normality. Fortunately, many instances of multivariate nonnormality are detectable through inspection of univariate distributions. Deletion of cases that are outliers may also contribute to multivariate normality.

Univariate Normality

Skew and kurtosis are two ways that a distribution can be nonnormal, and they can occur either separately or together in a single variable. Skew implies that the shape of a unimodal distribution is asymmetrical about its mean. **Positive skew** indicates that most of the scores are below the mean, and **negative skew** indicates just the opposite. For a unimodal, symmetrical distribution, **positive kurtosis** indicates heavier tails and a higher peak and **negative kurtosis** indicates just the opposite, both relative to a normal distribution with the same variance (DeCarlo, 1997). A distribution with positive kurtosis is described as **leptokurtic**, and a distribution with negative kurtosis is described as **platykurtic**.

Extreme skew is easy to spot by inspecting frequency distributions; normal probability plots, which show the relation of actual z scores to ones expected in a normal curve, are useful for spotting both skew and kurtosis. Perhaps the best known standardized measures of skew and kurtosis that permit the comparison of different distributions to the normal curve are calculated as follows:

$$\text{skew index} = \frac{S^3}{(S^2)^{3/2}} \text{ and kurtosis index} = \frac{S^4}{(S^2)^2} \quad (3.1)$$

where S^2, S^3, and S^4 are, respectively, the second through fourth **moments about the mean**:

$$S^2 = \Sigma(X - M)^2/N, \ S^3 = \Sigma(X - M)^3/N, \quad (3.2)$$
$$\text{and } S^4 = \Sigma(X - M)^4/N$$

The sign of the standardized skew index indicates the direction of the skew, positive or negative; a value of zero indicates a symmetrical distribution. The value of the standardized kurtosis index in a normal distribution equals 3.0, a value greater than 3.0 indicates positive kurtosis, and a value less than 3.0 indicates negative kurtosis. Some statistical computer programs subtract 3.00 from the kurtosis index before printing its value. The value of this rescaled index is zero for a normal distribution, and its sign indicates the type of kurtosis, positive or negative.

The ratio of the value of an unstandardized skew index or kurtosis index over its standard error is interpreted in large samples as a z test of the null hypothesis that there is no population skew or kurtosis, respectively. However, these tests may not be very useful in large samples because even slight departures from normality may be statistically significant. An alternative is to interpret the absolute values of standardized skew or kurtosis indexes, but there are few clear guidelines for doing so. Some suggestions can be offered, though, that are based on computer simulation studies of estimation methods used by SEM computer programs (e.g., Curran, West, & Finch, 1997). Variables with absolute values of the skew index greater than 3.0 seem to be described as "extremely" skewed by some authors of these studies. There is less consensus about the kurtosis index, however—absolute values from about 8.0 to over 20.0 of this index have been described as indicating "extreme" kurtosis. A conservative rule of thumb, then, seems to be that absolute values of the kurtosis index greater than 10.0 may suggest a problem and values greater than 20.0 may indicate a more serious one; see DeCarlo (1997) for additional information.

Transformations

One way to deal with univariate nonnormality (and thereby address multivariate nonnormality) is with **transformations**, meaning that the original scores are converted with a mathematical operation to new ones that may be more normally distributed. Because transformations alter the shape of the distribution, they can also be useful for dealing with outliers (discussed next). Examples of transformations that may normalize positively skewed distributions include square root ($X^{1/2}$), logarithmic (e.g., $\log_{10} X$), and inverse ($1/X$) functions. All the transformations just mentioned but applied to the original scores subtracted from the highest score plus 1 may remedy negative skew. Odd-root (e.g., $X^{1/3}$) and sine functions tend to bring outliers in from both tails of the distribution toward the mean, and odd-power polynomial transformations (e.g., X^3) may help for negative kurtosis. There are many other types of transformations, and this is one of their potential problems. That is, it may be necessary to try several different transformations before finding one that works for a particular distribution. Some distributions can be so severely nonnormal that, essentially, no transformation will work. Transformation means that the variable's original metric is lost and the interpretation of results for that variable must be made in the transformed metric. If the original metric is meaningful, this could be a sacrifice.

Outliers

Cases with scores that are very different from the rest are outliers. A case can be a **univariate outlier** if it has an extreme score on a single variable. There is no single definition of "extreme," but a common rule of thumb is that scores more than three standard deviations beyond the mean may be outliers. Univariate outliers are easy to find by inspecting frequency distributions of z scores. A **multivariate outlier** has extreme scores on two or more variables, or its pattern of scores is atypical. For example, a case may have scores between two and three standard deviations above the mean on all variables. Although none of the individual scores may be considered extreme, the case could be a multivariate outlier if this pattern is unusual in the sample. The detection of multivariate outliers without extreme individual scores is more difficult, but there are a few options. Some computer programs for SEM identify cases that contribute the most to multivariate nonnormality; such cases may be multivariate outliers. In order for cases to be screened by the computer, a raw data file must be analyzed.

Another method is based on the **Mahalanobis distance** (D) statistic, which indicates the distance in standard deviation units between a set of scores (vector) for an individual case and the sample means for all variables (centroids). Within large samples, D^2 is distributed as Pearson chi-square (χ^2) statistics with degrees of freedom equal to the number of variables. A value of D^2 with a relatively low p value in the appropriate chi-square distribution may lead to rejection of the null hypothesis that the case comes from the same population as the rest. A conservative level of statistical significance has been recommended for this test (e.g., $p < .001$). Some computer programs for general statistical analyses print D (or D^2) for individual cases; see Stevens (2002) for more information and examples.

Linearity and Homoscedasticity

Linearity and homoscedasticity were defined in Chapter 2. They are also aspects of multivariate normality that can be evaluated through the inspection of bivariate scatterplots. Heteroscedasticity may be caused by nonnormality in variables X or Y or by more random error (unreliability) at some levels of X or Y than at others. For example, scores from a cognitive test may not reliably measure the skills of persons of lower ability but could have adequate reliability for persons of higher ability. A transformation may remedy heteroscedasticity due to nonnormality but may not be helpful for heteroscedasticity due to differential reliability. Some heteroscedastic relations are expected, however, especially for developmental variables. For instance, age is related to height, but variation in height increases from childhood to adolescence.

Missing Data

It often happens that data sets have missing observations, typically because of factors beyond the researcher's control such as equipment failure or the attrition of cases from a longitudinal study. A *few* missing scores in a large sample may be of little concern; when there are *many* missing observations, however, that may well pose a more serious challenge. Entire books and special sections of journals (e.g., West, 2001) have been written about the problem of missing observations, which is fortunate, since it is not possible here to give a comprehensive account of it. The goal instead is to acquaint readers with analysis options related to SEM and provide references for further study.

Most methods to deal with incomplete observations assume that the data loss pattern is **ignorable**, which means not systematic. A systematic pattern means that incomplete cases differ from cases with complete records for some reason, rather than randomly; thus, results based only on the latter may not generalize to the whole population. There are two general kinds of ignorable missing data patterns, **missing at random** (MAR) and **missing completely at random** (MCAR). If the missing observations on some variable X differ from the observed scores on that variable only by chance, the data loss pattern is said to be MAR. If, in addition to the property just mentioned, the presence versus absence of data on X is unrelated to any other variable, the data loss pattern is said to be MCAR. Note that MCAR is just a stronger assumption about the randomness of data loss than is MAR, but it may be doubtful whether the assumption of MCAR holds in actual data sets. It is not always easy in practice to determine whether the data loss pattern is systematic or ignorable (i.e., MAR or MCAR), especially when each variable is measured only once (e.g., Allison, 2001; R. J. A. Little & Rubin, 2002). Also note that there is no magical statistical "fix" that will remedy systematic data loss. About the best that can be done is to attempt to understand the nature of the underlying data loss mechanism and take preventive measures.

Four general categories of methods for dealing with missing observations are described next (Vriens & Melton, 2002):

1. *Available case methods* are a component of many computer programs for general statistical analyses, not just for SEM. They typically assume a data loss pattern that is MCAR. Available case methods are also generally post-hoc in that they take little or no advantage of the structure in the data. This is because they analyze only the data available through deletion of cases with missing observations. In **listwise deletion**, cases with missing scores on any variable are excluded from all analyses. The effective sample size with listwise deletion includes only cases with complete records, and this number can be substantially smaller than the original sample size if missing observations are scattered across many records. An advantage of this method is that all analyses are conducted with the same number of cases. Not so with **pairwise deletion**, in which cases are excluded only if they have missing data on variables involved in a particular computation. This means that the effective sample size can vary from analysis to analysis. Suppose that $N = 300$ for a sample with missing observations on some variables. If 280 cases have no missing scores on variables X and Y, then the effective sample size for the covariance between X and Y is this number. If fewer or more cases have valid scores on X and W, however, then the effective sample size for the covariance between X and W will not be 280.

The feature of pairwise deletion just mentioned presents a potential drawback for SEM (and other multivariate methods). When individual values in a covariance matrix are based on different numbers of cases, it is possible that some of the values are mathematically out of range; that is, it would be impossible to derive them if the covariances were all calculated using data from the same cases (e.g., with listwise deletion). One way to look at this phenomenon is at the level of Pearson correlations, which are part of a covariance. Specifically, given three variables X, Y, and W, the value of the Pearson correlation between X and Y must fall within the following range:

$$r_{XW}\, r_{YW} \pm \sqrt{(1 - r_{XW}^2)(1 - r_{YW}^2)} \qquad (3.3)$$

If $r_{XW} = .60$ and $r_{YW} = .40$, for example, then the value of r_{XY} must be within the range $.24 \pm .73$ (i.e., $-.49$ to $.97$)—any other value would be out of bounds.

If an out-of-bounds correlation is part of a covariance matrix, then the matrix is **nonpositive definite** or **singular**, which means that certain mathematical operations with the matrix such as division (e.g., inverting the matrix) will fail because of problems such as denominators that equal zero. Some computer programs issue error messages after they try unsuccessfully to analyze a nonpositive definitive data matrix. Other symptoms of a singular data matrix that may be reported in program output are a matrix determinant that is zero or negative **eigenvalues**. The latter are types of variances for matrices, but variances cannot logically be less than zero. For these reasons, pairwise deletion is not generally recommended for use in SEM unless the number of missing observations is small.

2. *Single imputation methods* also generally assume that the data loss pattern is MCAR. Perhaps the most basic method is **mean substitution**, which involves replacing a missing score with the overall sample average. This method is simple, but it tends to distort the underlying distribution of the data, reducing variability and making distributions more peaked at the mean (Vriens & Melton, 2002). Other imputation methods take somewhat better advantage of the structure in the data. One is **regression-based imputation**, in which a missing observation is replaced with a predicted score generated by using multiple regression based on nonmissing scores on other variables. Ideally, these other vari-

ables should be ones related to the underlying data loss mechanism. The method of **pattern matching** replaces a missing observation with a score from another case with a similar profile of scores across other variables. The PRELIS program of LISREL 8 (Jöreskog & Sörbom, 2003) can use pattern matching to impute missing observations. Another method is **random hot-deck imputation**. This technique separates complete from incomplete records, sorts both sets of records so that cases with similar profiles on background variables such as gender or occupation are grouped together, randomly interleaves the incomplete records among the complete records, and replaces missing scores with those on the same variable from the nearest complete record. A disadvantage of all these methods is that if the proportion of missing observations is relatively high, error variance may be substantially underestimated due to imputing just a single value (Vriens & Melton, 2002).

3. *Model-based imputation methods* are generally more sophisticated than any of the methods described earlier and have recently become available in some SEM computer programs such as LISREL 8 and EQS 6 (Bentler, 2003). These methods can replace a missing score with one or more imputed (estimated) values from a predictive distribution that explicitly models the underlying data loss mechanism. In nontechnical terms, a model for both the complete data and missing data is defined under these methods. The computer then estimates means and variances in the whole sample that satisfy a statistical criterion. In SEM, this criterion is usually associated with the method of maximum likelihood, which is the most widely used estimation algorithm (Chapter 5). A related method for missing values analysis is based on the **expectation–maximization** (EM) algorithm, which has two steps. In the E (estimation) step, missing observations are imputed by predicted scores in a series of regressions where each missing variable is regressed on the remaining variables for a particular case. In the M (maximization) step, the whole imputed data set is submitted for maximum likelihood estimation. These two steps are repeated until a stable solution is reached across the M steps. See Peters and Enders (2002) for more information about model-based methods for analyses with missing data.

4. There are some special multivariate estimation methods that do not delete cases with incomplete records or impute missing observa-

tions. They also generally assume that the data loss pattern is MAR, not the more strict assumption of MCAR. In SEM, these methods are based on special forms of maximum likelihood estimation available in computer programs such as Amos 5 (Arbuckle, 2003) and Mx Graph (Neale, Boker, Xie, & Maes, 2002). This method partitions the cases into subsets with the same patterns of missing observations. All available statistical information is extracted from each subset, and all cases are retained in the analysis. Arbuckle (1996) and Peters and Enders (2002) found in computer simulation studies that special maximum likelihood-based methods for incomplete data generally outperformed traditional (available case) methods.

It seems that researchers too often neglect to inform their readers about how missing observations were handled in the analysis. For example, P. L. Roth (1994) examined 134 analyses in 75 articles published in two psychology journals. A total of 86 were conducted with data that contained missing values, but in more than a third of the cases (31, or 36%) the authors did not report how they dealt with missing observations. See Allison (2003) for further information about options for dealing with missing data in SEM.

Multicollinearity

Another cause of singular covariance matrices is **multicollinearity**, which occurs when intercorrelations among some variables are so high (e.g., >.85) that certain mathematical operations are either impossible or unstable because some denominators are close to zero. Multicollinearity can occur because what appear to be separate variables actually measure the same thing. Suppose that X is a measure of poverty and Y is a measure of unemployment. If $r_{XY} = .90$, for example, then variables X and Y are basically redundant. Either one or the other variable could be included in the same analysis, but it makes little sense to include both. In this case, the measurement of poverty is not distinct from the measurement of unemployment, so only one should be included in the analysis. Researchers can also inadvertently cause multicollinearity when composite variables and their constituent variables are analyzed together. Suppose that a questionnaire has 10 items and the total score is summed across all items. Although the bivariate correlations between the total score and each of the individual items may not be very high, the multiple correlation between the total score and the 10 items must equal 1.00, which is multicollinearity in its most extreme form.

It is easy to spot pairwise multicollinearity simply by inspecting the correlation matrix. Detecting multicollinearity among three or more variables is not so straightforward. Recall the example of the 10-item questionnaire where none of the bivariate correlations of the individual items with the total score will necessarily be high. One method is to calculate a squared multiple correlation (R^2_{smc}) between each variable and all the rest; $R^2_{smc} > .90$ suggests multicollinearity. A related statistic is **tolerance**, which equals $1 - R^2_{smc}$ and indicates the proportion of total standardized variance that is unique (i.e., not explained by all the other variables). Tolerance values less than .10 may indicate multicollinearity. Another statistic is the **variance inflation factor** (VIF). It equals $1/(1 - R^2_{smc})$, the ratio of the total standardized variance to unique variance. If the first is more than 10 times greater than the second (i.e., VIF > 10), the variable may be redundant.

There are two basic ways to deal with multicollinearity: eliminate variables or combine redundant ones into a composite variable. For example, if X and Y are highly correlated, one could be dropped or their scores could be summed to form a single new variable, but note that the total score must replace both X and Y in the analysis. Multicollinearity can also happen between latent variables when their estimated correlation is so high that it is clear they are not distinct variables. This problem is considered in later chapters.

Relative Variances

Covariance matrices where the ratio of the largest to the smallest variance is greater than, say, 10 are known as **ill scaled**. Analysis of an ill-scaled covariance matrix in SEM can cause problems. As discussed in Chapter 5, the most widely used estimation methods in SEM are iterative, which means that initial estimates are derived by the computer and then modified through subsequent cycles of calculations. The goal of iterative estimation is to derive better estimates at each stage, ones that improve the overall fit of the model to the data. When the improvements from step to step become very small, iterative estimation stops because the solution is stable. However, if the estimates do not converge to stable values, then the process may fail. One cause of failure of iterative estimation is variances of observed variables that are very different in magnitude (e.g., $s_X^2 = 12.00$, $s_Y^2 = .12$). When the computer adjusts the estimates from one step to the next in an iterative process for an ill-scaled covariance matrix, the sizes of these changes may be huge for variables with small variances but trivial for others with large variances. Consequently, the entire set of estimates may head toward worse rather than better fit of the model to the data. To prevent this problem, variables with extremely low or high variances can be rescaled by multiplying their scores by a constant, which changes the variance by a factor that equals the squared constant. For example, multiplication of scores on X by 5 will increase X's variance by 25-fold; likewise, multiplication by 1/5 will reduce its variance by 1/25. Note that rescaling a variable this way changes its mean and variance but not its correlation with other variables.

3.3 SCORE RELIABILITY AND VALIDITY

Reliability and validity are attributes of scores in a particular sample, not measures. This is because a measure is not reliable versus unreliable or valid versus not valid across all conceivable uses of it (B. Thompson, 2003). It is essential that the scores analyzed in SEM (or any other kind of statistical method for behavioral data) are both reliable and valid. These concepts are reviewed next; see Bryant (2000), Strube (2000), and Nunnally and Bernstein (1994) for more information.

Score Reliability

Reliability concerns the degree to which the scores are free from random measurement error. Examples of random error include inadvertent clerical errors in scoring and especially good luck in guessing the correct alternative in a multiple-choice item. Reliability is estimated as one minus the proportion of the observed variance that is due to random error. These estimates are called reliability coefficients, and a reliability coefficient for the scores of variable X is often designated with the symbol r_{XX}. Because r_{XX} is a proportion of variance, its theoretical range is 0–1.00. For example, if $r_{XX} = .80$, then it is estimated that 20%

of the observed variance is due to random error. As r_{XX} approaches zero, the scores are more and more like random numbers, and random numbers measure nothing in particular. However, it can happen that an empirical reliability coefficient is less than zero. A negative reliability coefficient is usually interpreted as though its value were zero, but such a result (i.e., $r_{XX} < 0$) often indicates a serious problem with the scores.

Because there are different types of random error, it is often necessary to evaluate different aspects of score reliability. The most commonly reported estimate of reliability is Cronbach's coefficient alpha (α). This statistic measures **internal consistency reliability**, the degree to which responses are consistent across the items within a single measure. If internal consistency reliability is low, the content of the items may be so heterogeneous that the total score is not the best possible unit of analysis for the measure. Estimation of other kinds of score reliability may require multiple measurement occasions, test forms, or examiners. For example, **test–retest reliability** involves the readministration of a measure to the same group on a second occasion. If the two sets of scores are highly correlated, then random error due to temporal factors may be minimal. **Alternate-forms reliability** involves the evaluation of the stability of scores across different versions of the same test. **Interrater reliability** is relevant for subjectively scored measures: if independent evaluators do not consistently agree in their scoring, then examiner-specific factors may contribute unduly to observed score variability.

Although there is no gold standard as to how high coefficients should be in order to consider score reliability as "good," some rough guidelines are offered: generally, reliability coefficients around .90 are considered "excellent," values around .80 are "very good," and values around .70 are "adequate." The researcher can either evaluate the reliability of scores in his or her own samples or rely on published sources (test manuals, journal articles, etc.). Note that published reliability coefficients may not generalize to a researcher's particular sample. Be careful about using a measure with scores of unknown reliability.

Score Validity

Validity concerns the soundness of the inferences based on the scores—that is, whether the scores measure what are they supposed to measure, but also *not* measure what they are not supposed to measure (B. Thompson, 2003). Score reliability is a necessary but insufficient requirement for validity. That is, reliable scores may also be valid, but unreliable scores cannot be valid.

Most forms of score validity are subsumed under the concept of **construct validity**, which concerns whether the scores measure the hypothetical construct the researcher believes they do. Hypothetical constructs are not directly observable and thus can be measured only indirectly through observed scores. There is no single, definitive test of construct validity, nor is it typically established in a single study. The SEM method of confirmatory factor analysis (Chapter 7) is a valuable tool for evaluating construct validity, but there are others, including experimental manipulation of some variable to evaluate whether scores change in a predicted way. A facet of construct validity is **content validity**, which concerns whether test items are representative of the domain they are supposed to measure. Expert opinion is the basis for establishing whether item content is representative.

Another facet of construct validity is **criterion-related validity**, which concerns whether a measure relates to an external standard (criterion) against which the measure can be evaluated. These relations are usually assessed with correlations called validity coefficients, often represented with the symbol r_{XY}, where X stands for the predictor (i.e., the measure) and Y for the criterion. The term **concurrent validity** is used when scores on the predictor and criterion are collected at the same time; **predictive validity**, when the criterion is measured later; and **postdictive validity**, when the criterion is measured before the predictor. **Convergent validity** and **discriminant validity** involve the evaluation of measures against each other instead of against an external criterion. A set of variables presumed to measure the *same* construct shows convergent validity if their intercorrelations are at least moderate in magnitude. In contrast, a set of variables presumed to measure *different* constructs shows discriminant validity if their intercorrelations are not too high. If $r_{XY} = .90$, for example, then we can hardly say that variables X and Y measure different constructs. The evaluation of convergent validity and discriminant validity is a common part of confirmatory factor analysis.

Unreliability in the scores of either X (predictor) or Y (criterion) attenuates their correlation. This formula from classical measurement theory shows the exact relation:

$$\text{theoretical maximum absolute value of } r_{XY} = \sqrt{r_{XX}r_{YY}} \quad (3.4)$$

In words, the value of an observed validity coefficient can equal ±1.00 only if the scores from both measures are perfectly reliable. Suppose that $r_{XX} = .90$ and $r_{YY} = .10$. Given these score reliabilities, the theoretical absolute value of r_{XY} can be no higher than $(.90 \times .10)^{1/2} = .30$. A variation of Equation 3.4 is the **correction for attenuation**:

$$\hat{r}_{XY} = \frac{r_{XY}}{\sqrt{r_{XX}r_{YY}}} \quad (3.5)$$

where $\hat{r}_{XY}$ is the estimated validity coefficient if scores on both measures were perfectly reliable. In general, $\hat{r}_{XY}$ is greater than r_{XY}. For example, $\hat{r}_{XY} = .50$, given $r_{XY} = .30$, $r_{XX} = .90$, and $r_{YY} = .40$. Because disattenuated correlations are only estimates, it can happen that their absolute values exceed 1.00. Disattenuating observed correlations is one way to take measurement error into account, but note that estimates of r_{XX} and r_{YY} are required. Perhaps a better way to take measurement error into account in SEM is to use multiple measures of each construct and specify a measurement model. This idea is elaborated in Chapter 4.

3.4 SUMMARY

The most widely used estimation methods in SEM require careful screening of the raw data for multivariate normality. It is also critical to select an appropriate method for dealing with missing data. These methods generally assume that the missing data pattern is random. The pairwise deletion of cases with missing observations can be problematic because it can lead to covariance matrices that cannot be analyzed by SEM computer programs (or other programs for multivariate analyses). Computer programs for SEM typically accept as input either raw data files or matrix summaries of the data. Because standard estimation methods in these programs assume the analysis of unstandardized variables, a covariance matrix is preferred over a correlation matrix when a matrix summary is the input to a SEM computer program and means are not analyzed. The fundamental concepts discussed in this chapter and the previous one set the stage for the overview of core techniques in the SEM family presented in the next chapter.

3.5 RECOMMENDED READINGS

Allison, P. D. (2003). Missing data techniques for structural equation modeling. *Journal of Abnormal Psychology, 112,* 545–557.

Bryant, F. B. (2000). Assessing the validity of measurement. In L. G. Grimm & P. R. Yarnold (Eds.), *Reading and understanding more multivariate statistics* (pp. 99–146). Washington, DC: American Psychological Association.

Thompson, B. (Ed.). (2003). *Score reliability: Contemporary thinking on reliability issues.* Thousand Oaks, CA: Sage.

4

Core SEM Techniques
and Software

The core SEM techniques—path analysis, confirmatory factor analysis, and the evaluation of structural regression models with features of both path and factor models—are reviewed in this chapter. This presentation is based on research examples that are dealt with in more detail later in this book (Part II). Data analysis options for these examples are considered from two perspectives: first from that of standard statistical procedures, and then from that of core SEM techniques. This discussion also introduces many of the graphical elements used in model diagrams in SEM. The main goal of this discussion is to build a broader context for SEM, one that gives the reader a better sense of the connections between core SEM techniques and other analytical methods with which he or she may be more familiar. Major software tools for SEM are also described.

4.1 STEPS OF SEM

The six basic steps of SEM are listed next. They are actually iterative because problems at a later step may require a return to an earlier one. Later chapters elaborate specific issues at each step for particular SEM techniques:

1. *Specify the model*, which means that the researcher's hypotheses are expressed in the form of a structural equation model. Although

many researchers begin the process of specification by drawing a diagram of a model using a set of more-or-less standard symbols (defined later), the model can alternatively be described as a series of equations. These equations define the model's parameters, which correspond to presumed relations among observed or latent variables that the computer eventually estimates with sample data.

2. *Determine whether the model is identified*, which means that it is theoretically possible for the computer to derive a unique estimate of every model parameter. Different types of structural equation models must meet certain requirements in order to be identified. If a model fails to meet the relevant identification requirements, attempts to estimate it may be unsuccessful.

3. *Select measures* of the variables represented in the model (i.e., operationalize the constructs) and *collect, prepare,* and *screen the data* (Chapters 2–3).

4. *Use a computer program to estimate the model* (i.e., conduct the analysis). Several things take place at this step:

   a. *Evaluate model fit,* which means determine how well the model as a whole explains the data. Perhaps more often than not, researchers' initial models do not fit the data very well. When (not if) this happens to you, go to step 5 (i.e., skip the rest of this step).
   b. *Interpret the parameter estimates.* Once it is determined that the fit of a structural equation model to the data is adequate, too many researchers in written summaries of the results do not interpret the parameter estimates for specific effects. It seems that the concern for overall model fit is sometimes so great that little attention is paid to whether estimates of its parameters are actually meaningful (Kaplan, 2000).
   c. *Consider equivalent models.* An equivalent model explains the data just as well as the researcher's preferred model but does so with a different configuration of hypothesized relations. An equivalent model thus offers a competing account of the data. For a given structural equation model, there may be many—and in some cases infinitely many—equivalent variations; thus, it behooves the researcher to explain why his or her preferred model should not be rejected in favor of statistically equivalent ones.

5. If necessary (and it often is), *respecify the model* and evaluate the fit of the revised model to the same data. As with a model's initial specification, its respecification should be guided by the researcher's hypotheses.

6. Given a satisfactory model, *accurately and completely describe the analysis* in written reports. MacCallum and Austin (2000) reviewed about 500 applications of SEM published in 16 different psychology research journals from 1993 to 1997. They found problems with the reporting of the results in many of these reports. For example, in about 50% of the articles, the reporting of parameter estimates was incomplete (e.g., unstandardized estimates were omitted); in about 25% it was not specified whether a covariance or correlation matrix was analyzed; and in about 10% the model specified or the indicators of latent variables were not clearly described. These are serious shortcomings, especially considering that there are published guidelines for the reporting of results in SEM (Boomsma, 2000; Hoyle & Panter, 1995; McDonald & Ho, 2002).

Two optimal steps could be added to the basic ones just described:

7. *Replicate the results.* Replication is relatively rare in SEM. That is, models are seldom estimated across independent samples either by the same researchers who collected the original data (e.g., internal replication) or by different researchers who did not (e.g., external replication). The general need for large samples in SEM undoubtedly complicates replication. Nevertheless, it is critical to eventually replicate a structural equation model if it is ever to represent anything beyond a mere statistical exercise.

8. *Apply the results.* Kaplan (2000) notes that despite more than 30 years of application of SEM in the behavioral sciences, it is rare that results from SEM analyses are used for policy or clinically relevant prediction studies. Neglecting to correctly carry out steps 4–6 may be part of the problem.

The next three sections describe research examples that introduce core SEM techniques. Each example is also considered in greater detail in later chapters devoted to each technique. Do not worry that you do not now understand all of the concepts introduced here; they are dealt with in more detail later in the book.

4.2 PATH ANALYSIS: A STRUCTURAL MODEL OF ILLNESS FACTORS

D. L. Roth, Wiebe, Fillingim, and Shay (1989) administered measures of exercise, hardiness, fitness, stress, and illness within a sample of 373 university students. Hardiness refers to dispositional traits such as resiliency and willingness to look for opportunities in difficult situations. (These are also desirable attributes in those who are learning about SEM!) D. L. Roth et al. hypothesized that (1) exercise and hardiness affect fitness; (2) exercise, hardiness, and fitness affect stress; and (3) all four variables just mentioned affect illness. The variables fitness and stress are accorded special roles in these hypotheses because they are viewed as both causes and effects of other variables. However, there was no particular hypothesis about causal relations between exercise and hardiness; that is, these variables were simply assumed to covary.

A standard statistical technique that might be used here is multiple regression. Three separate analyses might be conducted: the regression of (1) fitness on exercise and hardiness; (2) stress on exercise, hardiness, and fitness; and (3) illness on all four variables just mentioned. Each analysis would yield the R^2 for each criterion and regression coefficients for each predictor. But note that fitness or stress cannot be represented in multiple regression as both a predictor and a criterion in the same analysis—each must be one or the other. Conducting three separate regression analyses would also ignore likely intercorrelations among the criterion variables, fitness, stress, and illness. The technique of canonical correlation can simultaneously analyze sets of multiple predictors and criterion variables and control for intercorrelations within each set, but the fitness or stress variables must be specified as belonging to one set or the other, not both.

Path analysis (PA) from the SEM family is a possible technique when there is only a single measure of each theoretical variable and the researcher has prior hypotheses about causal relations among these variables. The starting point is the specification of a **structural model** that represents all causal hypotheses. A **path model** is a structural model for observed variables. Consider the path model presented in Figure 4.1. This model uses symbols from an approach to causal modeling called **reticular action modeling** (RAM; e.g., McArdle & McDonald, 1984). The RAM symbolism is used in this book because it explicitly represents in diagrams every model parameter that requires a statistical estimate. This property helps to avoid mistakes when one is translating a diagram to the syntax of a particular SEM computer program.

Observed variables in Figure 4.1 are represented with rectangles; in other diagrams they are also represented with squares. The variables exercise and hardiness are **exogenous** because their causes are unknown and thus are not represented in the model. Instead, exogenous variables are specified as causes of other variables. The curved line with two arrowheads (⌣) that connects the rectangles for exercise and hardiness in the figure represents the observed covariance between the two variables if they are unstandardized or their correlation if they are standardized. The same symbol also designates an **unanalyzed association** between two exogenous variables. Note that

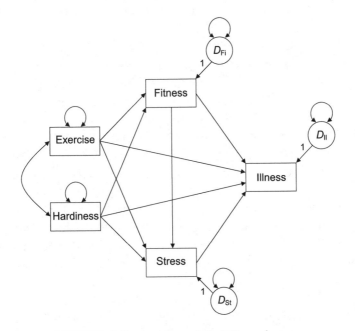

FIGURE 4.1. A path model of illness factors.

although such associations are estimated by the computer, they are unanalyzed in the sense that no prediction is put forward about *why* the two variables covary (e.g., does one cause the other?—do they have a common cause?). The two-headed curved arrows in Figure 4.1 that exit and reenter the same variable ($\curvearrowright$) represent the variance of an exogenous variable. Because the causes of exogenous variables are not represented in path models, they are typically considered free to vary and covary. The symbols $\curvearrowright$ and $\smile$, respectively, reflect these assumptions.

Each line with a single arrowhead ($\rightarrow$) in Figure 4.1 represents a hypothesized *direct effect* of one variable on another. The arrowhead points to the presumed effect and the line originates from a presumed cause. Direct effects are also called *paths*, and statistical estimates of directs effects are **path coefficients**. Path coefficients are interpreted as regression coefficients in multiple regression, which means that they control for correlations among multiple presumed causes of the same variable. For example, the coefficient for the path Exercise $\rightarrow$ Fitness in the figure controls for the correlation between exercise and hardiness.

The variables fitness, stress, and illness in Figure 4.1 are all **endogenous**. Unlike exogenous variables, presumed causes of endogenous variables are explicitly represented in the model. Observe that the endogenous variables fitness and stress in Figure 4.1 are also specified as direct causes of other endogenous variables (e.g., Fitness $\rightarrow$ Stress, Stress $\rightarrow$ Illness). These specifications give fitness and stress each a dual role as, in the language of regression, both a predictor and a criterion. This dual role is described in PA as an **indirect effect** or a **mediator effect**. Indirect effects involve one or more **intervening variables** presumed to "transmit" some of the causal effects of prior variables onto subsequent variables. Intervening variables in indirect effects are also called **mediator variables**. A total of nine different indirect effects are represented in Figure 4.1. One corresponds to the path Exercise $\rightarrow$ Fitness $\rightarrow$ Illness, and it reflects the hypothesis that exercise affects fitness, which in turn influences illness. Just as direct causal effects are estimated in a PA, so too are indirect causal effects.

Another standard feature of path models is the representation of hypothesized spurious associations. Observe in Figure 4.1 that fitness and stress are specified to have two common causes, exercise and hardiness. The coefficient for the path Fitness → Stress thus controls for these presumed common causes. Like a partial correlation, if the value of this coefficient is close to zero, the observed correlation between fitness and stress may reflect solely a spurious association. However, if this coefficient is substantial, the hypothesis of spuriousness is rejected. Together with the ability to estimate direct and indirect effects and to control for correlations among presumed causal variables, PA can be seen as a way to "decompose" observed correlations into their constituent parts, spurious and nonspurious (causal). A path model is said to fit the data if these decompositions can reproduce the observed correlations.

Circles or ellipses in diagrams of structural equation models usually represent unobserved or latent variables. These variables in path models are **disturbances**, and every endogenous variable has a disturbance. In Figure 4.1, disturbances are represented with an uppercase D. For example, the term D_{Fi} represents variance in fitness unexplained by the variables specified as its direct causes, exercise and hardiness; the other two disturbances in Figure 4.1 have similar interpretations. Disturbances are analogous to residuals in regression but have a connotation based more in causal modeling than just prediction. Theoretically, disturbances represent all causes of an endogenous variable that are omitted from the structural model. For example, there are almost certainly things that affect stress besides exercise, hardiness, and fitness: factors such as coping mechanisms or genetic predispositions, among others, quickly spring to mind. A disturbance can be seen as a "proxy" or composite variable that represents all unmeasured causes, and the line that points from a disturbance to an endogenous variable represents the combined effects of all the omitted causes of that variable. Because the nature and number of these omitted causes is unknown as far as the model is concerned, disturbances can be viewed as unmeasured exogenous variables. For this reason, the symbol for the variance of an exogenous variable ($\curvearrowright$) appears next to each disturbance in Figure 4.1. The constants (1.0) that appear in the figure next to the paths from disturbances to endogenous variables represent the assignment of a scale (metric) to each unobserved exogenous variable. The concept behind this specification is explained in the next chapter. Analysis of the path model in Figure 4.1 is discussed in Chapter 6.

4.3 CONFIRMATORY FACTOR ANALYSIS: A MEASUREMENT MODEL OF AROUSAL

The Visual Similes Test II (VST II; Eaves, 1995) is intended to measure levels of arousal among persons ages 5–21 years. It consists of two forms, Affective and Cognitive. Items for both forms consist of visual stimuli where a checkerboard pattern obscures 50% of the image: Affective form items (30 in total) are pictures that depict scenes related to survival, such as predation and disasters, but Cognitive form items (25 in total) depict stimuli that require abstractions in order to interpret them (e.g., a picture of the American flag should be recognized as that nation's flag by children in the United States). Examinees are to correctly identify each picture within 60 seconds. T. O. Williams, Eaves, and Cox (2002) administered the VST II to 216 children ages 10–12 years old, and they created 10 different item parcels, 5 for each form. A parcel is a total score across a group of homogeneous items and is usually considered a continuous variable. (The analysis of item parcels is discussed in more detail in Chapter 7.)

T. O. Williams et al. (2002) used the technique of confirmatory factor analysis (CFA) from the SEM family to evaluate whether the 10 different item parcels of the VST II seem to measure two distinct factors that may correspond to affective arousal and cognitive arousal. As concisely defined by Nunnally and Bernstein (1994, p. 85), a construct

> *reflects the hypothesis (often incompletely formed) that a variety of behaviors will correlate with one another in studies of individual differences and/or will be similarly affected by experimental manipulations.*

Hypothetical constructs are not directly observable. Instead, they can be only inferred or measured indirectly through observed variables, also called **indicators**. For two reasons, it is probably unrealistic to expect that a hypothetical construct could be adequately measured by any single indicator. First, indicators are not generally free from the effects of random error, which implies that their scores are not perfectly reliable. Second, not all of the systematic part of an indicator's variance may reflect the construct that the researcher wishes to assess (e.g., self-reports may be susceptible to a response set), which implies that the scores are not perfectly valid.

One way around the aforementioned problems of measuring a construct with a single indicator is to use multiple indicators. Scores across a set of measures tend to be more reliable and valid than scores on any individual measure. Also, multiple indicators may each assess a somewhat different facet of the construct, which enhances score validity. However, multiple indicators of every construct are not always available; if so, the researcher must settle for single-indicator measurement. Obviously, it is crucial that a single indicator have good psychometric characteristics. Either multiple- or single-indicator measurement can be represented in SEM, but path analysis assumes only the latter (see Figure 4.1).

A standard statistical technique for evaluating a measurement model is **exploratory factor analysis** (EFA). Originally developed by psychologists to test theories of intelligence, EFA is not generally considered a member of the SEM family. The term EFA actually refers to a class of procedures that include centroid, principal components, and principal axis factor analysis, among many others, that differ in the statistical criteria used to derive factors. As its name suggests, EFA does not require a priori hypotheses about how indicators are related to underlying factors or even the number of factors. For example, all of the indicators are typically allowed to correlate with every factor in EFA. Hence the term "exploratory," which in this context means that the researcher has little direct influence on the correspondence between indicators and factors. There are ways to conduct EFA in a more confirmatory mode, such as when the computer is instructed to extract a certain number of factors based on theory, but the point is that EFA does not require specific hypotheses in order to apply it. Fabrigar, Wegener, McCallum, and Strahan (1999) evaluate the use of EFA in psychological research.

The technique of CFA analyzes a priori measurement models in which both the number of factors and their correspondence to the indicators are explicitly specified. Presented in Figure 4.2 is a two-factor CFA measurement model of the VST II analyzed by T. O. Williams et al. (2002). The two factors in this model, Affective Arousal and Cognitive Arousal, are each represented by a symbol for a latent variable, an ellipse; in other diagrams, factors are also represented with circles. The curved line that connects the ellipses in the figure ($\smile$) has the same meaning as in PA in that it designates an unanalyzed association. Here,

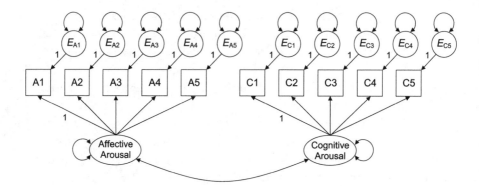

FIGURE 4.2. A confirmatory factor analysis measurement model of arousal.

there is no hypothesis that one of these factors causes the other; instead, they are simply assumed to covary. In this way, the two factors in Figure 4.1 are exogenous variables, but ones that are not directly measured. Because the factors are exogenous, the symbol for a variance ($\curvearrowright$) appears next to each of them in Figure 4.2.

The 10 different item parcels of the VST II (5 per scale) analyzed by T. O. Williams et al. (2002) are represented in Figure 4.2 with the symbol for an observed variable, a square. Analogous to their counterparts in PA are the paths in the figure that point from the factors to the indicators, which represent direct effects—but here of the factors on the indicators. Conceptually, these paths represent causal effects of the factor on an indicator, that is, the extent to which the factor is reflected in the scores of that indicator. In this sense, a measurement model can be viewed as a structural model of presumed causal effects of latent variables on observed scores. Whereas statistical estimates of direct effects in PA are called path coefficients, the corresponding term in factor analysis for such estimates is **factor loading**. In CFA, factor loadings are usually interpreted as regression coefficients that may be in standardized or unstandardized form. In some cases (defined in Chapter 7), standardized factor loadings can be interpreted as estimated Pearson correlations between an indicator and a factor. One of these cases is when an indicator is specified to reflect (measure, load on) a single factor and its measurement error term is unrelated to those of all other indicators. This description corresponds to the measurement model of

Figure 4.2. But in other cases, these coefficients in standardized form are interpreted as standardized regression weights (i.e., beta weights). The constants (1.0) that appear in Figure 4.2 next to the paths from the factors to just one of their indicators (e.g., Affective → A1) represent the assignment of a metric to the factors. The scaling of factors in CFA measurement models is discussed in Chapter 7.

Each term in Figure 4.2 designated with an uppercase E is a **measurement error**, which represents **unique variance**, a factor-analytic term for indicator variance not explained by the factors. Like disturbances in path models, measurement errors are proxy variables for all sources of residual variation in indicator scores that is not explained by the factors; that is, they are unmeasured exogenous variables. Accordingly, the symbol for a variance ($\curvearrowright$) appears next to each of the measurement error terms in Figure 4.2. Two types of unique variance are represented by measurement error terms: random error (score unreliability) and all sources of systematic variance not due to the factors. Examples of the latter include effects due to a particular measurement method or the particular stimuli that make up a task. When it is said that SEM takes account of measurement error, it is the E terms to which this statement refers, although E terms reflect more than just score unreliability. The paths in the figure that point to the indicators from the measurement errors represent the direct effects of all unmeasured sources of unique variance on the indicators. The constants (1.0) that appear in Figure 4.2 next to these paths represent the assignment of a metric to each residual term.

The results of a CFA include estimates of covariances between the factors, loadings of the indicators on their respective factors, and the amount of measurement error (unique variance) for each indicator. If the researcher's a priori measurement model is reasonably correct, then one should see the following pattern of results: (1) indicators specified to measure a common underlying factor all have relatively high standardized loadings on that factor, and (2) estimated correlations between the factors are not excessively high (e.g., >.85). The former result indicates convergent validity; the latter, discriminant validity. For example, if the estimated correlation between the Affective Arousal and the Cognitive Arousal factors in the model of Figure 4.2 is .95, then the 10 indicators can hardly be said to measure two distinct constructs. If the results of a CFA do not support the researcher's a priori hypotheses, the measurement model can be respecified and reanalyzed. The ideas of convergent validity and discriminant validity are discussed in more detail later in this book. The analysis of the CFA measurement model in Figure 4.2 is considered in Chapter 7.

4.4 A STRUCTURAL REGRESSION MODEL OF FAMILY RISK AND CHILD ADJUSTMENT

The most general kind of basic structural equation model is a structural regression (SR) model, also called a hybrid model or a LISREL model. The last term reflects the fact that LISREL was one of the first computer programs to analyze SR models, but essentially any contemporary SEM computer program can do so now. An SR model is the synthesis of a structural model and a measurement model. As in PA, the specification of an SR model allows tests of hypotheses about direct and indirect causal effects. Unlike path models, though, these effects can involve latent variables because an SR model also incorporates a measurement component that represents observed variables as indicators of underlying factors, just as in CFA. The capability to test hypotheses about both structural and measurement relations within a single model affords much flexibility.

Worland, Weeks, Janes, and Strock (1984) measured within a sample of 158 adolescents the degree of parental psychopathology (none, schizophrenia or affective disorder, other psychiatric or medical disorder) and low family socioeconomic status (SES). The cognitive status of the adolescents was assessed with an IQ test that yielded standard scores in three areas: verbal ability, visual–spatial ability, and short-term memory ability. Their scholastic skills were measured with other standardized tests of reading, arithmetic, and spelling. Finally, the adolescents' teachers completed rating scales about classroom adjustment in four areas: motivation, extraversion, social relationships, and emotional stability. Worland et al. (1984) hypothesized that greater familial risk as indicated by the presence of significant parent psychopathology and low family SES affects classroom adjustment only indirectly, first through cognitive ability and then through scholastic achievement (i.e., high familial risk → low ability → poor achievement → problematic classroom adjustment).

Worland and colleagues' use of multiple measures of each domain implies a measurement model—here, one with four factors each assessed with either two (familial risk), three (cognitive ability, achievement), or four (classroom adjustment) indicators. Using CFA, one could test whether the 12 indicators in this study indeed seem to measure four factors. Results of a CFA would also yield estimates of correlations among these four factors. However, Worland et al. (1984) did not simply assume that these four factors are correlated. Instead, they hypothesized a specific pattern of direct and indirect causal relations among them. The technique of CFA estimates only unanalyzed associations among factors, not direct causal effects. Presumed causal effects can be specified and tested in PA, but this technique analyzes observed variables, not latent variables that correspond to hypothetical constructs.

What is needed here is an analytic approach that combines features of both CFA and PA. It is possible in SEM to specify an SR model that has a structural component (like a path model) and a measurement component (like a factor model). Consider the model presented in Figure 4.3 specified to reflect Worland and colleagues' hypotheses (1984). The measurement part of this SR model concerns an a priori pattern of loadings of the indicators on the factors, just as in a CFA model. The structural portion of the model involves direct effects among the four latent variables. Here, the familial risk factor is specified as exogenous and the other three factors as endogenous. The cognitive ability factor is specified to mediate the effects of the familial risk factor on the scholastic achievement factor, which in turn mediates the effect of the cognitive ability factor on the classroom adjustment factor, just as hypothesized by Worland et al. (1984). The evaluation of an SR model is thus akin to conducting a PA but among factors instead of observed variables.

Note another feature of the SR model in Figure 4.3: it has both measurement errors and disturbances. Each indicator in the model has its own measurement error term, just as in a CFA model. Like a path model, the endogenous factors in Figure 4.3 each have a disturbance, but these disturbances reflect omitted causes of latent rather than observed variables. The representation of both kinds of residual terms in an SR model allows measurement error in the indicators to be estimated apart from direct or indirect causal effects among the factors. In

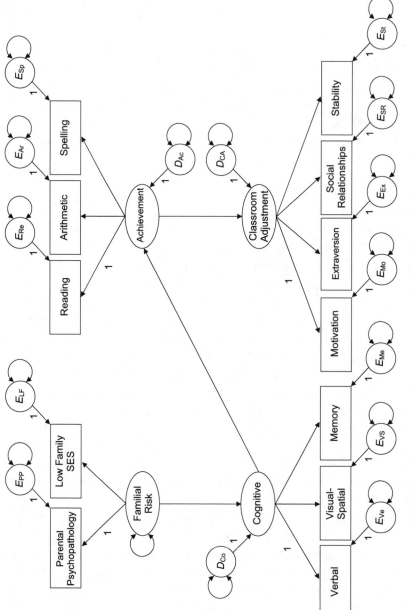

FIGURE 4.3. A structural regression model of familial risk and child adjustment.

contrast, estimation of structural relations in path models, which do not have factors and thus no measurement error terms (see Figure 4.1), does not control for measurement error. The ability to do so with an SR model in the evaluation of presumed causal relations is thus an important advantage over a path model. Analysis of the SR model in Figure 4.3 is discussed in Chapter 8.

4.5 EXTENSIONS

As demonstrated in Part II of this book, path, CFA measurement, or SR models can be specified to test a wide variety of hypotheses about how variables are presumed to relate to each other. All of these core kinds of models have just a **covariance structure**, which includes a structural model or a measurement model (or both). Models with a covariance structure are estimated with sample covariances (or the raw scores). Discussed in Part III of this book are ways that these core models can be extended to represent additional kinds of statistical effects. For example, it is possible to add a **mean structure** to the basic covariance structure of just about any kind of structural equation model. A latent growth model, among other kinds of models that represent means, is basically an SR model with a mean structure (Chapter 10). Unlike standard statistical techniques—such as the analysis of variance (ANOVA)—that analyze only means of observed variables, means of latent variables can also be estimated in SEM taking account of error in the indicators. Models with mean structures are estimated with sample covariances and means (or the raw scores). The ability to analyze basically any kind of structural equation model across multiple samples further extends the range of hypotheses that can be tested in SEM (Chapter 11). For example, group differences on latent variable means can be estimated when a model with a mean structure is simultaneously estimated across multiple samples.

4.6 SEM COMPUTER PROGRAMS

Described next are characteristics of the most widely used computer programs for SEM and ways of using them.

Human–Computer Interaction

There are now several different computer programs for SEM that run on personal computers. There are basically three ways to specify models in these programs. The first is batch mode, which is for users who already know a program's syntax. Lines of code that describe the model, data, and analysis are entered directly into an editor window that may be saved as an ASCII (text) file. Program code entered directly by the user this way is then executed through some form of a "run" command, and the output appears in a new window or is saved in a separate file. Virtually all SEM computer programs support batch mode. The two other ways to specify the model do not require knowledge of program syntax, but they are not available in all SEM computer programs. One method uses "wizards," which are series of templates (dialog boxes) that build the model, data, or analysis, which is done by the user clicking with the mouse cursor on graphical user interface (GUI) elements such as text fields, check boxes, or buttons. Once the wizard has all the information, it automatically writes the program code, which can then be run. Another method provides a GUI through which the user conducts an analysis by drawing the model on the screen. The user is typically provided with a palette of tools in a graphical editor for drawing the model using the symbols described earlier. Some drawing editors attempt to prevent the user from making illegal specifications with the drawing tools such as associating a disturbance with an exogenous variable. When the diagram is finished, the analysis is run from within the program's GUI.

Specifying a structural equation model by drawing it on the screen allows beginners to be productive right away. However, there are some drawbacks to working this way. It can be quite tedious to specify a complex model in a drawing editor, and it is even more tedious to generate a diagram of publication quality. (This is true in any drawing program though.) In fact, it can sometimes be easier to specify a relatively complicated model through a wizard that presents a series of templates. Conducting multiple-sample analyses through a drawing editor can also be awkward, especially if there are more than two groups. This is because it may be necessary to look through several different screens or windows to get all the information about model specifications and data for each group. As users become more familiar with the program, they may find it is more efficient to specify the model by writing code themselves and working in batch mode. For example, all program code for a multiple-sample analysis in batch mode is usually placed in one file, which eliminates the need to look through different windows in a drawing editor to verify whether model specification is correct.

Individual Programs

A total of eight different SEM computer programs for personal computers are briefly described next. Listed alphabetically, they include Amos, the CALIS procedure of SAS/STAT, EQS, LISREL, Mplus, Mx Graph, the RAMONA module of SYSTAT, and the SEPATH module of STATISTICA. There are free student versions of some of the programs just mentioned that place a limit on the size of model or number of variables that can be analyzed. And one of the programs, Mx Graph, is available at no cost because it is not a commercial product. There are other software programs that can analyze structural equation models, but they are not used as often as those listed above.

The programs described next can analyze all of the core types of structural equation models discussed earlier. Most of these programs can also analyze means or models across multiple samples. They differ mainly in their support for more advanced types of analyses and ways of interacting with the program. The descriptions that follow emphasize the major features and relatively unique characteristics of each program. Because specific features or capabilities of computer programs can change quickly when new versions are released, readers should refer to the Web sites listed here for the most recent information. Presented as appendixes in later chapters are examples of syntax from most of these programs applied to various research examples.

Amos[1]

Version 5 of Amos (Analysis of Moment Structures; Arbuckle, 2003) is a Microsoft Windows program made up of two core modules, Amos Graphics and Amos Basic. Amos Graphics provides a GUI through which the user can specify the model by drawing it on the screen. All other aspects of the analysis are also controlled through this GUI. A complete set of tools is available under Amos Graphics for drawing, modifying, or

[1]spss.com/amos

aligning graphical elements of model diagrams. Amos Graphics attempts to prevent mistakes in model specification. For example, it does not allow the user to connect two endogenous variables with ⌣, the symbol for an unanalyzed association between two exogenous variables. A set of preprogrammed graphical dialogs (wizards) is also available that automatically draw covariances among a set of exogenous variables, resize the squares or rectangles that represent observed variables, or draw an entire latent growth model, among other tasks.

If the analysis terminates normally, Amos Graphics can display either the unstandardized or standardized estimates in their proper places in the model diagram. A special utility is the Amos Modeling Laboratory, in which the user can select an individual parameter, change its value, and observe how this change affects model fit. Amos Graphics also has extensive capabilities for more exploratory analyses. For example, the Specification Search function allows the user to designate particular paths in the model diagram as optional. The Amos program then fits the model to the data, using every possible subset of optional paths. The resulting candidate models can be sorted by values of various statistics that measure the fit of the model to the data.

Amos Basic works in batch mode, which means that the model and data are specified in Amos's text-based syntax before all statements are run to execute the analysis. Amos Basic syntax is quite flexible in that it does not use a fixed set of symbols to designate things such as observed versus latent variables or disturbances. Instead, labels for all variables are supplied by the user. Amos Basic is also a full-featured Microsoft Visual Basic language interpreter. This means that it is possible in Amos Basic to write, compile, and debug scripts for Microsoft Visual Basic that control or modify the functionality of Amos Graphics.

Other special features of Amos include the capability to generate bootstrapped estimates of standard errors and confidence intervals for all parameter estimates. Both nonparametric bootstrapping (when a raw data file is analyzed) and parametric bootstrapping that assumes multivariate normality (when a matrix summary of the data is analyzed) are available in Amos. The program also offers a special maximum likelihood method for raw data files where some observations are missing at random. A free student version is also available.[2]

---

[2]www.amosdevelopment.com/download/

CALIS[3]

The CALIS (Covariance Analysis and Linear Structural Equations) procedure of SAS/STAT 8, a comprehensive software package for general statistical analysis that runs under Microsoft Windows (SAS Institute Inc., 2000), analyzes a wide variety of structural equation models. It can also estimate parameters in analyses such as multiple or multivariate linear regression. The CALIS procedure runs only in batch mode; that is, the user must type commands in an editor window that describe the data and model and then run the program in the SAS environment. Models can be specified in CALIS using one of four different representational notations, including LISREL-type matrix-based syntax, EQS-type equations-based syntax, the matrix representation system of the McArdle–McDonald RAM approach, or the matrix-based syntax used in an older SEM program for Microsoft DOS called COSAN (Covariance Structure Analysis; Fraser, 1990).[4] A person familiar with any one of these representational notations should be able to specify structural equation models in CALIS without much difficulty.

Many statistical aspects of the analysis can be controlled through options in CALIS. For example, the user can select among four different methods for calculating start values (initial estimates of model parameters; Chapter 5). Several other options control the estimation process, such as the particular statistical search method used to find optimal parameter estimates. Output from one analysis in CALIS can be automatically saved for input into the next run of the program for the same model and data. This capability can be handy for checking whether a model is identified. (This point is elaborated in later chapters.) However, multiple-sample analyses in CALIS are limited to cases where the sizes of all groups are equal.

EQS[5]

Version 6 of EQS (Equations; Bentler, 2003) is a Microsoft Windows program that can be used for all stages of the analysis from data entry

[3]www.sas.com/technologies/analytics/statistics/stat/index.html

[4]COSAN can be freely downloaded from the Web site of the Jefferson Psychometric Laboratory (Department of Psychology, University of Virginia) at kiptron.psyc.virginia.edu/Programs/software.html

[5]www.mvsoft.com

and screening to exploratory statistical analyses to SEM. The EQS data editor has many of the capabilities of a general statistical package, including conditional case selection, variable transformation, merging of separate data files, and the coding of missing values. Data can be displayed in several different kinds of graphical charts or plots, such as histograms, bar charts, scatterplots, and boxplots, among other types. Exploratory statistical analyses that can be conducted in EQS include the calculation of descriptive statistics, the *t* test, the analysis of variance (ANOVA) for one-way or factorial designs with or without covariates, multiple regression, nonparametric statistics, exploratory factor analysis, and intraclass correlation. There are also options for the analysis of missing data patterns and mean-, regression-, or model-based imputation of missing observations.

The user can interact with EQS in three different ways: in batch mode, through wizards that collect information about the model and data and automatically write EQS programming syntax, or through a drawing editor. The latter two ways do not require knowledge of EQS syntax. The drawing editor in EQS is its Diagrammer, which offers graphical tools for drawing the model on the screen. Tools available in the Diagrammer can automatically draw an entire path, factor, or latent growth curve model after the user completes a few templates about the variables, direct effects, measurement occasions, or residual terms. Like Amos Graphics, the EQS Diagrammer attempts to prevent the user from making illegal specifications with its drawing tools. The second way to specify a model in EQS is to bypass the Diagrammer and use the templates available under the "Build_EQS" menu, which prompt the user to enter information about the analysis. As the user completes each template, EQS syntax is automatically written line-by-line onto a background window. After all dialogs are completed, the whole set of EQS statements is executed by the user after he or she selects the "Run EQS" command under the "Build_EQS" menu.

The third way to run EQS is for users who know its programming syntax. Lines of code that describe the data, model, and analysis can be entered directly into an editor window that EQS saves as an ASCII file. The code is then executed through the "Run EQS" command of the "Build_EQS" menu. The syntax of EQS is based on the Bentler–Weeks representational system, in which the parameters of any covariance structure are regression coefficients for effects on dependent variables and the variances and covariances of independent variables. In the Bentler–Weeks model, independent variables include observed or unobserved exogenous variables (e.g., disturbances, measurement errors) and a dependent variable is any variable with an error term (i.e., it is endogenous). All types of models in EQS are thus set up in a consistent way.

A special strength of EQS is that it offers several different estimation methods for nonnormal data. They all require the analysis of a raw data file. Some of these methods allow for kurtosis in the univariate or multivariate distributions. Other methods assume that the distributions can assume any form but very large samples may be required. The EQS program also calculates for most methods— including standard methods that assume multivariate normality— standard errors and test statistics that are corrected for nonnormal distributions. The methods and corrected statistics just mentioned are described in Chapter 7. The EQS program also offers model-based bootstrapping and a special maximum likelihood estimation method for raw data files with randomly missing observations. The program can also estimate multilevel structural equation models with hierarchical data (Chapter 13).

LISREL[6]

Version 8 of LISREL (Linear Structural Relationships) for Microsoft Windows (Jöreskog & Sörbom, 2003) is an integrated suite of programs for all stages of the analysis, from data entry and management to exploratory data analyses to the evaluation of a wide range of structural equation models. Included in the program suite is PRELIS, which is designed to screen raw data files and prepare matrix summaries for analysis in LISREL. Many multivariate data screening and summarization options are available for raw data stored in PRELIS data files. Included among these options are extensive capabilities for the imputation of missing observations such as pattern matching and model-based multiple imputation. The PRELIS module can also generate bootstrapped samples and estimates, conduct simulation studies with variables specified to have particular distributional characteristics, and

[6]www.ssicentral.com

produce corrected correlation matrices when some of the indicators are not continuous (Chapter 7).

Interactive LISREL has been available in version 8.20 of the program or later. It consists of a series of wizards that prompt the user for information about the model and data and then automatically write command syntax in a separate window. Interactive LISREL also allows the user to specify the model by drawing it on screen through the Path Diagram function. Users already familiar with one of two different LISREL command syntaxes can as an alternative directly enter code into the LISREL editor and then run it by clicking with the mouse cursor on an icon in the main menu bar. The classic original syntax is based on matrix algebra. Its symbol set consists of numerous double-subscripted Greek characters that correspond to elements of various matrices that define the parameters of the model. This command syntax is not easy to use until after one has memorized the whole system.

The other LISREL programming syntax is SIMPLIS, which is not based on matrix algebra or Greek characters, nor does it generally require familiarity with LISREL's matrix-based syntax. Programming in SIMPLIS requires little more than naming the observed and latent variables and specifying paths with equation-type statements. Similar to Amos Basic syntax, the names of all variables are supplied by the user. One does not specify disturbances or measurement errors in SIMPLIS because these terms are automatically generated. If the statement "Path Diagram" is included in the appropriate place in a SIMPLIS command file, LISREL automatically creates the model diagram and displays it with the unstandardized estimates. This feature is very helpful for checking whether the model analyzed is the one the researcher intended to specify.

As befitting of the senior computer program for SEM, the statistical features and capabilities of LISREL are comprehensive. For example, a longstanding strength of LISREL is its ability to analyze models where the indicators of latent variables are discrete (i.e., categorical or ordinal) instead of continuous variables. Specifically, polyserial or polychoric correlations among discrete indicators are calculated in PRELIS, and these estimated Pearson correlations can be analyzed in LISREL or other SEM computer programs (Chapter 7). Multilevel structural equation models for hierarchical data (Chapter 13) can also be estimated in LISREL. A free student edition is also available.[7]

Mplus[8]

The Mplus 3 program (L. Muthén & B. Muthén, 1998–2004) runs under Microsoft Windows and is divided into a basic program for SEM, the Mplus Base program, and three add-on modules for analyzing additional kinds of latent variable models. Mplus Base analyzes path models, factor analysis models, and SR models including latent growth models. The Mplus Base user interacts with the program in one of two different ways, in batch mode by writing programs in the Mplus language that specify the model and data or through a graphical language generator wizard that prepares input files for batch analysis. Through the language generator, the Mplus user completes a few templates about the analysis details such as where the data file is to be found and variable names, and the user's responses are automatically converted to Mplus language statements that are written to an editor window. However, the statements that specify the model must be directly typed in the editor window by the user. Fortunately, the syntax of Mplus is quite straightforward. There is no model diagram input or output in Mplus Base.

Some notable features of Mplus Base include the availability of a special maximum likelihood estimation method for raw data files where some observations are missing at random. Robust estimation of test statistics and standard errors for nonnormal data is also available. Other estimation methods available in Mplus Base do not assume normality but may require very large sample sizes. Mplus Base can correctly analyze a correlation matrix, but only when all variables are continuous and the data come from a single group. There are also built-in capabilities for representing data from multiple cohorts in longitudinal designs or in complex sampling designs where data on continuous outcomes are clustered in units such as "household." Monte Carlo methods available in Mplus can generate simulated random samples based on a model specified by the user and report average results across these

[7]www.ssicentral.com/lisrel/student.html
[8]www.statmodel.com

samples with estimates of their variabilities. Indicators of continuous latent variables can be continuous, binary, ordered categorical (ordinal), count, censored,[9] or combinations of these variable types.

Two optional add-on modules extend the capabilities of Mplus Base even further. For example, the multilevel add-on module is for the analysis of hierarchical data and multilevel models (Chapter 13). The mixture add-on module analyzes models with categorical latent variables. Recall that the levels of a categorical latent variable represent a mixture of subpopulations where membership is not known but inferred from the data. Thus, Mplus Base with the mixture add-on module can analyze "classical" structural equation models with continuous latent variables, latent structure models with categorical latent variables, and models with both continuous and categorical latent variables (e.g., B. Muthén, 2001). Because of its flexibility in the kinds of models that can be analyzed, Mplus Base with the mixture add-on module blurs the distinction between SEM and other techniques for models with latent categorical variables such as latent class analysis, latent profile analysis, and finite mixture modeling, among others.

Mx Graph[10]

The program Mx (Matrix; Neale et al., 2002) is freely available over the Internet. It is a matrix algebra processor and a numerical optimizer that can analyze structural equation models and other kinds of multivariate statistical models. The Mx Graph version of this program is for personal computers with Microsoft Windows. It features a GUI through which the user controls the analysis. There are two different ways to specify a model in Mx Graph. The first is to write a script in the Mx programming language that describes the data and model and then run it in batch mode. The syntax of Mx is based on the McArdle–McDonald RAM matrix formulation, which represents structural equation models with three different matrices: S (symmetric) for unanalyzed associations, A (asymmetric) for direct effects, and F (filter) for identifying the observed variables; see Loehlin (1998, pp. 43–47) for examples. The second way to specify a model in Mx Graph is to use its drawing editor.

---

[9]A censored variable has a high proportion of its scores at the lower or upper end of its distribution.

[10]www.vcu.edu/mx/index.html

This method does not require knowledge of the Mx programming language. After defining an external data file, the user can click with the mouse cursor on a list of variables and these variables are automatically displayed in the drawing editor. Model diagrams in Mx Graph use the McArdle–McDonald RAM symbolism (as does this book). After using the Mx Graph drawing tools to complete the model diagram, one then clicks with the mouse cursor on a "run" button. Mx Graph automatically writes the Mx syntax for the analysis that is then executed. If the analysis terminates normally, the parameter estimates are displayed in their proper places in the model diagram. There is also a graphical Project Manager available in Mx Graph. Through the Project Manager, the user can view or control all aspects of the analysis.

Special features of Mx Graph for SEM include the ability to calculate confidence intervals and statistical power for individual parameter estimates and analyze special types of latent variable models for genetics data. Examples of Mx scripts for continuous or categorical variables of the kind analyzed in genetics research (e.g., in a linkage analysis) can be freely downloaded over the Internet.[11]

RAMONA[12]

M. W. Browne's RAMONA (Reticular Action Model or Near Approximation) is the module for SEM in SYSTAT 10 (Systat Software Inc., 2002), a comprehensive program for general statistical analysis that runs under Microsoft Windows. There is no drawing editor in RAMONA, nor does the program automatically generate a model diagram. The user interacts with RAMONA in the general SYSTAT environment by submitting a text (batch) file with commands that describe the model and data or by typing these commands at a prompt for interactive sessions. An alternative method is to use a wizard with graphical dialogs for naming the observed and unobserved variables (including disturbances and measurement errors), indicating the type of data matrix to be analyzed (correlation or covariance), and controlling other aspects of the analysis, but commands that specify the model in RAMONA must be directly typed in a text window by the user. Fortu-

[11]www.psy.vu.nl/mxbib/

[12]www.systat.com/products/systat/

nately, RAMONA syntax is quite straightforward and involves only two parameter matrices, one for direct effects and the other for covariance relations such as unanalyzed associations between exogenous variables.

Raw data files with missing observations can be prepared for analysis with RAMONA after analyzing them with general procedures for missing values analysis in SYSTAT. The RAMONA program can, as an option specified by the user, correctly analyze a correlation matrix using the method of constrained estimation (Chapter 7). There is also a "Restart" command that automatically creates a new batch file that can be submitted for analysis in a second run of the program. This second program run takes parameter estimates from the prior analysis as initial estimates in the new analysis. This capability is convenient for determining whether a structural equation model is identified. However, the RAMONA program cannot analyze a structural equation model across multiple samples, and there is no direct way to analyze means.

SEPATH[13]

J. H. Steiger's SEPATH (Structural Equation Modeling and Path Analysis) is the SEM module in STATISTICA 6 (StatSoft Inc., 2003), an integrated program for general statistical analyses, data mining, and quality control. All data management tasks and exploratory statistical analyses are carried out in the STATISTICA environment. Structural equation models are specified in SEPATH with the text-based PATH1 programming language that mimics that appearance of a model diagram based on McArdle–McDonald RAM symbolism. Because SEPATH does not generate model diagrams, the user cannot specify a model by drawing it on the screen.

There are three ways to enter PATH1 code in SEPATH. Users already familiar with the PATH1 language can enter statements directly into a window in the SEPATH start-up dialog. Two other ways offered in the start-up dialog do not require knowledge of the PATH1 language. One is a path construction tool that presents, in graphical dialogs, separate lists of the latent and observed variables and buttons that repre-

[13]www.statsoft.com

sent different types of paths for direct effects or covariances among exogenous variables. The user selects the variable(s) and path type with the mouse cursor, and the path construction tool automatically writes the corresponding PATH1 statements, which are then displayed in a separate window. The other way to specify a model that does not require knowledge of the PATH1 language is to use one of two different wizards, one for a CFA model and the other for an SR model. Graphical dialogs in these wizards ask the user to associate latent variables with their indicators, specify the relations between the factors, and indicate whether measurement errors or factor disturbances are independent or covary.

A special feature of SEPATH is that it offers the user several options for dealing with estimation problems that can arise under program default settings in basically any SEM computer program. These options afford the user quite precise control over the estimation, but effective use of them requires technical knowledge of nonlinear optimization procedures. Similar to the RAMONA program, SEPATH can correctly and automatically analyze a correlation matrix with the method of constrained estimation (Chapter 7). It also has extensive capabilities for Monte Carlo studies where simulated samples are drawn by the computer from a population data structure specified by the user. This data structure can either correspond to the data, model, or parametric versus nonparametric bootstrapping if raw data are analyzed. There is also a power analysis module in STATISTICA (also by J. H. Steiger) that estimates the power of statistical tests of overall model fit in SEM (Chapter 6).

4.7 SUMMARY

Examples of the types of research questions that can be addressed with the core SEM techniques were considered in this chapter. Path analysis allows researchers to specify and test structural models that reflect a priori assumptions about spurious associations and direct or indirect causal effects among observed variables. Measurement models that represent a priori hypotheses about relations between indicators and factors can be evaluated with the technique of confirmatory factor analysis. Structural regression models with both a structural component and a measurement component can also be analyzed. A total of eight different SEM computer programs were also described in this chapter. Most SEM analyses reported in the research literature are conducted using one of these software tools.

4.8 RECOMMENDED READINGS

Dilalla, L. F. (2000). Structural equation modeling: Uses and issues. In H. E. A. Tinsley & S. D. Brown (Eds.), *Handbook of applied multivariate statistics and mathematical modeling* (pp. 440–464). New York: Academic Press.

Klem, L. (2000). Structural equation modeling. In L. G. Grimm & P. R. Yarnold (Eds.), *Reading and understanding more multivariate statistics* (pp. 227–259). Washington, DC: American Psychological Association.

MacCallum, R. C., & Austin, J. T. (2000). Applications of structural equation modeling in psychological research. *Annual Review of Psychology, 51,* 201–236.

Part II

Core Techniques

5

Introduction to Path Analysis

This chapter introduces path analysis (PA), the original SEM technique for analyzing structural models with observed variables. Due to its relative seniority in the SEM family and the fact that it lacks a direct way to represent latent variables (other than disturbances), PA is sometimes seen as a less interesting or facile procedure than other varieties of SEM. But there are three reasons why this impression is mistaken. First, sometimes researchers use only a single indicator of some variables they are studying. Whether by design or default, due to things such as resource limitations, a multiple-indicator approach to construct measurement is not always possible. Second, it is important to know the principles of PA because many of these same concepts hold true for more complicated model types. Third, about 25% of roughly 500 applications of SEM published in 16 different psychology research journals from 1993 to 1997 concerned path models (MacCallum & Austin, 2000), so PA is still widely used. *Readers who master the fundamentals of PA will thus be better able to understand and critique a wider variety of structural equation models.*

5.1 CORRELATION AND CAUSATION

The technique of PA involves the estimation of presumed causal relations among observed variables. However, the basic datum of PA—and of all SEM techniques when means are not analyzed—is the covariance, which includes correlation: $cov_{XY} = r_{XY} \, SD_X \, SD_Y$. The reader is probably familiar with the expression "correlation does not imply causation."

This mantra-like principle is apt because although a substantial correlation could indicate a causal relation, variables can also be associated in ways that have nothing to do with causality—spurious associations are one example. It is also true that an observed correlation of zero does not preclude a true causal relation—the phenomenon of suppression is an example.

The path analytic approach to the study of causality with correlations is as follows. Using the basic building blocks of path models described below, the researcher specifies a model that attempts to explain why X and Y (and other observed variables) are correlated. Part of this explanation may include presumed causal effects (e.g., X causes Y). Other parts of the explanation may reflect presumed noncausal relations, such as a spurious association between X and Y due to common causes. The overall goal of a PA is to estimate causal versus noncausal aspects of observed correlations. Part of the evaluation of a path model involves assessing how well it accounts for the data, that is, the observed correlations or covariances. If the model is not rejected, however, the researcher *cannot* automatically conclude that the hypotheses about causality are correct. This is because the failure to reject a path model (or any type of structural equation model) does *not* prove that it is correct. (This point is elaborated on later.)

The inference of causality requires much more than just acceptable correspondence between the model and the data. For example, to reasonably infer that X is a cause of Y, all of the following conditions must be met: (1) there is time precedence, that is, X precedes Y in time; (2) the direction of the causal relation is correctly specified, that is, X causes Y instead of the reverse or X and Y cause each other in a direct feedback loop; and (3) the association between X and Y does not disappear when external variables such as common causes of both are held constant (i.e., it is not spurious). These conditions are a tall order. For example, the hypothesis that X causes Y would be bolstered if the magnitude of their association is substantial and X is measured before Y (i.e., the design is longitudinal). However, the expected value of r_{XY} may not be zero even if Y causes X and the effect (X) is measured before the cause (Y) (e.g., see Bollen, 1989, pp. 61–65). Even if X actually causes Y, the magnitude of r_{XY} may be low if the interval between their measurement is either too short (e.g., effects on Y take time to materialize) or too long (e.g., the effects are temporary and have dissipated).

Despite the problems just described, the assessment of variables at different times at least provides a measurement framework consistent with the specification of directional causal effects. However, longitudinal designs pose potential difficulties, such as subject attrition and the need for additional resources. Probably because of these reasons, most path analytic studies feature concurrent rather than longitudinal measurement. When the variables are concurrently measured, it is not possible to demonstrate time precedence. Therefore, the researcher needs a very clear, substantive rationale for specifying that X causes Y instead of the reverse or that X and Y mutually influence each other when all variables are measured at the same time.

It is only from a solid base of knowledge about theory and research that one can even begin to address these requirements for inferring causation from correlation. Although facility with the statistical details of SEM is essential, it is not a substitute for what could be called wisdom about one's research area. This point is emphasized time and again in this book. It is also why one should adopt the view that just as correlation does not imply causation, statistical causal modeling does not prove causation either. It is why Wilkinson and the Task Force on Statistical Inference (1999) emphasize that use of SEM computer programs "rarely yields any results that have any interpretation as causal effects" (p. 600). What additional evidence is required in order to infer causality after a PA (or any other form of SEM) is considered later.

5.2 SPECIFICATION OF PATH MODELS

The problems of specifying which variables to include in path models and the directionalities of presumed causal effects among them are considered next.

What to Include

This is perhaps the most basic specification issue: given some phenomenon of interest, what are all the variables that affect it? The literature for newer research areas can be limited, so decisions about what to include in the model must sometimes be guided more by the researcher's experience than by published reports. Consulting with experts in the field about plausible specifications may also help. In more established areas, however, sometimes there is *too much* information. That is, there may be so many potential causal variables mentioned in the literature that it is virtually impossible to include them all. To deal with this situation, the researcher must again rely on his or her judgment about the most crucial variables.

The specification error of omitting causal variables from a path model has the same potential consequence as omitting predictors from a regression equation does: estimates of causal effects of variables included in the model may be inaccurate if there are omitted causal variables that covary with those in the model. The direction of this inaccuracy could be either underestimation of true causal effects or overestimation, depending on the correlations between included and excluded variables. Note that overestimation probably occurs more often than underestimation. However, just as it is unrealistic to expect that all relevant predictors are included in a regression analysis, the same is true about including all causal variables in a path model. Given that most path models may be misspecified in this regard, the best way to minimize potential bias is preventive: make an omitted variable an included one through careful review of extant theory and research.

How to Measure the Hypothetical Construct

The selection of measures is a recurrent research problem. This is especially true in PA because there is only one observed measure of each construct. It is therefore crucial that measures have good psychometric characteristics; that is, their scores should be both reliable and valid. Score reliability is especially critical because one assumption of PA is that the exogenous variables are measured without error. Although this assumption is not required of the endogenous variables, the general consequence of error-prone measures of either exogenous or endogenous variables in PA is that the statistical estimates of presumed causal effects may be inaccurate. However, the nature of this potential inaccuracy is different for exogenous and endogenous variables. The consequences of measurement error in PA are discussed later after prerequisite concepts are introduced. Recall that disattenuating correlations for measurement error is one way to take reliability into account (see Equation 3.5), but it is not a standard part of PA.

Building Blocks

The basic elements of path models were introduced earlier but are briefly reviewed here. Let X refer to observed exogenous variables, Y to observed endogenous variables, D to disturbances (i.e., unobserved exogenous variables), $\curvearrowright$ and $\cup$ to, respectively, the variances and covariances (i.e., unanalyzed associations) of exogeneous variables, $\rightarrow$ to presumed direct causal effects, and $\rightleftarrows$ to reciprocal causal effects. An account of why observed variables are correlated with a path model can reflect two kinds of causal relations or two kinds of noncausal associations. The first kind of causal relation reflects presumed unidirectional influence and includes direct effects of one variable on another (e.g., $X \rightarrow Y$) or indirect effects through at least one mediating variable (e.g., $X \rightarrow Y_1 \rightarrow Y_2$). The second kind concerns feedback loops, either direct or indirect: **direct feedback** involves only two variables in a reciprocal relation (e.g., $Y_1 \rightleftarrows Y_2$); **indirect feedback** involves three or more variables (e.g., $Y_1 \rightarrow Y_2 \rightarrow Y_3 \rightarrow Y_1$). Feedback loops represent mutual influence among variables that are concurrently measured. As an example of a possible feedback relation, consider vocabulary breadth and reading: a bigger vocabulary may facilitate reading, but reading may result in an even larger vocabulary.

The two kinds of noncausal relations are unanalyzed associations and spurious associations. Most path models with more than one observed exogenous variable assume unanalyzed associations between them (e.g., $X_1 \cup X_2$). An unanalyzed association means just that: the two variables are assumed to covary, but the reasons why they covary— do they affect each other? do they have common causes?—are unknown. It is also possible to represent in path models unanalyzed associations between disturbances (e.g., $D_1 \cup D_2$). Recall that a disturbance represents all omitted causes of the corresponding endogenous variable. An unanalyzed association between a pair of disturbances is called a **disturbance correlation** (for standardized variables) or a **disturbance covariance** (for unstandardized variables); the former term is used herein from this point regardless of whether the variables are standardized or not. A disturbance correlation reflects the assumption that the corresponding endogenous variables share at least one common omitted cause. Accordingly, the *absence* of the symbol for an unanalyzed association between two disturbances reflects the presumption of independence of unmeasured causes. It also represents the hypothesis that the observed correlation between that pair of endogenous variables can be entirely explained by other observed variables in the model. Unlike unanalyzed associations between measured exogenous variables, which are routinely represented in path models, the inclusion of disturbance correlations in a structural model is not so simple. The reasons why this is so are elaborated later.

One other point about disturbances and unanalyzed associations: if measured exogenous variables have unanalyzed associations and disturbances can have them, too, can a disturbance have an unanalyzed association with a measured exogenous variable (e.g., $X \smile D$)? Theoretically, it can, and such a correlation would imply the presence of an omitted variable (e.g., W) that causes both X and the endogenous variable Y. That is, part of the covariance of X with Y is spurious due to a common cause. However, it is usually assumed in PA that the measured exogenous variables and disturbances are unrelated. (For an example of the estimation of $X \smile D$ and conditions required to do so, see Kenny, 1979, pp. 93–95.) Part of the reason for this assumption is statistical. Specifically, when multiple regression is used to estimate recursive path models (defined later), it must be assumed that the predictors (observed exogenous variables) and residuals (disturbances) are uncorrelated. Another reason is more conceptual: assuming the independence of disturbances and observed exogenous variables permits the estimation of direct effects of the latter (e.g., $X \rightarrow Y$), with omitted causal variables held constant. Recall that the derivation of regression coefficients accomplishes the same thing but among observed variables. The assumption of unrelated observed exogenous variables and disturbances provides what Bollen (1989) calls **pseudoisolation** of the former from all other unmeasured causes of the corresponding endogenous variable. This is a strong assumption, one that is probably violated in most applications of SEM. As noted earlier, the seriousness of violating this assumption increases with the magnitudes of the correlations between excluded and included variables, which once again highlights the importance of accurate specification.

Spurious associations in path models are represented by specifying common causes. For example, if X is specified as a direct cause of both Y_1 and Y_2, then at least part of the observed correlation between these two endogenous variables is presumed to be spurious. If the model contains no other direct or indirect causal effects between these variables (e.g., $Y_1 \rightarrow Y_2$), the entire association between them is presumed to be spurious. Spurious associations can also involve multiple common causes.

Directionality

The specification of the directionalities of presumed causal effects is a crucial part of a PA. The measurement of some variables before others provides one means to specify directionality. When variables are concurrently measured, however, the specification of directionality requires a clear rationale. For example, Lynam, Moffitt, and Stouthamer-Loeber (1993) estimated a path model where poor verbal ability was specified as a direct cause of delinquency, but both variables were concurrently measured in their sample, which raises the question: why this particular direction? Is it not also plausible that certain behaviors associated with delinquency, such as drug use or withdrawal from school, could impair verbal ability? The arguments offered by Lynam et al. for their original specification included the following: their participants were relatively young (about 12 years old), which may rule out delinquent careers long enough to affect verbal skills; the authors also cited results of prospective research that suggest that low verbal ability precedes antisocial acts. Although these particular arguments have been criticized (Block, 1995), they at least exemplify the types of arguments that researchers should provide for their specifications of directionality. Unfortunately, few path analytic articles even consider these issues, which is a serious problem.

What if a researcher is fundamentally uncertain about the directionalities of effects? There are basically three options: (1) forgo PA in favor of techniques that require fewer a priori assumptions, such as multiple regression; (2) specify and test alternative path models each with different directionalities; or (3) include reciprocal effects in the model as a way to cover both possibilities (e.g., $Y_1 \rightleftarrows Y_2$). The last two alternatives may seem appealing to someone who is keen to conduct a PA, but neither is a magical solution. In fact, the first option may be preferred. As already mentioned, it is possible in PA (or any other SEM technique) that different models may fit the same data equally well (i.e., equivalent models, defined later). When (not if!) this occurs, there is no statistical basis for choosing one model over another. Also, the inclusion of reciprocal effects is not a simple matter. The addition of even one reciprocal effect to a model makes it nonrecursive (defined later), which makes the model more difficult to analyze. Thus, there are potential costs to the specification of reciprocal causal effects as a hedge against uncertainty about directionality.

Model Complexity

Given the directionality problems just discussed, why not make life easier for yourself and just specify a path model wherein everything causes everything else? There is a problem with doing so because there is a limit on how many parameters can be represented in a structural equation model. A **parameter** is a characteristic of a population, and it is estimated with a sample statistic. The limit on the number of model parameters that can be estimated is determined by the number of **observations**, which is the number of variances and covariances among the observed variables. If v is the number of observed variables, the number of observations equals $v(v + 1)/2$. Suppose that there are four observed variables in a path model. The number of observations here is $4(5)/2$, or 10; thus, there are 10 observations altogether. Note that this number includes only the *unique* entries in a covariance matrix of four variables. That is, only entries above or below the diagonal (i.e., the covariances) are counted and added to the number of entries in the diagonal, which are the variances. The number of observations remains the same regardless of the sample size. If four variables are measured for 100 or 1,000 cases, the number of observations is still 10. Thus, adding cases does not increase the number of observations; only adding *variables* can do so.

The number of observations for a path model sets the upper limit for the number of parameters that can be estimated. Specifically, *the number of such model parameters cannot exceed the number of observations*. A model may have fewer parameters than observations but no more. The difference between the number of observations and the number of its parameters is the **model degrees of freedom**, df_M. The requirement that there be at least as many observations as parameters to be estimated can be expressed as the requirement that $df_M \geq 0$. The general rule for counting the number of parameters in a path model is as follows:

The total number of variances and covariances (i.e., unanalyzed associations) of exogenous variables that are either observed or unobserved (i.e., disturbances) and direct effects on endogenous variables from other observed variables equals the number of parameters.

Note that the variances and covariances of the endogenous variables are not considered model parameters. This is because endogenous variables are represented in path models as the effects of other measured variables in the model and their own disturbances. Thus, endogenous variables are not free to vary or covary. Instead, the path model as a whole attempts to account for variances of the endogenous variables and their covariances with other variables.

Although the reasons are outlined later, a model with more parameters than observations ($df_M < 0$) is not amenable to empirical analysis. Such models are said to be not identified, which means that it is mathematically impossible to derive unique estimates of each parameter. The most likely symptom of this problem is that an SEM computer program may terminate its run prematurely with error messages. Analogous situations can occur in multiple regression when there are more predictors than cases: the computer cannot carry out the analysis because the model is too complex to be estimated with the available information.

Constraints

The status of each model parameter can be free, fixed, or constrained depending on the researcher's specifications. A **free parameter** is to be estimated by the computer with sample data. In contrast, a **fixed parameter** is specified to equal a constant; that is, the computer "accepts" this constant as the estimate of the parameter regardless of the data. For the present example, the hypothesis that the direct effect of X on Y is zero corresponds to the specification that the coefficient for this path is fixed to zero. The computer will then estimate all other model parameters while holding this path coefficient constant (i.e., equal to 0). It is common in SEM to test hypotheses by specifying that a previously fixed-to-zero parameter becomes a free parameter or vice versa. Results of such analyses may indicate whether to respecify a model by making it more complex (an effect is added) or more parsimonious (an effect is dropped).

A **constrained parameter** is estimated by the computer within some restriction, but it is not fixed to equal a constant. The restriction typically concerns the relative values of other constrained parameters. An **equality constraint** means that the estimates of two or more parameters are forced to be equal. Suppose that an equality constraint is imposed on the two direct effects that make up a direct feedback loop (e.g., $Y_1 \rightleftarrows Y_2$). This constraint simplifies the analysis because only one path coefficient is needed rather than two. In a multiple-sample SEM analysis, a **cross-group equality constraint** forces the computer to derive equal estimates of that parameter across all groups. This specification corresponds to the null hypothesis that the parameter is equal in all populations from which the samples were drawn (Chapter 11).

Other kinds of constraints are not seen nearly as often in the literature. A **proportionality constraint** forces one parameter estimate to be some proportion of the other. For example, the path coefficient for one direct effect in a reciprocal relation may be forced to be three times the value of the other coefficient. An **inequality constraint** forces the value of a parameter estimate to be less than or greater than a specified value. The specification that the value of an unstandardized path coefficient must be at least 5.00 is an example of an inequality constraint. The imposition of proportionality or inequality constraints generally requires knowledge about the relative magnitudes of effects, but such knowledge is relatively rare in the behavioral sciences. A **nonlinear constraint** imposes a nonlinear relation between two parameter estimates. For example, the value of one estimate may be forced to equal the square of another. A method to correctly analyze a correlation matrix instead of a covariance matrix referred to as constrained estimation uses nonlinear constraints (Chapter 7). So does the Kenny–Judd method, one of two different methods for estimating nonlinear effects of latent variables described in Chapter 13.

5.3 TYPES OF PATH MODELS

There are two basic kinds of path models. **Recursive models** are the most straightforward and have two basic features: their disturbances are uncorrelated, and all causal effects are unidirectional. **Nonrecursive models** have feedback loops or may have correlated disturbances. Consider the path models in Figure 5.1. The model of Figure 5.1(a) is recursive because its disturbances are independent and no variable is both a cause and an effect of another variable, directly or indirectly. For example, X_1, X_2, and Y_1 are specified as direct or indirect causes of Y_2, but Y_2 has no effect back onto one of its presumed causes. In contrast, the model of Figure 5.1(b) is nonrecursive because it has a direct feedback loop in which Y_1 and Y_2 are specified as both causes and effects of each other ($Y_1 \rightleftarrows Y_2$). The model of Figure 5.1(b) also has a disturbance correlation. Note that models with indirect feedback loops, such as $Y_1 \rightarrow Y_2 \rightarrow Y_3 \rightarrow Y_1$, are also nonrecursive.

There is another type of path model, one that has directional effects and correlated disturbances, two examples of which are pre-

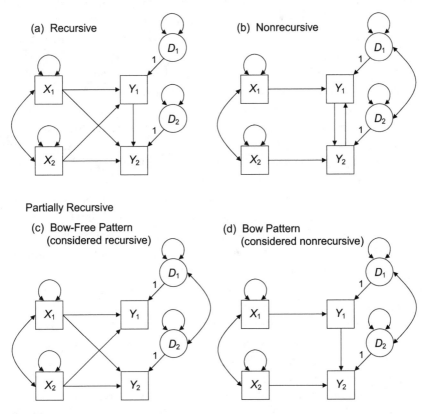

FIGURE 5.1. Examples of recursive, nonrecursive, and partially recursive path models.

sented in Figures 5.1(c) and 5.1(d). Unfortunately, the classification of such models in the SEM literature is not consistent. Some authors call these models nonrecursive, whereas others use the term **partially recursive**. But more important than the label for these models is the distinction made in the figure. Although the reasons are explained later, partially recursive models with a **bow-free pattern** of disturbance correlations can be treated in the analysis just like recursive models. A bow-free pattern means that correlated disturbances are restricted to pairs of endogenous variables *without* direct effects between them (see Figure 5.1(c)). In contrast, partially recursive models with a **bow pattern** of disturbance correlations must be treated in the analysis as nonrecursive models. A bow pattern means that a disturbance correlation occurs *with* a direct effect between the endogenous variables (see Figure 5.1(d); Brito & Pearl, 2003; Kenny, 1979). All ensuing references to recursive and nonrecursive models include, respectively, partially recursive models without and with direct effects among the endogenous variables.

The distinction between recursive and nonrecursive path models has several implications. The assumptions of recursive models that all causal effects are unidirectional and that the disturbances are independent when there are direct effects among the endogenous variables simplify the statistical demands for their analysis. For example, multiple regression can be used to estimate path coefficients for direct effects and disturbance variances in recursive models. Many social scientists are familiar with multiple regression, and computer programs with regression modules are widely available, some even freely available over the Internet. The same assumptions of recursive models that ease the analytical burden are also very restrictive, however. For example, causal effects that are not unidirectional (e.g., as in a feedback loop) or disturbances that are correlated in a model with direct effects between the corresponding endogenous variables (e.g., Figure 5.1(d)) cannot be represented in a recursive model. Although these effects can be represented in nonrecursive models, such models cannot be analyzed with standard multiple regression. Nonrecursive models require more sophisticated methods and may also require additional assumptions. The likelihood of a problem in the analysis of a nonrecursive model is also greater than for a recursive model. One of these problems is that of identification, which is discussed in the next section. Perhaps due to these difficulties, one sees relatively few nonrecursive path models in the behavioral science literature. But in some disciplines, especially economics, they are much more common, which suggests that the challenges of nonrecursive models can be overcome. The analysis of nonrecursive structural models is discussed in Chapter 9.

Before we continue, let us apply the rules for counting observations and parameters to the four path models of Figure 5.1. Because there are four observed variables in every model, the number of observations for each is 4(5)/2 = 10. It is assumed that the constants (1) in the figure are fixed parameters that scale the disturbances (Chapter 4; this point is also elaborated later). Summarized in Table 5.1 are the numbers and types of free parameters for each model. Note there that all four models meet the requirement for at least as many observations as parameters. Also note that a reciprocal effect (e.g., $Y_1 \rightleftarrows Y_2$ in the model of Figure 5.1(b)) counts as two direct effects when no equality constraint is imposed. Readers are encouraged to match the parameters listed in Table 5.1 against the corresponding path models of Figure 5.1.

5.4 PRINCIPLES OF IDENTIFICATION

If life were fair, the researcher could proceed directly from specification to collection of the data to estimation. Unfortunately, just as life is sometimes unfair, the analysis of a path model is not always so straightforward. The problem that potentially complicates the evaluation of a path model (or any other kind of structural equation model) is that of **identification**. A model is said to be identified if it is *theoretically* possible to derive a unique estimate of each parameter. If not, the model is not identified. The word "theoretically" emphasizes identification as a property of the model and not of the data. For example, if a model is not identified, then it remains so regardless of the sample size (100, 1,000, etc.). Therefore, models that are not identified should be respecified; otherwise, attempts to analyze them may be fruitless.

There are two basic requirements for the identification of any kind of structural equation model: (1) there must be at least as many observations as free model parameters ($df_M \geq 0$), and (2) every unobserved (latent) variable must be assigned a scale (metric). Models that violate the first requirement are not identified; specifically, they are

TABLE 5.1. Number and Types of Parameters for Path Models in Figure 5.1

Model	Variances	Covariances	Direct effects on endogenous variables		Total
(a) Recursive	X_1, X_2	$X_1 \cup X_2$	$X_1 \rightarrow Y_1$	$X_2 \rightarrow Y_1$	10
	D_1, D_2		$X_1 \rightarrow Y_2$	$X_2 \rightarrow Y_2$	
			$Y_1 \rightarrow Y_2$		
(b) Nonrecursive	X_1, X_2	$X_1 \cup X_2$	$X_1 \rightarrow Y_1$	$X_2 \rightarrow Y_2$	10
	D_1, D_2	$D_1 \cup D_2$	$Y_1 \rightarrow Y_2$	$Y_2 \rightarrow Y_1$	
(c) Partially recursive (considered recursive)	X_1, X_2	$X_1 \cup X_2$	$X_1 \rightarrow Y_1$	$X_2 \rightarrow Y_1$	10
	D_1, D_2	$D_1 \cup D_2$	$X_1 \rightarrow Y_2$	$X_2 \rightarrow Y_2$	
(d) Partially recursive (considered nonrecursive)	X_1, X_2	$X_1 \cup X_2$	$X_1 \rightarrow Y_1$	$X_2 \rightarrow Y_2$	9
	D_1, D_2	$D_1 \cup D_2$	$Y_1 \rightarrow Y_2$		

underidentified. As an example of how a deficit of observations leads to nonidentification, consider the following equation:

$$a + b = 6 \qquad (5.1)$$

Look at this expression as a model, the "6" as an observation (i.e., a datum), and a and b as parameters. Because Equation 5.1 has more parameters (2) than observations (1), it is impossible to find unique estimates for its parameters. In fact, there are an infinite number of solutions, including ($a = 4$, $b = 2$), ($a = 8$, $b = -2$), and so on, all of which satisfy Equation 5.1. A similar thing happens when a computer tries to derive unique estimates for an underidentified structural equation model: it is impossible to do so, and thus the attempt fails.

Assuming that all disturbances are assigned a scale (discussed next), it is impossible to specify a recursive path model with more parameters than observations. Look again at the path model of Figure 5.1(a). This recursive model already has as many parameters as observations (10). However, it is not possible to add another parameter to this model and still have it be recursive. For example, the addition to this model of a disturbance correlation or a direct effect from Y_2 to Y_1 (which would result in a direct feedback loop) would make it nonrecursive.

It can be shown that due to their particular characteristics, recursive path models are always identified (e.g., Bollen, 1989, pp. 95–98). Thus, although it is *theoretically* possible (that word again) to derive unique estimates of the parameters of recursive path models, their analysis can still be foiled by other types of problems. (Remember, life isn't fair!) Data-related problems are one such difficulty. For example, multicollinearity can result in what Kenny (1979) referred to as **empirical underidentification**: if two observed variables are very highly correlated (e.g., $r_{XY} = .90$), then, practically speaking, they are the same variable, which reduces the effective number of observations below the value of $v(v + 1)/2$. The analysis of a recursive path model can also be foiled if the user of an SEM computer program specifies inaccurate initial estimates of model parameters, also called start values. This problem is discussed later. The good news here is that neither of these potential problems is due to inherent features of a recursive model. The first (multicollinearity) can be addressed through data screening; the second (bad start values), through additional computer runs with better initial estimates.

The situation for nonrecursive path models is more complicated. First, it is possible to inadvertently specify a nonrecursive model with more parameters than observations. Look again at the path model of Figure 5.1(b), which is nonrecursive. Although it appears that this model has "room" for two more direct effects (e.g., $X_1 \rightarrow Y_2$), it already has as many parameters as observations (10). Second, particular configurations of paths in a nonrecursive model can make it nonidentified even if there are as many observations as parameters. As a simple example of how a model with equal numbers of parameters and observations can nevertheless fail to have a unique solution, consider the following set of formulas:

$$a + b = 6 \qquad\qquad (5.2)$$
$$3a + 3b = 18$$

Again, look at both expressions as a model, the total scores as observations, and a and b as parameters. Although this model has two observations and two parameters, it does not have a unique solution. In fact, there are an infinite number of solutions that satisfy Equation 5.2, such as ($a = 4$, $b = 2$), ($a = 8$, $b = -2$), and so on. This happens due to an inherent characteristic of the model: the second formula in Equation 5.2 ($3a + 3b = 18$) is not unique. Instead, it is simply three times the first formula ($a + b = 6$), which means that it cannot narrow the range of solutions that satisfy the first formula. These two formulas can also be described as linearly dependent.

Although the example just presented oversimplifies the identification issue for nonrecursive models, it points out one of the difficulties in their analysis: a nonrecursive model with at least as many observations as parameters is not necessarily identified. Fortunately, there are some ways that a researcher can determine whether some (but not all) types of nonrecursive models are identified. These procedures are described in Chapter 9, but it is worthwhile to make the following point now: adding exogenous variables is one way to remedy an identification problem of a nonrecursive structural model, but this typically can only be done *before* the data are collected. *Thus, it is crucial to evaluate whether a nonrecursive model is identified right after it is specified and before the study is conducted.*

Two other terms require definition: **just-identification** and **overidentification**. A just-identified model has equal numbers of parameters and observations *and* is identified. As discussed, a nonrecursive model with equal numbers of parameters and observations is not necessarily identified, so the term "just-identified" does not automatically apply to it. It does, however, apply to recursive models with the same property. As a demonstration of just-identification, consider the following formulas as a model with two observations (6, 10) and two parameters (a, b). Note that the second formula is not linearly dependent on the first:

$$a + b = 6 \qquad\qquad (5.3)$$
$$2a + b = 10$$

This two-observation, two-parameter model has a single solution ($a = 4$, $b = 2$); therefore, it is just-identified. Note something else about Equation 5.3: given estimates of its parameters, it can perfectly reproduce the observations (i.e., 6, 10). The same thing is generally true for just-identified path models: not only do they theoretically have unique solutions, but given such they will also perfectly fit the data. The implication of this characteristic for hypothesis testing in PA is discussed later.

A path model can also have fewer parameters than observations. If such models are also identified (true for a recursive model; perhaps not for a nonrecursive one), they are called *overidentified*. As an example of parameter estimation for an overidentified model, consider the following set of formulas with three observations (6, 10, 12) and two parameters (a, b):

$$a + b = 6 \qquad\qquad (5.4)$$
$$2a + b = 10$$
$$3a + b = 12$$

Try as you might, you will be unable to find values of a and b that satisfy all three formulas. For example, the solution $(a = 4, b = 2)$ works only for the first two formulas in Equation 5.4. At first, the absence of a solution appears paradoxical, but there is a way to solve this problem: the imposition of a statistical criterion leads to unique estimates for the parameters of an overidentified model. An example of such a criterion for Equation 5.4 could be the following: find values of a and b that are positive and yield totals such that the sum of the squared differences between the observations (6, 10, 12) and these totals is as small as possible. Applying this criterion to the estimation of a and b in Equation 5.4 yields a solution that not only gives the smallest total squared difference (.67) but that is also unique (using only one decimal place, we obtain $a = 3.0$ and $b = 3.3$). Note that this solution does not perfectly reproduce the observations in Equation 5.4.

Thus, although it is possible to find a unique solution for overidentified models, it may not perfectly reproduce the observations. By the same token, an overidentified path model may not perfectly fit the data. Although this characteristic may at first glance seem like a drawback, it actually has an important role in model testing, one that is explored later.

The second general requirement for identification is that every latent variable must be assigned a scale. This is necessary in order for the computer to be able to calculate estimates of effects that involve latent variables. Disturbances are the only kind of latent variable in path models. In PA, scales are usually assigned to disturbances through a **unit loading identification** (ULI) **constraint**. This means that the path coefficient for the direct effect of a disturbance—also called a **residual path coefficient**—is fixed to equal 1.0.[1] This specification has the consequence of assigning to a disturbance a scale that is related to that of the unexplained variance of the corresponding endogenous variable. This scale is not typically identical to that of the endogenous variable because it reflects the predictive power of the presumed causes of the latter. For example, the disturbance D_1 in Figure 5.1 is assigned a scale related to that of the unexplained variance of Y_1 through the imposition of a ULI constraint (i.e., $D_1 \rightarrow Y_1 = 1.0$). Because the residual path coefficient is here a fixed parameter, the computer needs only to estimate the disturbance variance. There is another method to scale latent variables that is discussed in Chapter 7, but it is rarely applied to disturbances in path models. Moreover, most SEM computer programs make it easier to specify a ULI constraint for disturbances.

5.5 SAMPLE SIZE

As already mentioned, the number of cases has no bearing on whether a path model is identified. What, then, is the role of sample size in PA—and all other SEM techniques? Basically the same as for other kinds of statistical methods: results derived within larger samples have less sampling error than within smaller samples. The researcher must then answer the next logical question: how large a sample is required in order for the results to be reasonably stable? Some guidelines about absolute sample size in estimation methods were offered earlier (small, $N < 100$; medium, N between 100 and 200; large, $N > 200$). Another consideration is model complexity. That is, more complex models— those with more parameters—require larger samples than more parsimonious models in order for the estimates to be comparably stable. Thus, a sample size of 200 or even much larger may be necessary for a very complicated path model. Although there are no absolute standards

---

[1]The specification of *any* constant, such as 2.0 or 17.3, for the residual path coefficient would identify the disturbance, but it is much more common for this constant to equal 1.0.

in the literature about the relation between sample size and path model complexity, the following recommendations are offered: a desirable goal is to have the ratio of the number of cases to the number of free parameters be 20:1; a 10:1 ratio, however, may be a more realistic target. Thus, a path model with 20 parameters should have a minimum sample size of 200 cases. If the cases/parameter ratio is less than 5:1, the statistical precision of the results may be doubtful. Other, more precise ways to estimate minimum sample sizes, such as power analysis, are considered in the next chapter.

5.6 OVERVIEW OF ESTIMATION OPTIONS

There are basically two options for the analysis of recursive path models: (1) multiple regression or (2) estimation with an SEM computer program. The latter typically offers users the choice of different procedures, the most widely used of which is maximum likelihood (ML) estimation. In fact, ML estimation is the default method in most SEM computer programs. For just-identified recursive path models, multiple regression and ML estimation yield identical estimates of direct effects (path coefficients); estimates of disturbance variances may vary slightly because the two procedures use somewhat different denominators in these terms. Values of path coefficients for overidentified recursive path models may be slightly different, but the two procedures generally yield similar results within large samples (i.e., their estimates are asymptotic).

Notwithstanding the similarity of results yielded by multiple regression and ML estimation for recursive path models, there are three reasons why it is well worth the effort to learn how to use an SEM computer program. First, there are numerous statistical indexes of the overall fit of the model to the data that are available in the output of SEM computer programs that are not generated by regression programs. These fit indexes, introduced in Chapter 6, are very useful for testing certain types of hypotheses, especially those that involve the comparison of different models evaluated with the same data. Second, there are several types of results that are automatically calculated by SEM computer programs that must be derived by hand when one uses a regression program. For simple models, these hand calculations are not too burdensome a chore. For complex models, though, it's a real advantage to let the computer do the work. In contrast, nonrecursive path models and other kinds of structural equation models, such as CFA measurement models or structural regression (SR) models, can be estimated with ML but not multiple regression. Indeed, it would be no exaggeration to describe ML estimation as the motor of SEM. (You are the driver.)

5.7 MAXIMUM LIKELIHOOD ESTIMATION

This section reviews basic characteristics of ML estimation for any kind of structural equation model. Other estimation options, including multiple regression for recursive path models only, are described in the next chapter.

Description

The term **maximum likelihood** describes the statistical principle that underlies the derivation of parameter estimates: the estimates are the ones that maximize the likelihood (the continuous generalization) that the data (the observed covariances) were drawn from this population. That is, ML estimators are those that maximize the likelihood of a sample that is actually observed (Winer, Brown, & Michels, 1991). It is a **normal theory** method because ML estimation assumes that the population distribution for the endogenous variables is multivariate normal. Other methods are based on different parameter estimation theories, but they are not currently used as often. In fact, the use of an estimation method other than ML requires explicit justification (Hoyle, 2000).

Most forms of ML estimation in SEM are simultaneous, which means that estimates of model parameters are calculated all at once. For this reason, ML estimation is described in the statistical literature as a **full-information method**. (There are some partial-information forms of ML estimation, but they are not described in this book.) In contrast, techniques that analyze the equation for only one endogenous variable at a time are known as **partial-information** or **limited-information methods**. Multiple regression used to estimate a recursive path model is an example of a partial-information method. So is two-stage least squares, a special type of regression method described in Chapter 9 that can analyze nonrecursive path models. Implications of the difference between full-information versus partial-information estimation when there is specification error are considered in Chapter 6.

The statistical criterion minimized in ML estimation—also known as the **fitting function** or **discrepancy function**—is related to discrepancies between the observed covariances and those predicted by the researcher's model. (How model-implied covariances are calculated is discussed in Chapter 6 after prerequisite concepts are introduced here.) In this sense, the ML fitting function is analogous (but not equivalent) to the least squares criterion of multiple regression. The mathematics of how ML estimation actually goes about generating a set of parameter estimates that minimize its fitting function are complex, and it is beyond the scope of this section to describe them in detail (e.g., Eliason, 1993; Kaplan, 2000, pp. 25–28; a less technical presentation is available in Nunnally & Bernstein, 1994, pp. 147–155). The similarities between ML estimates and those derived with multiple regression for recursive path models is reassuring for nonstatisticians, however.

The method of ML estimation is usually so complicated that it is often iterative, which means that the computer derives an initial solution and then attempts to improve these estimates through subsequent cycles of calculations. "Improvement" means that the overall fit of the model to the data generally becomes better from step to step. For most just-identified structural equation models, the fit will eventually be perfect. For overidentified models, the fit of the model to the data may be imperfect, but iterative estimation will continue until the increments of the improvement in model fit fall below a predefined minimum value. **Iterative estimation** may converge to a solution quicker if the procedure is given reasonably accurate **start values**, which are initial estimates of a model's parameters. If these initial estimates are grossly inaccurate—for instance, the start value for a path coefficient is positive when the actual direct effect is negative—then iterative estimation may fail to converge, which means that a stable solution has not been reached. Iterative estimation can also fail if the relative variances among the observed variables are very different; that is, the covariance matrix is ill scaled.

Computer programs typically issue a warning message if iterative estimation is unsuccessful. When this occurs, whatever final set of esti-mates was derived by the computer may warrant little confidence. Also, some SEM computer programs automatically generate their own start values. *It is important to understand, however, that computer-derived start values do not always lead to converged solutions.* Although the com-puter's "guesses" about start values are usually pretty good, sometimes it is necessary for the researcher to provide better start values for the solution to converge. The guidelines for calculating start values for path models presented in Appendix 5.A may be helpful. Another tactic is to increase the program's default limit on the number of iterations to a higher value (e.g., from 30 to 100). Allowing the computer more "tries" may lead to a converged solution.

Although usually not a problem with recursive path models, it can happen in ML and other iterative methods that a converged solution is **inadmissible**. This is evident by a parameter estimate with an illogical value such as **Heywood cases**, which include negative variance esti-mates or estimated correlations between a factor and an indicator with an absolute value greater than 1.0. Heywood cases can be caused by specification errors, nonidentification of the model, the presence of outlier cases that distort the solution, a combination of small sample sizes (e.g., $N < 100$) and only two indicators per factor in a measure-ment model, bad start values, or extremely high or low population cor-relations that result in empirical underidentification (Chen, Bollen, Paxton, Curran, & Kirby, 2001). An analogy may help give a context for Heywood cases: ML estimation (and related methods) is like a reli-gious fanatic in that it so believes the model's specification that it will do anything, no matter how implausible, to force the model on the data (e.g., estimated correlations > 1.0). Note that some SEM computer pro-grams do not permit certain Heywood cases to appear in the solution. For example, EQS does not allow the estimate of an error variance to be less than zero; that is, it sets a lower bound of zero (i.e., an inequality constraint) that prevents a negative variance estimate. However, solu-tions in which one or more estimates have been constrained by the computer to prevent an illogical value may indicate a problem (i.e., they should not be trusted). Researchers should also attempt to deter-mine the source of the problem instead of constraining an error vari-ance to be positive in a computer program for SEM and then rerunning the analysis (Chen et al., 2001).

The ML method is generally both **scale free** and **scale invariant**. The former means that if a variable's scale is linearly transformed, a parameter estimated for the transformed variable can be algebraically converted back to the original metric. The latter means the value of the ML fitting function in a particular sample remains the same regardless of the scale of the observed variables (Kaplan, 2000). However, ML estimation may lose these properties if a correlation matrix is analyzed instead of a covariance matrix. Some special methods to correctly analyze a correlation matrix are discussed in Chapter 7.

When a raw data file is analyzed, standard ML estimation assumes there are *no* missing values. A special form of ML estimation available for raw data files where some observations are missing at random was described earlier (section 3.2). The statistical assumptions of ML estimation include independence of the observations, multivariate normality of the endogenous variables, independence of the exogenous variables and disturbances, and correct specification of the model. The requirement for correct specification is critical because full-information methods, such as ML estimation, tend to propagate errors throughout the whole model. That is, specification error in one parameter can affect results for other parameters elsewhere in the model. It is difficult to predict the specific direction and magnitude of this error because it depends in part upon the relation between the incorrect parameters and other parameters, but the more serious the specification error, the more serious may be the resulting bias. An additional assumption when a path model is analyzed is that the exogenous variables are measured without error, but this requirement is not specific to ML estimation. See Kaplan (2000, chap. 5) for more information about the statistical assumptions underlying SEM.

Reviewed in Chapter 7 are results of some computer simulation studies of the robustness of ML estimation against violation of the assumption of multivariate normality. Briefly summarized, these results suggest that although the values of parameter estimates generated by ML are relatively robust against nonnormality, results of statistical tests may be positively biased, which means that they lead to the rejection of the null hypothesis too often. Ways to deal with this problem are discussed in Chapter 7, but it can be said here that corrective measures should be taken if distributions of endogenous variables are severely nonnormal.

Interpretation of Parameter Estimates

However complex the mathematics of ML estimation, the interpretation of ML estimates for path models is relatively straightforward. Path coefficients are interpreted as regression coefficients in multiple regression, which means that they control for correlations among multiple presumed causes. In the unstandardized solution, disturbance variances are estimated in the metric of the unexplained variance of the corresponding endogenous variable. Suppose that the observed variance of Y_1 in a recursive path model is 25.00 and the estimated variance of its disturbance is 15.00. From these results it can be concluded that 15.00/25.00 = .60, or 60%, of the variability in Y_1 is *not* explained by the observed variables presumed to directly affect it. Accordingly, the term $1 - .60 = .40$, or 40%, is the proportion of total variance in Y_1 explained by the model; it also equals the squared multiple correlation (R_{smc}^2) for this endogenous variable. A technical problem with R_{smc}^2 as a measure of the proportion of explained variance for an endogenous variable in a feedback loop (i.e., the path model is nonrecursive) and a corrected measure are discussed in Chapter 9.

In the standardized solution, the variances of all variables (including the disturbances) equal 1.0. However, some SEM computer programs report standardized estimates for disturbances that are proportions of unexplained variance; that is, they equal $1 - R_{smc}^2$ for each endogenous variable. The square root of $1 - R_{smc}^2$ equals the standardized residual path coefficient for the direct effect of the disturbance on the corresponding endogenous variable. For example, if the proportion of explained variance is $R_{smc}^2 = .40$, then the proportion of unexplained variance is $1 - .40 = .60$ and the standardized residual path coefficient equals $.60^{1/2} = .775$. This example shows that when residual path coefficients are fixed to 1.0 in the unstandardized solution to scale the disturbance (i.e., by imposing a ULI constraint), their values are typically not also 1.0 in the standardized solution.

In standard ML estimation, standard errors are calculated only for the unstandardized solution. This means that results of statistical tests (i.e., ratios of parameter estimates over their standard errors) are available only for the unstandardized solution. Users of SEM computer programs often assume that results of statistical tests of unstandardized estimates apply to the corresponding standardized estimates. For samples that are large and representative, this assumption may not be problematic. Readers should realize, however, that the level of statistical significance of an unstandardized estimate does not automatically apply to its standardized counterpart. Furthermore, standard ML estimation may derive incorrect standard errors when the variables are standardized. The reasons for this potential inaccuracy are technical (e.g., Bollen, 1989, pp. 123–126; Cudeck, 1989), but this is another argument against the analysis of a correlation matrix instead of a covariance matrix with standard ML estimation. However, there are basically two ways to obtain more accurate estimated standard errors for the standardized solution. Some SEM computer programs, such as Amos, use bootstrapping to generate standard errors for standardized estimates. Another method is constrained estimation, which is available as a user-specified option in some SEM computer programs including SEPATH and RAMONA (Chapter 7).

A common question about path coefficients is this: what indicates a "large" direct effect?—a "small" one? Statistical tests of path coefficients do not really provide an answer to this question. Results of statistical tests reflect not only the absolute magnitudes of path coefficients but also other factors, such as the sample size and intercorrelations among the variables. Because SEM is generally a large-sample technique, it may happen more often than in other kinds of analyses that truly small effects are statistically significant. The interpretation of standardized path coefficients is an alternative, but there are few guidelines about what is a "large" versus a "small" effect. Some suggestions for the interpretation of effect size magnitude for standardized path coefficients are offered in Appendix 5.B.

5.8 OTHER ISSUES

Other conceptual issues about PA are addressed below, but many generalize to other SEM methods.

What to Do after a Path Analysis

General requirements for estimating causality from covariances were discussed earlier. The statistical methods used in PA, such as ML estimation, usually require additional assumptions about the population distributions of either the observed endogenous variables (i.e., multivariate normal) or the disturbances (i.e., normal and homoscedastic). Given a single study, it would be almost impossible to believe that all of these logical and statistical requirements were met. Thus, the interpretation that direct effects in a path model correspond to causal relations in the real world is typically unwarranted. It is only with the accumulation of the following types of evidence that the results of a PA may indicate causality: (1) replication of the model across independent samples; (2) elimination of plausible equivalent models; (3) corroborating evidence from experimental studies of variables in the model that are manipulable; and (4) the accurate prediction of the effects of interventions; see Mulaik (2000) for more information.

Consequences of Measurement Error

An assumption of PA is that the exogenous variables are measured without error. The consequences of minor violations of this requirement are not very critical. More serious violations result in biased estimates of direct effects. This bias affects not only the path coefficients of exogenous variables measured with error but also those of other exogenous variables in the model. However, it is difficult to anticipate the direction of this bias. Depending on the intercorrelations among the exogenous variables, some path coefficients may be biased upward (i.e., they are too high) but others may be biased in the other direction. For example, a direct effect that is actually zero may have a nonzero path coefficient, a true negative direct effect may have a positive path coefficient, or the absolute value of the path coefficient may be less than the true value (i.e., attenuation), all the result of measurement error. In an actual analysis, though, the direction of bias for individual path coefficients is difficult to predict. The amount of bias may be less if intercorrelations among measures of exogenous variables are low or if the magnitudes of true direct effects on the endogenous variables are low.

Although there is no assumption that the endogenous variables are measured without error, the use of psychometrically deficient measures of them has somewhat different consequences than for exogenous variables. The effect of measurement error on endogenous variables is manifested through their disturbances in addition to the effects of omitted causes. This leads to a potential interpretive confound, but one that affects *standardized* estimates of direct effects on the endogenous variables but not *unstandardized* ones. Standardized path coefficients tend to be too small when endogenous variables are measured with error. Values of unstandardized path coefficients for the same direct effects, on the other hand, are not biased by measurement error. This pattern of bias due to measurement error in the endogenous variables assumes that the exogenous variables have no error. If the exogenous variables are measured with error, these effects for the endogenous variables could be amplified, diminished, or even canceled out. It is best not to hope for the latter, however.

The use of more than a single measure of a construct is the most common way to deal with the problem of measurement error; this topic is introduced in Chapter 7. Scores from multiple indicators tend to be more reliable and valid than those from a single indicator. The technique of PA does not readily accommodate a multiple-indicator approach to measurement, but other SEM techniques do. In particular, the evaluation of an SR model with both measurement and structural components can be viewed as a type of latent variable PA that allows the use of multiple indicators. This topic is covered in Chapter 8, as is a method to correct for measurement error in single indicators. Readers who wish to learn more about measurement error in SEM are referred to Bollen (1989, chap. 5), Kenny (1979, chap. 5), and Maruyama (1998, chap. 5).

Suppression in Path Models

Suppression can also occur among variables in path models. A general definition is that suppression is indicated when the path coefficient for a predictor has a different sign or is greater in absolute value than that predictor's bivariate correlation with the endogenous variable. Because suppression is the result of correction for correlated causes, at least two causal variables must be involved in suppression. Maasen and Bakker (2001) describe various types of suppression effects that can be observed in path models, and generally they are counterparts of forms of suppression in regression analyses, including classical, reciprocal, and negative suppression. Maasen and Bakker also note that measurement error can mask the presence of a suppression effect in PA.

5.9 SUMMARY

This chapter has introduced the basic logic of specifying structural models with observed variables (path models). It is the same logic that underlies the specification of structural models with latent variables that represent hypothetical constructs. Specification is primarily a rational exercise, that is, it should be based on theory and results of prior empirical studies. Also introduced in this chapter was maximum likelihood estimation, the most widely used method for analyzing most kinds of structural equation models. It is a normal-theory, full-information method that simultaneously analyzes all model equations in an iterative algorithm. General statistical assumptions include independence of observations, independence of exogenous variables and disturbances, multivariate normality, and correct specification of the model. With these concepts in mind, we are ready to delve into the details of path analysis.

5.10 RECOMMENDED READINGS

Kenny, D. A. (1979). *Correlation and causality*. New York: Wiley. (Chaps. 3–5)

Klem, L. (1995). Path analysis. In L. G. Grimm & P. R. Yarnold (Eds.), *Reading and understanding multivariate statistics* (pp. 65–98). Washington, DC: American Psychological Association.

Recommendations for Start Values

These recommendations for the generation of start values for path coefficients and disturbance variances are based on the guidelines about effect size magnitude outlined in Appendix 5.B. If the researcher is using different numerical interpretations of these effect size magnitudes, they can be substituted in the following equations. Suppose that a researcher believes that the direct effect of X on Y is positive and of "medium" magnitude. A reasonable start value for the standardized coefficient for the path $X \rightarrow Y$ would be .30; for the unstandardized coefficient, the start value would be .30 (SD_Y/SD_X). If the expected magnitude were "small" or "large," then, respectively, .10 or .50 would be substituted for .30. Also suppose that a researcher believes that the magnitude of the predictive power of all variables with direct effects on Y (including X) is "large." A component of the start value for the disturbance variance for Y in standardized terms could be .75, which corresponds to 25% explained variance and 75% unexplained. (The former is the square of a "large" correlation, $.50^2$.) The start value for the unstandardized disturbance variance would be .75 (s_Y^2). If instead the researcher believed that the magnitude of the predictive power is "small" or "medium," then .99 (i.e., 1% explained variance, or $.10^2$) or .91 (i.e., 9% explained, or $.30^2$), respectively, would be substituted for .75.

Effect Size Interpretation of Standardized Path Coefficients

It is difficult to suggest interpretive guidelines that will prove useful across different research areas. This is because what may be considered a "large" effect in one area may be seen as modest in another. Also, some types of endogenous variables are more difficult to predict than others. For example, the predictive validity of IQ scores against scholastic achievement is quite strong, but it is less so against other variables such as occupational success.

Given these limitations, some suggestions about the interpretation of the absolute magnitudes of path coefficients are offered. They are based on recommendations by J. Cohen (1988) about effect size interpretations of correlations in the social sciences. Standardized path coefficients with absolute values less than .10 may indicate a "small" effect; values around .30 a "typical" or "medium" effect; and "large" effects may be indicated by coefficients with absolute values ≥.50. These guidelines are intended for cases where the researcher has little theoretical or empirical basis to differentiate between smaller versus larger effects, which is most likely to happen in new research areas. In more established areas, one should look to the research literature (e.g., meta-analytic studies) to gauge whether an observed effect size is smaller or larger. The above guidelines should *not* be rigidly interpreted. For example, one standardized path coefficient of .49 and another of .51 should not be considered as qualitatively different because the former indicates a "medium" effect and the latter a "large" effect. See Bollen (1989, pp. 137–138) for other recommendations about effect size interpretations of standardized path coefficients.

6

Details of Path Analysis

This chapter deals with the details of conducting a path analysis (PA). The discussion begins with the analysis of the path model of illness factors introduced earlier (section 4.2). How to interpret parameter estimates, calculate indirect and total effects, and compare observed correlations or covariances with their predicted counterparts are discussed in the context of this example. Also introduced here are statistical indexes of overall model fit and strategies for testing hypotheses about path models. Most of these analysis details generalize to the other types of structural equation models considered in later chapters, so they warrant careful review.

6.1 DETAILED ANALYSIS OF A RECURSIVE MODEL OF ILLNESS FACTORS

Briefly reviewed here is the work of D. L. Roth, Wiebe, Fillingim, and Shay (1989), who administered measures of exercise, hardiness, fitness, stress, and illness to 373 university students. Reported in Table 6.1 is a matrix summary of these data. The difference between the smallest and largest observed variances (i.e., $3.80^2 = 14.44$ and $624.80^2 = 390,375.04$ for, respectively, hardiness and illness) is so great that the covariance matrix for the original data is ill scaled, which can cause iterative estimation to fail. To avoid this potential problem, the original variables were multiplied by the constants listed in Table 6.1 in order to make their variances more homogeneous.

Presented in Figure 6.1 is the recursive path model specified by

TABLE 6.1. Input Data (Correlations, Standard Deviations) for Analysis of a Path Model of Illness Factors

Variable	1	2	3	4	5
1. Exercise	1.00				
2. Hardiness	−.03	1.00			
3. Fitness	.39	.07	1.00		
4. Stress	−.05	−.23	−.13	1.00	
5. Illness	−.08	−.16	−.29	.34	1.00
M	40.90	0.00	67.10	4.80	716.70
Original *SD*	66.50	3.80	18.40	6.70	624.80
Constant	1.00	10.00	4.00	10.00	.10
New *SD*	66.50	38.00	36.80	67.00	62.48

Note. These data are from D. L. Roth et al. (1989); N = 373. Means are reported but not analyzed. Note that low scores on the hardiness measure used by these authors indicate greater hardiness. In order to avoid confusion due to negative correlations, the signs of the correlations that involve the hardiness measure were reversed before they were recorded in this table.

D. L. Roth et al. (1989). The direct effects in the figure depicted with dashed lines were predicted by the authors to be zero. These predictions represent the hypotheses that (1) the effect of exercise on illness is indirect and mediated only by fitness, (2) the effect of hardiness on illness is indirect and mediated only by stress, and (3) the direct effect of fitness on stress is zero. These paths are included in the model analyzed next in order to eventually test these hypotheses. This path model is just-identified: with 5 observed variables, there are 5(6)/2 = 15 observations; the number of free model parameters is also 15, including the variances of 5 exogenous variables (2 observed and 3 unobserved, that is, the disturbances), 1 covariance between the observed exogenous variables, and a total of 9 direct effects. Thus, the model degrees of freedom are zero (df_M = 0).

Parameter Estimates

The path model of Figure 6.1 was fitted to a covariance matrix constructed from the correlations and standard deviations of Table 6.1

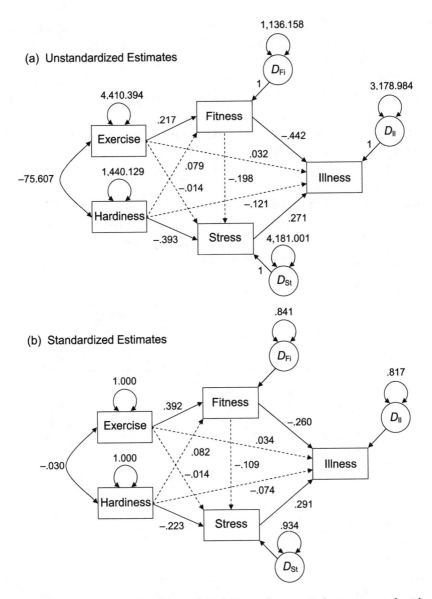

FIGURE 6.1. A recursive path model of illness factors. Paths represented with dashed lines were presumed zero by D. L. Roth et al. (1989). Standardized estimates for the disturbances are proportions of unexplained variance.

with Amos 5 (Arbuckle, 2003). The analysis converged to an admissible solution. Reported in Table 6.2 are the maximum likelihood (ML) estimates of model parameters. Let us consider first the unstandardized solution, which is also reported in Figure 6.1(a). For example, the unstandardized estimate of the direct effect of exercise on fitness is .217. This means that a 1-point increase on the exercise variable predicts a .217-point increase on the fitness variable, when we control for hardiness. The estimated standard error for this direct effect is .026 (Table 6.2), so $z = .217/.026 = 8.35$, which exceeds the critical value of 2.58 for two-tailed statistical significance at the .01 level. The unstandardized path coefficient for the direct effect of hardiness on fitness is .079; thus, a 1-point increase on the hardiness variable predicts a .079-point increase on the fitness variable, when we control for exercise. The estimated standard error is .046, so $z = .079/.046 = 1.72$. This

TABLE 6.2. Maximum Likelihood Parameter Estimates for a Just-Identified Path Model of Illness Factors

Parameter	Unstandardized	SE	Standardized
	Direct effects		
Exercise → Fitness	.217**	.026	.392
Hardiness → Fitness	.079	.046	.082
Exercise → Stress	−.014	.055	−.014
Hardiness → Stress	−.393**	.089	−.223
Fitness → Stress	−.198*	.099	−.109
Exer → Illness	.032	.048	.034
Hardiness → Illness	−.121	.079	−.074
Fitness → Illness	−.442**	.087	−.260
Stress → Illness	.271**	.045	.291
	Variances and covariances		
Exercise	4,410.394**	323.386	1.000
Hardiness	1,440.129**	105.595	1.000
Exercise ⌣ Hardiness	−75.607	130.726	−.030
D_{Fi}	1,136.158**	83.307	.841
D_{St}	4,181.001**	306.566	.934
D_{Il}	3,178.984**	233.094	.817

Note. Standardized estimates for disturbance variances are proportions of unexplained variance.

$*p < .05; **p < .01.$

value is less than that required for statistical significance at the .05 level, 1.96. Other unstandardized path coefficients in Table 6.2 and Figure 6.1(a) are interpreted in similar ways. Overall, the pattern of direct effects with statistically significant unstandardized path coefficients is consistent with the predictions of D. L. Roth et al. (1989). The only exception is for the path Fitness → Stress, for which the unstandardized coefficient (–.198) is statistically significant at the .05 level (Table 6.2).

Estimates of the unstandardized variances and covariances of the observed exogenous variables, exercise and hardiness, are just the observed values (Table 6.2, Figure 6.1(a)). The Amos program calculates variances of observed variables as $S^2 = SS/N$ instead of $s^2 = SS/df$, but note that $df/N \times s^2 = S^2$. The estimated disturbance variances reflect unexplained variability for each endogenous variable. For example, the estimated disturbance variance for fitness is 1,136.158. The observed variance of this variable is $s^2 = 36.80^2$ (Table 6.1), so $S^2 = (372/373)1354.24 = 1,350.609$. The ratio of the disturbance variance over the observed variance is $1,136.158/1,350.609 = .841$. That is, the proportion of total variance in fitness not explained by its presumed direct causes, exercise and hardiness, is .841. The proportion of explained variance for fitness thus equals $R^2_{smc} = 1 - .841 = .159$. The estimated disturbance variances for the two other endogenous variables, stress and illness, are interpreted in similar ways. Values of R^2_{smc} for these variables are, respectively, .066 and .183. (Readers should verify these results.)

Because not all variables have the same scale, the unstandardized estimates for different variables cannot be directly compared. However, this is not a problem for the standardized solution, which is reported in Table 6.2 and Figure 6.1(b). Note that there are no standard errors for the standardized estimates, which is typical for the default ML method in most SEM computer programs. (Amos can use bootstrapping to generate standard errors for standardized estimates, but these results are not reported here.) For example, the estimated standardized path coefficients for the direct effects of exercise and hardiness on fitness are, respectively, .392 and .082. That is, a level of exercise one full standard deviation above the mean predicts a fitness level almost .40 standard deviations above the mean, controlling for hardiness. Likewise, a level of hardiness one full standard deviation above the mean is associated with a fitness level about .10 standard deviations above the mean, when we control for exercise. The magnitude of the standardized direct effect of exercise on fitness is thus about four times greater than that of hardiness. Results for the seven other standardized direct effects are interpreted in similar ways. Overall, the pattern of the standardized direct effects is consistent with D. L. Roth and colleagues' hypotheses (1989); specifically, paths predicted to be zero generally have standardized coefficients less than .10 in absolute value (see Figure 6.1(b)). The only exception is the path Fitness $\rightarrow$ Stress (standardized coefficient = $-.109$).

Indirect and Total Effects

Indirect effects are estimated statistically as the product of direct effects, either standardized or unstandardized, that comprise them. They are also interpreted just as path coefficients. For example, the standardized indirect effect of fitness on illness through stress is estimated as the product of the standardized coefficients for the paths Fitness $\rightarrow$ Stress and Stress $\rightarrow$ Illness, or $-.109$ (.291) = $-.032$ (see Figure 6.1(b)). The rationale for this derivation is as follows: fitness has a certain direct effect on stress ($-.109$), but only part of this effect, .291 of it, is transmitted to illness. The result $-.032$ says that illness level is expected to decrease by about .03 standard deviations for every increase in fitness of one full standard deviation via its prior effect on stress.

The unstandardized indirect effect of fitness on illness through stress is estimated as the product of the unstandardized coefficients for the same two paths, or $-.198$ (.271) = $-.054$ (see Figure 6.1(a)). That is, the score on the illness variable in its original metric is expected to decrease by about .05 points for every 1-point increase on the fitness variable in its original metric via its prior effect on stress. A full standard deviation on the fitness variable is $S = (372/373)^{1/2}\ 36.80 = 36.751$ (Table 6.1). Therefore, an increase of one full standard deviation on the fitness variable predicts a decrease of 36.751 ($-.054$), or -1.985 points on the illness variable through the mediator of fitness. The standard deviation of the illness variable is $S = (372/373)^{1/2}\ 62.48 = 62.396$. A raw score change of -1.985 points thus corresponds to $-1.985/62.396 = -.032$ standard deviations, which matches the standardized estimate of this indirect effect calculated earlier.

Total effects are the sum of all direct and indirect effects of one variable on another. For example, the standardized total effect of fitness on illness is the sum of its direct effect, –.260 (see Figure 6.1(b)), and indirect effect through stress, –.032, or –.292 altogether. Total standardized effects are also interpreted as path coefficients, and the value of –.292 means that increasing fitness by one standard deviation reduces illness by this amount via all presumed direct and indirect causal links between these variables. Unstandardized estimates of total effects are calculated the same way but with unstandardized coefficients. For example, the unstandardized total effect of fitness on illness is the sum of its direct effect, –.442, and indirect effect through fitness, –.198 (.271) = –.054 (see Figure 6.1(a)), or –.496 altogether. That is, for every 1-point increase on the fitness variable in its original metric, we expect about a half-point decrease on the illness variable in its original metric via all presumed causal pathways between these variables.

Some SEM computer programs optionally generate an **effects decomposition**, a tabular summary of estimated direct, indirect, and total effects. This is fortunate because it can be tedious and error prone to calculate these effects by hand. The Amos program can print both total effects and total indirect effects. The latter is the sum of all indirect effects of a causally prior variable on a subsequent one. For example, fitness is specified to have a single indirect effect on illness (through stress; see Figure 6.1). However, the exercise and hardiness variables each have three possible indirect effects on illness, including one though fitness, another through stress, and the third through both variables (e.g., Exercise → Fitness → Stress → Illness).

In standard ML estimation, Amos does not report standard errors for total effects or total indirect effects. However, Amos can use the method of bootstrapping to estimate the standard error for unstandardized or standardized total effects and total indirect effects. Reported in Table 6.3 is the effects decomposition printed by Amos with standard errors for the unstandardized results only estimated across 1,000 random samples generated by the computer from the observed covariance matrix (Table 6.1). The bootstrapped standard errors for the unstandardized direct effects in Table 6.3 are very similar to the corresponding ones in Table 6.2 from the standard ML analysis. Note in Table 6.3 that stress has only a direct effect on illness, which is also its total effect. The variable fitness has just one indirect effect on illness

TABLE 6.3. Effects Decomposition for a Just-Identified Path Model of Illness Factors

| | Endogenous variables | | | | | | | | |
| | Fitness | | | Stress | | | Illness | | |
Causal variable	Unst.	*SE*	St.	Unst.	*SE*	St.	Unst.	*SE*	St.
Exercise									
Direct effect	.217**	.026	.392	−.014	.055	−.014	.032	.047	.034
Total indirect effects	—	—	—	−.043*	.022	−.043	−.112**	.026	−.119
Total effect	.217**	.026	.392	−.057	.050	−.057	−.080	.047	−.085
Hardiness									
Direct effect	.079	.046	.082	−.393**	.091	−.223	−.121	.076	−.074
Total indirect effects	—	—	—	−.016	.013	−.009	−.146**	.039	−.089
Total effect	.079	.046	.082	−.409**	.091	−.232	−.267**	.082	−.163
Fitness									
Direct effect	—	—	—	−.198*	.097	−.109	−.442**	.085	−.260
Total indirect effects	—	—	—	—	—	—	−.054	.028	−.032
Total effect	—	—	—	−.198*	.097	−.109	−.496**	.090	−.292
Stress									
Direct effect	—	—	—	—	—	—	.271**	.045	.291
Total indirect effects	—	—	—	—	—	—	—	—	—
Total effect	—	—	—	—	—	—	.271**	.045	.291

Note. Unst., unstandardized; St., standardized.
*p < .05; **p < .01.

(through stress), but only the unstandardized direct and total effects of this predictor are statistically significant. The unstandardized direct effects of exercise and hardiness on illness are also not statistically significant, but the total indirect effects of both variables are so. This pattern of results—statistically significant indirect effects but not direct effects—represents the strongest demonstration for a mediator effect, assuming correct directionality specifications. This pattern of results is also consistent with predictions by D. L. Roth and colleagues (1989;

see Figure 6.1). For more information about the estimation of indirect effects in SEM, see Shrout and Bolger (2002) and Cole and Maxwell (2003).

The Amos program does not calculate standard errors for individual indirect effects of variables with multiple indirect effects on other variables, such as exercise and hardiness in the present example. (This is a characteristic of some other SEM computer programs that report effects decompositions.) However, Baron and Kenny (1986) describe some hand-calculable statistical tests for unstandardized indirect effects in recursive path models that involve only one mediator (e.g., Exercise → Fitness → Illness). The best known of these tests is based on an estimated standard error developed by Sobel (1986), which is described in Appendix 6.A.

Model-Implied or Predicted Covariances and Correlations

The standardized total effect of one variable on another approximates the part of their observed correlation due to presumed causal relations. The sum of the standardized total effects and all other noncausal (e.g., spurious) associations represented in the path model equal **model-implied (predicted) correlations** that can be compared against the observed correlations. **Model-implied covariances** have the same general meaning, but they concern the unstandardized solution. All SEM computer programs that calculate model-implied correlations or covariances use matrix algebra methods (e.g., Loehlin, 1998, pp. 43–47). There is an older method for recursive path models amenable to hand calculation known as the **tracing rule**. It is worthwhile to know about the tracing rule more for its underlying principles than for its now limited utility. The tracing rule is as follows: *a model-implied correlation is the sum of all the causal effects and noncausal associations from all valid tracings between two variables in a recursive path model.* A "valid" tracing means that a variable is not (1) entered through an arrowhead and exited by the same arrowhead nor (2) entered twice in the same tracing.

As an example of the application of the tracing rule to calculate model-implied correlations with the standardized solution, look again at Figure 6.1(b) and find the exercise and stress variables. There are four valid tracings between them. Two of these tracings make up the standardized total effect (Exercise → Stress, Exercise → Fitness → Stress), which equals –.057 (see Table 6.3). The other two tracings involve the unanalyzed association of exercise with another variable, hardiness, that has direct or indirect effects on stress. These two tracings are Exercise ∪ Hardiness → Stress and Exercise ∪ Hardiness → Fitness → Stress. Estimates for both tracings are calculated in the same way as indirect effects; that is, as the products of the relevant path coefficients and correlations. The estimate for the Exercise ∪ Hardiness → Stress tracing is calculated as –.030 (–.223) = .007, and the estimate for the Exercise ∪ Hardiness → Fitness → Stress tracing is calculated as –.030 (.082) (–.109) = .0003. The implied correlation between exercise and stress equals the total effect plus both of the tracings that involve unanalyzed associations between the exogenous variables, or –.057 + .007 + .0003 = –.0497. Note that this value rounded to two decimal places (–.05) equals the observed correlation between exercise and stress (see Table 6.1). This result is just what we expect because this path model is just-identified ($df_M = 0$).

The difference between a model-implied and an observed correlation is known as a **correlation residual**. Correlation residuals are standardized **covariance residuals**—also known as **fitted residuals**—which the are differences between observed and predicted covariances.[1] For the just-identified path model in Figure 6.1, all correlation residuals are zero. For an overidentified path model ($df_M > 0$), however, not all correlation residuals may be zero. There is a rule of thumb in the SEM literature that correlation residuals with absolute values greater than .10 suggest that the model does not explain the corresponding observed correlation very well. Although it is difficult to say how many absolute correlation residuals greater than .10 are "too many," the more there are, the worse the explanatory power of the model for specific observed associations. There is no comparable rule of thumb about values of covariance residuals that suggest a poor expla-

---

[1]In EQS output, correlation residuals are labeled as **standardized residuals**, but in LISREL the same label designates the ratio of a covariance residual over its standard error, which is interpreted in large samples as a z test of whether the population covariance residual is zero.

nation because covariances are affected by the scales of the original variables.

Use of the tracing rule is error prone even for relatively simple recursive models because it can be difficult to spot all of the valid tracings. For example, there are a total of 10 different valid tracings between the stress and illness variables of the model in Figure 6.1. All but one of these tracings are for either spurious associations or ones that involve unanalyzed associations between the exogenous variables. This is even another reason to appreciate that many SEM computer programs automatically calculate model-implied correlations as a user-specified option. Note that the tracing rule does not apply to nonrecursive path models. Estimation of indirect and total effects for such models is discussed in Chapter 9.

6.2 ASSESSING MODEL FIT

Overidentified path models with more observations than parameters usually do not perfectly fit the data. There is thus a need to measure the degree of fit of such models. Discussed next are various statistical indexes of overall model fit.

Overview

There are dozens of model fit indexes described in the SEM literature, and new indexes are being developed all the time. Evaluation of the statistical properties of various fit indexes in computer simulation studies is also an active research topic (e.g., Kenny & McCoach, 2003; Marsh, Balla, & Hau, 1996), so the state of knowledge in this area is continuously changing. It is also true that many SEM computer programs print in their output the values of more fit indexes than are typically reported for the analysis.

The availability of so many different fit indexes presents a few problems. One is that different fit indexes are reported in different articles, and another is that different reviewers of the same manuscript may request indexes that they know about or prefer (Maruyama, 1998). This means that it can be difficult for a researcher to decide as to which particular indexes and which values to report. There is also the possibility for selective reporting of values of fit indexes. For example, a researcher keen to demonstrate good model fit may report only those fit indexes with favorable values. Another problem is that one can become so preoccupied with overall model fit that other crucial information, such as whether the parameter estimates make sense, is overlooked.

Described next is a minimal set of fit indexes that should be reported and interpreted when reporting the results of SEM analyses. This particular set reflects the current state of practice and recommendations about what to report in written summaries of the analysis (e.g., Boomsma, 2000; McDonald & Ho, 2002). These statistics include (1) the model chi-square, (2) the Steiger–Lind root mean square error of approximation (RMSEA; Steiger, 1990) with its 90% confidence interval, (3) the Bentler comparative fit index (CFI; Bentler, 1990), and (4) the standardized root mean square residual (SRMR). Before any of these statistics are described, it is useful to keep in mind the following limitations of basically all fit indexes in SEM:

1. Values of fit indexes indicate only the average or overall fit of a model. It is thus possible that some parts of the model may poorly fit the data even if the value of a particular index seems favorable. See Tomarken and Waller (2003) for discussion of potential problems with models that seem to fit the data well based on values of fit statistics.

2. Because a single index reflects only a particular aspect of model fit, a favorable value of that index does not by itself indicate good fit. This is also why model fit is usually assessed based in part on the values of more than one index. That is, there is no single "magic index" that provides a gold standard for all models.

3. Fit indexes do not indicate whether the results are theoretically meaningful. For example, the signs of some path coefficients may be unexpectedly in the opposite direction. Even if values of fit indexes appear to be favorable, results so anomalous require explanation.

4. Values of fit indexes that suggest adequate fit do not indicate that the predictive power of the model is also high. For example, disturbances of models with even perfect fit to the data can still be large, which means that the model accurately reflects the relative lack of predictive validity among the variables.

5. The sampling distributions of many fit indexes used in SEM are unknown (the RMSEA may be an exception), and the interpretive guidelines suggested later for individual indexes concerning good fit are just that.

Model Chi-Square

The most basic fit statistic is the product $(N - 1)$ F_{ML}, where $N - 1$ are the overall degrees of the freedom in the sample and F_{ML} is the value of the statistical criterion minimized in ML estimation. In large samples and assuming multivariate normality, $(N - 1)$ F_{ML} is distributed as a Pearson chi-square statistic with degrees of freedom equal to that of the researcher's model, df_M. This statistic is referred to here as the **model chi-square**, χ^2_M; it is also known as the **likelihood ratio chi-square** or **generalized likelihood ratio**. The value of χ^2_M for a just-identified model generally equals zero and has no degrees of freedom. If $\chi^2_M = 0$, the model perfectly fits the data (i.e., the predicted correlations and covariances equal their observed counterparts). As the value of χ^2_M increases, the fit of an overidentified model becomes increasingly worse. Thus, χ^2_M is actually a "badness-of-fit" index because the higher its value, the worse the model's correspondence to the data.

We continue to assume large samples and multivariate normality. Under the null hypothesis that the researcher's model has perfect fit in the population, χ^2_M approximates a **central chi-square distribution**. The only parameter of a central chi-square distribution is its degrees of freedom. Other applications of chi-square as a test statistic perhaps more familiar to readers, such as the test of association for two-way contingency tables, also approximate central chi-square distributions as N increases. Also, tables of critical values of chi-square in most statistics textbooks are based on central chi-square distributions.

For an overidentified model, χ^2_M tests the null hypothesis that the model is correct (i.e., it has perfect fit in the population). Suppose that $\chi^2_M = 10.00$ for a model where $df_M = 5$. The exact level of statistical significance associated with this statistic is $p = .075$.[2] Given this result, the researcher would *not* reject the null hypothesis at the .05

---

[2]This result was obtained from a central chi-square probability calculator freely available over the Internet; see http://members.aol.com/johnp71/javastat.html

level. However, if $\chi_M^2 = 12.00$ for the same model degrees of freedom, then $p = .035$ and the hypothesis that the model is correct would be rejected at the .05 level (but not at the .01 level). Therefore, it is the *failure* to reject the null hypothesis that supports the researcher's model. This logic is "backward" from the usual *reject–support* context for statistical tests where it is the rejection of the null hypothesis that supports the researcher's theory. However, it is perfectly consistent with an *accept–support* context where the null hypothesis represents the researcher's belief (Steiger & Fouladi, 1997).

Another way of looking at χ_M^2 is that it tests the difference in fit between a given overidentified model and a just-identified version of it. Suppose for an overidentified path model that $\chi_M^2 > 0$ and $df_M = 5$. Adding five more paths to this model would make it just-identified and reduce both χ_M^2 and df_M to zero. This is because almost all just-identified models perfectly explain the data. However, models that are just as complex as the data (i.e., $df_M = 0$) are not very interesting. Raykov and Marcoulides (2000) described each degree of freedom for χ_M^2 as a dimension along which the model can *potentially* be rejected. This is also why, given two different plausible models of the same phenomenon, the one with greater degrees of freedom (i.e., fewest parameters) is generally preferred because it has withstood a greater potential to be rejected. The same idea underlies the **parsimony principle**: given two different models with similar explanatory power for the same data, the simpler model is to be preferred.

There are some problems with relying solely on χ_M^2 as a fit statistic. The hypothesis tested by χ_M^2 is likely to be implausible. That is, it may be unrealistic to expect a model to have perfect population fit. It is sensitive to the size of the correlations: bigger correlations generally lead to higher values of χ_M^2. This happens in part because larger correlations tend to allow for the possibility of greater differences between observed and model-implied correlations. The model chi-square is also affected by sample size. Specifically, if the sample size is large, which is required in order to interpret the index as a test statistic, the value of χ_M^2 may lead to rejection of the model even though differences between observed and predicted covariances are slight. Indeed, rejection of basically any overidentified model based on χ_M^2 requires only a sufficiently large number of cases. To reduce the sensitivity of χ_M^2 to sample size, some researchers divide its value by the degrees of freedom (χ_M^2/df_M), which generally results in a lower value called the **normed chi-square** (NC). However, there is no clear-cut guideline about what value of the NC is minimally acceptable. Bollen (1989) notes that values of the NC of 2.0, 3.0, or even as high as 5.0 have been recommended as indicating reasonable fit and that the NC does not completely correct for the influence of sample size. Other, more sophisticated fit indexes described next are less affected by sample size and have interpretive norms.

Despite problems with χ_M^2 as a fit index, it is reported in virtually all reports of SEM analyses. One reason is that the formulas of most if not all other indexes include χ_M^2, so it is a key ingredient. The model chi-square is also useful in the comparison of hierarchical models evaluated with the same data, a topic considered in the next section. Problems with χ_M^2 have also motivated the development of numerous supplemental fit statistics, some described next. Basically all of these indexes—and χ_M^2 on which they are based—assume multivariate normality for the endogenous variables. If the distributions are severely nonnormal, the value of χ_M^2 tends to be too high. This means that (1) true models will be rejected too often when χ_M^2 is interpreted as a test statistic and (2) values of supplemental fit indexes based on χ_M^2 may be distorted. Corrective measures should be taken if the distributions are severely nonnormal (Chapter 7).

Root Mean Square Error of Approximation

The RMSEA has attracted much interest of late due to a relatively unique combination of properties. It is a **parsimony-adjusted index** in that its formula includes a built-in correction for model complexity. This means that given two models with similar overall explanatory power for the same data, the simpler model will be favored. It does not approximate a central chi-square distribution. The RMSEA instead approximates a **noncentral chi-square distribution**, which does not require a true null hypothesis. In this case it means that fit of the researcher's model in the population is *not* assumed to be perfect. A noncentral chi-square distribution has an additional parameter known as the **noncentrality parameter**, designated here as δ. This parameter measures the degree of falseness of the null hypothesis. Specifically, if the null hypothesis is true, then $\delta = 0$ and a central chi-square distribution is indicated. That is, a central chi-square distribution is just a special case of a noncentral chi-square distribution. The value of δ increases as the null hypothesis becomes more and more false. It also serves to shift the noncentral chi-square distribution to the right compared with the central chi-square distribution with the same degrees of freedom (e.g., MacCallum, Browne, & Sugawara, 1996, p. 136.)

In SEM, the parameter δ can be seen as reflecting the degree of misspecification of the researcher's model. It is often estimated as the difference between χ^2_M and df_M or zero, whichever is greater (i.e., the estimate cannot be negative). This estimator is designated here as $\hat{\delta}_M$, which is expressed as follows:

$$\hat{\delta}_M = \max(\chi^2_M - df_M, 0) \qquad (6.1)$$

where "max" refers to the maximum value of either of the two expressions in parentheses. Fit indexes, such as the RMSEA, based in part on $\hat{\delta}_M$ reflect the view that the researcher's model is an approximation of reality, not an exact copy of it (Raykov & Marcoulides, 2000).

Along the same lines, Browne and Cudeck (1993) distinguished between two different sources of lack of model fit. One is the **error of approximation**, which concerns the lack of fit of the researcher's model to the population covariance matrix. The RMSEA measures the error of approximation, and for this reason it is sometimes referred to as a **population-based index**. The other source of poor model fit concerns the **error of estimation**, the difference between the fit of the model to the sample covariance matrix and to the population covariance matrix. The error of estimation is affected by sample size—there is greater error in smaller samples—but the error of approximation is not. These two different kinds of errors contribute to **overall error**, the difference between the population covariance matrix and the model-implied covariance matrix estimated with the sample data. Fit indexes, such as χ^2_M and others that approximate central chi-square distributions, measure overall error and thus are described as **sample-based indexes**.

The RMSEA is a "badness-of-fit" index in that a value of zero indicates the best fit and higher values indicate worse fit. The formula is

$$\text{RMSEA} = \sqrt{\frac{\hat{\delta}_M}{df_M(N-1)}} \tag{6.2}$$

This equation shows that the RMSEA estimates the amount of error of approximation per model degree of freedom and takes sample size into account. Note that the result RMSEA = 0 says only that $\chi_M^2 < df_M$, not that $\chi_M^2 = 0$ (i.e., the fit is perfect; see Equation 6.1). A rule of thumb is that RMSEA $\leq$ .05 indicates close approximate fit, values between .05 and .08 suggest reasonable error of approximation, and RMSEA $\geq$ .10 suggests poor fit (Browne & Cudeck, 1993).

Computer programs for SEM that calculate the RMSEA typically also print a 90% confidence interval for the population parameter estimated by the RMSEA, designated here as ε. Confidence intervals for ε are based on the estimated noncentrality parameter $\hat{\delta}_M$, and the lower and upper bounds of such a confidence interval may not be symmetrical around the sample value of the RMSEA (see Steiger & Fouladi, 1997). This interval reflects the degree of uncertainty associated with RMSEA as a point estimate at the 90% level of statistical confidence. It also explicitly acknowledges that the RMSEA (and all other model fit indexes) are sample statistics subject to sampling error.

If the lower bound of a particular 90% confidence interval for ε is less than .05, we would not reject the directional null hypothesis H_0: $\varepsilon_0 \leq$ .05, which says that the researcher's model has close approximate fit in the population. (Ideally, zero is the lower bound of a 90% confidence interval for ε.) If it is also true that the upper bound of the same confidence interval does not exceed whatever cutoff value is selected as indicating poor fit (e.g., .10), we can reject the null hypothesis that the fit of the model in the population is just as bad or even worse (e.g., H_0: $\varepsilon_0 \geq$ .10). Suppose that RMSEA = .045 with the 90% confidence interval is 0–.150. Because the lower bound of this interval (0) is less than .05, the null hypothesis of close approximate fit is not rejected. However, the upper bound of the same confidence interval (.150) exceeds .10, so we cannot reject the hypothesis of poor approximate fit. Thus, the result RMSEA = .045 for this example is subject to a fair amount of sampling error because it is just as consistent with the hypothesis of good approximate fit as it is with the hypothesis of poor approximate fit. This type of "mixed" outcome is more likely to happen in smaller samples. A larger sample may be required in order to obtain more precise results.

Comparative Fit Index

The CFI was originally associated with EQS but is now printed by other SEM computer programs. It is one of a class of fit statistics known as **incremental** or **comparative fit indexes**, which are among the most widely used in SEM. All these indexes assess the relative improvement in fit of the researcher's model compared with a **baseline model**. The latter is typically the **independence model**—also called the **null model**—which assumes zero population covariances among the observed variables. When means are not analyzed, the only parameters of the independence model are the population variances of these variables. Because the independence model assumes unrelated variables, the value of its model chi-square, χ_B^2, is often quite large compared with that of the researcher's model, χ_M^2. To the extent that χ_M^2 is less than χ_B^2, the researcher's model is an improvement over the independence model; otherwise, there is no improvement and thus no reason to prefer the researcher's model.

Unlike some older incremental fit indexes described later, the CFI does *not* assume zero error of approximation (i.e., perfect population fit of the researcher's model). The formula is

$$CFI = 1 - \hat{\delta}_M / \hat{\delta}_B \qquad (6.3)$$

where $\hat{\delta}_M$ and $\hat{\delta}_B$ estimate the noncentrality parameter of a noncentral chi-square distribution for, respectively, the researcher's model and the baseline model. The estimator $\hat{\delta}_B$ has the same general form as that of $\hat{\delta}_M$ except that the former concerns the difference between χ_B^2 and df_B (see Equation 6.1). A rule of thumb for the CFI and other incremental indexes is that values greater than roughly .90 may indicate reasonably good fit of the researcher's model (Hu & Bentler, 1999). However, CFI = 1.0 means only that $\chi_M^2 < df_M$, not that the model has perfect fit.

All incremental fit indexes have been criticized when the baseline model is the independence (null) model (which is almost always true). This is because the assumption of zero covariances is scientifically implausible in many (probably most) applications of SEM. Therefore, finding that the researcher's model has better relative fit than the corresponding independence model may not be very impressive. Although it is possible to specify a different, more plausible baseline model and compute by hand the value of an incremental fit index with its equation, this is rarely done in practice. Widaman and J. Thompson (2003) describe how to specify more plausible baseline models for different kinds of SEM analyses. The Amos 5 program (Arbuckle, 2003) allows the specification of baseline models where covariances among the observed variables are required to be equal instead of zero, which is more realistic. See Marsh et al. (1996) for more information about statistical properties of incremental fit indexes.

Standardized Root Mean Square Residual

The indexes described next are based on covariance residuals, differences between observed and predicted covariances. Ideally, all these residuals should be about zero for good model fit. A statistic called the root mean square residual (RMR) was originally associated with LISREL but is now calculated by other SEM computer programs. It is a measure of the mean absolute value of the covariance residuals. Perfect model fit is indicated by RMR = 0, and increasingly higher values indicate worse fit (i.e., it is a badness-of-fit index). One problem with the RMR is that because it is computed with unstandardized variables, its range depends upon the scales of the observed variables. If these scales are all different, it can be difficult to interpret a given value of the RMR. The standardized root mean square residual (SRMR), on the other hand, is based on transforming both the sample covariance matrix and the predicted covariance matrix into correlation matrices. The SRMR is thus a measure of the mean absolute correlation residual, the overall difference between the observed and predicted correlations. Values of the SRMR less than .10 are generally considered favorable.

In addition to the statistics just described, it is also informative to view visual summaries of distributions of the residuals. Specifically, frequency distributions of the correlation residuals or covariance residuals should be generally normal in shape, and a Q-plot of the standardized residuals ordered by their size against their position in the distribution represented by normal deviates (z scores) should follow a diagonal line. Obvious departures from these patterns may indicate serious misspecification or violation of multivariate normality for the endogenous variables.

Other Fit Indexes

A class of statistics known as **predictive fit indexes** assess model fit in *hypothetical* replication samples of the same size and randomly drawn from the same population as the researcher's original sample. For this reason, these indexes may be seen as population based rather than sample based. Perhaps the best known predictive fit index under ML estimation is the Akaike information criterion (AIC). It is based on an information theory approach to data analysis that combines estimation and model selection under a single conceptual framework (e.g., D. R. Anderson, Burnham, & W. Thompson, 2000). It is also a parsimony-adjusted index because it favors simpler models. Confusingly, two different formulas for the AIC are reported in the SEM literature. The first is

$$AIC_1 = \chi^2_M + 2q \qquad (6.4)$$

where q is the number of free model parameters. Equation 6.4 thus *increases* the chi-square for the researcher's model by a factor of 2 times the number of free parameters. The second formula is

$$AIC_2 = \chi^2_M - 2df_M \qquad (6.5)$$

which *decreases* the model chi-square by a factor of 2 times the degrees of freedom. Though the two formulas are different, the key is that the relative change in the AIC is the same in both versions, and this change is a function of model complexity.

The AIC and other predictive fit indexes are generally used in SEM to select among competing nonhierarchical models estimated with the same data. (The difference between hierarchical vs. nonhierarchical models is defined in the next section.) Specifically, the model with the smallest AIC is chosen as the one most likely to replicate. This is the model with relatively better fit and fewer parameters compared with competing models. In contrast, more complex models with comparable overall fit may be less likely to replicate due to greater capitalization on chance.

Table 6.4 summarizes the characteristics of some miscellaneous fit indexes that readers may see reported in written summaries of SEM analyses. Some of these indexes are older than ones described earlier or have special problems that argue against their use. None are recommended over the indexes described earlier. Listed in the top part of the table are incremental fit indexes, including the Bentler–Bonett normed fit index (NFI) and the non-normed fit index[3] (NNFI; Bentler & Bonett, 1980) and the parsimony-adjusted NFI (PNFI; James, Mulaik, & Brett, 1982). The latter two statistics correct for model complexity (i.e., they favor simpler models), but note that the PNFI is quite sensitive to model size. This means that the penalty for complexity tends to be greater when the total number of observed variables in the model is relatively small, such as 10 or fewer. In small samples, it is possible for values of the NNFI to be much lower than those of other fit indexes. The relative noncentrality index (RNI; McDonald & Marsh, 1990) is similar to the CFI except that its values can be negative. In this regard the CFI is a better index because its range is 0–1.0.

Described in the middle part of Table 6.4 are miscellaneous predictive fit indexes. Like the AIC, they can be used to select among competing nonhierarchical models fitted to the same data; specifically, the model with the lowest values of these indexes is preferred. The expected cross-validation index (ECVI; Browne & Cudeck, 1993) results in the same rank ordering of competing models as the AIC, and some SEM computer programs print a 90% confidence based on the ECVI. The consistent Akaike information criterion (CAIC; Bozdogan, 1987) takes direct account of sample size, unlike the AIC. Another index known as the Bayes information criterion (BIC; Raftery, 1993), penalizes complexity more than either the AIC or the CAIC.

Listed in the bottom part of Table 6.4 are **absolute fit indexes** that estimate the proportion of variability in the sample covariance matrix explained by the model (i.e., the predicted covariance matrix). The goodness-of-fit index (GFI) was the very first standardized fit index (Jöreskog & Sörbom, 1981). Originally associated with LISREL, the GFI is now calculated by some other SEM computer programs. It is

---

[3]Also known as the Tucker–Lewis index.

TABLE 6.4. Formulas and Descriptions of Miscellaneous Fit Indexes

Index	Formula	Comment
Incremental fit indexes		
NFI	$1 - \chi_M^2/\chi_B^2$	Sample-based
NNFI	$(NC_B - NC_M)/(NC_B - 1)$	Sample-based, parsimony-adjusted, value can fall outside of range 0–1.0
PNFI	$(df_M/df_B)NFI$	Sample-based, parsimony-adjusted, sensitive to model size
RNI	$1 - (\chi_M^2 - df_M)/(\chi_B^2 - df_B)$	Population-based, value can be negative
PCFI	$(df_M/df_B)CFI$	Population-based, parsimony-adjusted, sensitive to model size
Predictive fit indexes		
ECVI	$(\chi_M^2 + 2q)/(N - 1)$	Population-based, parsimony-adjusted
CAIC	$\chi_M^2 + q(\ln N + 1)$	Population-based, parsimony-adjusted, takes account of sample size
BIC	$\chi_M^2 + q\ln[Nv(v + 1)/2]$	Population-based, parsimony-adjusted, takes account of sample size, greater penalty for complexity
Absolute fit indexes		
GFI	$1 - F_{ML}/F_0$	Sample-based, analogous to R^2, value can fall outside of range 0–1.0
AGFI	$1 - (1 - GFI)[v(v + 1)/2df_M]$	Sample-based, parsimony-adjusted, analogous to corrected R^2, value can fall outside of range 0–1.0
PGFI	$\{df_M/[v(v + 1)/2]\}GFI$	Sample-based, parsimony-adjusted, analogous to corrected R^2, value can fall outside of range 0–1.0, sensitive to model size

Note. NC, normed chi-square; q, number of free parameters; v, number of observed variables; F_{ML}, value of fit function for the researcher's model; F_0, value of fit function when all model parameters are zero; NFI, normed fit index; NNFI, non-normed fit index; PNFI, parsimony NFI; RNI, relative noncentrality index; PCFI, parsimony comparative fit index; ECVI, expected cross-validation index; CAIC, consistent Akaike information criterion; BIC, Bayes information criterion; GFI, goodness-of-fit index; AGFI, adjusted GFI; PGFI, parsimony GFI.

analogous to a squared multiple correlation (R^2) except that the GFI is a kind of matrix proportion of explained variance. Thus, GFI = 1.0 indicates perfect model fit, GFI > .90 may indicate good fit, and values close to zero indicate very poor fit. However, values of the GFI can fall outside the range 0–1.0. Values greater than 1.0 can be found with just-identified models or with overidentified models with almost perfect fit; negative values are most likely to happen when the sample size is small or when model fit is extremely poor. Another index originally associated with LISREL is the adjusted goodness-of-fit index (AGFI; Jöreskog & Sörbom, 1981). It corrects downward the value of the GFI based on model complexity; that is, there is a greater reduction for more complex models. However, the AGFI has not performed well in some computer simulation studies, which may explain why it is seen less often in the literature nowadays. The parsimony goodness-of-fit index (PGFI; Mulaik et al., 1989) corrects the value of the GFI by a factor that reflects model complexity, but it is sensitive to model size.

6.3 TESTING HIERARCHICAL MODELS

This section concerns ways to test hypotheses about hierarchical path models with the same data, but the general principles apply to all kinds of hierarchical structural equation models. Two path models are **hierarchical**—also known as **nested**—if one is a subset of the other. For example, if a path is dropped from model A to form model B, the two models are hierarchically related (i.e., model B is nested under model A).

Model Trimming and Building

There are two contexts in which hierarchical path models are usually compared. In **model trimming**, the researcher typically begins the analysis with a just-identified model and simplifies it by eliminating paths. This is done by specifying that at least one path previously freely estimated is now constrained to equal zero. The starting point for **model building** is usually a bare-bones, overidentified model to which paths are added. Typically, at least one previously fixed-to-zero path is specified as a free parameter. As a model is trimmed, its overall fit to the data typically becomes worse (e.g., χ^2_M increases). Likewise, model fit generally improves as paths are added (e.g., χ^2_M decreases). However, the goal of both trimming and building is to find a parsimonious model that still fits the data reasonably well.

Models can be trimmed or built according to one of two different standards, theoretical or empirical. The first represents tests of specific, a priori hypotheses. Suppose that a path model contains a direct effect of X on Y_2 and an indirect effect through Y_1. If the researcher believed that the relation of X to Y_2 is entirely mediated by Y_1, then he or she could test this hypothesis by constraining the coefficient for the path $X \rightarrow Y_2$ to zero (i.e., the path is trimmed). If the overall fit of this constrained model is not appreciably worse than the one with $X \rightarrow Y_2$ as a free parameter, the hypothesis about a mediated relation of X to Y_2 is supported. The main point, though, is that respecification of a model to test hierarchical versions of it is guided by the researcher's hypotheses. This is not the case, however, for empirically based respecification, in which paths are deleted or added according to statistical criteria. For example, if the sole basis for trimming paths is that their coefficients are not statistically significant, then model respecification is guided by purely empirical considerations. The distinction between theoretically or empirically based respecification has implications for the interpretation of the results of model trimming or building, which are considered after a model comparison test statistic is introduced.

The **chi-square difference** statistic, χ^2_D, can be used to test the statistical significance of the decrement in overall fit as paths are eliminated (trimming) or the improvement in fit as paths are added (building). As its name suggests, χ^2_D is simply the difference between the χ^2_M values of two hierarchical models estimated with the same data; its degrees of freedom, df_D, equal the difference between the two respective values of df_M. The χ^2_D statistic tests the null hypothesis of identical fit of the two hierarchical models in the population. Specifically, smaller values of χ^2_D lead to the failure to reject the equal-fit hypothesis, but larger values lead to the rejection of this hypothesis. In model trimming, rejection of the equal-fit hypothesis suggests that the model has been oversimplified; the same result in model building, however, supports retention of the path that was just added. Ideally, the more complex of the two models compared with χ^2_D should fit the data reasonably well. Otherwise, it makes little sense to compare the relative fit of two hierarchical models neither of which adequately explains the data.

Suppose for an overidentified path model that $\chi^2_M(5) = 18.30$. A single path is added to the model (which reduces the degrees of freedom by 1), and the result is $\chi^2_M(4) = 13.20$. Given both results, $\chi^2_D(1) = 18.30 - 13.20 = 5.10$, which has the exact level of statistical significance $p = .024$. Thus, the overall fit of the new model with an additional path is statistically better than that of the original model at the .05 level (but not at the .01 level). In this example, the chi-square difference test is a univariate one because it concerned a single path (i.e., $df_D = 1$). When two hierarchical models that differ by two or more paths are compared (i.e., $df_D \geq 2$), the chi-square difference test is essentially a multivariate test of all the added (or deleted) paths together. If $p < .05$ for χ^2_D in this case, at least one of the paths is nonzero. The paths may be statistically significant at the .05 level if tested individually, but this is not guaranteed.

Empirical versus Theoretical Respecification

The interpretation of χ^2_D as a test statistic depends in part upon whether the new model is derived empirically or theoretically. For example, if individual paths that are not statistically significant are dropped from the model, it is likely that χ^2_D will not be statistically significant. But if the deleted path is also predicted in advance to be zero, χ^2_D is of utmost theoretical interest. Also, if model specification is entirely driven by empirical criteria such as statistical significance, the researcher should worry about capitalization on chance. That is, a path may be statistically significant due only to chance variation, and its inclusion in the model would be akin to a Type I error. Likewise, a path that corresponds to a true nonzero causal effect may not be statistically significant in a particular sample, and its exclusion from the model would be essentially a Type II error. A sort of buffer against the problem of sample-specific results, though, is a greater role for theory in model respecification.

The issue of capitalization on chance is especially relevant when the researcher uses an "automatic modification" option available in some SEM computer programs such as LISREL. Such purely exploratory options drop or add paths according to empirical criteria such as statistical significance at the .05 level of a **modification index**, which is calculated for every path that is fixed to zero. A modification index is actually a univariate version of something known as a **Lagrange Multiplier** (LM), which in this case is expressed as a χ^2 statistic with a single degree of freedom. The value of an LM in the form of a modification index estimates the amount by which the overall model chi-square statistic, χ^2_M, would *decrease* if a particular fixed-to-zero path were freely estimated. That is, a modification index estimates $\chi^2_D(1)$ for adding that path. Thus, the greater the value of a modification index, the better the predicted improvement in overall fit if that path were added to the model. Likewise, a multivariate LM estimates the effect of allowing a set of constrained-to-zero paths to be freely estimated. For example, an LM with 5 degrees of freedom approximates the value of $\chi^2_D(5)$ for adding the same 5 paths. Some SEM computer programs, such as Amos and EQS, allow the user to generate modification indexes for specific parameters, which lends a more a priori sense to the use of this statistic.

The Wald W statistic is a related index but one used for model trimming. A univariate Wald W statistic approximates the amount by which the overall χ^2_M statistic would *increase* if a particular freely estimated path were fixed to zero. That is, a univariate Wald W statistic estimates $\chi^2_D(1)$ for dropping the same path. A value of univariate Wald W that is not statistically significant at, say, the .05 level predicts a decrement in overall model fit that is not statistically significant at the same level. Model trimming that is entirely empirically based would thus delete paths with Wald W statistics that are not statistically significant. A multivariate Wald W statistic approximates the value of χ^2_D for trimming a set of two or more paths from the model. Loehlin (1998) gives us some good advice: A researcher should *not* feel compelled to drop every path that is not statistically significant from the model, especially when the sample size is not large or power is low. Removing such paths might also affect the solution in an important way. It might be better to leave them in the model until replication indicates that the corresponding direct effect is of negligible magnitude.

All of the test statistics just described are sensitive to sample size; thus, even a trivial change in overall model fit due to adding or dropping a path could be statistically significant within a large sample. In addition to noting the statistical significance of a modification index, the researcher should also consider the absolute magnitude of the

change in the coefficient for the path if it is allowed to be freely estimated or constrained to equal zero. If the magnitude of the change is
small, the statistical significance of the modification index may reflect
the sample size more than it does the magnitude of the direct effect (see
Kaplan, 2000, pp. 121–122).

Specification Searches

MacCallum (1986) and Silvia and MacCallum (1988) conducted computer simulation studies of **specification searches**. They took known
structural equation models, imposed different types of specification
errors on them (e.g., a nonzero path is omitted), and evaluated the
erroneous models using data generated from populations in which the
known models were true. In MacCallum's study (1986), models were
modified using empirically based methods (e.g., modification indexes).
Most of the time the changes suggested by empirically based
respecification were incorrect, which means that they typically did not
recover the true model. This pattern was even more apparent for small
samples (e.g., $N = 100$). Silvia and MacCallum (1988) followed a similar procedure except that the application of automatic modification was
guided by theoretical knowledge, which improved the chances of dis-
covering the true model. The implication of these studies is clear: learn
from your data, but your data should not be your teacher.

A relatively new research area in SEM concerns the development of
automated yet "intelligent" specification searches based on heuristics
that attempt to optimize respecification compared with "dumb" specification searches (e.g., automatic model modification). These algorithms
are generally based on principles of machine learning or data mining in
computer science. For example, Marcoulides and Drezner (2001)
describe an adaptive search algorithm based on principles of genetics
and natural selection that evaluates models through successive "gener-
ations" from parent to child models. Marcoulides and Drezner (2003)
describe a search algorithm that mimics the behavior of an ant colony
as it collectively tries to achieve a certain goal, in this case model optimization. Intelligent specification search algorithms are not yet widely
implemented in SEM computer programs, but this may change. It
remains to be seen whether such algorithms are as intelligent as they
are claimed to be.

Example of Model Trimming

Model trimming guided by both a priori and empirical considerations is demonstrated for the just-identified path model of illness analyzed earlier. Recall that D. L. Roth et al. (1989) believed that five direct effects in this model were actually zero (see Figure 6.1). To test this hypothesis, the model with these five paths deleted was fitted to the covariance matrix based on the data in Table 6.1 with Amos 5 (Arbuckle, 2003). Amos Basic syntax for this analysis is presented in Appendix 6.B. Values of selected fit indexes are $\chi^2_M(5) = 11.078$, $p = .050$, NC = 11.078/5 = 2.216, CFI = .961, SRMR = .051, and RMSEA = .057, with the 90% confidence interval .001–.103. These results present a mixed picture. For example, the null hypothesis of perfect model fit in the population is technically *not* rejected at the .05 level because the probability of the model chi-square (.050) is not below .05, but just barely so. The value of the RMSEA (.057) is just higher than the ideal value of .05, but the upper bound of its 90% confidence interval (.103) is consistent with the hypothesis of poor approximate model fit in the population (H_0: $\varepsilon_0 \geq .10$). On the other hand, values of the CFI (.961) and SRMR (.051) are both favorable.

Only one correlation residual had an absolute value greater than .10. This residual, –.13, is between the fitness and stress variables. Thus, the model with five deleted paths, including Fitness → Stress (see Figure 6.1), underpredicts this correlation by .13. The only statistically significant modification index, $\chi^2(1) = 5.096$, $p = .024$, is for the same path. Based on these results, the path Fitness → Stress was added back to the model and the respecified model with only four deleted paths was estimated with the same data. Values of selected fit indexes from this second analysis are $\chi^2_M(4) = 9.921$, $p = .205$, NC = 1.480, CFI = .988, SRMR = .034, and RMSEA = .036 with the 90% confidence interval 0–.092. The results of the chi-square difference test are

$$\chi^2_D(1) = \chi^2_M(5) - \chi^2_M(4) = 11.078 - 5.921 = 5.157, p = .023$$

which means that the improvement in overall fit due to adding back the path Fitness → Stress is statistically significant at the .05 level. [Note that values of $\chi^2_D(1)$ and of the modification index $\chi^2(1)$ are close but not identical: 5.157 and 5.096, respectively.] Also, all absolute correlation residuals are less than .10 for the respecified model with four deleted paths but including Fitness → Stress.

6.4 COMPARING NONHIERARCHICAL MODELS

Sometimes researchers specify alternative models that are not hierarchically related. Although the values of χ_M^2 from two different nonhierarchical models can still be compared, the difference between them cannot be interpreted as a test statistic. This is where the AIC and other predictive fit indexes come in handy: within a set of competing nonhierarchical models, the one with the lowest value is preferred. An example follows. Presented in Figure 6.2 are two different path models of recovery after cardiac surgery evaluated by Romney, Jenkins, and Bynner (1992). The *psychosomatic model* of Figure 6.2(a) represents the hypothesis that morale mediates the effects of neurological dysfunction and diminished socioeconomic status (SES) on physical symptoms and social relationships. The *conventional medical model* of Figure 6.2(b) depicts different assumptions about causal relations among the same variables.

Reported in Table 6.5 are the correlations among the observed variables reported by Romney et al. (1992) for a sample of 469 patients. Unfortunately, Romney et al. did not report variable means or standard deviations, and the analysis of a correlation matrix with standard ML estimation is not generally recommended. To deal with this problem, the correlation matrix in Table 6.5 was analyzed with the SEPATH module of STATISTICA 6 (StatSoft Inc., 2003). This module offers a program option that, if selected, results in the automatic use of the method of constrained estimation (described in Chapter 7), which can correctly analyze a correlation matrix. Each model of Figure 6.2 was fitted to the correlation matrix in Table 6.1 with the method of constrained ML estimation in SEPATH. Both analyses converged to admissible solutions. Values of selected fit indexes for the psychosomatic model (Figure 6.2(a)) are

$$\chi_M^2(5) = 40.402, p < .001, \text{CFI} = .918,$$
$$\text{SRMR} = .065, \text{RMSEA} = .120 \ (.086-.156)$$

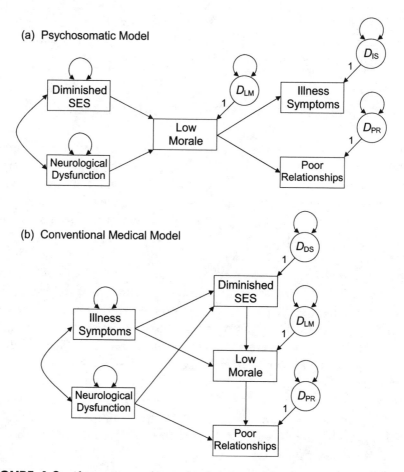

FIGURE 6.2. Alternative nonhierarchical path models of adjustment after cardiac surgery.

and corresponding values for the conventional medical model (Figure 6.2(b)) are

$$\chi^2_M (3) = 3.238, \, p = .283, \, \text{CFI} = .999,$$
$$\text{SRMR} = .016, \, \text{RMSEA} = .013 \, (0–.080)$$

It is not surprising that the overall fit of the more complex conventional medical model ($df_M = 3$) is better than that of the more parsimonious psychosomatic model ($df_M = 5$). However, the fit advantage of the

TABLE 6.5. Input Data (Correlations) for Analysis of Nonhierarchical Path Models of Recovery after Cardiac Surgery

Variable	1	2	3	4	5
1. Low Morale	1.00				
2. Illness Symptoms	.53	1.00			
3. Neurological Dysfunction	.15	.18	1.00		
4. Poor Relationships	.52	.29	−.05	1.00	
5. Diminished SES	.30	.34	.23	.09	1.00

Note. These data are from Romney et al. (1992); $N = 469$.

more complex model is enough to offset the penalty for having more parameters imposed by the AIC as defined by Equation 6.4. For the conventional medical model, AIC = 27.238, but for the psychosomatic model, AIC = 60.402. Because the former model has the lowest AIC value, it is preferred over the latter model.

6.5 EQUIVALENT MODELS

After a final path model is selected from among hierarchical or nonhierarchical alternatives, then **equivalent models** should be considered. Equivalent models yield the same predicted correlations or covariances but with a different configuration of paths among the same observed variables. Equivalent models also have equal goodness-of-fit indexes, including χ_M^2 (and df_M) and all other fit statistics described earlier. For a given path model—or any structural equation model—there may be many equivalent variations; thus, it behooves the researcher to explain why his or her final model should be preferred over mathematically identical ones.

Readers already know that just-identified path models perfectly fit the data. By default, any variation of a just-identified path model exactly matches the data, too, and thus is an equivalent model. Equivalent versions of overidentified path models can be generated using the **Lee–Herschberger replacing rules** (Herschberger, 1994; Lee & Herschberger, 1990), which are summarized below:

1. Within a block of variables at the beginning of a model that is just-identified and with unidirectional relations to subsequent variables, direct effects, correlated disturbances, and equality-constrained reciprocal effects (i.e., the two unstandardized direct effects are specified to be equal) are interchangeable. For example, $Y_1 \rightarrow Y_2$ may be replaced by $Y_2 \rightarrow Y_1$, $D_1 \cup D_2$, or $Y_1 \rightleftarrows Y_2$. If two variables are specified as exogenous, then an unanalyzed association may be substituted, too.

2. At subsequent places in the model where two endogenous variables have the same causes and their relations are unidirectional, all of the following may be substituted for one another: $Y_1 \rightarrow Y_2$, $Y_2 \rightarrow Y_1$, $D_1 \cup D_2$, and the equality-constrained reciprocal effect $Y_1 \rightleftarrows Y_2$.

Note that substituting reciprocal direct effects ($\rightleftarrows$) for other types of paths would make the model nonrecursive, but it is assumed that the new model is identified. How to tell whether a nonrecursive structural model is identified is considered in Chapter 9. Also, some equivalent versions of a structural model may be implausible due to the nature of the variables or the time of measurement. For example, a model that contains a direct effect from an acculturation variable to gender would be illogical; also, the assessment of Y_1 before Y_2 is inconsistent with the specification $Y_2 \rightarrow Y_1$. When an equivalent model cannot be disregarded, however, it is up to the researcher to provide a rationale for preferring one over the other.

Relatively simple structural models may have few equivalent versions, but more complicated ones may have hundreds or even thousands (e.g., MacCallum et al., 1993). We learn in Chapter 7 that measurement models can have infinitely many equivalent versions. Thus, it is unrealistic that researchers consider all possible equivalent models. As a compromise, researchers should generate at least a few substantively meaningful equivalent models. Unfortunately, even this limited step is often neglected. MacCallum et al. (1993) reviewed 53 articles published in behavioral science research journals in which SEM results were reported. Although nonhierarchical models were considered in about a dozen works, none of the authors explicitly acknowledged the existence of equivalent models. In their review of about 500 applications of SEM published in 16 different research journals, MacCallum

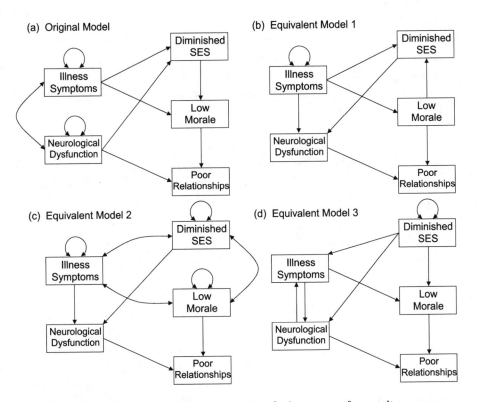

FIGURE 6.3. Four equivalent path models of adjustment after cardiac surgery. Disturbances are omitted.

and Austin (2000) found that researchers are still mainly unaware of the phenomenon of equivalent models or choose to ignore it. This particular kind of confirmation bias is one of the most serious limitations of today's practice of SEM.

Presented in Figure 6.3(a) is Romney and associates' original *conventional medical model* (1992) shown without disturbances to save space. The other three models in Figure 6.3 are generated from the original using the Lee–Herschberger replacing rules and thus are equivalent to it. For example, the equivalent model of Figure 6.3(b) substitutes a direct effect for a covariance between the illness symptoms and neurological dysfunction variables; it also reverses the direct effects between diminished SES and low morale and between diminished SES and neurological dysfunction. The equivalent model of Figure 6.3(c) replaces two of three direct effects that involve diminished SES with unanalyzed associations. The equivalent model of Figure 6.3(d) replaces the unanalyzed association between illness symptoms and neurological dysfunction with an equality-constrained direct feedback loop. It also reverses the direct effects between illness symptoms and diminished SES and between neurological dysfunction and diminished SES. Because all four path models of Figure 6.3 are equivalent, they explain the data in Table 6.5 equally well. For example, $\chi^2_M (3) = 3.238$ for all four models. Therefore, the choice among them must be based on theoretical rather than statistical grounds. Applying the Lee–Herschberger replacing rules to any of the models in Figure 6.3 may generate even more equivalent models. See Meehl and Walker (2002) and Reichardt (2002) for additional discussions about the testing of alternative directionality specifications for structural models.

6.6 POWER ANALYSIS

Power analysis can determine the probability that the results of a statistical test will lead to rejection of the null hypothesis when it is false. A power analysis in SEM can be conducted at the level of individual paths or for the whole model. One way to estimate the power of the test for a particular unstandardized path coefficient in a recursive path model is to use a method for the technique of multiple regression (J. Cohen, 1988, chap. 9). This method is amenable to hand calculation and estimates the power of tests of individual unstandardized regression coefficients. It requires the specification of the population proportion of unique variance explained by the direct effect of interest. This is the amount by which the proportion of total explained variance in the endogenous variable is expected to increase due to adding that direct effect to the model. (It also equals the squared part correlation.) The researcher also specifies in this method the level of α (usually .05 or .01), calculates the noncentrality parameter for the appropriate F distribution, λ, and then uses special tables in J. Cohen (1988) to estimate power. A variation is to specify a desired level of power (e.g., .80) and then estimate the minimum sample size needed to obtain it.

A method by Saris and Satorra (1993) for estimating power to detect an added path is more specific to SEM, and it can be used with basically any kind of structural equation model. Suppose that a researcher believes that the population unstandardized direct effect of X on Y is 5.0 (i.e., a 1-point increase in X leads to an increase on Y of 5 points when all other causal variables are held constant). Using this and the other a priori values of the parameters of the model of interest, the researcher's next step is to generate a predicted covariance matrix by employing the tracing rule (recursive path models only) or methods based on matrix algebra (e.g., Loehlin, 1998, pp. 43–47). This model-implied covariance matrix is then specified as the input data to an SEM computer program. The model analyzed does *not* include the path $X \rightarrow Y$ (i.e., it is fixed to zero), and the sample size specified is a planned value for the study (e.g., $N = 200$). The χ^2_M statistic from this analysis approximates a noncentral chi-square statistic. Next, the researcher consults a special table for noncentral chi-square for estimating power as a function of degrees of freedom and level of α (e.g., Loehlin, 1998, p. 263). The researcher uses $df = 1$ in these tables to obtain the estimated probability of detecting the added path when testing for it.

An approach to power analysis at the model level by MacCallum et al. (1996) is based on the RMSEA and noncentral chi-square distributions for the three different kinds of null hypotheses: (1) H_0: $\varepsilon_0 \leq .05$ (the model has *close fit* in the population); (2) H_0: $\varepsilon_0 \geq .05$ (there is *not close fit*); and (3) H_0: $\varepsilon_0 = 0$ (there is *exact fit*). The exact fit hypothesis is tested by χ^2_M, but because this hypothesis may be typically implausible, only the close-fit and not-close-fit hypotheses are considered here. Higher power for a test of the close-fit hypothesis means that we are better able to reject an incorrect model. In contrast, higher power for a test of the not-close-fit hypothesis implies better ability to detect a reasonably correct model. A power analysis for either null hypothesis (or both) would be conducted by specifying N, α, df_M, and a suitable value of the parameter estimated by the RMSEA under the alternative hypothesis, ε_1. For example, ε_1 could be specified for the close-fit null hypothesis as .08, the recommended upper limit for reasonable approximation error, or ε_1, could be specified for the not-close-fit null hypothesis as .01, which represents the case of a very good model. A variation is to determine the minimum sample size needed to reach a target level of power (e.g., .80) given α, ε_0, and ε_1.

Estimated power or minimum sample sizes can be obtained by consulting special tables in MacCallum et al. (1996) or Hancock and

Freeman (2001) or by using a computer program. MacCallum et al. (1996) give syntax for the SAS/STAT program (SAS Institute Inc., 2000) for a power analysis based on the method just described. Another option is to use the Power Analysis module in STATISTICA 6 (StatSoft Inc., 2003), which can estimate power for a structural equation model over ranges of ε_1 (with ε_0 fixed to .05), α, df_M, and N. The ability to inspect power curves as functions of sample size is very useful for planning a study.

The Power Analysis module of STATISTICA was used to estimate the power to reject the close-fit hypothesis, H_0: $\varepsilon_0 \leq .05$, assuming $\varepsilon_1 = .08$ and $\alpha = .05$ for the Romney et al. *conventional medical model* (1992), where $df_M = 3$ (see Figure 6.2). The sample size in this analysis was specified as $N = 469$, the size of the original sample. The estimated power calculated by the Power Analysis program is .276. That is, if this model actually does *not* have close fit in the population, then the estimated probability that we can reject this incorrect model is just somewhat greater than 25% for a sample size of 469 cases, given the other assumptions for this analysis. These results reflect a general trend that power at the model level may be low when there are few model degrees of freedom even for reasonably large samples. For models with only one or two degrees of freedom, sample sizes in the thousands may be required in order for model-level power to be greater than .80 (e.g., Loehlin, 1998, p. 264). Sample size requirements for the same level of power drop to some 300–400 cases for models when df_M is about 10. Even smaller samples may be needed for 80% power if $df_M > 20$, but the sample size should not be less than 100 in any event. As noted by Loehlin (1998), the results of power analysis in SEM can be sobering. Specifically, if an analysis has a low probability of rejecting a false model, this fact should temper the researcher's enthusiasm for his or her preferred model.

6.7 OTHER ESTIMATION OPTIONS

Some other estimation procedures for data with multivariate normal distributions available in many SEM computer programs are briefly described here. Two iterative methods include **generalized least squares** (GLS) and **unweighted least squares** (ULS). Both are based on the least squares criterion, but unlike multiple regression (i.e., ordinary least squares) they are full-information methods that estimate all parameters at once. A drawback of the ULS method is that it requires all observed variables to have the same scale; that is, this method is neither scale free nor scale invariant. It is also generally less efficient than ML estimation, which means that standard errors tend to be somewhat larger in ULS estimation. The GLS method is a member of a larger family of estimation methods known as weighted least squares (WLS), and some other WLS methods can be used for severely non-normal data (Chapter 7). One potential advantage of ULS and GLS over ML estimation is that they may require less computation time and presumably less computer memory. However, this potential advantage is not as meaningful nowadays given fast processors and abundant memory available in relatively inexpensive personal computers.

Two partial-information methods that analyze only one equation at a time are described next. Neither method is iterative, so no start values are required. Neither method assumes multivariate normality, and both are available in many software programs for general statistical analyses. The first is standard multiple regression, which was the "classical" estimation method for PA before SEM computer programs such as LISREL were introduced in the early 1970s. Recall that one requirement of multiple regression is that the residuals are uncorrelated with the predictors. This aspect of least squares estimation requires in PA the assumption that the disturbances are uncorrelated with all presumed causes of the corresponding endogenous variable. This assumption explains why standard multiple regression cannot be used to estimate nonrecursive path models. It also cannot be used to analyze models with latent variables that represent hypothetical constructs. How to estimate a recursive path model with multiple regression is described in Appendix 6.C. Although there are ways to estimate the overall fit of overidentified recursive path models to the data with multiple regression (e.g., Kline, 1998, pp. 152–154; Schumacker & Lomax, 1996, pp. 44–45), they require tedious and error-prone hand calculations. It is generally better to use an SEM computer program.

Another partial-information, noniterative method is two-stage least squares (2SLS). Unlike standard multiple regression, 2SLS can be used to estimate nonrecursive path models. There are also forms of 2SLS for models with latent variables, such as measurement models.

For example, LISREL uses a type of 2SLS estimation to calculate start values that are then passed to iterative, full-information methods such as ML estimation. The method of 2SLS is also widely used in other areas, such as econometrics, and its range of potential application for model estimation is much wider than that of standard multiple regression. The 2SLS method is described in Chapter 9.

Because partial-information methods such as 2SLS estimate only one equation at a time, they may be more robust against specification error propagation than full-information methods. However, results of a study by Kaplan and Wenger (1993) indicate that it is difficult to predict exactly how specification error in one part of the model will affect estimates for other parts of the model. This is because error propagation is determined first by the initial model specification and then by how the model is subsequently respecified. Bollen (2001) found that 2SLS estimates were generally less biased by specification error propagation than ML estimates, but only under the restrictive assumptions that specification error elsewhere in the model does not affect the equation being analyzed and that this equation is correctly specified. Thus, it is difficult at present to recommend partial-information over full-information estimation methods such as ML.

The availability of so many different estimation methods can sometimes seem overwhelming for newcomers to SEM. Loehlin (1998, p. 54) cites the following proverb that may describe this experience: a person with one watch always knows what time it is; a person with two never does. Actually, the situation is not so bewildering because ML estimation works just fine for most types of structural equation models if the data have been properly screened and the distributions of the endogenous variables are reasonably multivariate normal. Also, these different estimation procedures tend to yield similar solutions for such "well-behaved" data.

6.8 SUMMARY

The details of conducting a path analysis and testing hypotheses were the subject of this chapter. Researchers often begin the analysis with a just-identified model that is trimmed; that is, the model is simplified by eliminating paths. As models are trimmed, their fit to the data usually becomes progressively worse. Researchers can also test models in the opposite direction: an initial, overidentified model can be made more complex by adding paths. At each step, the fit of each respecified model can be compared against that of the original model with the chi-square difference test. The goal of both model trimming and building is to a find in a series of hierarchical models one that is parsimonious and yet fits the data reasonably well. Model testing should be guided as much as possible by theoretical rather than empirical considerations (e.g., paths are added solely according to their statistical significance levels). After the researcher selects a final path model, it is critical to generate and evaluate some plausible equivalent models that explain the data just as well but with a different configuration of paths.

Given an understanding of path analysis, one knows essentially half the rationale of SEM—that of structural models. The other half concerns measurement models, in which observed variables are represented as indicators of underlying latent variables, the subject of Chapter 7. Once the reader understands the principles of measurement models, then he or she will have acquired the conceptual framework necessary to understand the whole of SEM for the analysis of covariance structures as variations on these two major themes, structural analysis and measurement.

6.9 RECOMMENDED READINGS

MacCallum, R. C., Wegener, D. T., Uchino, B. N., & Fabrigar, L. R. (1993). The problem of equivalent models in applications of covariance structure analysis. *Psychological Bulletin, 114,* 185–199.

Shrout, P. E., & Bolger, N. (2002). Mediation in experimental and nonexperimental studies: New procedures and recommendations. *Psychological Methods, 7,* 422–445.

Tomarken, A. J., & Waller, N. G. (2003). Potential problems with "well-fitting" models. *Journal of Abnormal Psychology, 112,* 578–598.

Appendix 6.A

Statistical Tests for Indirect Effects in Recursive Path Models

Suppose that a is the unstandardized coefficient for the path $X \rightarrow Y_1$ and that SE_a is its standard error; let b and SE_b, respectively, represent the same things for the path $Y_1 \rightarrow Y_2$. The product ab estimates the unstandardized indirect effect of X on Y_2 through Y_1. Sobel's (1986) estimated standard error of ab is

$$SE_{ab} = \sqrt{b^2 SE_a^2 + a^2 SE_b^2} \qquad (6.6)$$

In a large sample, the ratio ab/SE_{ab} is interpreted as a z test of the unstandardized indirect effect and is called the **Sobel test**. There is also a Web page that automatically calculates the Sobel test after the required information is entered in graphical dialogs.[4] Results of the Sobel test for the individual unstandardized indirect effects of exercise on illness for the recursive path model of Figure 6.1 based on the results reported in Table 6.2 are summarized in the accompanying table.

Indirect effect	a	SE_a	b	SE_b	ab	SE_{ab}	z
Exer $\rightarrow$ Fit $\rightarrow$ Ill	.217	.026	−.442	.087	−.096	.022	−4.34**
Exer $\rightarrow$ Stress $\rightarrow$ Ill	−.014	.055	.271	.045	−.004	.015	.25
Hardi $\rightarrow$ Fit $\rightarrow$ Ill	.079	.046	−.442	.087	−.035	.021	−1.63
Hardi $\rightarrow$ Stress $\rightarrow$ Ill	−.393	.089	.271	.045	−.107	.030	−3.56**

**$p < .01$.

The author is unaware of a hand-calculable test of the statistical significance of indirect effects through two or more mediators, but a rule of thumb by J. Cohen and P. Cohen (1983) seems reasonable: if all of its component unstandardized path coefficients are statistically significant at the same level of α, then the whole indirect effect can be taken as statistically significant at that level of α, too. All three of the component unstandard-

[4]www.psych.ku.edu/preacher/sobel/sobel.htm

ized coefficients of the path Exercise → Fitness → Stress → Illness meet this requirement at the .05 level (see Table 6.2), so the whole indirect effect can be considered statistically significant at the same level. Note that the only other indirect effect through two mediators, Hardiness → Fitness → Stress → Illness, fails to meet this standard because the unstandardized path coefficient of its first component direct effect is not statistically significant at the .05 level (Table 6.2). See Shrout and Bolger (2002) for more information about the analysis of mediator effects.

Appendix 6.B

Amos Basic Syntax

```
Sub Main()
    Rem Figure 6.1
    Dim SEM As New AmosEngine
    SEM.TextOutput
    SEM.Standardized
    SEM.Smc
    SEM.SampleMoments
    SEM.BeginGroup "Roth.csv"
        SEM.Structure "Fitness = Exercise + (p1) Hardiness" _
            & "+ D_Fi (1)"
        SEM.Structure "Stress = (p2) Exercise + Hardiness" _
            & "+ (p3) Fitness + D_St (1)"
        SEM.Structure "Illness = (p4) Exercise + (p5) _
            Hardiness" & "+ Fitness + Stress + D_Il (1)"
        SEM.Model "Trim 5", "p1 = p2 = p3 = p4 = p5 = 0"
        SEM.Model "Trim 4", "p1 = p2 = p4 = p5 = 0"
End Sub
```

Appendix 6.C

Estimation of Recursive Path Models with Multiple Regression

Follow these steps:

1. *Variances and covariances (i.e., unanalyzed associations) of observed exogenous variables.* These are simply the observed values. For example, the unstandardized estimate of an unanalyzed association is the covariance, and the standardized estimate is the Pearson correlation.

2. *Direct effects on endogenous variables from other observed variables.* For each endogenous variable, enter all observed variables specified to directly affect it as predictors in a regression equation. The unstandardized regression coefficients are the unstandardized path coefficients, and the beta weights are the standardized path coefficients.

3. *Disturbance variances.* Record R^2 from each analysis in the previous step. The term $1 - R^2$ is the proportion of unexplained variance. The product $(1 - R^2)s_Y^2$, where s_Y^2 is the observed variance of the corresponding endogenous variable, equals the unstandardized disturbance variance. The term $(1 - R^2)^{1/2}$ is the standardized residual path coefficient.

4. *Disturbance covariances (i.e., unanalyzed associations).* This step concerns only partially recursive models with disturbance correlations restricted to pairs of endogenous variables without direct effects between them (see Figure 5.1). The unstandardized estimate is the partial covariance between the endogenous variables when we control for their common causes, and the standardized estimate is the corresponding partial correlation (e.g., Kenny, 1979, pp. 52–61).

7

Measurement Models and Confirmatory Factor Analysis

A limitation of path analysis is the use of a single measure of each construct represented in the model. Not only does this force the researcher to choose among alternative measures (if available), but also basically any single indicator is susceptible to measurement error. An alternative is to use multiple measures of each construct, which tends to reduce the effect of measurement error in any individual indicator on the accuracy of the results. Although path models do not readily accommodate multiple-indicator measurement, other types of structural equation models do. These models feature the distinction between indicators and the underlying latent variables (factors) that the indicators are presumed to measure, which together make up a measurement model. This chapter deals with the analysis of measurement models with confirmatory factor analysis (CFA). In measurement models evaluated by CFA, the factors are simply assumed to covary with each other; that is, all of their associations are specified as unanalyzed. The next chapter deals with structural regression (SR) models where some unanalyzed associations between factors are replaced by direct causal effects, which gives the model a structural as well as a measurement component.

7.1 SPECIFICATION OF CFA MODELS

Presented in Figure 7.1 is an example of a standard CFA model, the type evaluated most often in the behavioral sciences; the indicators are depicted with Xs, their measurement errors with Es, and the factors

(a) Unstandardized Factors

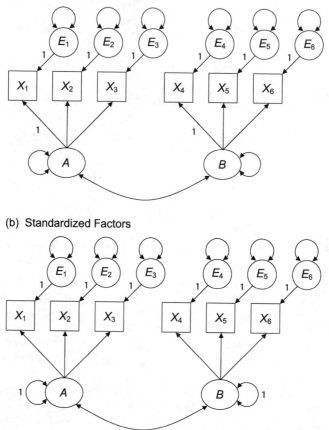

(b) Standardized Factors

FIGURE 7.1. Standard confirmatory factor analysis measurement models with (a) unstandardized factors and (b) standardized factors.

with the letters A and B. This model represents the hypotheses that X_1 to X_3 measure factor A, X_4 to X_6 measure factor B, and the two factors covary. Standard CFA models have the characteristics listed below and described afterward:

1. Each indicator is a continuous variable represented as having two causes—a single underlying factor that the indicator is supposed to measure and all other unique sources of causation that are represented by the error term.

2. The measurement errors are independent of each other and of the factors.

3. All associations between the factors are unanalyzed.

The lines with single arrowheads that point from a factor to an indicator (e.g., $A \rightarrow X_1$ in Figure 7.1) represent the presumed causal effect of the factor on the observed scores. Statistical estimates of these direct effects are called **factor loadings** or **pattern coefficients**, and they are generally interpreted as regression coefficients that may be in unstandardized or standardized form. Indicators assumed to be caused by underlying factors are referred to as **effect indicators** or **reflective indicators**. In this sense, indicators in standard CFA models are endogenous and the factors are exogenous. The lines that point from an error term to an indicator (e.g., $E_1 \rightarrow X_1$ in Figure 7.1) represent the combined effect of all other sources of influence on the observed scores besides that of the factor the indicator is supposed to measure. Like disturbances in path models, measurement errors in CFA models can also be seen as unobserved exogenous variables. Measurement errors reflect two kinds of unique variance: (1) random error of the type estimated by the complements of reliability coefficients (i.e., $1 - r_{XX}$), and (2) systematic variance due to things that the indicator measures besides its underlying factor, such as the effects of a particular method of measurement.

The specifications that each indicator depends on just one factor and that the error terms are independent are described by J. C. Anderson and Gerbing (1988) as **unidimensional measurement**. If an indicator has loadings on two or more factors or if its error term is assumed to covary with that of another indicator, then **multidimensional measurement** is specified. For example, adding a direct effect from factor B to indicator X_1 ($B \rightarrow X_1$) in the model of Figure 7.1 would specify multidimensional measurement. Readers should note that there is some controversy in the SEM literature about allowing indicators to load on multiple factors. On the one hand, Cattell (1978) noted that some indicators may actually measure more than one domain (i.e., they are factorially complex). An engineering aptitude test with text and diagrams, for example, may measure both verbal and nonverbal reasoning. Allowing this indicator to load on two different factors in a CFA model would be consistent with this possibility. On the other hand,

J. C. Anderson and Gerbing (1988) argued that unidimensional measurement models are more generally useful because they offer more precise tests of the convergent and discriminant validity of factor measurement. For example, if every indicator of Figure 7.1 were allowed to load on both factors, an exploratory factor analysis model that allows correlated factors (i.e., an oblique rotation) would be specified.

The specification of correlated error terms is the second way to represent multidimensional measurement. A measurement error correlation reflects the assumption that the two corresponding indicators measure something in common that is not explicitly represented in the model. Because error correlations are unanalyzed associations between unobserved exogenous variables (e.g., $E_1 \cup E_2$), what this "something" may be is unknown as far as the model is concerned. Error term correlations can be included in a model as a way to test hypotheses about shared sources of variability other than that due to the underlying factors. For example, it is relatively common in SEM to specify error correlations for indicators that are repeated measures variables, which represents the hypothesis of autocorrelated errors. Specification of error correlations can also reflect the hypothesis of a common method effect. In contrast, the absence of a measurement error correlation between a pair of indicators reflects the assumption that their observed correlation can be explained by the factors presumed to underlie them. This refers to the **local independence assumption** that the indicators are independent, given the (correctly specified) latent variable model (W. Wothke, personal communication, November 24, 2003).

Either form of multidimensionality—indicators that depend on multiple factors or correlated measurement errors—has implications for the identification of CFA models that are considered in the next section. Adding either characteristic to a standard CFA model also increases the number of parameters, which reduces parsimony. As with other types of specification decisions in SEM, though, the choice between unidimensional versus multidimensional measurement should be guided by substantive considerations.

There is another variation on standard CFA models that feature hierarchical relations among the factors. Hierarchical CFA models depict at least one construct as a second-order factor that is not directly measured by any indicator. This exogenous second-order factor is also presumed to have direct causal effects on the first-order factors, which have indicators. These first-order factors are endogenous and thus do not have unanalyzed associations with each other. Instead, their common direct cause, the second-order factor, is presumed to explain the correlations among the first-order factors. Hierarchical models of intelligence, in which a general ability factor (g) is presumed to underlie more specific ability factors (verbal, visual–spatial, etc.), are examples of theoretical models that have been tested with hierarchical CFA. Hierarchical CFA is considered in more detail later.

The assumption that the indicators are caused by underlying factors is not always appropriate. Some indicators may be viewed as **cause indicators** or **formative indicators** that affect a factor instead of the reverse. Consider an example by Bollen and Lennox (1991): Three variables, income, education, and occupation, are used to measure socioeconomic status (SES). In a standard model, these variables would be specified as effect indicators that are caused by an underlying SES factor (and by measurement errors). But we usually think of SES as being "caused" by all these variables, not the other way around. For example, a change in any one of these indicators, such as a salary increase, may affect SES. In this case, SES can be seen as a composite variable that is caused by the three observed exogenous variables just mentioned. The specification of even one observed variable as a cause indicator makes the factor endogenous and the whole model an SR model. A special type of measurement model with a single cause indicator that is an equivalent version of a single-factor CFA model is considered later. See Diamantopoulos and Winklhofer (2001) and Kline (in press) for more information.

7.2 IDENTIFICATION OF CFA MODELS

Requirements for the identification of different types of CFA models are outlined next.

Necessary Requirements

Any kind of CFA model must meet two necessary conditions in order to be identified: (1) the number of free parameters is less than or equal to the number of observations (i.e., $df_M \geq 0$), and (2) every latent variable, which includes the measurement errors and factors, must have a scale. The number of observations equals v $(v + 1)/2$, where v is the number of observed variables, which is the same as for path models. Parameters of CFA measurement models are counted as follows:

> *The total number of variances and covariances (i.e., unanalyzed associations) of the exogenous variables (the factors and measurement errors) plus direct effects of the factors on the indicators (i.e., the loadings) equals the number of parameters.*

Just as for disturbances in path models, measurement errors in CFA models are almost always assigned a scale through a unit loading identification (ULI) constraint. In CFA, this fixes the unstandardized residual path coefficient for the direct effect of a measurement error on the corresponding indicator to 1.0. This specification has the consequence of assigning to a measurement error a scale related to that of the unexplained (unique) variance of its indicator. For example, the specification $E_1 \rightarrow X_1 = 1.0$ in Figure 7.1 assigns to E_1 a metric that corresponds to that of the unique variance of X_1. Although fixing the residual path coefficient to any other constant, such as 2.0 or 4.5, would also identify a measurement error, most SEM computer programs make it easier to specify a ULI constraint for these terms or do so automatically.

There are two options for scaling a factor. One is to use the same method as for the measurement errors, that is, by imposing ULI constraints. For a factor this means to fix the unstandardized coefficient (loading) for the direct effect on one of its indicators to equal 1.0. (Again, specification of any other constant would do, but 1.0 is the default in most SEM computer programs.) The indicator with the ULI constraint is known as the **reference variable**. This specification assigns to a factor a scale related to that of the explained (common) variance of the reference variable. For example, the specification $A \rightarrow X_1 = 1.0$ in the model of Figure 7.1(a) makes X_1 the reference variable and assigns a scale to A based on the common variance of X_1; the specification $B \rightarrow X_4 = 1.0$ has a similar interpretation. Assuming that scores on each of multiple indicators are equally reliable, the choice of which indicator is to be the reference variable is generally arbitrary. Otherwise, it makes sense to select the indicator with the most reliable scores. The second option is fix the factor variance to a constant. Specification of any constant would do, but it is much more common to impose a **unit variance identification** (UVI) **constraint**, which fixes the factor variance to 1.0 and also standardizes the factor. When a factor is scaled through a UVI constraint, all factor loadings for its indicators are free parameters. A UVI constraint is represented in model diagrams in this book with the constant 1.0 next to the symbol for the variance of an exogenous variable ($\curvearrowright$). For example, the variance of factor A is fixed to 1.0 in the model of Figure 7.1(b). This specification not only assigns a scale to A, it also implies that the loadings of all three of its indicators can be freely estimated with sample data. The UVI constraint for factor B in the model of Figure 7.1(b) has a similar interpretation. Note that scaling factors through either ULI or UVI constraints reduces the total number of free parameters by one for each factor.

Both methods of scaling the factors generally result in the same overall fit of the model to same data, but not always. A special problem known as constraint interaction occurs when the choice between either method affects overall model fit. This phenomenon is described later after prerequisite concepts about model testing are introduced, but most of the time constraint interaction may not be a problem. The choice between these two methods, then, is usually based on the relative merits of analyzing factors in standardized versus unstandardized form. When a CFA model is analyzed in a single sample, either method is probably acceptable. Fixing the variance of a factor to 1.0 to standardize it has the advantage of simplicity. A shortcoming of this method, though, is that it is usually applicable only to exogenous factors. This is because although basically all SEM computer programs allow the imposition of constraints on any model parameter, the variances of endogenous variables are not considered parameters. Only some programs, including SEPATH and RAMONA, allow the predicted variances of endogenous factors to be constrained to equal 1.0. This is not an issue for CFA models, wherein all factors are exogenous, but it can be for SR models, where some factors are endogenous. However, the analysis of standardized factors is *not* generally appropriate when a structural equation model is analyzed across independent samples, a point discussed in Chapter 11.

Sufficient Requirements

Meeting both necessary requirements just described does not guarantee that a CFA model is identified. Fortunately, there is a sufficient condition for identification that concerns minimum numbers of indicators that applies to standard CFA models, those that feature unidimensional measurement and all possible unanalyzed associations among the factors:

> *If a standard CFA model with a single factor has at least three indicators, the model is identified. If a standard model with two or more factors has at least two indicators per factor, the model is identified.*

Bollen (1989) referred to the second sufficient condition just listed as the **two-indicator rule**. However, note that models with factors that have only two indicators are more prone to estimation problems, especially when the sample size is small. Both points are elaborated later, but a minimum of three indicators per factor is recommended.

There is no comparable easily applied sufficient condition for CFA models that specify multidimensional measurement. Although the identification status of such models is more ambiguous, some suggestions for dealing with them are offered below. However, it is important to evaluate whether such CFA models are identified when they are specified and before the data are collected. This is because one way to respecify a nonidentified CFA model is to add indicators, which increases the number of observations available to estimate effects. This may be possible only before the study is carried out.

The specification of either correlated measurement errors or loadings of indicators on multiple factors may not be problematic. The presence of both in the same CFA model, however, may cause identification problems. A necessary but insufficient condition for the identification of a model that specifies multidimensional measurement is that an SEM computer program can generate a converged, admissible solution that passes empirical checks of its uniqueness. These empirical checks can be applied to the actual data. Instead, it is suggested to use an SEM computer program as a diagnostic tool with made-up data arranged in a covariance matrix and based on correlations and standard deviations that are anticipated to approximate actual values. (This suggestion assumes that the actual data are not yet collected.) Care must be taken not to generate hypothetical correlations that are out of bounds or that may result in empirical underidentification. If the researcher is uncertain about a particular hypothetical covariance matrix, then others with somewhat different but still plausible values can be constructed. The model is then analyzed with the hypothetical data. If a computer program is unable to generate a converged, admissible solution, the CFA model may not be identified. Otherwise, if the solution passes the uniqueness tests described next, it may be identified.

One empirical check is to use the predicted covariance matrix from a successful analysis of a CFA model as the input data for a second analysis of the same model. The second analysis should yield the same solution as the first because the input data (i.e., the predicted covariances) were generated based on the parameter estimates from the first analysis. If not, the solution is not unique and the model is not identified. Note that this empirical check works only if $df_M > 0$ (i.e., there are more observations than parameters). If $df_M = 0$, the predicted covariances will almost always equal the corresponding made-up values. A second uniqueness test is to conduct a second analysis using different start values than in the first analysis. If estimation converges to the same solution working from different initial estimates, the model may be identified.

A third empirical test involves inspection of the matrix of estimated correlations among the parameter estimates. Although parameters are fixed values that do not vary in the population, their estimates are considered random variables with their own distributions and covariances. Estimates of these covariances are based on what is known as the **information matrix**, which is associated with iterative methods, including maximum likelihood (ML) estimation. The number of rows and columns of this square matrix equals the number of free parameters, and its elements are related to the statistical criterion minimized in the analysis. If the model is identified, the information matrix has an inverse (i.e., it is positive definite) and this inverse is the matrix of covariances among the parameter estimates. Some SEM computer programs optionally print the associated correlations. An identification problem is indicated if any of these correlations are close to 1.0 in absolute value. Correlations so high literally say that one parameter estimate cannot be derived independently of another estimate. Remember, though, that all three of the empirical checks just described and other more complicated ones based on linear algebra methods (e.g., Bollen, 1989, pp. 246–251) do not guarantee that a CFA model that specifies multidimensional measurement is actually identified.

Let's apply the identification requirements just discussed to the standard CFA models presented in Figure 7.2. The model of Figure 7.2(a) has a single factor with two indicators. This model is underidentified: with two observed variables, there are three observations but four parameters, including three variances of exogenous variables (of factor A and two measurement errors) and one factor loading (of X_2; the other is fixed to 1.0 to scale A). The imposition of a constraint, such as one of equality (e.g., $A \rightarrow X_1 = A \rightarrow X_2 = 1.0$), in the unstandardized solution may make this model estimable. However, Kenny (1979) noted for such models that if the correlation between the two indicators is negative, then the just-identified model that results by imposing an equality constraint on the factor loadings does not exactly reproduce the observed correlation. This is an example of a just-identified model that does not perfectly fit the data. Because the single-factor model in Figure 7.2(b) has three indicators, it is identified (specifically, just-identified): There are 3(4)/2 = 6 observations available to estimate the six model parameters, including four variances (of factor A and three measurement errors) and two factor loadings. Note that a standard single-factor CFA model must have at least four indicators in order to be overidentified. Because each of the two factors in the model of Figure 7.2(c) each has two indicators, it is identified (specifically, overidentified): a total of 4(5)/2 = 10 observations is available to estimate nine parameters, including six variances (of two factors and four measurement errors), one unanalyzed association between the factors, and two factor loadings.

Just as with other types of structural equation models, CFA models that are theoretically identified are still susceptible to empirical underidentification. For example, suppose that the estimated loading for the path $A \rightarrow X_2$ in the model of Figure 7.2(b) is close to zero. Practically speaking, this model would resemble the one in Figure 7.2(a) in that factor A has only two indicators, which is too few for a single-factor model. The model of Figure 7.2(c) may be empirically underidentified if the estimate of the correlation between factors A and B is close to zero. The virtual elimination of the path from this model transforms it into two single-factor, two-indicator models, each of

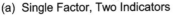

(a) Single Factor, Two Indicators   (b) Single Factor, Three Indicators

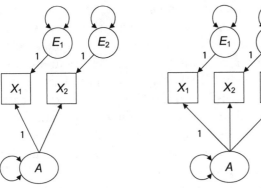

(c) Two Factors, Two Indicators

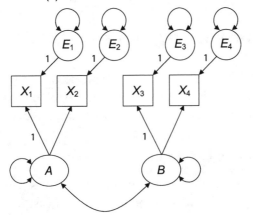

FIGURE 7.2. Identification status of three standard confirmatory factor analysis models.

which is underidentified. See Kenny, Kashy, and Bolger (1998) and Bollen (1989, pp. 238–246) for more information about identification requirements for CFA models.

7.3 NAMING AND REIFICATION FALLACIES

Factors in the CFA models considered to this point were designated with letters, such as A and B. In real analyses, researchers are more likely to assign meaningful labels to factors, such as "working memory." However, it is important to avoid two logical errors concerning factor labels. The first is the **naming fallacy**; that is, just because a factor is named does not mean that the hypothetical construct is understood or even correctly labeled. Factors require some type of designation, however, if for no other reason than communication of the results. Although verbal labels are more "user friendly" than more abstract symbols, such as ξ or η (both are from LISREL's matrix algebra notation), they should be viewed as conveniences and not as substitutes for critical thinking. The second logical error to avoid is **reification**, the belief that a hypothetical construct *must* correspond to a real thing. For example, a general cognitive ability factor, g, is a hypothetical construct. To automatically consider g as real, however, is a potential reification error that may affect the interpretation of the results.

7.4 ESTIMATION OF CFA MODELS

This section deals with basic issues that concern the estimation of all CFA models. A later section outlines more specialized methods that can be used to analyze indicators with severely nonnormal distributions.

Interpretation of Estimates

Unstandardized estimates are interpreted as follows. Unanalyzed associations between either a pair of factors or measurement errors are covariances. Factor loadings (pattern coefficients) are interpreted as unstandardized regression coefficients that estimate the direct effects of the factors on the indicators. Note that loadings of indicators fixed to 1.0 to scale the corresponding factor remain so in the unstandardized solution and are not tested for statistical significance because they are constants (i.e., they have no standard errors). The ratio of the estimated measurement error variance over the observed variance of the corresponding indicator equals the proportion of unexplained (unique) variance. One minus this ratio is the proportion of explained indicator variance, R^2_{smc}. Recall that estimated disturbance variances in path analysis are similarly interpreted.

In the standardized solution, estimates of unanalyzed associations are correlations. When indicators are specified to measure just one factor, standardized factor loadings are also estimated correlations. The square of these standardized loadings equals the proportion of explained (common) indicator variance, or R^2_{smc}. If an indicator is specified to measure multiple factors, however, its standardized factor loadings are interpreted as standardized regression coefficients (i.e., beta weights) that control for correlations among underlying factors. Because beta weights are not correlations, one should not square their values to derive proportions of explained variance. However, one minus the ratio of the unstandardized measurement error variance over the observed variance always equals the proportion of explained variance (R^2_{smc}) regardless of the number of factors an indicator is specified to measure.[1]

The estimated correlation between an indicator and a factor is known as a **structure coefficient**. If an indicator is specified to measure just one factor, its standardized loading is a structure coefficient; otherwise it is not. Graham, Guthrie, and B. Thompson (2003) remind us that the specification that the direct effect of a factor on an indicator is zero does *not* mean that the correlation between the two must be zero. That is, a zero pattern coefficient does *not* imply that the structure coefficient for the same factor and indicator is zero. For example, X_1 in Figure 7.2(c) is specified to measure factor A but not B; therefore, the pattern coefficient for the direct effect $B \rightarrow X_1$ is zero. Assuming the factor correlation is not zero, however, the predicted correlation between B and X_1 is not zero because B covaries with a cause of X_1, factor A. In general, indicators are expected to be correlated with *all* factors in CFA models, but they should have higher estimated correlations with the factors they are believed to measure; see Graham et al. (2003) for additional discussion and examples.

Problems

Failure of iterative estimation can be caused by poor start values; suggestions for calculating start values in CFA are presented in Appendix

---

[1]This description corresponds to the completely standardized solution in LISREL where the variances of all variables (factors, indicators, residuals) are rescaled to equal 1.0 (option SC). LISREL can also print a different solution where just the factors are standardized, but results for other measures are reported in the original metrics (option SS).

7.A. Inadmissible solutions in CFA include Heywood cases, such as negative variance estimates or estimated absolute correlations greater than 1.0. Results of some computer simulation studies indicate that nonconvergence or improper solutions are more likely to occur for CFA models with only two indicators per factor and sample sizes less than 100–150 cases (e.g., Marsh & Hau, 1999). If possible, at least three indicators per factor are recommended, especially if a researcher's sample is so small. The suggestion offered earlier that researchers also think about minimum sample size in terms of the ratio of cases to free parameters (i.e., 10:1 or, even better, 20:1) may also be appropriate for CFA (e.g., Jackson, 2003). Marsh and Hau (1999) give the following suggestions for analyzing CFA models when the sample size is not large:

1. Use indicators with good psychometric characteristics that will each also have relatively high standardized factor loadings (e.g., > .60).
2. Estimation of the model with equality constraints imposed on the unstandardized loadings of the indicators of the same factor may help to generate more trustworthy solutions. (Equality constraints for CFA models are discussed later.)
3. When the indicators are categorical items instead of continuous scales, it may be better to analyze them in groups known as parcels rather than individually. However, the analysis of parcels is controversial; this topic is considered later.

Effect of Nonnormality

Standard ML estimation assumes multivariate normal distributions for the indicators. Results of several computer simulation studies indicate that it is best not to ignore this requirement. When the indicators are continuous but have severely nonnormal distributions, ML parameter estimates are generally accurate in large samples, but their estimated standard errors tend to be too low (i.e. negatively biased), perhaps by as much as 25–50% depending on the data and model. This results in rejection of the null hypothesis that the population parameter is zero more often than is correct (i.e., Type I error rate is inflated). In contrast, the value of the model chi-square, χ^2_M, tends to be too high, which implies that true models will be rejected too often in exact fit tests. The actual rate of this type of error may be as high as 50% when the expected rate assuming normal distributions is 5%, again depending upon the data and model (e.g., Chou & Bentler, 1995; Curran et al., 1997).

The effect of analyzing categorical indicators on the accuracy of results from normal theory methods, such as ML, has been examined in other computer simulation studies. Distributions of variables with small numbers of categories (e.g., two to four) are not generally normal. These simulation studies generally assume a true population measurement model with continuous indicators. Within generated samples, the indicators are categorized to approximate data from non-continuous variables. Bernstein and Teng (1989) found that when there is only a single factor in the population but the indicators have few categories, one-factor CFA models tend to be rejected too often. That is, categorization can spuriously suggest the presence of multiple factors. DiStefano (2002) found that ML parameter estimates and their standard errors were both generally too low when the data analyzed are from categorical indicators, and the degree of this negative bias was higher as the distributions became increasingly nonnormal.

The lesson from these studies is quite clear: results from standard ML estimation may be inaccurate if the multivariate normality requirement for the indicators is violated. Options to deal with this problem are described later.

Fitting Models to Correlation Matrices

This is a good point at which to describe the method of **constrained estimation** or **constrained optimization** (Browne, 1982) for correctly fitting a model to a correlation matrix instead of a covariance matrix. It can be used in CFA or any other SEM procedure. Recall that standard ML estimation assumes the analysis of unstandardized variables. If the variables are standardized, ML results may be inaccurate, including the value of χ^2_M or estimates of standard errors. This can happen if a model is not scale invariant, which means that its overall fit to the data depends on whether the variables are standardized or unstandardized. Whether a particular model is scale invariant or not is determined by a rather complex combination of elements, including how the factors are

scaled (i.e., ULI vs. UVI constraints) and the presence of equality constraints on estimates of factor loadings (Cudeck, 1989). The method of
constrained estimation involves the imposition of nonlinear constraints
on certain parameter estimates to guarantee that the model is scale
invariant. These nonlinear constraints can be quite complicated to program manually (e.g., Steiger, 2002, p. 221), and not all SEM computer
programs support this type of constraint (LISREL, Mx, and CALIS do).
However, the SEPATH and RAMONA programs both allow constrained
estimation to be performed automatically by selecting an option, which
is very convenient.

7.5 TESTING CFA MODELS

This discussion begins with the analysis of the measurement model for
the Visual Similes Test II (VST II) introduced earlier (section 4.3).
Briefly reviewed, T. O. Williams et al. (2002) tested the two-factor CFA
model of the VST II presented in Figure 4.2. The indicators of this
model are 10 different item parcels, 5 from the Affective form of the
VST II and 5 from the Cognitive form. Presented in Table 7.1 are the
correlations and standard deviations among the parcels within a sample
of 216 children ages 10–12 years old.

Test for a Single Factor

When theory is not specific about the number of constructs, this is
often the first step in a series of analyses: if a single-factor model cannot be rejected, there is little point in evaluating more complex ones.
Even when theory is more precise about the number of factors (e.g.,
two for the VST II), it should be determined whether the fit of a simpler, one-factor model is comparable. A covariance matrix based on the
data in Table 7.1 was submitted to EQS 6 (Bentler, 2003) for ML estimation of a single-factor CFA model. The unstandardized loading of the
first parcel (A1) was fixed to 1.0 scale the factor. With 10 indicators, there
are $10(11)/2 = 55$ observations available to estimate a total of 20
parameters, including 11 variances (of the factor and 10 measurement
errors) and 9 factor loadings. Estimation in EQS did not converge to a
stable solution after the default number of iterations (30). It was neces-

TABLE 7.1. Input Data (Correlations, Standard Deviations) for Analyses of Measurement Models for the Visual Similes Test II

Parcel	A1	A2	A3	A4	A5	C1	C2	C3	C4	C5
Affective form										
A1	1.000									
A2	.822	1.000								
A3	.852	.839	1.000							
A4	.814	.831	.779	1.000						
A5	.840	.846	.910	.819	1.000					
Cognitive form										
C1	.582	.637	.643	.580	.680	1.000				
C2	.634	.660	.662	.623	.704	.731	1.000			
C3	.605	.607	.628	.603	.673	.784	.757	1.000		
C4	.587	.575	.622	.570	.674	.750	.758	.703	1.000	
C5	.674	.662	.685	.659	.716	.724	.782	.771	.789	1.000
SD	45.145	43.956	36.247	45.102	45.408	25.110	27.235	32.976	29.245	26.994

Note. These data are from T. O. Williams et al. (2002); $N = 216$.

sary to increase this limit before estimation converged to an admissible solution. Values of selected fit indexes are $\chi^2_M (35) = 409.286$, $p < .001$, NC = 11.694, CFI = .845, SRMR = .083, and RMSEA = .223 with the 90% confidence interval .203–.242. These results clearly indicate poor fit of the single-factor model of the VST II to the data in Table 7.1.

The test for a single factor is relevant not just for CFA models. For example, Kenny (1979) noted that such models could also be tested as part of a path analysis. The inability to reject a single-factor model in this context would mean the same thing as in CFA: the observed variables do not show discriminant validity; that is, they seem to measure only one domain. A test for single factoredness was conducted for the five variables of the D. L. Roth et al. (1989) path model of illness analyzed in the previous chapter (see Figure 6.1). A single-factor model for these variables was fitted to a covariance matrix based on the data summarized in Table 6.1 with the ML method of EQS. Values of selected fit indexes clearly show that a single-factor model poorly explains the data: $\chi^2_M (5) = 60.386$, $p < .001$, NC = 12.007, CFI = .644, SRMR = .096, and RMSEA = .173 with the 90% confidence interval .134–.212, providing a "green light" to proceed with evaluation of the path model.

Test for Multiple Factors

The specification of a multifactor CFA model in which each indicator loads on only one factor provides a precise test of convergent and discriminant validity. For example, the two-factor model of the VST II predicts that the five parcels from the Affective form measure one factor and that the five parcels from the Cognitive form measure another (see Figure 4.2). To scale the factors, the unstandardized loadings of the A1 and C1 parcels on their respective factors were each fixed to 1.0. A total of 21 parameters remain to be estimated, including 12 variances (of 2 factors and 10 error terms), 8 factor loadings (4 on each factor), and 1 factor covariance. With 10 observed variables and 55 observations, $df_M = 55 - 21 = 34$.

The two-factor model of the VST II was fitted to the data of Table 7.1 with the ML method of EQS, and a converged, admissible solution was obtained. Values of selected fit indexes are as follows: $\chi^2_M (34) = 88.159$, $p < .001$, NC = 2.593, CFI = .978, SRMR = .022, and RMSEA = .086 with the 90% confidence interval .086–.108. These results are generally favorable except for the RMSEA. On the other hand, the largest absolute correlation residual is .053, so the two-factor model explains the observed correlations relatively well. The only statistically significant modification index, $\chi^2 (1) = 4.933$, $p = .026$, is for the loading of the A5 parcel on the cognitive arousal factor. That is, specifying that this indicator measures both factors would reduce the overall model chi-square by about 5 points, an amount that may be statistically significant. Even without this respecification, however, the original two-factor model seems to be at least minimally adequate, so it is retained here.

The fit of the two-factor model is also clearly better than that of the single-factor model to the same data. Can we compare the relative fits of these two models with the chi-square difference test? Recall that this test is only for hierarchical models. Is this true of the one- and two-factor models of the VST II? Yes, and here is why: the one-factor model is actually a restricted version of the two-factor model. Look at Figure

4.2. If the correlation between the two factors is fixed to equal 1.0, then the two factors are identical, which is the same thing as replacing both factors with just one. The results of the chi-square difference test are

$$\chi_D^2(1) = \chi_M^2(35) - \chi_M^2(34) = 409.286 - 88.159$$
$$= 321.127, p < .001$$

which says that the fit of the two-factor model is statistically better than that of the single-factor model. The comparison just described can be generalized to models with more factors. With a four-factor model, for instance, fixing all of the factor correlations to 1.0 generates a single-factor model that is nested under the unrestricted model.

Reported in Table 7.2 are the parameter estimates for the two-factor model. Values of the unstandardized factor loadings estimate the expected change in the original metric of each indicator given a 1-point increase on its factor. For example, scores on the A2 parcel are expected to increase by .976 points for every 1-point increase in the affective arousal factor. The estimated unstandardized measurement error variance for this parcel is 358.602. Because EQS calculates the variance of observed variables as $s^2 = SS/df$, the ratio of this error variance over the observed variance of the A2 parcel (see Table 7.1), or $358.602/43.956^2$, equals .186. The proportion of explained variance for this parcel is thus $R_{smc}^2 = 1 - .186 = .814$. Unstandardized estimates for the other indicators are interpreted in similar ways. Because each indicator is specified to measure just one factor, the standardized factor loadings are also structure coefficients that estimate indicator–factor correlations. For each set of indicators, the standardized factor loadings are all relatively high, which suggests convergent validity. The evidence for discriminant validity is less strong. This is because the estimated factor correlation, .811, is high enough to suggest that the two arousal factors, affective and cognitive, may not be clearly distinct.

Reported in Table 7.3 are values of structure coefficients (estimated correlations with each factor) for all 10 parcels (indicators) in the two-factor model of the VST II. Coefficients presented in boldface in the table are also standardized factor loadings for indicators specified to measure either the affective arousal factor or the cognitive arousal factor. For example, the A1 indicator is specified to measure the affective arousal factor but not the cognitive arousal factor (Figure 4.2).

TABLE 7.2. Maximum Likelihood Parameter Estimates for a Two-Factor Model of the Visual Similies Test II

Parameter	Unstandardized	SE	Standardized
	Factor loadings		
Affective → A1	1.000[a]	—	.901
Affective → A2	.976	.046	.902
Affective → A3	.837	.036	.939
Affective → A4	.964	.050	.869
Affective → A5	1.063	.043	.952
Cognitive → C1	1.000[a]	—	.852
Cognitive → C2	1.115	.065	.876
Cognitive → C3	1.330	.080	.863
Cognitive → C4	1.173	.071	.858
Cognitive → C5	1.126	.064	.893
	Measurement error variances		
E_{A1}	385.166	43.419	.189
E_{A2}	358.602	40.583	.186
E_{A3}	155.933	20.160	.119
E_{A4}	498.373	53.584	.245
E_{A5}	193.521	27.807	.094
E_{C1}	172.458	19.704	.274
E_{C2}	172.770	20.671	.233
E_{C3}	277.148	32.275	.255
E_{C4}	225.216	25.991	.263
E_{C5}	147.591	18.539	.203
	Factor variances and covariance		
Affective	1,652.905	194.331	1.000
Cognitive	458.054	59.439	1.000
Affective ⌣ Cognitive	705.473	86.359	.811

Note. Standardized estimates for measurement errors are proportions of unexplained variance.
[a]Not tested for statistical significance; $p < .01$ for all other unstandardized estimates.

Therefore, the pattern coefficient for the relation between this indicator and the cognitive arousal factor is zero. The structure coefficients for the A1 indicator are .901 and .730 (Table 7.3). The former (.901) equals the standardized loading of this indicator on the affective arousal factor (Table 7.2). The latter (.730) is the model-implied correlation between the A1 indicator and the cognitive arousal factor. It is calculated using the tracing rule as the product of the structure coefficient for A1 and the estimated correlation between the two factors, or .901 (.811) = .730. Thus, the A1 indicator is estimated to have a substantial correlation with the factor (cognitive arousal) it is not specified to measure. The results in Table 7.3 clearly show that the structure coefficients are typically not zero for corresponding zero pattern coefficients when the factors are substantially correlated.

Respecification

In the face of adversity, the protagonist of Kurt Vonnegut's novel *Slaughterhouse-Five* often remarks, "So it goes." And so it often does in CFA that an initial model does not fit the data very well. The respecification of a CFA model is even more challenging than that of a path model because there are more possibilities for change. For example, the number of factors, their relations to the indicators, and patterns of measurement error correlations are all candidates for modification. Given so many potential variations, respecification of CFA models should be guided as much as possible by substantive considerations rather than solely by empirical ones. Otherwise, the respecification process could put the researcher in the same situation as the sailor in

TABLE 7.3. Structure Coefficients for a Two-Factor Model of the Visual Similies Test II

	Factor	
Parcel	Affective	Cognitive
A1	.901	.730
A2	.902	.732
A3	.939	.761
A4	.869	.704
A5	.952	.772
C1	.691	.852
C2	.710	.876
C3	.700	.863
C4	.696	.858
C5	.724	.893

this adage attributed to Leonardo da Vinci: one who loves practice without theory is like the sailor who boards ship without a rudder and compass and never knows where he or she may be cast.

There are two general classes of problems that can be considered in respecification. The first concerns the indicators. Sometimes indicators fail to have substantial loadings on the factors to which they are originally assigned (e.g., standardized loading = .20). One option is to specify that an indicator loads on a different factor. Inspection of the correlation residuals can help to identify the other factor to which the indicator's loading may be switched. Suppose that an indicator is originally specified to measure factor A but the correlation residuals between it and the indicators of factor B are large and positive. This would suggest that the indicator may measure factor B more than it does factor A. Note that an indicator can have relatively high loadings on its own factor but also have high correlation residuals between it and the indicators of another factor. The pattern just described suggests that the indicator in question measures more than one construct. This can be represented in the model by allowing the indicator to load on multiple factors. Another possibility consistent with this same pattern of correlation residuals is that these indicators share something that is unique to them, such as a particular method of measurement. This possibility could be represented by allowing that pair of measurement errors to covary. The second class of problems concerns the factors. For example, the researcher may have specified the wrong number of factors. Poor discriminant validity as evidenced by very high factor correlations may indicate that the model has too many factors. On the other hand, poor convergent validity within sets of indicators suggests that the model may have too few factors.

This example of respecification concerns the Kaufman Assessment Battery for Children (K-ABC; A. S. Kaufman & N. L. Kaufman, 1983). Three tasks on the K-ABC's Sequential Processing scale require the correct recall of the order in which auditory or visual stimuli are presented. In contrast, the five tasks of the Simultaneous Processing scale are intended to measure more holistic, integrative, less order-dependent reasoning. There are several examples in the literature of the use of CFA to evaluate whether these eight tasks altogether measure two factors (e.g., Cameron et al., 1997). This analysis concerns the data summarized in Table 7.4, which are from the test's standardization sample for 10 year-old children ($N = 200$).

A covariance matrix assembled from the correlations and standard deviations in Table 7.4 was submitted to the CALIS module of SAS/STAT (SAS Institute Inc., 2000) for ML estimation of the two-factor model presented in Figure 7.3. The CALIS syntax for the analysis of this model with 19 degrees of freedom (readers should verify this) is presented in Appendix 7.B. The analysis in CALIS converged to an admissible solution. Values of selected fit indexes are $\chi_M^2 (19) = 38.129$, $p = .006$, NC = 2.007, CFI = .959, and RMSEA = .071 with the 90% confidence interval .037–.104 (CALIS does not calculate the SRMR). The result for the RMSEA is not favorable. Specific problems with the two-factor model are suggested in the standardized solution, presented in Figure 7.3. Some factor loadings and associated values of R_{smc}^2 are so low that convergent validity seems doubtful. For example, the loadings

TABLE 7.4. Input Data (Correlations, Standard Deviations) and Correlation Residuals for Analysis of a Two-Factor Model of the Kaufman Assessment Battery for Children

Variable	1	2	3	4	5	6	7	8
Sequential scale								
1. Hand Movements	—	-.01	-.05	.07	.12	.22	.23	.17
2. Number Recall	.39	—	.02	-.12	-.06	-.01	.06	-.06
3. Word Order	.35	.67	—	-.07	-.04	-.02	.04	.02
Simultaneous scale								
4. Gestalt Closure	.21	.11	.16	—	.02	-.03	.01	.03
5. Triangles	.32	.27	.29	.38	—	-.01	-.01	.01
6. Spatial Memory	.40	.29	.28	.30	.47	—	.02	.00
7. Matrix Analogies	.39	.32	.30	.31	.42	.41	—	-.04
8. Photo Series	.39	.29	.37	.42	.58	.51	.42	—
SD	3.40	2.40	2.90	2.70	2.70	4.20	2.80	3.00

Note. Input data are from A. S. Kaufman and N. L. Kaufman (1983); $N = 200$. The input correlations are below the diagonal, and the correlation residuals are above the diagonal.

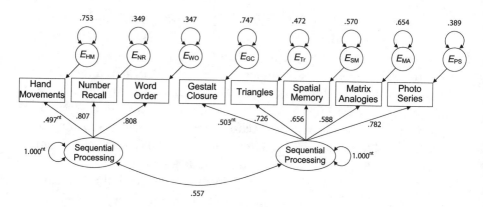

FIGURE 7.3. Two-factor model of the Kaufman Assessment Battery for Children with the completely standardized solution. Estimates for the measurement errors are proportions of unexplained variance. The unstandardized counterparts of the above estimates are all statistically significant at the .01 level except for those designated "nt," which means not tested.

of the Hand Movements and Gestalt Closure tasks on their respective factors are both only about .50, and $R^2_{smc} < .50$ for a total of four out of eight indicators. On the other hand, the estimated factor correlation (.557) is only moderate in size, which suggests discriminant validity.

A starting point for respecification often includes inspection of the correlation residuals, which for the two-factor model of the K-ABC are reported in Table 7.4 (absolute residuals greater than .10 are shown in boldface). Most of the larger residuals concern one of the indicators of the sequential factor, Hand Movements, and most of the indicators of the simultaneous factor. All of these residuals are positive, which means that the two-factor model underestimates correlations between the Hand Movements task and other tasks specified to measure the other factor. Because the standardized loading of the Hand Movements task on its original factor is at least moderate (.497), it is possible that this task may actually measure both factors.

Another type of information relevant to respecification are values of modification indexes for parameter estimates constrained to equal zero. A total of five such indexes were statistically significant at the .05 level. The χ^2 (1) statistic for the path Simultaneous → Hand Movements is about 20.00. However, the χ^2 (1) statistic for a different path, $E_{NR} \cup E_{WO}$, is also about 20.00. Thus, either allowing the Hand Movements task to also load on the simultaneous factor or adding an error covariance between the Word Order and Number Recall tasks would reduce the overall value of χ^2_M by about 20 points. Other changes suggested by the modification indexes would result in smaller improvements in overall fit, but among these, two have almost exactly the same χ^2 (1) value (about 7.00): allow the errors of the Number Recall and Word Order tasks to covary or allow the Number Recall task to also load on the sequential factor. Obviously, the researcher needs some rationale for choosing among these potential respecifications.[2]

Other Tests

Some other kinds of tests with CFA models are briefly described. Whether a set of indicators is **congeneric**, **tau-equivalent**, or **parallel** can be tested in CFA by comparing hierarchical models with the chi-square difference test. Congeneric indicators measure the same construct but not necessarily to the same degree. The CFA model for congenerity does not impose any constraints except that a set of indicators is specified to load on the same factor. If this model fits the data reasonably well, one can proceed to test the more demanding assumptions of tau-equivalence and parallelism. Tau-equivalent indicators are congeneric and have equal true score variabilities. This hypothesis is tested by imposing equality constraints on the unstandardized factor loadings (i.e., they are all fixed to 1.0). If the fit of the tau-equivalence model is not appreciably worse than that of the congenerity model, then additional constraints can be imposed that test for parallelism. These additional constraints require equal error variances. If the fit of this model is not appreciably worse than that of the model for tau-equivalence, the indicators may be parallel. All these models assume independent errors and must be fitted to a covariance matrix, not a correlation matrix. See Raykov and Marcoulides (2000, pp. 113–120) for examples.

It was noted earlier that fixing all factor correlations to 1.0 in a multifactor model generates a single-factor model that is nested under the original. In the factor analysis literature, the comparison with the chi-square difference test just described is referred to as the **test for redun-**

---

[2]Based on my familiarity with the K-ABC, allowing the Hand Movements task to load on both factors is plausible.

dancy. A variation is to fix the covariances between multiple factors to zero, which provides a test for **orthogonality**. If the model has only two factors, this procedure is not necessary because the statistical test of the factor covariance in the unconstrained model provides the same information. For models with three or more factors, the test for orthogonality is akin to a multivariate test of whether all the factor covariances together differ statistically from zero. Note that each factor should have at least three indicators for the redundancy test; otherwise, the model may not be identified. See Nunnally and Bernstein (1994, pp. 576–578) for examples.

A brief comment is needed. Estimates of equality-constrained factor loadings are equal in the unstandardized solution, but the corresponding standardized coefficients are typically unequal. This will happen when the two indicators have different variances. *Thus, it makes no sense to compare standardized coefficients from equality-constrained factor loadings.* If it is really necessary to constrain a pair of standardized loadings to be equal, then one option is to fit the model to a correlation matrix using the method of constrained estimation.

Constraint Interaction

For most CFA models, the choice between ULI or UVI constraints to scale the factors (see Figure 7.1) has no impact on model fit. That is, model fit is generally invariant to whether the factors are unstandardized or standardized. Steiger (2002) describes an exception called **constraint interaction** that can occur for CFA models where some factors have only two indicators and loadings of indicators on *different* factors are constrained to be equal. Specifically, it can happen in some cases that the value of χ_D^2 for the test of the equality constraint depends on how the factors are scaled. An example follows. Suppose that a researcher specifies a standard two-factor CFA model where the indicators of factor A are X_1 and X_2 and the indicators of factor B are X_3 and X_4. The sample covariance matrix where the order of the variables is X_1 to X_4 and $N = 200$ is as shown here.

$$\begin{bmatrix} 25.00 & & & \\ 7.20 & 9.00 & & \\ 3.20 & 2.00 & 4.00 & \\ 2.00 & 1.25 & 1.20 & 4.00 \end{bmatrix}$$

It is believed that the unstandardized loadings of X_2 and X_4 on their respective factors are equal. To test this hypothesis, an equality constraint is imposed on the estimates of these loadings (i.e., $A \rightarrow X_2 = B \rightarrow X_4$), and this restricted model is compared to the one without this equality constraint. Ideally, the value of $\chi_D^2(1)$ for this comparison should be unaffected by how the factors are scaled, but this ideal is not realized for this example. If X_1 and X_3 are the reference variables for, respectively, factors A and B (i.e., they are scaled through ULI constraints), then $\chi_D^2(1) = 0$. However, if instead the factor variances are fixed to 1.0 (i.e., they are scaled through UVI constraints), then $\chi_D^2(1) = 14.017$ for the same comparison as calculated in LISREL! (Use an SEM computer program to verify these results. The chi-square difference statistics should be similar within rounding error to these results if a program other than LISREL is used.)

The unexpected result just described is an example of constraint interaction, which means that the value of χ_D^2 for the test of the equality constraint depends on how the factors are scaled. It happens in this example because the imposition of the cross-factor equality constraint has the unintended consequence of making unnecessary one of the two identification constraints. However, removing the unnecessary identification constraint from the model with the equality constraint would result in two nonhierarchical models with equal degrees of freedom; that is, we could not conduct the chi-square difference test. Steiger (2002) describes the following simple test for the presence of constraint interaction: Obtain χ_M^2 for the model with the equality constraint. If the factors have been scaled with ULI constraints, change one of these constraints to a new constant (e.g., 2.0 instead of 1.0). If the factors have instead been scaled with UVI constraints, then fix the variance of one of these factors to a constant other than 1.0. Fit the model so modified to the same data. If the value of χ_M^2 for the modified model is not identical to that of the original, constraint interaction is present. If so, then the choice of how to scale the factors should be based on substantive grounds. If no such grounds exist, the test results for the equality constraint may not be very meaningful. See Steiger (2002) for more information about constraint interaction. See also Gonzalez and Griffin (2001) for a discussion about how the estimation of standard errors for latent variables models is not in all cases invariant to how the factors are scaled.

7.6 EQUIVALENT CFA MODELS

There are two sets of principles for generating equivalent CFA models—one for models with multiple factors and another for single-factor models. As an example of the former, consider the two-factor model of self-perception of ability and achievement aspiration by Kenny (1979) presented in Figure 7.4(a) without measurement errors to save space. The method of constrained ML estimation in the RAMONA module of SYSTAT 10 (Systat Software Inc., 2002) was used to fit this model to the correlation matrix reported in Kenny (1979, p. 144) from a sample of 556 Grade 8 students (Calsyn & Kenny, 1977). Values of selected fit indexes indicate good overall fit of the model: χ^2_M (8) = 9.256, p = .321, NC = 1.157, CFI = .999, SRMR = .012, and RMSEA = .012 with the 90% confidence interval .017–.054.

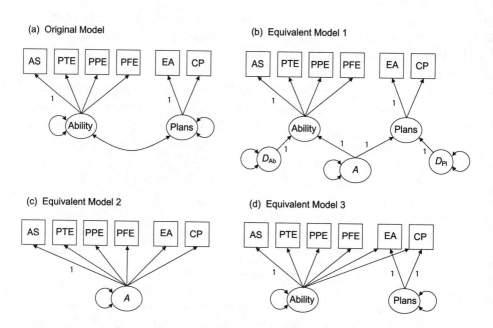

FIGURE 7.4. Four equivalent measurement models of self-perceived ability and educational plans. Measurement errors are omitted. The measurement errors of the EA and CP indicators covary in model (c). *Key:* AS, Ability Self-Concept; PTE, Perceived Teacher Evaluation; PPE, Perceived Parental Evaluation; PFE, Perceived Friends' Evaluation; EA, Educational Aspiration; CP, College Plans.

The three other CFA models presented in Figure 7.4 are equivalent versions of the original model that yield the same predicted correlations and values of fit statistics. The equivalent model in Figure 7.4(b) is actually a hierarchical CFA model in which the unanalyzed association between the factors of the original model is replaced by a second-order factor (A), which has no indicators and is presumed to have direct effects on the first-order factors (ability, plans). This specification provides an alternative account of why the two lower-order factors (which are endogenous in this model) covary. Because the second-order factor has only two indicators, it is necessary to constrain its direct effects on the first-order factors to be equal (i.e., A → Ability = A → Plans = 1.0). The other two equivalent variations are unique to models wherein some factors have only two indicators. The equivalent model in Figure 7.4(c) features the substitution of the plans factor with a correlation between the measurement errors of its indicators. The equivalent model in Figure 7.4(d) features replacement of the correlation between the ability and plans factors with the specification that some indicators are multidimensional. Although the factors are assumed to be orthogonal in this model, all six indicators have loadings on a common factor (ability), which accounts for their observed correlations just as well as the original model. Note that because the factors are specified as independent in the model of Figure 7.4(d), it is necessary to constrain the factor loadings of the educational aspiration and college plans indicators to be equal in order to identify this model.

For two reasons, the situation regarding equivalent versions of CFA models with multiple factors is even more complex than suggested by the above example. First, it is possible to apply the Lee–Herschberger replacing rules to substitute factor covariances (i.e., unanalyzed associations) with direct effects, which makes some factors endogenous. The resulting model is not a CFA model; it is an SR model—but it will fit the data equally well. For example, substitution of the factor covariance Ability ⌣ Plans in the original model of Figure 7.4(a) with the direct effect Ability → Plans generates an equivalent model. Second, Raykov and Marcoulides (2001) show that there is actually a set of infinitely many equivalent models for standard multifactor CFA models. For each equivalent model in this set, the factor covariances are eliminated (i.e., the factors are assumed to be independent) and replaced by one or more factors not represented in the original model with fixed unit loadings

(1.0) on all indicators. These models with additional factors explain the data just as well as the original.

Equivalent versions of single-factor CFA models can be derived using Herschberger's (1994) **reversed indicator rule**, which involves the specification of one of the observed variables as a cause indicator while the rest remain as effect indicators. Consider the hypothetical single-factor CFA model of reading presented in Figure 7.5(a). The effect indicators of this model represent different tasks, including word and letter recognition, word attack (i.e., correct pronunciation of non-sense words), and phonics skills. An equivalent version is presented in Figure 7.5(b), and it features phonics skill as a cause of reading, a specification for which there is evidence. Note that the factor in this equivalent model is no longer exogenous: because a causally prior variable (phonics skill) has a direct effect on it, the factor here is endogenous and thus has a disturbance. Also, the phonics skill indicator is exogenous in the equivalent model of Figure 7.5(b), not endogenous as in the original. For these reasons, this equivalent model is actually an SR model. A total of three other such equivalent models could potentially be generated, one with each of the remaining indicators specified as causes of reading. Not all of these equivalent versions may be theoretically plausible, but at least the one with phonics skill as a cause indicator offers a logical alternative to the original one-factor CFA model. See Herschberger (1994) for additional examples.

The model in Figure 7.5(b) is an example of a **multiple indicators and multiple causes** (MIMIC) model. A MIMIC model is a measurement model with both cause indicators and effect indicators. The cause indicators are measured exogenous variables, and they can be continuous as in the previous example or categorical. A categorical cause indicator represents group membership. We will see in Chapter 11 that a MIMIC model with a categorical cause indicator is a special case of the SEM approach to estimating group differences on latent variables.

7.7 ANALYZING INDICATORS WITH NONNORMAL DISTRIBUTIONS

There are basically four options by which to avoid bias when the indicators are continuous but their distributions are severely nonnormal.

(a) Original Model with Effect Indicators

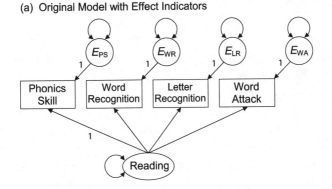

(b) Equivalent Model with a Cause Indicator

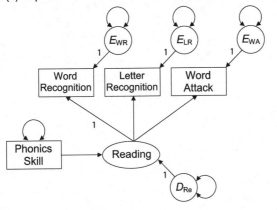

FIGURE 7.5. Application of the reversed indicator rule to generate an equivalent one-factor model of reading.

The first option is to normalize the variables with transformations and then analyze the transformed data with standard ML estimation. The second option is to use a **corrected normal theory method**. This means to analyze the original data with a normal theory method, such as ML, but use robust standard errors and corrected test statistics. The former are estimates of standard errors that are supposed to be relatively robust against nonnormality. An example of the latter is the Satorra–Bentler statistic (Satorra & Bentler, 1994), which adjusts downward the value of χ^2_M from standard ML estimation by an amount that reflects the degree of observed kurtosis. The Satorra–Bentler statistic was originally associated with EQS but is now calculated by other SEM computer programs. Results of computer simulation studies of the Satorra–Bentler statistic are generally favorable (e.g., Chou & Bentler, 1995). However, note that the difference between the corrected model chi-squares of two hierarchical models fitted to the same data cannot generally be interpreted as a statistic that tests the equal-fit hypothesis.

The third option is to use an estimation method that does not assume multivariate normality. A method known as **asymptotic distribution free** or **arbitrary distribution function** (ADF) estimation makes *no* distributional assumptions (Browne, 1984). This is because it estimates the degree of both skew and kurtosis in the raw data. However, ADF estimation typically requires very large samples in order for the results to be reasonably accurate. For example, relatively simple models may require sample sizes of 200–500, and thousands of cases may be needed for more complex models. These requirements are impractical for many researchers. Another class of estimators based on **elliptical distribution theory** requires only symmetrical distributions (Bentler & Dijkstra, 1985). These methods estimate the degree of kurtosis in raw data. If all indicators have a common degree of kurtosis, positive or negative skew is allowed; otherwise, zero skew is assumed. These methods may not require as many cases as required by arbitrary distribution estimators such as ADF. Various elliptical distribution estimators are available in EQS.

Arbitrary and elliptical distribution estimators are generally special cases of a family of methods known as weighted least squares (WLS).[3] Other estimators within this family include **mean-adjusted weighted least squares** and **variance-adjusted weighted least squares** (B. Muthén, 1993)—designated in Mplus as, respectively, WLSM and WLSMV—and **diagonally weighted least squares** (DWLS), available in LISREL. The methods just mentioned may be used to estimate models with categorical indicators. All of these methods can be more difficult to apply than corrected normal theory methods. Also, not all of the indexes of model fit described in Chapter 6 are available under these methods. Therefore, corrected normal theory methods may be the best overall choice for researchers without especially strong quantitative skills.

[3]The method of generalized least squares (GLS) is also a member of this family, but it assumes multivariate normal distributions for the indicators.

The fourth option is to use a normal theory method with nonparametric bootstrapping, which assumes only that the population and sample distributions have the same basic shape. In a bootstrap approach, parameters, standard errors, and model test statistics are estimated within empirical sampling distributions from large numbers of generated samples (e.g., Yung & Bentler, 1996). Results of a computer simulation study by Nevitt and Hancock (2001) indicate that bootstrapped estimates for a CFA model were generally less biased compared with those from standard ML estimation under conditions of nonnormality and for sample sizes of $N \geq 200$. For $N = 100$, however, bootstrap estimates had relatively large standard errors and many generated samples were unusable due to problems such as nonpositive definite covariance matrices. Because there are at present few other studies of the bootstrap method as a way to deal with nonnormality in SEM, it is difficult to recommend it now with confidence.

There are two basic options by which to avoid bias when some or all indicators are categorical. The first is to use special estimation methods (e.g., B. Muthén, 1984) that are supported in some SEM computer programs, including EQS, LISREL, and Mplus. These methods generate **asymptotic covariance matrices** when there are both continuous and categorical indicators or **asymptotic correlation matrices** when all indicators are categorical. These asymptotic matrices are typically based on non-Pearson correlations, such as polyserial or polychoric correlations, that estimate what the Pearson r between two variables would be if both were continuous and normally distributed in the population. Either type of asymptotic matrix is then analyzed by a form of WLS estimation. A problem with this approach is that asymptotic data matrices are not always positive definite, which can cause the analysis to fail. The second option is for discrete indicators that are individual items with Likert-type response formats (e.g., *agree, neutral, disagree*). It involves the analysis of parcels instead of individual items. A **parcel** is a total score (linear composite) across a set of homogeneous items (i.e., it is a miniscale). Parcels are treated as continuous indicators. Also, the score reliability of parcels tends to be greater than that for the individual items. If the distributions of all parcels are roughly normal, a normal theory method such as ML may be used to estimate the model. Readers should be aware that parceling is a somewhat controversial technique. This is in part because it requires that items within each set are unidimensional, which means that they are known to measure a single construct. This knowledge may come from familiarity with the item domain or results of prior statistical analyses (e.g., exploratory factor analysis) that indicate unidimensional measurement. Parceling is not recommended if the assumption of unidimensionality is not tenable. Specifically, parceling should not be part of an analysis aimed at determining whether a set of items is unidimensional. This is because it is possible in some cases that parceling can mask a multidimensional factor structure in such a way that a seriously misspecified CFA model may nevertheless fit the data reasonably well (Bandalos, 2002). There are also different ways to parcel items, including random assignment of items to parcels and grouping of items based on rational grounds (e.g., the items refer to the same stimulus material) versus statistical grounds (e.g., based on item intercorrelations) (T. D. Little, Cunningham, Shahar, & Widaman, 2002). It is not always clear which method is best, however, and the choice can affect the results. See Bandalos and Finney (2001) for a comprehensive review of parceling in SEM.

7.8 SPECIAL TYPES OF CFA MODELS

Two types of special CFA models are described next. Each extends the range of hypotheses that can be tested in CFA.

Hierarchical CFA Models

It is possible to represent hypotheses about hierarchical relations between constructs in CFA models through the specification of higher-order factors with presumed direct causal effects on lower-order factors. Suppose that indicators X_1 to X_9 are tasks from a cognitive ability test battery. The hierarchical CFA model in Figure 7.6 represents the hypothesis that X_1 to X_3 measure verbal ability, X_4 to X_6 measure visual–spatial ability, and X_7 to X_9 measure memory ability. It also represents the hypothesis that each of these **first-order factors** has two direct causes. One is a **second-order factor**, g, which represents a general ability construct that has no indicators. This is because higher-order factors are measured indirectly through the indicators of the first-order factors. The specification of a common direct cause of all first-order

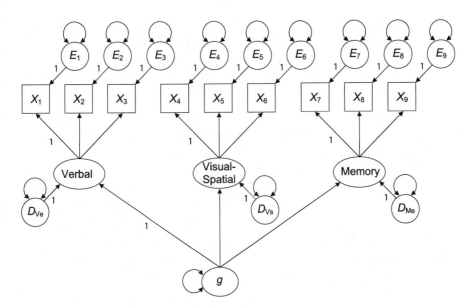

FIGURE 7.6. A hierarchical confirmatory factor analysis model of the structure of cognitive ability.

factors implies that their associations are believed to be spurious. The second presumed direct cause of each first-order factor is a disturbance, which represents all omitted causes (i.e., other than g). That is, all first-order factors are endogenous but the second-order general ability factor is exogenous. Accordingly, the symbol for the variance of an exogenous variable ($\curvearrowright$) appears next to g in Figure 7.6.

In order for a CFA model with a second-order factor to be identified, there must be at least three first-order factors. (The analogous requirement for a standard single-factor CFA model is that it have at least three indicators.) Otherwise, the direct effects of the second-order factor on the first-order factors or the disturbance variances may be underidentified (see Figure 7.4). Also, each first-order factor should have at least two indicators. The model in Figure 7.6 satisfies both of these requirements. To set scales for the first-order factors (verbal, visual–spatial, memory), one unstandardized loading for each is represented in Figure 7.6 as fixed to 1.0 (i.e., these factors are unstandardized). This tactic cannot be used with the second-order factor, g, because it has no indicators. One way to assign a scale to g is to fix one of its unstandardized effects on a first-order factor to 1.0. This tactic corresponds to the specification $g \rightarrow$ Verbal Ability = 1.0 that is represented in Figure 7.6. Another option is to fix the variance of g to 1.0 (i.e., standardize it). This approach leaves all three direct effects of g on the first-order factors as free parameters. Either means of scaling g in a single-sample analysis is probably fine. In a multiple-sample analysis, however, it would be typically inappropriate to standardize higher-order factors (or any other factors; Chapter 11).

The parameters of the model in Figure 7.6 include 14 variances (of 10 measurement errors, 3 disturbances, and g) and 8 direct effects (6 on indicators from first-order factors, 2 on first-order factors from g) for a total of 22. With 10 indicators, there are 10 (11)/2 = 55 observations, so $df_M = 55 - 22 = 33$. For examples of the analysis of hierarchical CFA models, see Cheung (2000), who analyzed a hierarchical model of student ratings of teacher effectiveness, and Neuman, Bolin, and Briggs (2000), who analyzed a hierarchical model of ability similar to that represented in Figure 7.6 for a group-administered aptitude test. T. O. Williams et al. (2002) analyzed a hierarchical model of the VST II that is an equivalent version of the two-factor model analyzed earlier (see Figure 4.2).

Models for Multitrait–Multimethod Data

The method of CFA can also be used to analyze data from a **multitrait–multimethod** (MTMM) study, the logic of which was first articulated by Campbell and Fiske (1959). In an MTMM study, two or more traits are measured with two or more methods. Traits are hypothetical constructs that concern cognitive abilities, personality attributes, or other stable characteristics, and methods refer to multiple test forms, occasions, specific measurement methods, such as self-report, or specific informants (e.g., parents; Marsh & Grayson, 1995). The main goals of an MTMM study are to (1) evaluate the convergent and discriminant validity of a set of tests that vary in their measurement method and (2) derive separate estimates of the effects of traits versus methods on the observed scores.

The earliest method for analyzing data from an MTMM study involved inspection of the correlation matrix of scores from all variables. For example, convergent validity would be indicated by the observation of relatively high correlations among variables that supposedly measured the same trait but with different methods. In contrast, discriminant validity would be indicated by the observation of relatively low correlations among variables that are supposed to measure different traits with different methods. If correlations among variables that should measure different traits but use the same method are relatively high, then common method effects are indicated. This would imply that correlations among different variables based on the same method may be relatively high even if they measured different traits.

The method of CFA offers a more systematic way to analyze data from an MTMM study than inspection of correlations. When CFA was first applied to this problem in the 1970s, researchers typically specified models like the one presented in Figure 7.7, a **correlated trait–correlated method** (CTCM) model. Such models have separate trait and method factors that are assumed to covary, but method factors are assumed to be independent of trait factors. It is specified in the model of Figure 7.7 that X_1 to X_3 are based on one method, X_4 to X_6 are based

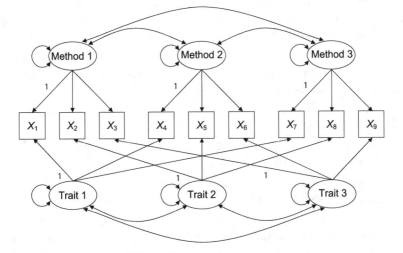

FIGURE 7.7. A correlated-trait correlated method (CTCM) model for multitrait–multimethod data. Measurement errors are omitted and assumed to be independent.

on another method, and X_7 to X_9 are based on a third method. This model also specifies that one trait is measured by the set of indicators (X_1, X_4, X_7), a different trait is measured by the set (X_2, X_5, X_8), and a third trait by the set (X_3, X_6, X_9). According to the rationale of this model, relatively high loadings on trait factors would suggest convergent validity, high loadings on the method factors would indicate common method effects, and moderate correlations among the trait factors would suggest discriminant validity.

Although there are reports of successful analyses of CTCM models in the literature (e.g., Bollen, 1989, pp. 190–195), others have found that analyses of such models yield inadmissible or unstable solutions (e.g., Wothke, 1996). Marsh and Bailey (1991) found in computer simulation studies that illogical estimates were derived about three-quarters of the time for CTCM models. Kenny and Kashy (1992) noted part of the problem: CTCM models are not identified if the loadings on the trait or method factors are equal; if the loadings are different but similar in value, then CTCM models may be empirically underidentified.

Several simpler alternative CFA models for MTMM data have been proposed, including ones with multiple but uncorrelated method factors, a single method factor specified to affect all the indicators, and a model like the one presented in Figure 7.8, which is called a **correlated uniqueness** (CU) model (Marsh & Grayson, 1995). This model features measurement error correlations among indicators based on the same method instead of separate method factors (compare Figure 7.7 with Figure 7.8). In this representation, method effects are assumed to be a property of each indicator and relatively high correlations among their residuals are taken as evidence for common method variance for each pair of indicators. Note that the similarity of methods for different traits is only one possible explanation for high measurement error correlations in CU models for MTMM data. Saris and Alberts (2003) evaluated alternative CFA models that could account for correlated residuals in CU models in survey research, including models that represented response biases, effects due to relative answers (i.e., when respondents compare their answers across different questions), and method effects. See Bollen and Paxton (1998) and Lance, Noble, and Scullen (2002) for additional discussion about the relative merits of CU models versus other kinds of CFA models for MTMM data.

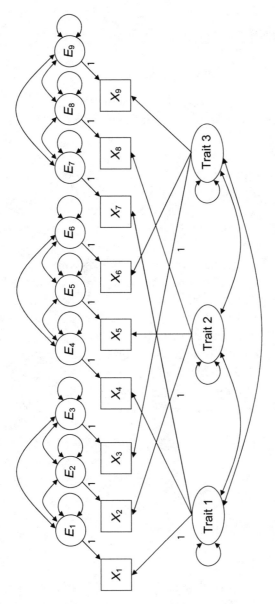

FIGURE 7.8. A correlated uniqueness (CU) model for multitrait–multimethod data.

7.9 OTHER ISSUES

Some additional issues in the application of CFA are outlined in the following subsections.

Estimated Factor Scores

When raw data are analyzed, it is possible to calculate factor scores for
each case. Because factors are not measured directly but instead through
their indicators, such scores are only estimates of cases' relative standings
on the factor. There is more than one way to calculate factor scores,
however, and although scores derived using different methods tend to be
highly correlated, they generally do not all yield identical rank orderings
of the cases. For example, given estimated correlations between a factor
and its indicators, multiple regression can be used to derive estimated
factor scores that are weighted linear combinations of the indicators and
the factor. The weights derived in multiple regression are those that lead
to the closest correspondence between the underlying factor(s) and
the estimated factor scores, given estimates of correlations among the
indicators and the factor(s). However, such weights are subject to capitalization on chance variation within a particular sample. An alternative
to empirically derived weights is simply to add the scores for each case
across the indicators, which weights each variable equally. The application of equal weights is called **unit weighting**. This method has the
advantage of simplicity and less susceptibility to sample-specific variation, but unit weights may not be optimal ones within a particular sample. Given that there is more than one way to derive estimated factor
scores, Bollen's (1989) perspective on this matter is pertinent: researchers should probably refrain from making too fine a comparison on estimated factor scores. See Loehlin (1998, pp. 181–192) for more information.

CFA after EFA

It is not entirely appropriate to specify a CFA model based on results of
an exploratory factor analysis (EFA) and to estimate the former using
the same data. That is, the CFA would not in this case "confirm" the

results of the EFA. This is because EFA results are subject to capitalization on chance variation, and specification of a CFA model based on the EFA outcomes and analyzed with the same data may just compound this problem. Besides, there is some evidence that factor structures identified in EFA may turn out to have poor fit to the same data when evaluated with CFA. This may be especially likely when all relatively high factor loadings from EFA are specified as free parameters in CFA, but all relatively low (secondary) EFA factor loadings (e.g., those with absolute values less than .30) are fixed to zero in CFA (van Prooijen & van der Kloot, 2001). Secondary loadings in EFA often account for relatively high proportions of the variance, so constraining them to zero in CFA may be too conservative. It is preferable to validate a factor structure across different samples and to use the same method, either EFA or CFA, in both samples. Specific methods are available to evaluate whether EFA results for the same variables replicate across different samples. There is also multiple-sample CFA, which is discussed in Chapter 11. See Hurley et al. (1997) for more information.

An Alternative to CFA for Item Analysis

An alternative to CFA for item-level analyses is the generation of **item-characteristic curves** (ICC) according to **item-response theory** (IRT). Briefly described, IRT yields estimates about characteristics of individual items, including their precision of measurement of a latent variable or susceptibility to guessing effects on multiple-choice items. It is also assumed in IRT that the relations between items and factors as represented by the ICCs are nonlinear. For example, the probability of correctly answering a difficult item may be slight for low-ability examinees but increases geometrically toward an asymptotic level at increasing higher levels of ability. The IRT method is also oriented toward the development of "tailored tests," subsets of items that may optimally assess a particular person. Items from tailored tests are typically selected by a computer, and their order of presentation depends upon the examinee's pattern of responses. For instance, if the examinee fails initial items, then easier ones are presented. Testing stops when more difficult items are consistently failed. See Reise, Widaman, and Pugh (1993) for a comparison of CFA and IRT for item-level analyses.

7.10 SUMMARY

The specification of a CFA measurement model reflects hypotheses about the correspondence among observed variables (indicators), factors that represent hypothetical constructs, and measurement errors. A standard CFA model is one where all factors are first-order factors, the indicators are each specified to load on a single factor, and the measurement error terms are independent. The latter two characteristics describe unidimensional measurement. The specification of multidimensional measurement may be appropriate when an indicator is believed to assess more than one construct or when the unique variances of some indicators are expected to overlap. However, multidimensional measurement should not be specified in a post hoc attempt to improve model fit. Many types of hypotheses about measurement can be tested with standard CFA models. For example, the evaluation of a model with multiple factors that specifies unidimensional measurement provides a specific test of convergent and discriminant validity. Respecification of a CFA model can be challenging problem because there may be many possible changes that could be made to a given model. Another difficult problem is that of equivalent CFA models. The only way to deal with both of these challenges is to rely more on substantive knowledge than on statistical considerations in model evaluation.

Next, Chapter 8 is about structural regression (SR) models. Similar to CFA models, SR models allow the evaluation of hypotheses about measurement. Unlike standard CFA models, they also permit the specification of presumed causal effects among the factors. In this way, SR models represent the pinnacle in SEM for the analysis of covariances.

7.11 RECOMMENDED READINGS

Graham, J. M., Guthrie, A. C., & Thompson, B. (2003). Consequences of not interpreting structure coefficients in published CFA research: A reminder. *Structural Equation Modeling, 10,* 142–153.

Hoyle, R. H. (2000). Confirmatory factor analysis. In H. E. A. Tinsley & S. D. Brown (Eds.), *Handbook of applied multivariate statistics and mathematical modeling* (pp. 465–497). New York: Academic Press.

Recommendations for Start Values

These recommendations assume the factors are unstandardized. Initial estimates of factor variances should probably not exceed 90% of that of the observed variance for the corresponding reference variable. Start values for factor covariances follow the initial estimates of their variances; that is, they are the product of each factor's standard deviation (i.e., the square root of the initial estimates of their variances) and the expected correlation between them. If the indicators of a construct have similar variances to that of the reference variable, then initial estimates of their factor loadings can also be 1.0. If the reference variable is, say, one-tenth as variable as another indicator of the same factor, the initial estimate of the other indicator's factor loading could be 10.0. Conservative starting values of measurement error variances would be 90% of the observed variance of the associated indicator, which assumes only 10% of the variance will be explained. Bentler (1995) suggests that it is probably better to overestimate the variances of the exogenous variables than to underestimate them. This advice is also appropriate for Heywood cases of the type where a variance estimate is negative: in the reanalysis of the model, try a start value that is higher than in the previous run.

Appendix 7.B

CALIS Syntax

```
Title "Figure 7.3";
Data KABC(TYPE=COV); _type_ = 'cov';
Input _name_ $ V1-V8;
Label V1='HM' V2='NR' V3='WO'
      V4='GC' V5='Tr' V6='SM' V7='MA' V8='PS';
```

```
Datalines;
V1    11.560     .      .      .      .      .      .      .
V2     3.182   5.760    .      .      .      .      .      .
V3     3.451   4.663  8.410    .      .      .      .      .
V4     1.928    .713  1.253  7.290    .      .      .      .
V5     2.938   1.750  2.271  2.770  7.290    .      .      .
V6     5.712   2.923  3.410  3.402  5.330 17.640    .      .
V7     3.713   2.150  2.436  2.344  3.175  4.822  7.840    .
V8     3.978   2.088  3.219  3.402  4.698  6.426  3.528  9.000
;
Proc CALIS cov data=KABC nobs=200 pall;
Lineqs
    V1 = F1 + E1,  V2 = LD2 F1 + E2,  V3 = LD3 F1 + E3,
    V4 = F2 + E4,  V5 = LD5 F2 + E5,  V6 = LD6 F2 + E6,
    V7 = LD7 F2 + E7,  V8 = LD8 F2 + E8;
Std
    E1-E8 = Err1-Err8,  F1-F2 = FVar1-FVar2;
Cov
    F1 F2 = FCov;
Run;
```

8

Models with Structural and Measurement Components

Structural regression (SR) models (also called hybrid or LISREL models) can be viewed as syntheses of path and measurement models. They are the most general of all the types of structural equation models considered to this point. As in path analysis, the specification of an SR model allows tests of hypotheses about patterns of causal effects. Unlike path models, though, these effects can involve latent variables because an SR model also incorporates a measurement model that represents observed variables as indicators of underlying factors, just as in confirmatory factor analysis (CFA). The capability to test hypotheses about both structural and measurement relations with a single model affords much flexibility. Discussed next are characteristics of SR models, requirements for identification, and estimation strategies. All of the advanced techniques described in later chapters extend the rationale of SR models to other kinds of analyses, such as estimation of latent variable means.

8.1 CHARACTERISTICS OF SR MODELS

Presented in Figure 8.1(a) is a structural model with observed variables—a path model—that features the use of a single measure of each construct. The observed exogenous variable of this model, X_1, is assumed to be measured without error, an assumption usually violated in practice. This assumption is not required for the observed endoge-

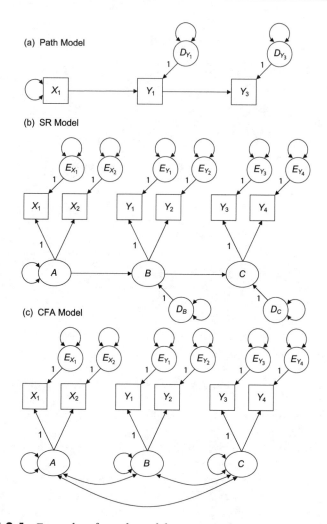

FIGURE 8.1. Examples of a path model, a structural regression (SR) model, and a confirmatory factor analysis (CFA) model.

nous variables of this model, but measurement error in Y_1 or Y_3 is manifested in their disturbances. The model of Figure 8.1(b) is an SR model with both structural and measurement components. Its measurement model has the same three observed variables represented in the path model, X_1, Y_1, and Y_3. Unlike the path model, each of these three variables is specified as one of a pair of indicators of an underlying factor.

Consequently, all the observed variables in Figure 8.1(b) have measurement errors. This SR model also has a structural component that depicts the same basic pattern of direct and indirect causal effects as the path model but among latent instead of observed variables. Each latent endogenous variable of this SR model has a disturbance. Unlike the path model, the disturbances of the SR model reflect only omitted causes and not measurement error. For the same reason, estimates of the direct effects (i.e., the path coefficients) for the SR model ($A \rightarrow B$, $B \rightarrow C$) are corrected for measurement error but those for the path model ($X_1 \rightarrow Y_1$, $Y_1 \rightarrow Y_3$) are not. A CFA model is represented in Figure 8.1(c). It features the same multiple-indicator approach to measurement, but all associations among the factors are specified as unanalyzed.

The SR model of Figure 8.1(b) could be described as "fully latent" because every variable in its structural model is latent. Although this characteristic is desirable because it implies multiple-indicator measurement, it is also possible to represent in SR models an observed variable that is the single indicator of a construct. Such models could be called "partially latent" because at least one variable in their structural model is a single indicator. However, unless measurement error in a single indicator is taken into account, partially latent SR models have the same limitations as path models outlined earlier. How to deal with this problem for SR models with single indicators is dealt with later. The discussion that follows assumes a fully latent SR model.

8.2 ANALYSIS OF HYBRID MODELS

If one understands the fundamentals of path analysis and CFA, there is relatively little new to learn about SR models because their analysis can be decomposed into two parts. The specification of the structural component of an SR model follows the same basic rationale as in path analysis. Likewise, the specification of the measurement component of an SR model requires consideration of basically the same issues as in CFA. The evaluation of whether an SR model is identified and its subsequent estimation should also both be conducted separately for each part, measurement and structural. There is also a common theme to identification and analysis: a valid measurement model is needed before the structural component of an SR model can be evaluated.

Identification of SR Models

Any SR model must satisfy the same two necessary requirements for identification as any other kind of structural equation model: the number of observations, which equals $v(v + 1)/2$, where v is the number of observed variables, must equal or exceed the number of free parameters—that is, the model degrees of freedom must be at least zero ($df_M \geq 0$)—and each latent variable must have a scale. Parameters of SR models are counted as follows:

> *The total number of (1) variances and covariances (i.e., unanalyzed associations) of exogenous variables (measurement errors, disturbances, and exogenous factors) and (2) direct effects on endogenous variables (factor loadings of indicators, direct effects on endogenous factors from other factors) equals the number of parameters.*

It is generally assumed for SR models that the exogenous factors are uncorrelated with the disturbances of the endogenous factors and that the factors (exogenous or endogenous) and the measurement errors are independent. These assumptions parallel similar ones for path models and CFA models.

Disturbances and measurement errors in SR models are usually assigned a scale through unit loading identification (ULI) constraints that fix the residual path coefficients to 1.0. (Some SEM computer programs do so by default.) Exogenous factors can be scaled either by imposing a ULI constraint where the loading of one indicator per factor (that of the reference variable) is fixed to 1.0 (i.e., the factor is unstandardized) or by imposing a unit variance identification (UVI) constraint where the factor variance is fixed to equal 1.0 (i.e., the factor is standardized). However, most SEM computer programs allow only the first method just mentioned for scaling endogenous factors. This is because the variances of endogenous variables are not generally considered model parameters. This also implies that endogenous factors are unstandardized in perhaps most analyses. When an SR model is analyzed within a single sample, the choice between scaling an exogenous factor with either ULI or UVI constraints combined with the use of ULI constraints only to scale endogenous factors usually makes no difference. An exception for SR models where some indicators have only two indicators is when the identification constraints for scaling the factors interact with equality constraints imposed on either factor loadings or path coefficients. This is constraint interaction, which for SR models is considered later.

As with CFA models, meeting the necessary requirements that $df_M \geq 0$ and every latent variable is scaled does not guarantee the identification of an SR model. An additional requirement for identification reflects the view that the analysis of an SR model is essentially a path analysis conducted with estimated variances and covariances among the factors. Thus, it must be possible to derive unique estimates of the factor variances and covariances before specific causal effects among them can be estimated. That is, in order for the structural portion of an SR model to be identified, its measurement portion must be identified. Bollen (1989) described this requirement as the **two-step rule**, and the steps to evaluate it are outlined below:

1. Respecify the SR model as a CFA model with all possible unanalyzed associations among the factors. Evaluate this CFA model against the requirements for identification outlined in the previous chapter.
2. View the structural portion of the SR model as a path model. If it is recursive, the structural model is identified; if it is nonrecursive, then evaluate the structural model against the requirements for identification outlined in Chapter 9.

If both the measurement and structural portions of an SR model are identified, the whole model is identified. The two-step rule is thus a sufficient condition: SR models that meet both parts of it are in fact identified. Evaluation of the two-step rule is demonstrated for the SR model presented in Figure 8.2(a). This model meets the necessary requirements because every latent variable is scaled and there are more observations than free parameters. Specifically, with 6 observed variables, there are 6(7)/2 = 21 observations available to estimate this model's 14 parameters, which include 9 variances of exogenous variables (of factor A, 6 measurement errors, and 2 disturbances) and 5

(a) Original SR Model

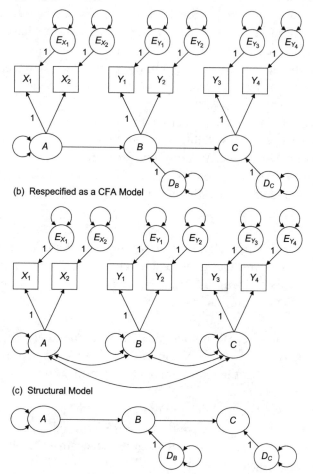

(b) Respecified as a CFA Model

(c) Structural Model

FIGURE 8.2. Evaluation of the two-step rule for identification for a structural regression (SR) model.

direct effects on endogenous variables (3 factor loadings [one per factor] and 2 paths: $A \rightarrow B$, $B \rightarrow C$); thus, $df_M = 7$. However, we still do not know whether the model of Figure 8.2(a) is identified. To find out, we can apply the two-step rule. The respecification of this SR model as a CFA model is presented in Figure 8.2(b). Because this standard CFA model has at least two indicators per factor, it is identified. The first part of the two-step rule is thus satisfied. The structural part of the SR model is presented in Figure 8.2(c). Because this structural model is recursive, it too is identified. Because the original SR model in Figure 8.2(a) meets the sufficient two-step rule, it is identified (specifically, overidentified).

Two important points must be noted about the two-step rule for SR models. First, the estimation of SR models that are identified can still be foiled by empirical underidentification. Suppose that the estimated correlations between any two pairs of factors in the CFA model of Figure 8.2(b) is close to zero. The consequence is that one of the factors may be underidentified because it has only two indicators and is essentially independent of the other two factors. Single-factor CFA models with only two indicators are not identified without additional constraints. Second, it is not always possible to determine the identification status of every SR model by using the two-step rule. For example, suppose that the measurement portion of an SR model expressed as a CFA model is not standard due to the presence of correlated measurement errors or indicators that load on two or more factors (i.e., multidimensional measurement). This means that there may be no easily applied rule to determine whether that CFA model is identified. The same thing can happen for certain types of nonrecursive structural models (addressed in Chapter 9). If either the measurement or structural portion of an SR model is "none of the above" such that its identification cannot be clearly established, the two-step rule may be too strict. That is, an SR model with the characteristics just mentioned may fail the two-step rule but still be identified. Partially latent SR models with single indicators that are actually identified may also fail the two-step rule, which is demonstrated later. If the researcher is uncertain about whether a particular SR model is identified, the empirical tests for solution uniqueness described in the previous chapter can be applied. See Bollen (1989, pp. 326–333) and Kenny, Kashy, and Bolger (1998, pp. 252–258) for more information about identification requirements for SR models.

Testing SR Models

There are two general approaches to testing SR models. One is based on an earlier method by J. C. Anderson and Gerbing (1988) known as two-step modeling. Another, more recent method described by Mulaik and Millsap (2000) is four-step modeling. Both methods generally require a fully latent SR model. Both methods also deal with the problem of how to locate the source of specification error in an SR model with poor fit to the data. An example is introduced that illustrates the nature of this problem.

A researcher has specified an SR model that is identified (e.g., Figure 8.2(a)). The data are collected and the researcher uses **one-step modeling** to estimate the model, which means that the measurement and structural components of the SR model are analyzed simultaneously in a single analysis. The results indicate that the overall fit of the SR model is poor. Now, where is the model misspecified?—the measurement portion?—the structural portion?—or both? With one-step modeling, it is difficult to precisely locate the source of poor model fit. **Two-step modeling** parallels the two-step rule for identification. In two-step modeling, an SR model is first respecified as a CFA measurement model. The CFA model is then analyzed in order to determine whether it fits the data. If the fit of this CFA model is poor, then not only may the researcher's hypotheses about measurement be wrong, but also the fit of the original SR model to the data may be even worse if its structural model is overidentified. For example, look again at Figure 8.2. Suppose that the fit of the three-factor CFA model in Figure 8.2(b) is poor. Note that this CFA model has three paths among the factors that represent all possible analyzed associations ($A \smile B$, $A \smile C$, $B \smile C$). In contrast, the structural portion of the SR model in Figure 8.2(a) has only two paths among the factors that represent direct effects ($A \rightarrow B$, $B \rightarrow C$). If the fit of the CFA model with three paths among the factors is poor, the fit of the SR model with only two paths among the factors may be even worse.

The first part of two-step modeling thus involves finding an acceptable CFA model. If the initial measurement model is rejected, the suggestions discussed in Chapter 7 for respecification can be followed. Given an acceptable measurement model, the second stage of two-step modeling is to compare the fits of the original SR model and those with different structural models to one another and to the fit of the CFA model with the chi-square difference test. (This assumes hierarchical structural models.) The procedure is as follows: if the structural portion of an SR model is just-identified, the fits of the original SR model and the CFA respecification of it are identical. In fact, these models are equivalent versions that generate the same predicted correlations and covariances. For example, if the path $A \to C$ were added to the SR model of Figure 8.2(a), then it would have just as many parameters as does the CFA measurement model of Figure 8.1(b). The original SR model of Figure 8.1(a) with its overidentified structural model is thus nested under the CFA model. However, it may be possible to trim a just-identified structural portion of an SR model without an appreciable deterioration in the overall fit of the whole model. In general, structural portions of SR models can be trimmed (or built) according to the same principles as in path analysis. The goal is also the same: to find a parsimonious structural model that still explains the data (here, estimated covariances among the factors) reasonably well.

One other point: given an acceptable measurement model, one should observe only slight changes in the factor loadings as SR models with alternative structural models are tested. If so, then the assumptions about measurement may be relatively invariant to changes in the structural relations among the factors. If the factor loadings change markedly when different structural models are specified, however, then the measurement model is not invariant. This phenomenon may lead to **interpretational confounding** (Burt, 1976), which in this context means that the empirical definitions of the constructs change depending on the structural model. This is another potential advantage of two-step modeling over one-step modeling: it is easier to avoid potential interpretational confounding with two-step modeling.

Four-step modeling can be seen as an extension of two-step modeling that is intended to even more precisely diagnose specification error in the measurement model. In this approach, the researcher specifies and tests a sequence of at least four hierarchical models. In order for these nested models to be identified, each factor in the original SR model should have at least four indicators (preferably not all based on the same measurement method). As in two-step modeling, if the fit of a model in four-step modeling with fewer constraints is poor, then a model with even more constraints should not even be considered (i.e., do not go to the next step). The least restrictive model specified at the first step is basically an exploratory common factor analysis model that allows all indicators to load on each factor and where the number of factors is the same as that in the original SR model. This model should be analyzed with the same method of estimation, such as maximum likelihood (ML), as used to analyze the final SR model. This first step is intended to test the provisional correctness of the hypothesis regarding the number of factors, but it cannot confirm that the correct number of factors has been specified if model fit is adequate (Hayduk & Glaser, 2000).

The second step of four-step modeling is basically the same as the first step of two-step modeling: a CFA model is specified wherein the loadings (pattern coefficients) of indicators on certain factors are fixed to zero. This specification for a pattern coefficient of zero reflects the prediction that the indicator does not depend on that factor. If the fit of the CFA model at the second step is acceptable, one goes on to test the original SR model; otherwise, the measurement model should be respecified. The third step of four-step modeling involves testing the SR model with the same set of zero pattern coefficients as are represented in the measurement model from the second step but where at least one unanalyzed association between two factors is respecified as a direct effect or reciprocal effect and some of the factors are respecified as endogenous. The last step of four-step modeling involves tests of a priori hypotheses about parameters free from the outset of model testing. These tests typically involve the imposition of zero or equality constraints, such as on pairs of reciprocal direct effects between two factors. The third and fourth steps of four-step modeling are basically a more specific statement of activities that could fall under the last step of two-step modeling.

Which approach to analyzing SR models is better, two-step or four-step modeling? Both methods have their critics and defenders (e.g., Hayduk, 1996; Herting & Costner, 2000). Both approaches also capitalize on chance variation when measurement and SR models are tested and respecified using data from the same sample. The two-step method has the advantage of simplicity, and it does not require models with at least four indicators per factor. Both two-step and four-step modeling are better than one-step modeling, where there is no separation of measurement issues from the estimation of causal effects among constructs. However, neither two-step nor four-step modeling is a "gold standard" for testing SR models, but unfortunately there is no such thing for model testing in SEM (Bentler, 2000). Bollen (2000) describes additional methods for testing SR models.

8.3 ESTIMATION OF SR MODELS

The same estimation methods described in the previous chapters for path models and CFA models can be used with SR models. Briefly, standard ML estimation would normally be the method of choice for SR models with continuous indicators that are normally distributed. If the distributions are severely nonnormal or the indicators are discrete with a small number of categories, however, then one of the alternative methods described in Chapter 7 should be used instead.

Interpretation of parameter estimates from the analysis of an SR model should not be difficult if one knows about path analysis and CFA. For example, path coefficients are interpreted for SR models as regression coefficients for effects on endogenous variables from other variables presumed to directly cause them, just as for path models. Total effects among the factors that make up the structural part of an SR model can be broken down into direct and indirect effects using the principles of effects decomposition from path analysis. Factor loadings are interpreted for SR models as regression coefficients for effects of factors on indicators, just as they are for CFA models. For CFA and SR models alike, a zero pattern coefficient does not imply a zero structural coefficient. That is, indicators typically have nonzero model-implied correlations with factors other than the one(s) they are specified to measure.

Some SEM computer programs print estimated squared multiple correlations (R_{smc}^2) for each endogenous variable. This includes for SR models the indicators and factors with direct effects on them from other factors. Values of R_{smc}^2 are usually computed for indicators in the unstandardized solution as one minus the ratio of the estimated measurement error variance over the observed variance of that indicator, just as for CFA models. Although variances of endogenous variables are not considered model parameters, they nevertheless have model-implied variances. Therefore, values of R_{smc}^2 are usually calculated for endogenous factors as one minus the ratio of the estimated disturbance variance over the predicted variance for that factor. Look out for Heywood cases in the solution, such as negative variance estimates, that suggest a problem with the data, specification, or identification status of the model. If iterative estimation fails due to poor start values set automatically by the computer, the guidelines in Appendix 5.A can be followed for generating user-supplied starting values for the structural part of an SR model and in Appendix 7.A for the measurement part.

Most SEM computer programs calculate a standardized solution for SR models by first finding the unstandardized solution with ULI constraints for endogenous factors and then transforming it to standardized form (i.e., it is derived in two steps). Steiger (2002) notes that this method assumes that the ULI constraints function only to scale the endogenous variables; that is, they do not affect overall model fit. This assumption is probably valid most of the time, but not when there is constraint interaction. Recall that constraint interaction for CFA models is indicated when the value of the chi-square difference (χ_D^2) statistic for the test of the equality of the loadings of indicators for different factors depends on how the factors are scaled (i.e., with ULI vs. UVI constraints). If all such identification constraints are used in this case, then the hypothesis of equality of factor loadings is not invariant under the method used to scale the factors. Steiger (2002) shows that the same phenomenon can happen with SR models where some factors have only two indicators and when estimates of direct effect on two or more different endogenous factors are constrained to be equal. Constraint interaction can also result in an incorrect standardized solution for an SR model if it is calculated in the way described earlier (i.e., in two steps).

The presence of constraint interaction can be detected the same way for SR and CFA models: while imposing the equality constraint, change the value of each identification constraint from 1.0 to another constant and rerun the analysis; if the value of the model chi-square (χ_M^2) changes by an amount that is more than expected by rounding error, there is constraint interaction. Steiger (2002) suggests a way to deal with constraint interaction in SR models: if the analysis of standardized factors can be justified, the method of constrained estimation (described in Chapter 7) can be used to test hypotheses of equal standardized path coefficients and generate a correct standardized solution. Recall that constrained estimation is a method that uses nonlinear constraints to correctly fit a structural equation model to a correlation matrix. Constrained estimation of an SR model standardizes all factors, exogenous and endogenous. This method also avoids the problem that ULI constraints imposed on endogenous factors do not generally standardize them.

8.4 A DETAILED EXAMPLE

This example of the specification of an SR model of family risk and child adjustment was introduced earlier (section 4.4). This example is briefly reviewed here. Worland et al. (1984) measured within a sample of 158 adolescents two indicators of familial risk (parental psychopathology, low family socioeconomic status [SES]), three of cognitive ability (verbal, visual–spatial, memory), three of achievement (reading, spelling, arithmetic), and four of classroom adjustment (teacher reports of motivation, extraversion, social relationships, emotional stability). Data from these 12 variables are summarized in Table 8.1. Worland et al. (1984) did not report standard deviations, so only the

TABLE 8.1. Input Data (Correlations) for Analysis of a Structural Regression Model of Familial Risk and Child Adjustment

Variable	1	2	3	4	5	6	7	8	9	10	11	12
Familial risk												
1. Par Psych	1.00											
2. Low SES	.42	1.00										
Cognitive ability												
3. Verbal	–.43	–.50	1.00									
4. Visual–Spatial	–.40	–.40	.66	1.00								
5. Memory	–.35	–.38	.67	.66	1.00							
Achievement												
6. Reading	–.39	–.43	.78	.56	.73	1.00						
7. Arithmetic	–.24	–.37	.69	.49	.70	.73	1.00					
8. Spelling	–.31	–.33	.63	.49	.72	.87	.72	1.00				
Classroom adjustment												
9. Motivation	–.25	–.25	.49	.32	.58	.53	.60	.59	1.00			
10. Extraversion	–.14	–.17	.18	.09	.17	.14	.15	.15	.25	1.00		
11. Harmony	–.25	–.26	.42	.25	.46	.42	.44	.45	.77	.19	1.00	
12. Stability	–.16	–.18	.33	.27	.35	.36	.38	.38	.59	–.29	.58	1.00

Note. These data are from Worland et al. (1984); N = 158.

correlations are available for this analysis. This problem is dealt with here by using the constrained estimation method of the SEPATH module in STATISTICA 6 (StatSoft Inc., 2003).

Worland et al. (1984) used the technique of path analysis to test their hypothesis that familial risk affects classroom adjustment only indirectly first through child cognitive status and then through achievement. An alternative is to specify an SR model that represents the use of multiple indicators and takes account of measurement error. Such a model is presented in Figure 4.3. The two-step evaluation of this SR model with four factors (familial risk, cognitive ability, achievement, classroom adjustment) is demonstrated below. Some problems are encountered along the way, but so it often goes in SEM when a relatively complex model is analyzed.

Considered first is whether the four-factor SR model of Figure 4.3 is identified. Presented in Figure 8.3(a) is the measurement portion of the SR model expressed as a four-factor CFA model. Assuming standardized factors (i.e., their variances are fixed to 1.0), this model has 30 free parameters, including 12 variances of measurement errors, 12 factor loadings, and 6 factor correlations. With 12 indicators, there are $12(13)/2 = 78$ observations, so $df_M = 48$. Because this is a standard CFA model with at least two indicators per factor, we can say it is identified. Presented in Figure 8.3(b) is the structural part of the four-factor SR model in Figure 4.3. This structural model is recursive, so it is also identified. Because both the measurement and structural models in Figure 8.3 are identified, we conclude that the original four-factor SR model in Figure 4.3 is identified.

In the first step of two-step modeling, the four-factor CFA model in Figure 8.3(a) was fitted to the correlation matrix of Table 8.1 with the constrained estimation method in SEPATH. Because this method also calculates correct standard errors for standardized estimates, a statistical test (i.e., a z test) of whether the population parameter is zero can be calculated directly for the standardized estimates. A converged, admissible solution was obtained, but values of selected indexes indicate poor overall fit of the four-factor CFA model: $\chi_M^2(48) = 188.050$, $p < .001$, NC = 3.918, CFI = .886, SRMR = .067, and RMSEA = .124 with the 90% confidence interval .103–.145. Inspection of the standardized ML solution (presented in Figure

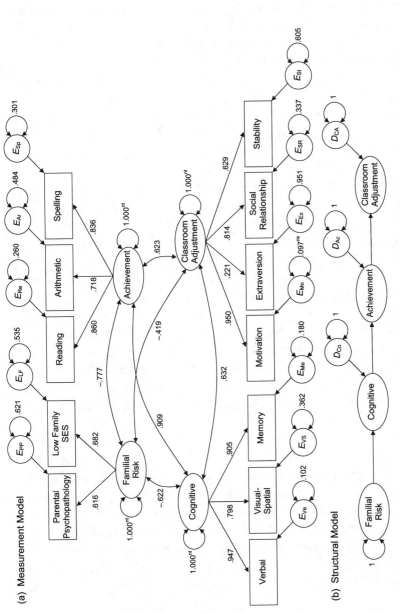

FIGURE 8.3. The measurement and structural parts of a structural regression model of familial risk and child adjustment with the standardized solution from constrained estimation for the measurement model. Estimates for the measurement errors are proportions of unexplained variance. All estimates above are statistically significant at the .05 level except for those designated "ns," which means not significant, and those designated "nt," which means not tested.

223

8.3(a)) indicates some specific problems.[1] The loading of the teacher-rated extraversion scale is quite low (.221), and consequently it has a relatively high proportion of unique variance (.951). The correlation residuals of this indicator with those of other factors were not high, which suggests that switching the loading of this indicator to a different factor would not substantially improve model fit. The estimated correlation between the cognitive ability factor and the achievement factor is so high (.909) as to suggest that these two factors are not distinct (i.e., poor discriminant validity). This result is consistent with the view that ability and achievement tests may not really measure distinct cognitive processes.

Additional problems were indicated by the correlation residuals. Some of the residuals among the indicators of cognitive ability and among the indicators of achievement were relatively high. This pattern suggests that the measurement errors within each set of tasks may covary. Considering that the three cognitive ability scores are from one test and the three achievement scores are from another test, such measurement error correlations may reflect common method variance. Two other residual correlations across these sets of indicators were also relatively high, one for the association between the verbal task and the spelling task and another between the memory task and the reading task. Measurement error correlations between the indicator pairs just mentioned may reflect the contribution of language-related skills and short-term memory, respectively, to task performance.

Based on the results just described, the measurement model in Figure 8.3(a) was respecified so that (1) the extraversion scale of the classroom adjustment factor was excluded from the analysis; (2) the cognitive ability and achievement factors were merged; (3) the measurement errors within each set of ability and achievement tasks were allowed to covary for a total of six such within-test correlations; and (4) the measurement errors for each of the two pairs of tasks mentioned earlier were allowed to covary across tests. The respecified three-factor CFA measurement model is presented in Figure 8.4(a).

[1]The standardized solution in Figure 8.3(a) from constrained estimation cannot be directly compared with a traditional standardized solution calculated in two steps with ULI constraints, including the one presented in the previous edition of this book for the same data (Kline, 1998, pp. 252–258).

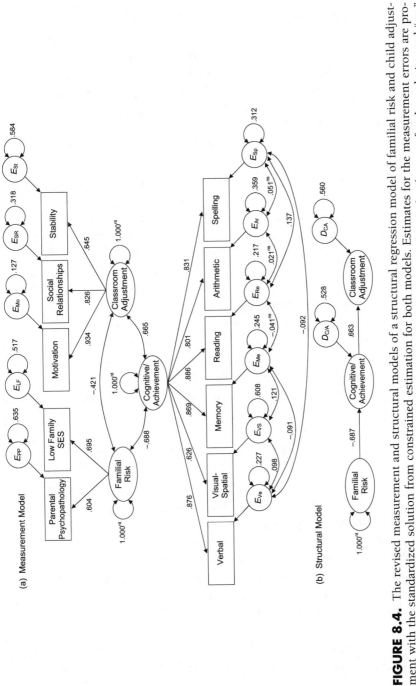

FIGURE 8.4. The revised measurement and structural models of a structural regression model of familial risk and child adjustment with the standardized solution from constrained estimation for both models. Estimates for the measurement errors are proportions of unexplained variance. All estimates above are statistically significant at the .05 level except for those designated "ns," which means not significant, and those designated "nt," which means not tested.

225

This model was estimated in SEPATH with the same data (Table 8.1). The analysis converged to an admissible solution, and values of selected indexes generally suggest reasonable overall model fit: $\chi^2_M (33)$ = 52.407, p = .107, NC = 1.588, CFI = .983, SRMR = .041, and RMSEA = .059 with the 90% confidence interval .022–.089. The standardized solution (presented in Figure 8.4(a)) suggests reasonable convergent validity among the indicators of each factor. The range of estimated factor correlations is –.688 to .665, and their absolute values are consistent with discriminant validity (i.e., they are not too high). The range of the estimated measurement error correlations is –.092 to .137. Although not high in absolute value, these error correlations as a set are necessary for reasonable model fit. For example, the following results were obtained for the three-factor measurement model with no error correlations, all of which indicate poor fit: $\chi^2_M (41)$ = 147.071, p < .001, NC = 3.587, CFI = .909, SRMR = .052, and RMSEA = .125 with the 90% confidence interval .103–.148.

With an adequate measurement model, the second stage of two-step modeling—the evaluation of the structural model—can proceed. The three-factor CFA model of Figure 8.4(a) was respecified as an SR model in which (1) the familial risk factor is exogenous and the cognitive/achievement factor and the classroom adjustment factor are both endogenous, and (2) the structural model has the following form:

$$\text{Familial Risk} \rightarrow \text{Cognitive/Achievement}$$
$$\rightarrow \text{Classroom Adjustment}$$

This structural model is overidentified because there is no direct effect from the familial risk factor to the classroom adjustment factor. Because the three-factor CFA measurement model in Figure 8.4(a) is an equivalent version of the corresponding three-factor SR model with a just-identified structural model, the version of the three-factor SR model with the overidentified structural model is nested under the CFA model. These results were calculated in SEPATH for the three-factor SR model with the overidentified structural model: $\chi^2_M (34)$ = 52.648, p = .021, NC = 1.548, CFI = .984, SRMR = .041, RMSEA = .058 with the 90% confidence interval .021–.088. These results are virtually identical to those reported earlier for the three-factor SR model with the just-identified structural model (i.e., with the path Familial Risk → Classroom Adjustment). For the model just mentioned, $\chi_M^2(33)$ = 52.407, so

$$\chi_D^2(1) = 52.648 - 52.407 = .241, p = .623$$

That is, the relative fit of the three-factor SR models with and without the path Familial Risk → Classroom Adjustment to the same data does not differ statistically at the .05 level. The same result also says that the path coefficient for this direct effect does not differ statistically from zero at the same level of probability.

Presented in Figure 8.4(b) is the standardized solution for just the structural portion of the three-factor SR model without the path Familial Risk → Classroom Adjustment (i.e., df_M = 34). The estimate of the direct effect of the familial risk factor on the cognitive/achievement factor is −.687, and the estimate for the direct effect of the cognitive/achievement factor on the classroom adjustment factor is .663. As expected, higher levels of familial risk are associated with lower levels of cognitive/achievement skills, which in turn predicts worse classroom adjustment. Using the tracing rule, the predicted correlation between the familial risk factor and the classroom adjustment factor equals the standardized indirect effect, which is estimated as −.687 (.663) = −.456. This predicted correlation is very close to the estimated correlation between these factors from the three-factor CFA model, −.421 (see Figure 8.4(a)). Thus, the overidentified structural model of the final SR model can essentially reproduce the estimated factor correlation, which supports Worland and colleagues' hypothesis (1984) that the effect of familial risk on classroom adjustment is entirely indirect through child cognitive/achievement status. Reported in Table 8.2 are the standardized ML estimates for all parameters of the three-factor SR model without the path Familial Risk → Classroom Adjustment. Note that the estimates for the measurement component of this SR model are very similar to their counterparts in the three-factor CFA measurement model of Figure 8.4(a). This is a desired result because it indicates no apparent interpretational confounding.

For additional examples of the analysis of an SR model, see Stew-

TABLE 8.2. Maximum Likelihood Parameter Estimates for a Three-Factor Structural Regression Model of Familial Risk and Child Adjustment

Parameter	Estimate	SE	Parameter	Estimate	SE
Factor loadings			Measurement error variances		
Fam Risk → Par Psych	.606	.075	E_{PP}	.632	.091
Fam Risk → Low SES	.693	.076	E_{LF}	.520	.105
Cog/Ach → Verbal	.879	.030	E_{Ve}	.227	.052
Cog/Ach → Vis–Spat	.626	.056	E_{VS}	.608	.070
Cog/Ach → Memory	.870	.033	E_{Me}	.242	.057
Cog/Ach → Read	.885	.029	E_{Re}	.217	.051
Cog/Ach → Arith	.800	.036	E_{Ar}	.360	.057
Cog/Ach → Spell	.829	.037	E_{Sp}	.312	.062
Class Adj → Motiv	.932	.027	E_{Mo}	.131	.051
Class Adj → Soc Rel	.828	.034	E_{SR}	.315	.056
Class Adj → Stabil	.646	.051	E_{St}	.582	.066
Direct effects			Disturbance variances		
Fam Risk → Cog/Ach	−.687	.077	$D_{C/A}$	.528	.106
Cog/Ach → Class Adj	.663	.052	D_{CA}	.560	.069
Measurement error covariances					
$E_{Ve} \smile E_{VS}$	.098	.046	$E_{Re} \smile E_{Ar}$	.022[a]	.040
$E_{VS} \smile E_{Me}$	.120	.049	$E_{Ar} \smile E_{Sp}$	.052[a]	.046
$E_{Ve} \smile E_{Me}$	−.094	.042	$E_{Re} \smile E_{Sp}$	.137	.048
$E_{Me} \smile E_{Re}$	−.042[a]	.026	$E_{Ve} \smile E_{Sp}$	−.092	.028

Note. Estimates for measurement errors and disturbances are proportions of unexplained variance.

[a]$p > .05$; $p < .05$ for all other estimates.

art, Simons, Conger, and Scarmella (2002), who evaluate the role of legal sanctions as a mediator of the effects of poor parenting practices on delinquent behavior, and Shahar, Chinman, Sells, and Davidson (2003), who within a sample of persons with severe mental illness test the hypothesis that the influence of maltreatment in childhood is mediated by current suspiciousness and hostility.

8.5 OTHER ISSUES

Some additional topics in the analysis of SR models are reviewed below.

Equivalent SR Models

Just as in path analysis and CFA, it is often possible to generate equivalent versions of SR models. An equivalent version of an SR model with a just-identified structural model was mentioned earlier: the measurement part of the SR model respecified as a CFA model, which assumes no causal effects among the factors, only unanalyzed associations. Regardless of whether the structural model is just-identified or not, it may be possible to generate equivalent versions of it using the Lee–Herschberger replacing rules for path models. Given no change in the measurement model, alternative SR models with equivalent structural models will fit the same data equally well. With the structural model held constant, it may also be possible to generate equivalent versions of the measurement model using Herschberger's reversed indicator rule, which involves reversing the direction of the causal effect between a factor and one of its indicators; that is, one indicator is specified as a cause indicator rather than as an effect indicator. Given no change in the structural model, alternative SR models with equivalent measurement models also fit the same data equally well. See Herschberger (1994) for several examples of the generation of equivalent SR models.

Single Indicators in Partially Latent SR Models

There are times when a researcher has only one measure of some construct. Scores from a single indicator are quite unlikely to have no measurement error, that is, to be both perfectly reliable and valid. There is an alternative to representing a single observed variable in the structural part of an SR model as one would in path analysis (i.e., without a measurement error term). This alternative requires an a priori estimate of the proportion of variance of the single indicator that is due to measurement error (10%, 20%, etc.). This estimate may be based on the researcher's experience with the measure or on results reported in the research literature. Recall that (1) one minus a reliability coefficient, $1 - r_{XX}$, estimates the proportion of observed variance due to random error, which is only one source of measurement error, and (2) specific types of reliability coefficients usually estimate only one kind of random error. Accordingly, the quantity $1 - r_{XX}$ probably underestimates the proportion of variance in a single indicator due to measurement error.

Suppose that variable X_1 is the only indicator of an exogenous construct A and that the researcher estimates that 20% of X_1's variance is due to measurement error. Given this estimate, it is possible to specify an SR model like the one presented in Figure 8.5(a). Note that X_1 in this model is specified as the single indicator of factor A and that X_1 has a measurement error term. The variance of this measurement error term is fixed to equal .20 times the observed variance, $.2s_{X_1}^2$, which is the estimated error variance expressed in the original metric of X_1. Because factor A must have a scale in order for the model to be identified, the loading of X_1 on A is fixed to equal 1.0. (An alternative for this exogenous factor is to fix its variance to 1.0 and leave the factor loading as a free parameter.) With the specification of a residual term for X_1, the direct effect of factor A is estimated controlling for measurement error in its single indicator. Now look at the SR model of Figure 8.5(b), in which Y_1 is specified as the sole indicator of the endogenous factor B. The proportion of measurement error in Y_1 is estimated to be .30. Given this estimate, the variance of the measurement error term for Y_1 is fixed to equal $.3s_{Y_1}^2$. Given that Y_1 has an error term, both the disturbance variance for B and the direct effect on this factor will be estimated while controlling for measurement error in the single indicator.

Three points should be noted about the method just described for single indicators: First, why not just specify the measurement error variance for a single indicator as a free parameter and let the computer estimate it? Such a specification may result in an identification problem (e.g., Bollen, 1989, pp. 172–175). A safer tactic with a single indicator is to fix the value of its measurement error variance based on a prior estimate. Second, what if the researcher is uncertain about his or her estimate of the measurement error variance for a single indicator? The model can be analyzed with a range of estimates, which allows the researcher to evaluate the impact of different assumptions about measurement error on the solution. Third, the models in Figure 8.5 illustrate why SR models with single indicators that are identified may nev-

(a) Single Indicator of an Exogenous Construct

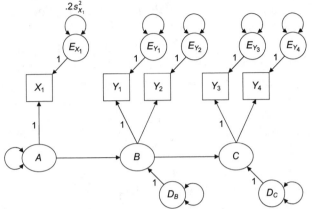

(b) Single Indicator of an Endogenous Construct

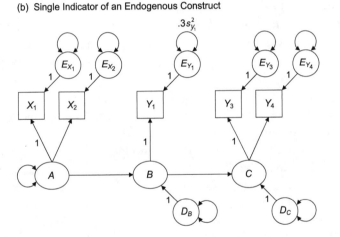

FIGURE 8.5. Two structural regression models with single indicators that correct for measurement error. It is assumed that the proportion of error variance for X_1 is .20 and for Y_1 is .30.

ertheless fail the two-step rule for identification: when either model in the figure is respecified as a CFA measurement model, one factor (A or B) will have only one indicator, which—according to the requirements already outlined in Chapter 7—is one less than the minimum. Fixing the measurement error variance of X_1 in the model of Figure 8.5(a) or Y_1 in the model of Figure 8.5(b) to a constant, however, identifies the model. See Bedeian, Day, and Kelloway (1997) for more information about the issues just discussed.

Cause Indicators

Observed variables of measurement models are usually represented as effect (reflective) indicators that are presumed to be caused by underlying factors and their measurement errors. The specification of observed variables as cause (formative) indicators reflects a different assumption about directionality—that the factor is affected by its indicators, instead of the other way around. Cause indicators were introduced in Chapter 7 in the context of CFA: the specification of one indicator in a single-factor CFA model as a cause indicator instead of as an effect indicator generates an equivalent model.

There are many examples in the literature of the analysis of SR models with factors that have both effect and cause indicators. Sometimes used to describe such factors is the term MIMIC, which stands for multiple indicators and multiple causes. A MIMIC factor is always endogenous. Herschberger (1994) described a MIMIC depression factor with indicators that represented various symptoms. Some of these indicators, such as "crying" and "feeling depressed," were specified as effect indicators because they are classical symptoms of depression. However, another indicator, "feeling lonely," was specified as a cause indicator of depression. This is because "feeling lonely" may be something that causes depression rather than vice versa. Beckie, Beckstead, and Webb (2001) analyzed a MIMIC model of women's quality of life after suffering a cardiac event that corrected for measurement error in all cause indicators using the method described above.

It is also theoretically possible to specify that all of the indicators of a factor are cause indicators rather than effect indicators. In Chapter 7 an example was cited showing that indicators such as education, income, and occupational prestige could all be causes of a socioeconomic (SES) factor instead of its effects. It turns out that the analysis of models with some factors that have only cause indicators can be tricky because such models require very specific patterns of direct effects among the factors in order to be identified. MacCallum and Browne (1993) discuss these requirements and present a detailed example.

8.6 SUMMARY

The evaluation of an SR model is essentially a simultaneous path analysis and CFA. Multiple-indicator assessment of constructs is represented in the measurement portion of an SR model, and presumed causal relations among latent variables are represented in the structural part. The analysis of an SR model can be broken down into these two models. In order for the structural component of an SR model to be identified, the measurement model must also be identified. To evaluate whether the measurement model is identified, respecify the original SR model as a CFA model with all possible factor covariances. If the identification status of the CFA model can be determined, next look at only the structural portion of an SR model. Evaluate whether the structural model is identified by using the same criteria as for path models. If this two-step process indicates that both the measurement and structural models are identified, the whole SR model is identified. It is also recommended that SR models be analyzed in at least two steps. In the first step, the SR model is respecified as a CFA measurement model. If the fit of the measurement model is unsatisfactory, then the fit of the original SR model may be even worse if its structural model is overidentified. With an acceptable measurement model, however, one can then test the SR model with alternative structural models. The researcher should also consider equivalent versions of his or her preferred SR model. Equivalent versions of the structural part of an SR model can be generated using the same rules as for path models, and equivalent measurement models can be created according to the same principles as for CFA models.

Structural regression models represent the apex in the SEM family for the analysis of covariances, and their review in this chapter completes our tour of core SEM techniques. The next few chapters consider some advanced methods, including the analysis of means and multiple-sample SEM. How to avoid fooling yourself with SEM is also discussed in an upcoming chapter (12), which may indeed be the most important chapter in this book.

8.7 RECOMMENDED READINGS

Bedeian, A. G., Day, D. V., & Kelloway, E. K. (1997). Correcting for measurement error attenuation in structural equation models: Some important reminders. *Educational and Psychological Measurement, 57*, 785–799.

MacCallum, R. C. (1995). Model specification: Procedures, strategies, and related issues. In R. H. Hoyle (Ed.), *Structural equation modeling* (pp. 16–36). Thousand Oaks, CA: Sage.

Appendix 8.A

SEPATH Syntax

```
*TABLE 8.2
*To save space, multiple commands are listed in the same
  line
*Note that SEPATH reads only one command per line
(FamRisk)-1->[ParPsych]  (FamRisk)-2->[LowSES]
(CogAch)-3->[Verbal]  (CogAch)-4->[VisSpat]
  (CogAch)-5->[Memory]
(CogAch)-6->[Read]  (CogAch)-7->[Arith]
  (CogAch)-8->[Spell]
(ClassAdj)-9->[Motiv]  (ClassAdj)-10->[SocRel]
(ClassAdj)-11->[Stable]
(E_PP)-->[ParPsych]  (E_SES)-->[LowSES]  (E_Ve)-->[Verbal]
(E_VS)-->[VisSpat]  (E_Me)-->[Memory]  (E_Re)-->[Read]
(E_Ar)-->[Arith]  (E_Sp)-->[Spell]  (E_Mo)-->[Motiv]
(E_SR)-->[SocRel]  (E_St)-->[Stable]
(E_PP)-12-(E_PP)  (E_SES)-13-(E_SES)  (E_Ve)-14-(E_Ve)
(E_VS)-15-(E_VS)  (E_Me)-16-(E_Me)  (E_Re)-17-(E_Re)
(E_Ar)-18-(E_Ar)  (E_Sp)-19-(E_Sp)  (E_Mo)-20-(E_Mo)
(E_SR)-21-(E_SR)  (E_St)-22-(E_St)
(FamRisk)-23->(CogAch)  (CogAch)-25->(ClassAdj)
(D_CogAch)-->(CogAch)  (D_ClassAdj)-->(ClassAdj)
(D_CogAch)-26-(D_CogAch)  (D_ClassAdj)-27-(D_ClassAdj)
(E_Ve)-28-(E_VS)  (E_Ve)-29-(E_Me)  (E_Me)-30-(E_VS)
(E_Re)-31-(E_Ar)  (E_Re)-32-(E_Sp)  (E_Ar)-33-(E_Sp)
(E_Ve)-34-(E_Sp)  (E_Me)-35-(E_Re)
```

Part III
Advanced Techniques; Avoiding Mistakes

9

Nonrecursive Structural Models

This chapter deals with nonrecursive structural models where either all variables are observed (i.e., a path model) or some variables are latent (i.e., a structural regression [SR] model). Recursive structural models assume that all causal effects are represented as unidirectional and that there are no disturbance correlations between endogenous variables with direct effects between them. These assumptions are very restrictive. For example, many "real world" causal processes are based on cycles of mutual influence, that is, feedback. The presence of a feedback loop in a structural model automatically makes it non-recursive. However, it is often more difficult to analyze nonrecursive models compared with recursive models. One source of this problem is identification: recursive models are always identified, but particular combinations of effects in a nonrecursive model can result in under-identification of one or more of its parameters even if there are more observations than freely estimated parameters and all latent variables are scaled. A major topic of this chapter thus concerns how to determine whether a nonrecursive model is identified. Also covered here are options for the estimation of nonrecursive models.

9.1 SPECIFICATION OF NONRECURSIVE MODELS

A feedback loop involves mutual causation among variables measured at the same time (i.e., the design is cross sectional). Recall that direct feedback involves only two variables in a reciprocal relation (e.g., $Y_1 \rightleftarrows Y_2$), but indirect feedback involves three or more variables (e.g.,

$Y_1 \rightarrow Y_2 \rightarrow Y_3 \rightarrow Y_1$). A direct feedback loop between Y_1 and Y_2 is represented in Figure 9.1(a) without disturbances or other variables. An alternative way to estimate reciprocal causal effects requires a longitudinal design where Y_1 and Y_2 are each measured at two or more different points in time. For example, the symbols Y_{11} and Y_{21} in the **panel model** shown in Figure 9.1(b) without disturbances or other variables represent, respectively, Y_1 and Y_2 at the first measurement occasion. Likewise, the symbols Y_{12} and Y_{22} represent scores from the same two variables at the second measurement. Reciprocal causation is represented in Figure 9.1(b) by the **cross-log** direct effects between Y_1 and Y_2 measured at different times, such as $Y_{11} \rightarrow Y_{22}$ and $Y_{21} \rightarrow Y_{12}$. A complete panel model may be recursive or nonrecursive depending upon its pattern of disturbance correlations.

Panel models for longitudinal data offer some potential advantages over models with feedback loops for cross-sectional data. These include the explicit representation of a finite causal lag that corresponds to the measurement occasions and the ability to measure stability versus change in rank order or variability over time. However, the analysis of a panel model is not a panacea for estimating reciprocal causal effects (Kenny, 1979). Not only are longitudinal designs more expensive and subject to loss of cases over time, but with such designs it can also be difficult to specify measurement occasions that match actual finite causal lags. Panel designs are also not generally useful for resolving causal priority between reciprocally related variables—for

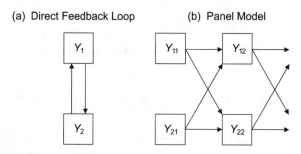

FIGURE 9.1. Reciprocal causal effects between Y_1 and Y_2 represented with (a) a direct feedback loop based on a cross-sectional design and (b) a cross-lag effect based on a longitudinal design (panel model).

example, does Y_1 cause Y_2 or vice versa?—unless some highly restrictive (i.e., unrealistic) assumptions are met. One of these is **stationarity**, the requirement that the causal structure does not change over time. Maruyama (1998) notes that the general requirement that there are no omitted causes correlated with those in the model is even more critical for panel models because of the repeated sampling of variables over time. The complexity of panel models can also increase rapidly as more variables in the form of repeated measurements are added to the model (e.g., Cole & Maxwell, 2003; Finkel, 1995). For many researchers, the estimation of reciprocal causation between variables measured at the same time is the only realistic alternative to a longitudinal design.

However, Kaplan, Harik, and Hotchkiss (2001) remind us that data from a cross-sectional design give only a "snapshot" of an ongoing dynamic process. Therefore, the estimation of reciprocal effects with cross-sectional data requires the assumption of **equilibrium**. This means that any changes in the system underlying a presumed feedback relation have already manifested their effects and that the system is in a steady state. This does *not* mean that the two direct effects that make up the feedback loop, such as $Y_1 \rightarrow Y_2$ and $Y_2 \rightarrow Y_1$, are equal. Instead, it means that the estimates of their values do not depend upon the particular time point of data collection. Heise (1975) describes equilibrium this way: it means that a dynamic system has completed its cycles of response to a set of inputs and that the inputs do not vary over time; in other words, estimation of the reciprocal effects with cross-sectional data requires that the causal process has basically dampened out and is not just beginning (Kenny, 1979).

Recall that the presence of a disturbance correlation reflects the assumption that the corresponding endogenous variables share at least one common omitted cause. The disturbances of variables involved in feedback loops are often specified as correlated. This specification also often makes sense because if variables are presumed to mutually cause each other, then it seems plausible to expect that they may have common omitted causes. The presence of disturbance correlations in particular patterns in nonrecursive models also helps to determine their identification status. Just as for measurement models, however, residuals should be specified as correlated only if there are substantive reasons for doing so.

9.2 IDENTIFICATION OF NONRECURSIVE MODELS

This discussion assumes that the two basic requirements for the identification of any type of structural equation model are satisfied—specifically, that the number of free parameters does not exceed the number of observations (i.e., $df_M \geq 0$) and every latent variable has a scale. The next few diagrams of nonrecursive structural models illustrate path models, but the same principles discussed here apply to the structural components of SR models.

Unlike recursive models, nonrecursive models are not always identified. Although there are algebraic means to determine whether the parameters of a nonrecursive model can be expressed as unique functions of its observations (e.g., Berry, 1984, pp. 27–35), these techniques are practical only for very simple models. Fortunately, there are alternatives that involve checking whether a nonrecursive model meets certain requirements for identification that can be readily evaluated by hand. Some of these requirements are only necessary for identification, which means that satisfying them does not guarantee that the model is really identified. If a nonrecursive structural model satisfies a sufficient condition, however, then it is identified.

The nature and number of conditions for identification that a nonrecursive model must satisfy depend upon its pattern of disturbance correlations. Specifically, the necessary **order condition** and the sufficient **rank condition** apply to models with unanalyzed associations between all pairs of disturbances either for the whole model or within blocks of endogenous variables that are recursively related to each other. Consider the two nonrecursive path models of Figure 9.2. For both models, $df_M \geq 0$ and all latent variables are scaled, but these facts are insufficient to identify either model.[1] The model of Figure 9.2(a) has an indirect feedback loop that involves Y_1 to Y_3 and all possible disturbance correlations (3). The model of Figure 9.2(b) has two direct feedback loops and a pattern of disturbance correlations described by some authors as **block recursive**. Note that one can partition the

---

[1]The model of Figure 9.2(a) has 21 observations and 18 parameters, including 6 variances (of 3 Xs and 3 Ds), 6 covariances (between 3 Xs and 3 Ds), and 6 direct effects, so $df_M = 3$. The model of Figure 9.2(b) has 21 observations and 17 parameters, including 6 variances (of 2 Xs and 4 Ds), 3 covariances (between 2 Xs and two different pairs of Ds), and 8 direct effects, so $df_M = 4$.

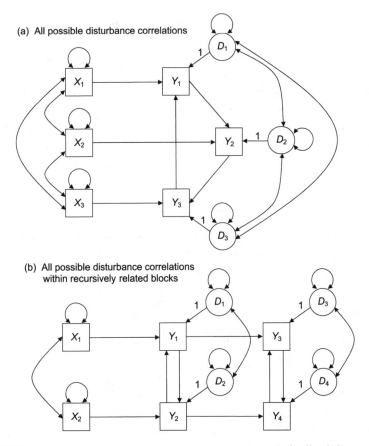

FIGURE 9.2. Two examples of nonrecursive models with feedback loops.

endogenous variables of this model into two blocks, one with Y_1 and Y_2 and the other made up of Y_3 and Y_4. Each block contains all possible disturbance correlations (i.e., $D_1 \cup D_2$ for the first block, $D_3 \cup D_4$ for the second), but the disturbances across the blocks are independent (e.g., D_1 is uncorrelated with D_3). Also, causal relations within each block are nonrecursive (e.g., $Y_1 \rightleftarrows Y_2$), but effects between the blocks are unidirectional. Therefore, the two blocks of endogenous variables in the model of Figure 9.2(b) are recursively related to each other even though the whole model is nonrecursive. Application of the order and rank conditions to determine the identification status of these models is considered shortly.

If a nonrecursive structural model has either no disturbance correlations or less than all possible disturbance correlations such that the model is not block recursive, the order and rank conditions are generally too conservative. That is, such "none-of-the-above" nonrecursive models that fail either condition could nevertheless be identified. Unfortunately, there may be no sufficient condition that can be readily evaluated by hand to determine whether a none-of-the-above nonrecursive model is actually identified. Thus, the identification status of such models may be more ambiguous. However, such models can be evaluated with the methods outlined in Chapter 7 for confirmatory factor analysis (CFA) models for which there is no easily applied sufficient condition for identification. These methods involve checking whether a converged solution from an SEM computer program passes empirical tests of uniqueness, but recall that such tests are only necessary conditions for identification.

Order Condition

The order condition is a counting rule applied to each endogenous variable in a nonrecursive model either with all possible disturbance correlations or that is block recursive. If the order condition is not satisfied, the equation for that endogenous variable is underidentified. One evaluates the order condition by tallying the numbers of variables in the structural model (except disturbances) that have direct effects on each endogenous variable versus the number that do not; let us call the latter excluded variables. The order condition has the following requirement:

> *The number of excluded variables for each endogenous variable equals or exceeds the total number of endogenous variables minus 1.*

For models with all possible disturbance correlations, the total number of endogenous variables equals that for the whole model. For example, the model of Figure 9.2(a) has all possible disturbance correlations, so the total number of endogenous variables equals 3. This means that there must be a minimum of $3 - 1 = 2$ variables excluded from the equation of each endogenous variable, which is true here: specifically, there are 3 variables excluded from the equation of every endogenous variable (e.g., X_2, X_3, and Y_2 for Y_1), which exceeds the minimum number. Thus, the model of Figure 9.2(a) meets the order condition.

For nonrecursive models that are block recursive, however, the total number of endogenous variables is counted separately for each block when the order condition is evaluated. For example, there are two recursively related blocks of endogenous variables in the model of Figure 9.2(b). Each block has two variables, so the total number of endogenous variables for each block is 2. To satisfy the order condition, there must be at least $2 - 1 = 1$ variables excluded from the equation of each endogenous variable in both blocks, which is true here: specifically, 1 variable is excluded from each equation for Y_1 and Y_2 in the first block (e.g., X_2 for Y_1), and 3 variables are excluded from each equation for Y_3 and Y_4 in the second block (e.g., X_1, X_2, and Y_2 for Y_3). Because the number of excluded variables for each endogenous variable in every block exceeds the minimum number, the order condition is satisfied for this model.

Rank Condition

Because the order condition is only necessary, we still do not know whether the nonrecursive models of Figure 9.2 are actually identified. Evaluation of the sufficient rank condition, however, will provide the answer. The rank condition is usually described in the SEM literature in matrix terms (e.g., Bollen, 1989, pp. 98–103), which is fine for those familiar with linear algebra but otherwise not. Berry (1984) devised an algorithm for checking the rank condition that does not require extensive knowledge of matrix operations, a simpler version of which is presented here. A nontechnical description of the rank condition is given next.

For nonrecursive models with all possible disturbance correlations, the rank condition can be viewed as a requirement that each variable in a feedback loop has a unique pattern of direct effects on it from variables outside the loop. Such a pattern of direct effects provides a sort of "statistical anchor" so that the parameters of variables involved in feedback loops can be estimated distinctly from one another. Look again at Figure 9.2(a). Note that each of the three endogenous variables of this model has a unique pattern of direct effects on it from variables external to their indirect feedback loop (i.e., $X_1 \rightarrow Y_1$, $X_2 \rightarrow Y_2$, $X_3 \rightarrow Y_3$).

Note that this analogy does not hold for those models considered in this book to be nonrecursive that do not have feedback loops, such as partially recursive models with correlated disturbances and direct effects among the endogenous variables (see Figure 5.1). Therefore, a more formal method of evaluating the rank condition is needed.

The starting point for checking the rank condition is to construct something that Berry (1984) called a **system matrix**, in which the endogenous variables of the structural model are listed on the left side of the matrix (rows) and all variables (excluding disturbances) along the top (columns). In each row, a "0" or "1" appears in the columns that correspond to that row. A "1" indicates that the variable represented by that column has a direct effect on the endogenous variable represented by that row. A "1" also appears in the column that corresponds to the endogenous variable represented by that row. The remaining entries are "0's," and they indicate excluded variables. The system matrix for the model of Figure 9.2(a) with all possible disturbance correlations is presented here (I):

$$
\begin{array}{c}
 \\
Y_1 \\
Y_2 \\
Y_3
\end{array}
\begin{array}{cccccc}
X_1 & X_2 & X_3 & Y_1 & Y_2 & Y_3 \\
\left[\begin{array}{cccccc}
1 & 0 & 0 & 1 & 0 & 1 \\
0 & 1 & 0 & 1 & 1 & 0 \\
0 & 0 & 1 & 0 & 1 & 1
\end{array}\right]
\end{array}
\qquad (I)
$$

"Reading" this matrix for Y_1 indicates three "1's" in its row, one in the column for Y_1 itself and the others in the columns of variables that, according to the model, directly affect it, X_1 and Y_3. Because X_2, X_3, and Y_2 are excluded from Y_1's equation, the entries in the columns for these variables are all "0's." Entries in the rows of this matrix for Y_2 and Y_3 are read in a similar way.

The rank condition is evaluated using the system matrix. Like the order condition, the rank condition must be evaluated for the equation of each endogenous variable. The steps to do so for a model with all possible disturbance correlations are outlined next:

1. Begin with the first row of the system matrix (i.e., the first endogenous variable). Cross out all entries of that row. Also cross out any column in the system matrix with a "1" in this

row. Use the entries that remain to form a new, reduced matrix. Row and column labels are not necessary in the reduced matrix.

2. Simplify the reduced matrix further by deleting any row with entries that are all zeros. Also delete any row that is an exact duplicate of another or that can be reproduced by adding other rows together. The number of remaining rows is the rank. (Readers who are familiar with matrix algebra may recognize this step as the equivalent of elementary row operations to find the rank of a matrix.) For example, consider the reduced matrix shown here (II):

$$\begin{bmatrix} 1 & 0 \\ 0 & 1 \\ 1 & 1 \end{bmatrix} \tag{II}$$

The third row can be formed by adding the corresponding elements of the first and second rows, so it should be deleted. Therefore, the rank of this matrix (II) is 2 instead of 3. *The rank condition is met for the equation of this endogenous variable if the rank of the reduced matrix is greater than or equal to the total number of endogenous variables minus 1.*

3. Repeat steps 1 and 2 for every endogenous variable. *If the rank condition is satisfied for every endogenous variable, then the model is identified.*

Steps 1 and 2 applied to the system matrix for the model of Figure 9.2(a) with all possible disturbance correlations are outlined here (III). Note that we begin with endogenous variable Y_1.

$$\begin{array}{c} \rightarrow \\ \\ \end{array} \begin{array}{c} \\ Y_1 \\ Y_2 \\ Y_3 \end{array} \begin{array}{cccccc} X_1 & X_2 & X_3 & Y_1 & Y_2 & Y_3 \\ \end{array} \tag{III}$$

$$\begin{array}{ccc} \rightarrow & Y_1 \\ & Y_2 \\ & Y_3 \end{array} \begin{bmatrix} \cancel{1} & \cancel{0} & \cancel{0} & \cancel{1} & \cancel{0} & \cancel{1} \\ \cancel{0} & 1 & 0 & \cancel{1} & 1 & \cancel{0} \\ \cancel{0} & 0 & 1 & \cancel{0} & 1 & \cancel{1} \end{bmatrix} \rightarrow \begin{bmatrix} 1 & 0 & 1 \\ 0 & 1 & 1 \end{bmatrix} \rightarrow \text{Rank} = 2$$

For step 1, all the entries in the first row of the system matrix (III) are crossed out. Also crossed out are three columns of the matrix with a "1" in this row (i.e., those with column headings X_1, Y_1, and Y_3. The resulting reduced matrix has two rows. Neither row has entries that are all zero or can be reproduced by adding other rows together, so the reduced matrix cannot be simplified further. This means that the rank of the equation for Y_1 is 2. This rank exactly equals the required minimum value, which is 1 less than the total number of endogenous variables in the whole model, or $3 - 1 = 2$. The rank condition is satisfied for Y_1.

We repeat this process for the other two endogenous variables of the model in Figure 9.2(a), Y_2 and Y_3. The steps for doing so are summarized in Table 9.1. Readers are encouraged to follow these steps for the sake of additional practice. The rank of the equations for each of Y_2 and Y_3 is 2, which exactly equals the minimum required value. Because the rank condition is satisfied for all three endogenous variables of this model, we conclude that it is identified.

The rank condition is evaluated separately for each block of endogenous variables in the block recursive model of Figure 9.2(b). The steps are as follows: First, construct a system matrix for each block. For example, the system matrix for the block that contains Y_1 and Y_2 lists only these variables plus prior variables (X_1 and X_2; see Table 9.2). Variables of the second block, Y_3 and Y_4, are not included in the matrix for the first block. The system matrix for the second block lists only Y_3 and Y_4 in its rows but represents all of the variables in the whole structural model in its columns. Next, the rank condition is

TABLE 9.1. Evaluation of the Rank Condition for the Model of Figure 9.2(a)

Evaluation for Y_2

	X_1	X_2	X_3	Y_1	Y_2	Y_3
Y_1	1	θ	0	‡	θ	1
→ Y_2	θ	‡	θ	‡	‡	θ
Y_3	0	θ	1	θ	‡	1

$$\rightarrow \begin{bmatrix} 1 & 0 & 1 \\ 0 & 1 & 1 \end{bmatrix} \rightarrow \text{Rank} = 2$$

Evaluation for Y_3

	X_1	X_2	X_3	Y_1	Y_2	Y_3
Y_1	1	0	θ	1	θ	‡
Y_2	0	1	θ	1	‡	θ
→ Y_3	θ	θ	‡	θ	‡	‡

$$\rightarrow \begin{bmatrix} 1 & 0 & 1 \\ 0 & 1 & 1 \end{bmatrix} \rightarrow \text{Rank} = 2$$

TABLE 9.2. Evaluation of the Rank Condition for the Model of Figure 9.2(b)

Evaluation for block 1

$$
\begin{array}{c}
\rightarrow \\
\\
\end{array}
\begin{array}{c}
Y_1 \\
Y_2
\end{array}
\begin{array}{cccc}
X_1 & X_2 & Y_1 & Y_2 \\
\end{array}
\left[
\begin{array}{cccc}
\cancel{+} & \theta & \cancel{+} & \cancel{+} \\
\theta & 1 & \cancel{+} & \cancel{+}
\end{array}
\right]
\rightarrow
\left[\; 1 \;\right]
\rightarrow \text{Rank} = 1
$$

$$
\begin{array}{c}
\\
\rightarrow
\end{array}
\begin{array}{c}
Y_1 \\
Y_2
\end{array}
\begin{array}{cccc}
X_1 & X_2 & Y_1 & Y_2 \\
\end{array}
\left[
\begin{array}{cccc}
1 & \theta & \cancel{+} & \cancel{+} \\
\theta & \cancel{+} & \cancel{+} & \cancel{+}
\end{array}
\right]
\rightarrow
\left[\; 1 \;\right]
\rightarrow \text{Rank} = 1
$$

Evaluation for block 2

$$
\begin{array}{c}
\rightarrow \\
\\
\end{array}
\begin{array}{c}
Y_1 \\
Y_2
\end{array}
\begin{array}{cccccc}
X_1 & X_2 & Y_1 & Y_2 & Y_3 & Y_4 \\
\end{array}
\left[
\begin{array}{cccccc}
\theta & \theta & \cancel{+} & \theta & \cancel{+} & \cancel{+} \\
0 & 0 & \theta & 1 & \cancel{+} & \cancel{+}
\end{array}
\right]
\rightarrow
\left[\; 0 \;\; 0 \;\; 1 \;\right]
\rightarrow \text{Rank} = 1
$$

$$
\begin{array}{c}
\\
\rightarrow
\end{array}
\begin{array}{c}
Y_3 \\
Y_4
\end{array}
\begin{array}{cccccc}
X_1 & X_2 & Y_1 & Y_2 & Y_3 & Y_4 \\
\end{array}
\left[
\begin{array}{cccccc}
0 & 0 & 1 & \theta & \cancel{+} & \cancel{+} \\
\theta & \theta & \theta & \cancel{+} & \cancel{+} & \cancel{+}
\end{array}
\right]
\rightarrow
\left[\; 0 \;\; 0 \;\; 1 \;\right]
\rightarrow \text{Rank} = 1
$$

evaluated for the system matrix of each block. These steps are outlined in Table 9.2. Because the rank of the equation of every endogenous variable of each system matrix equals the number of endogenous variables in each block minus 1 (i.e., 2 – 1), the rank condition is met. Thus, the model of Figure 9.2(b) is identified.

Respecification of Models That Fail the Order or Rank Condition

Consider the model presented in Figure 9.3. Let Y_1 and Y_2 represent, respectively, violence on the part of protesters and police. The direct feedback loop reflects the hypothesis of reciprocal causation: as protesters become more violent, so do the police, and vice versa. The two exogenous variables, X_1 and X_2, represent, respectively, seriousness of the civil disobedience committed by the protesters and availability of

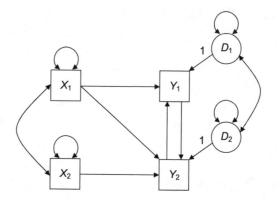

FIGURE 9.3. An example of a nonrecursive model that is not identified.

police riot gear (clubs, shields, tear gas, etc.). Immediately after this model is specified but before the data are collected, the researcher evaluates its identification status. Two problems are discovered: the model has more parameters (11) than observations (10), and the order condition is violated because there are no excluded variables for Y_2. Because this model fails the order condition, it will also fail the rank condition.

What can be done about this identification problem? Because the data are not yet collected, one possibility is to add exogenous variables to the model such that (1) the number of additional observations afforded by the new exogenous variables is greater than the number of parameters they add to the model; (2) the numbers of excluded variables for Y_1 and Y_2 are each at least 1; and (3) the respecified model also meets the rank condition. Suppose that it is decided that a new exogenous variable, X_3, would be protesters' level of commitment to nonviolence. The addition of the path $X_3 \rightarrow Y_1$ (Y_1 is protester violence) and unanalyzed associations between X_3 and the other two exogenous variables to the model of Figure 9.2 would accomplish the goals just listed. Thus, the model respecified in this way is identified. (Readers are encouraged to verify that the respecified model meets the order and rank conditions.) But now suppose that the identification status of the original model was not checked until after the data were collected. Because it is now too late to add exogenous variables, there is only one option: simplify the model. One way to do this is to trim paths (i.e., fix the value of the corresponding parameter estimate to zero). For instance, deleting the path $X_1 \rightarrow Y_2$ (riot gear $\rightarrow$ police violence) would yield an identified model, but doing so forces a change in the original hypotheses. That is, if the researcher believes that the availability of riot gear has a direct effect on police violence, then dropping this path is akin to intentionally making a specification error. In contrast, adding an exogenous variable does not sacrifice the original specifications about causal effects.

At first glance, the respecification of nonrecursive structural models so that they are identified can seem like a shell game: add this path, drop another, and—voilà!—the model is identified or—curses!—it is not. Although one obviously needs an identified model, it is crucial to modify structural models in a judicious manner. That is, any change to the original specification of a model for the sake of identification should by guided by the researcher's hypotheses and sense of relevant theory. For instance, the specification that a path is zero must be made on theoretical or logical grounds, not on empirical ones. That is, one cannot estimate a model, find that a path coefficient is close to zero, and then eliminate the path in order to identify a nonrecursive model. Don't lose sight of the ideas that motivated the analysis in the first place through willy-nilly specification.

9.3 ESTIMATION OF NONRECURSIVE MODELS

Some special issues in the analysis of nonrecursive structural models are considered next.

Problems

Technical problems are more likely when nonrecursive models are analyzed compared with recursive models. For example, iterative estimation of direct effects or disturbance variances–covariances for variables involved in feedback loops may fail without quite accurate start values. If the default start values of an SEM computer program do not lead to a converged solution, it is the researcher who should provide better initial estimates (e.g., see Appendix 5.A). A converged solution may contain Heywood cases (e.g., negative variance estimates) or other kinds of illogical parameter estimates (e.g., estimated standard errors so large that no interpretation is plausible). Estimation of nonrecursive models may be more susceptible to empirical underidentification, which can happen when estimates of certain key paths are close to zero. For example, suppose the coefficient for the path $X_2 \rightarrow Y_2$ in the model of Figure 9.2(b) is about zero. The virtual absence of this path alters the system matrix for the first block of endogenous variables. This consequence is outlined next, starting with the matrix (IV) for the model in Figure 9.2(b) without the path $X_2 \rightarrow Y_2$ (the rank for Y_1's equation is zero):

$$
\begin{array}{c}
\rightarrow Y_1 \\
Y_2
\end{array}
\begin{array}{cc}
\begin{array}{cccc} X_1 & X_2 & Y_1 & Y_2 \end{array} \\
\left[\begin{array}{cccc}
1 & 0 & 1 & 1 \\
0 & 0 & 1 & 1
\end{array}\right]
\end{array}
\rightarrow \left[\ 0\ \right] \rightarrow \text{Rank} = 0 \qquad \text{(IV)}
$$

Equality and Proportionality Constraints

The imposition of an equality or proportionality constraint on the direct effects of a feedback loop is one way to reduce the number of free model parameters without dropping paths. For example, the specification that both direct effects of the reciprocal relation $Y_1 \rightleftarrows Y_2$ are equal means that only one path coefficient is needed rather than two. A possible drawback of equality constraints on feedback loops is that they preclude the detection of unequal mutual influence. For example, Wagner, Torgeson, and Rashotte (1994) found in longitudinal studies that the effect of children's phonological abilities on their reading skills is about three times the magnitude of the effect in the opposite direction. If equality constraints are blindly imposed when bidirectional effects differ in magnitude, then not only may the model poorly fit the data but the researcher may also miss an important finding. In contrast, a proportionality constraint allows for unequal mutual influence but on an a priori basis. For instance, it may be specified that the coefficient for the path $Y_1 \rightarrow Y_2$ must be three times the value of that for the path $Y_2 \rightarrow Y_1$. Like equality constraints, proportionality constraints reduce the number of free parameters, one for each pair of direct effects. However, the imposition of proportionality constraints generally requires prior knowledge about the relative effect magnitudes. Also recall that equality or proportionality constraints usually apply only in the unstandardized solution. An exception is when a correlation matrix is analyzed using the method of constrained estimation.

Effects Decomposition

Variables in feedback loops have indirect effects (and thus total effects) on *themselves*, which is apparent in effects decompositions calculated by SEM computer programs for nonrecursive models. Consider the reciprocal relation $Y_1 \rightleftarrows Y_2$. Suppose that the standardized direct effect of Y_1 on Y_2 is .40 and that the effect in the other direction is .20. An indirect effect of Y_1 on itself would be the sequence $Y_1 \rightarrow Y_2 \rightarrow Y_1$, which is estimated as .40 × .20, or .08. There are additional indirect effects of Y_1 on itself through Y_2, however, because cycles of mutual influence in feedback loops are theoretically infinite. The indirect effect $Y_1 \rightarrow Y_2 \rightarrow Y_1 \rightarrow Y_2 \rightarrow Y_1$ is one of these, and its estimate is .40 × .20 × .40 × .20, or .0064. Mathematically, these product terms head fairly quickly to zero, but the total effect of Y_1 on itself is an estimate of the sum of all possible cycles through Y_2. Indirect and total effects of Y_2 on itself are similarly derived.

Calculation of indirect and total effects among variables in a feedback loop as just described assumes equilibrium. It is important to realize, however, that there is generally no statistical way to directly evaluate whether the equilibrium assumption is tenable when the data are cross sectional; that is, it must be argued substantively. Kaplan et al. (2001) note that rarely is this assumption explicitly acknowledged in the literature on applications of SEM where feedback effects are estimated with cross-sectional data. This is unfortunate because the results of a computer simulation by Kaplan et al. indicate that violation of the equilibrium assumption can lead to severely biased estimates. In their simulation, Kaplan et al. specified a true dynamic system that was perturbed at some earlier time and was headed toward but had not yet attained equilibrium in either a smooth or oscillatory manner. By *oscillatory* is meant that the sign of a direct effect in a feedback loop changes from positive to negative and back again over time as the system moves back toward stability after being perturbed. A *smooth* manner means that the sign of the direct effect is constant but its value tends to increase or decrease over time toward an asymptotic value as the system approaches equilibrium. Computer-generated data sets simulated cross-sectional studies conducted at different numbers of cycles before equilibrium is reached. Kaplan et al. found that estimates of direct effects in feedback loops can vary dramatically depending on when the simulated data were collected. As expected, this phenomenon was more striking for dynamic systems in oscillation before reaching equilibrium.

Kaplan et al. (2001) also found that the **stability index** did not accurately measure the degree of bias due to lack of equilibrium. The stability index is printed in the output of some SEM computer programs when a nonrecursive model is analyzed. It is based on certain mathematical properties of the matrix of coefficients for direct effects among all the endogenous variables in a structural model, not just those involved in feedback loops. These properties concern whether estimates of the direct effects would get infinitely larger over time. If so, the system is said to "explode" because it may never reach equilibrium, given the observed direct effects among the endogenous variables. The mathematics of the stability index are relatively complex (e.g., see Kaplan et al., 2001, pp. 317–322). A standard interpretation of this index is that values less than 1.0 are taken as positive evidence for equilibrium but values greater than 1.0 suggest the lack of equilibrium. However, this interpretation is not generally supported by Kaplan and colleagues' computer simulations results, which emphasizes the need to evaluate equilibrium on rational grounds.

Squared Multiple Correlations

Bentler and Raykov (2000) note that squared multiple correlations (R^2_{smc}) computed as one minus the ratio of the disturbance variance over the total variance may be inappropriate for endogenous variables involved in feedback loops. This is because the disturbances of such variables may be correlated with one of their presumed causes, which violates a requirement of least squares estimation that the residuals are unrelated to the predictors. They described a general approach to estimating explained variance in nonrecursive models that corrects for model-implied correlations between disturbances and predictors. Their proportion of explained variance for nonrecursive models, the Bentler–Raykov corrected R^2, is automatically calculated by EQS.

Two-Stage Least Squares Estimation

Maximum likelihood (ML) estimation is commonly used to analyze nonrecursive models. An older alternative for nonrecursive path models is **two-stage least squares** (2SLS) estimation. As its name suggests, 2SLS is a variation on multiple regression that gets around the problem of model-implied correlations between disturbances and presumed causes of endogenous variables. Recall that 2SLS is a partial-information method that analyzes one structural equation at a time. It is also a noniterative method, which means that it needs no start values.

For nonrecursive path models, 2SLS is nothing more than MR applied in two stages. The aim of the first stage is to replace every problematic observed causal variable with a newly created predictor. A "problematic" causal variable has a direct effect on an endogenous variable and a model-implied correlation with the disturbance of that endogeneous variable. Variables known as **instruments** are used to create the new predictors. An **instrumental variable** has a direct effect on the problematic causal variable but no direct effect on the endogenous variable (i.e., it is excluded from the equation of the latter). Note that both conditions are given by theory, not by statistical analysis. An instrument can be either exogenous or endogenous. In a direct feedback loop, the same variable cannot serve as the instrument for both variables in that loop. Also, one of the variables does not need an instrument if the disturbances of the variables in the loop are specified as uncorrelated (Kenny, 2002).

The 2SLS method works likes this: The problematic causal variable is regressed on the instrument. The predicted criterion variable in this analysis will be uncorrelated with the disturbance of the endogenous variable and replaces the problematic causal variable. When similar replacements are made for all problematic causal variables, we proceed to the second stage of 2SLS, which is just ordinary multiple regression conducted for each endogenous variable but using the predictors created in the first step whenever the original ones were replaced. As an example, look back at Figure 9.2(b). This nonrecursive path model specifies two direct causes of Y_1, the variables X_1 and Y_2. From the perspective of standard multiple regression, Y_2 is a problematic causal variable because of the model-implied correlation between this variable and the disturbance of Y_1. Note that there is no such problem with X_1, the other causal variable. The instrument here is X_2 because it is excluded from the equation of Y_1 and has a direct effect on Y_2, the problematic causal variable. Therefore, we regress Y_2 on X_2 in a standard regression analysis. The predicted criterion variable from this first analysis, $\hat{Y}_2$, replaces Y_2 as a predictor of Y_1 in a second regression analysis where X_1 is the other predictor. The regression coefficients from the second regression analysis are taken as the least squares estimates of the path coefficients for the direct effects of X_1 and Y_2 on Y_1. See Berry (1984, chap. 5), James and Singh (1978), and Kenny (1979, pp. 83–92, 103–107; 2002) for more information about 2SLS estimation for path models. Bollen (1996) describes forms of 2SLS estimation for latent variable models.

9.4 EXAMPLES

Two examples of analyzing nonrecursive models with direct feedback loops are presented next.

Transgenerational Relation of Adjustment Problems

Data for this example are from Cooperman (1996), who studied a sample of 84 mothers participating in a longitudinal study. Although the sample size here is small, the data set is interesting. When these women were in elementary school, their classmates completed rating scales about aggressive or withdrawn behavior, and these cases obtained extreme scores in either area. During evaluations some 10–15 years later, teachers completed rating scales about conduct or emotional problems of the children of these women. Descriptive statistics for all variables just mentioned and for educational levels and maternity ages are summarized in Table 9.3.

The nonrecursive path model presented in Figure 9.4 depicts the transgenerational relation of adjustment problems of these mothers and their children. A childhood history of aggression in mothers is specified as both a direct and an indirect cause of externalization in their children. Likewise, a maternal history of withdrawal is predicted to be both a direct and an indirect cause of internalization in their children. Specified as mediator variables are the mother's educational level and her maternity age. The latter is hypothesized to be directly affected by a maternal history of aggression, which may manifest itself in adolescence through more frequent or careless sexual activity. The mother's educational level, on the other hand, is assumed to be directly affected by the tendency to withdraw. The two mediators are

TABLE 9.3. Input Data (Correlations and Standard Deviations) for Analysis of a Nonrecursive Path Model of Transgenerational Relation of Adjustment Problems

Variable	1	2	3	4	5	6
Mother characteristics						
1. Aggression	1.00					
2. Withdrawal	.19	1.00				
3. Education	−.16	−.20	1.00			
4. Maternal Age	−.37	−.06	.36	1.00		
Child characteristics						
5. Internalization	−.06	−.05	−.03	−.25	1.00	
6. Externalization	.13	−.06	−.09	−.28	.41	1.00
M	.51	.47	10.87	20.57	.08	.15
SD	1.09	1.03	2.17	2.33	.28	.36

Note. These data are from Cooperman (1996); N = 84. Means are reported but not analyzed.

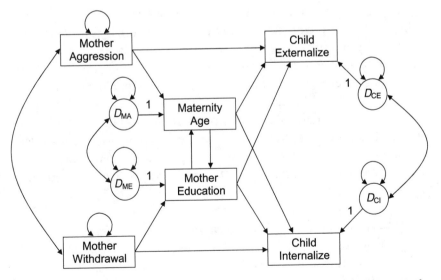

FIGURE 9.4. A nonrecursive path model of transgenerational adjustment problems.

specified as reciprocally related. For example, young women may be more likely to leave school if they are pregnant, but leaving school could itself be a risk factor for pregnancy. The disturbances of the mediators are assumed to covary as are the disturbances of the variables about the internalization and externalization status of the children. However, note that the pair of disturbances for the maternal variables is specified as unrelated to the pair of disturbances of the variables concerning the adjustment of the children (i.e., the model is block recursive).

With 6 observed variables in the model of Figure 9.4, there are 21 observations. The total number of free model parameters is 19, including 6 variances of exogenous variables, 3 unanalyzed associations between pairs of exogenous variables, and 10 direct effects, so $df_M = 2$. The model's structural equations satisfy the order and rank conditions for the equation of every endogenous variable. (Readers should verify this statement.) The model of Figure 9.4 is thus identified (specifically, overidentified). The covariance matrix assembled from the correlations and standard deviations in Table 9.3 was analyzed with the ML method of EQS 6 (Bentler, 2003). The program's default start values were used. The analysis terminated at the very first iteration with the error message "you have bad start values."

The guidelines in Appendix 5.A were followed to generate initial estimates for the reciprocal direct effects and disturbance variances for the variables mother education and maternity age. It was expected that maternity age would have a greater relative impact on mother education than the reverse. Specifically, a "medium" standardized effect size of .30 was assumed for the path Maternity Age → Mother Education, and a "small" standardized effect size of .10 was assumed for the path Mother Education → Maternity Age. Given the observed standard deviations of the mother education and maternity age variables—respectively, 2.17 and 2.33 (Table 9.3)—start values were computed as follows:

Maternity Age → Mother Education:	.30 (2.17/2.33)	= .28
Variance of D_{ME}:	$(1 - .30^2)\ 2.17^2$	= 4.29
Mother Education → Maternity Age:	.10 (2.33/2.17)	= .11
Variance of D_{MA}:	$(1 - .10^2)\ 2.33^2$	= 5.38

A second analysis using the start values just calculated terminated normally with a converged, admissible solution. The EQS syntax for this analysis is presented in Appendix 9.A. Values of selected fit indexes indicate reasonable overall model fit but one associated with a fair amount of sampling error because of the small sample size: $\chi^2_M (2)$ = 2.959, p = .228, NC = 1.480, CFI = .978, SRMR = .041, and RMSEA = .076 with the 90% confidence interval 0–.243. The ML estimates of the direct effects and disturbance variances–covariances are reported in Table 9.4. The statistical power of this analysis is probably low because of the small sample size. Accordingly, little attention is paid below to whether effects are statistically significant.

Standardized path coefficients from Table 9.4 are reported in parentheses below. Women described by their childhood peers as being one standard deviation above the mean in aggression tend to have their own first child at an age about one-third of a standard deviation below the mean (–.380), and a maternity age one standard deviation above the

TABLE 9.4. Maximum Likelihood Parameter Estimates for a Nonrecursive Path Model of Transgenerational Relation of Adjustment Problems

Parameter	Unstandard-ized	SE	Standard-ized	Parameter	Unstandard-ized	SE	Standard-ized
Direct effects				Disturbances variances and covariances			
Moth Agg→Mat Age	−.812**	.304	−.380	D_{MA}	4.904*	2.480	.457
Moth Educ→Mat Age	−.065	.648	−.061				
Moth With→Moth Educ	−.378	.215	−.180	D_{ME}	3.949**	.613	.839
Mat Age→Moth Educ	.317	.256	.340	$D_{MA} \smile D_{ME}$ .304		2.874	.069
Moth Agg→Child Ext	.032	.035	.097	D_{CE}	.120**	.019	.923
Moth Educ→Child Ext	.003	.019	.015				
Mat Age→Child Ext	−.039*	.018	−.248				
Moth With→Child Int	−.005	.027	−.018	D_{CI}	.073**	.011	.936
Moth Educ→Child Int	.008	.015	.065	$D_{CE} \smile D_{CI}$ .035**		.011	.379
Mat Age→Child Int	−.033*	.014	−.275				

Note. Standardized estimates for the disturbances are proportions of unexplained variance.
*p < .05; **p < .01.

mean (i.e., the mother is older) is associated with a level of education about one-third of a standard deviation above average (.340). Level of education is also affected by withdrawal: Women described by their childhood peers as being one full standard deviation above average in withdrawal have lower educational levels by about two-tenths of a standard deviation (–.180). The direct effect of the mother's education on maternity age was actually negative but only about 6% of a standard deviation in magnitude (–.061). Of all six direct effects on the externalization and internalization variables for the children of these women, the magnitude of the effect of maternity age is clearly the largest. Specifically, a maternity age that is one full standard deviation above the mean predicts lower levels of conduct problems in the children by about a quarter of a standard deviation (–.248). Values of the Bentler–Raykov corrected R^2 reported by EQS are .100 for maternity age, .162 for mother education, .086 for externalization, and .067 for internalization.

Reciprocal Effects between Stress and Depression

Shen and Takeuchi (2001) administered within a stratified random sample of 983 native-born Chinese Americans and immigrants of Chinese descent measures of the degree of acculturation, socioeconomic status (SES), stress, and depression. Descriptive statistics for these variables are summarized in Table 9.5.

Presented in Figure 9.5 is an SR model where the structural component contains a direct feedback loop between stress and depression plus a disturbance covariance. Also, degree of acculturation and SES are specified as direct causes of, respectively, stress and depression. The measurement error covariance between two indicators of acculturation is as per Shen and Takeuchi's original model (2001). With 8 observed variables, there are 36 observations available to estimate the 22 parameters of this model. These include 11 variances (of 2 exogenous factors, 7 measurement errors, and 2 disturbances), 3 covariances (between 1 pair of exogenous factors and 2 pairs of disturbances), 4 factor loadings, and 4 direct effects, so df_M = 14. The structural portion of the model is identified because it satisfies the necessary order condition and the sufficient rank condition. The measurement portion is not fully latent, but it is identified. Therefore, the whole SR model of Figure 9.5 is identified (specifically, overidentified).

TABLE 9.5. Input Data (Correlations and Standard Deviations) for Analysis of a Model with a Direct Feedback Loop between Stress and Depression

Variable	1	2	3	4	5	6	7	8
Acculturation indicators								
1. Acculturation Scale	1.00							
2. Generation Status	.44	1.00						
3. Percent Life in U.S.	.69	.54	1.00					
Socioeconomic status indicators								
4. Education	.37	.08	.24	1.00				
5. Income	.23	.05	.26	.29	1.00			
Stress indicators								
6. Interpersonal	.12	.08	.08	.08	−.03	1.00		
7. Job	.09	.06	.04	.01	−.02	.38	1.00	
Single indicator								
9. Depression	.03	.02	−.02	−.07	−.11	.37	.46	1.00
SD	.78	.41	.24	3.27	3.44	.37	.45	.32

Note. These data are from Shen and Takeuchi (2001); $N = 983$.

The model of Figure 9.5 was fitted to the covariance matrix assembled from the correlations and standard deviations in Table 9.5 using the ML method of LISREL 8 (Jöreskog & Sörbom, 2003). The analysis converged normally to an admissible solution. Values of selected fit indexes indicate reasonable overall fit: $\chi^2_M (14) = 58.667$, $p < .001$, NC = 4.191, CFI = .976, SRMR = .031, RMSEA = .057 with the 90% confidence interval .044–.073. Also, all absolute correlation residuals were less than .10. To save space, only the completely standardized solution is presented (see Figure 9.5). Briefly, the model of Figure 9.5 explains 31.7% and 47.0% of the variance of the stress and depression variables, respectively. (These are uncorrected R^2_{smc} values.) The magnitude of the standardized direct effect of stress on depression (.795) is roughly three times the magnitude of the direct effect in the opposite direction (.274). The latter is also not statistically significant at the .05 level. It is not unexpected that greater stress predicts more depression symp-

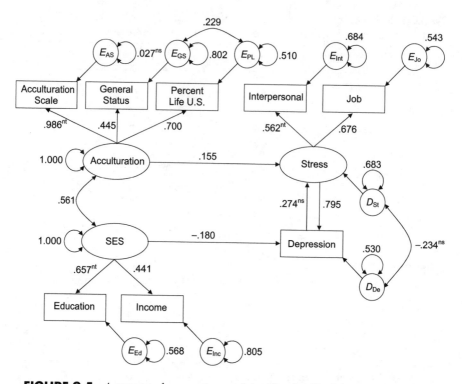

FIGURE 9.5. A structural regression model with a feedback loop between stress and depression and the completely standardized solution. Estimates for the residual terms are proportions of unexplained variance. The unstandardized counterparts of the above estimates are all statistically significant at the .05 level except for those designated "ns," which means not significant, and those designated "nt," which means not tested because this parameter is fixed to 1.0 in the unstandardized solution.

toms and vice versa. However, it is surprising that greater acculturation is associated with higher levels of stress (standardized direct effect = .155), controlling for SES. Higher SES is also associated with fewer symptoms of depression (standardized direct effect = −.180).

9.5 SUMMARY

Compared with recursive models, nonrecursive models are more difficult to analyze. One of the main reasons is identification: recursive models are always identified, but certain configurations of paths in nonrecursive models can render at least one of their parameters underidentified. Fortunately, there are ways to definitely evaluate the identification status of at least some kinds of nonrecursive models. The order condition and rank condition apply to nonrecursive models with all possible disturbance correlations or that are block recursive. The order condition requires that the number of variables omitted from each structural equation at least equals or exceeds the number of endogenous variables in the corresponding system matrix minus 1. This condition is only necessary. The rank condition, in contrast, is sufficient, which means that meeting it implies identification. This condition requires that the rank of every structural equation at least equals or exceeds the number of endogenous variables in the corresponding system matrix minus 1. Estimation of direct effects in a feedback loop requires the assumption of equilibrium when the data are cross sectional. Whether this assumption is reasonable must be established primarily on rational grounds, not statistical ones. Next, Chapter 10 concerns the analysis of means in SEM.

9.6 RECOMMENDED READINGS

Berry, W. D. (1984). *Nonrecursive causal models.* Beverly Hills, CA: Sage.
Heise, D. R. (1975). *Causal analysis.* New York: Wiley. (Chap. 6)

Appendix 9.A

EQS Syntax

```
/Title
   Figure 9.4
/Specifications
   Cases = 84; Variables = 6; Data_file='Cooperman.ess';
/Labels
   V1 = MOM_AGG; V2 = MOM_WITH; V3 = MOM_EDUC;
   V4 = MATN_AGE; V5 = CHILD_INT; V6 = CHILD_EXT;
/Equations
   V3 = *V2 + .28*V4 + E3; V4 = *V1 + .11*V3 + E4;
   V5 = *V3 + *V4 + *V2 + E5; V6 = *V4 + *V3 + *V1 + E6;
/Variances
   V1-V2 = *; E3 = 4.29*; E4 = 5.38*; E5-E6 = *;
/Covariances
   V1,V2 = *; E3,E4 = *; E5,E6 = *;
/Print
   Fit = All;
/End
```

10

Mean Structures
and Latent Growth Models

The basic datum of SEM, the covariance, does not convey information about means. If only covariances are analyzed, then all observed variables are mean deviated (centered) so that latent variables must have means of zero. Sometimes this loss of information (i.e., the means) is too restrictive. For example, means of repeated measures variables may be expected to differ. Means are estimated in SEM by adding a mean structure to the model's basic covariance structure (i.e., its structural or measurement components). The input data for the analysis of a model with a mean structure are covariances and means (or the raw scores). The SEM approach to the analysis of means is distinguished by the capability to test hypotheses about the means of latent variables and the covariance structure of the error terms. In contrast, other statistical methods such as the analysis of variance (ANOVA) are concerned mainly with the means of observed variables and are not as flexible in the analysis of error covariances. The basic rationale for the analysis of means in SEM is outlined next. Also considered in this chapter is the analysis in a single sample of latent growth models for longitudinal data.

10.1 INTRODUCTION TO MEAN STRUCTURES

The representation of means in structural equation models is based on the general principles of regression. For example, consider the scores on variables X and Y presented in Table 10.1. (For the moment ignore

TABLE 10.1. Example Bivariate Data Set

	Raw scores		Constant
Case	X	Y	△
A	3	24	1
B	8	20	1
C	10	22	1
D	15	32	1
E	19	27	1
M	11.000	25.000	—
SD	6.205	4.690	—
s^2	38.500	22.000	—

Note. $r_{XY} = .601$.

the column in the table labeled △.) The unstandardized regression equation for predicting Y from X for these data is

$$\hat{Y} = .455\,X + 20.000$$

The regression coefficient (.455) can be seen as the covariance structure of the prediction equation for these data. This coefficient says something about the association between X and Y, but it conveys no information about the mean of either variable. In contrast, the intercept (20.000) reflects the means of both variables and the regression coefficient, albeit with a single number. Given $M_X = 11.000$, $M_Y = 25.000$, and $r_{XY} = .601$ (Table 10.1), the intercept for these data can be expressed as

$$\text{intercept} = 20.000 = 25.000 - .455\,(11.000)$$

How a computer calculates the intercept of an unstandardized regression equation provides a key to understanding the analysis of means in SEM. Look again at Table 10.1 and in particular at the column labeled △, which represents a constant that equals 1.0 for every case in the McArdle–McDonald symbolism for SEM. The results of two regression analyses with the constant $\triangle$ are summarized in Table 10.2. Both analyses were conducted by instructing the computer to omit from the analysis the intercept term it would otherwise automatically calculate. (This is an option in most regression modules.) In the first analysis summarized in Table 10.2, variable Y is regressed on both X and the constant. Note that the regression coefficient for X is the same as before, .455, and for the constant it is 20.000, which equals the intercept. This result indicates a general principle: *when a criterion is regressed on a predictor and a constant, the unstandardized coefficient for the constant is the intercept.* The second analysis summarized in Table 10.2 concerns the regression of X on the constant. Note that the regression coefficient in this analysis is 11.000, which equals the mean of X. A second principle is thus: *when a predictor is regressed on a constant, the unstandardized coefficient is the mean of the predictor.*

A path analytic representation of the regression analyses just described is presented in Figure 10.1. Unlike a standard path model, the one in this figure has both a covariance structure and a mean structure. The covariance structure includes the direct effects of the measured and unmeasured exogenous variables (X and D, respectively) and their variances. Estimating this covariance structure with the data in Table 10.1 yields an unstandardized path coefficient of .455 (the same as the unstandardized regression coefficient) and a disturbance variance of 14.045. No information about the means of X or Y is represented in this covariance structure.

The mean structure of Figure 10.1 consists of the direct effects of the constant $\triangle$ on both observed variables. Although the constant is depicted as exogenous in this figure, it is not an exogenous variable in the usual sense because it has no variance. The unstandardized path

TABLE 10.2. Results of Regression Analyses with a Constant for the Data in Table 10.1

Regression	Predictor(s)	Unstandardized coefficient(s)
1. Y on X and $\triangle$	X	.455
	$\triangle$	20.000
2. X on $\triangle$	$\triangle$	11.000

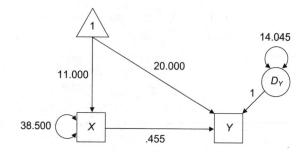

FIGURE 10.1. A path model with a mean structure.

coefficient for the direct effect of the constant on the exogenous variable X is 11.000, which is the mean of X and the same value obtained by regressing X on the constant (see Table 10.2). The mean of X is thus explicitly represented in the mean structure in the form of an unstandardized path coefficient. (The standardized coefficient for the path $\triangle \rightarrow X$ is zero because the means of standardized variables are zero.) Also note that because the constant has no direct effect on X through other variables, the coefficient for the path $\triangle \rightarrow X$ is also a total effect. The unstandardized path coefficient for the direct effect of the constant on the endogenous variable Y is 20.000, which is the intercept. In addition to this direct effect, the constant also has an indirect effect on Y through X. Using the tracing rule for his model, we obtain this result:

$$\text{total effect of } \triangle \text{ on } Y = \text{direct effect} + \text{indirect effect}$$
$$= 20.000 + .455 \, (11.000) = 25.000$$

which equals the mean of Y. A third principle about mean structures can thus be expressed in path analytic language: *the mean of an endogenous variable Y is a function of three parameters—the intercept* (20.000 for the data of Table 10.1), *the unstandardized path coefficient* (.455), *and the mean of the exogenous variable* (11.000). There is a related fourth principle: *the model-implied (predicted) mean for an observed variable is the total effect of the constant on that variable.* Because the mean structure of the model in Figure 10.1 is just-identified, the predicted means for X and Y equal their observed counterparts. This point is elaborated below.

When an SEM computer program analyzes means, it automatically creates a constant on which variables in the model are regressed. A variable is included in the mean structure by specifying in the program's syntax that the constant has a direct or indirect effect on it. This leads to a fifth principle: *for exogenous variables, the unstandardized path coefficient for the direct effect of the constant is a mean; for endogenous variables, though, the direct effect of the constant is an intercept but the total effect is a mean.* If a variable is excluded from the mean structure, then the mean of that variable is assumed to be zero. Note that error terms (disturbances and measurement errors) are *not* included in a mean structure because their means are typically assumed to be zero. In fact, the mean structure may not be identified if the mean of an error term is inadvertently specified as a free parameter.

Three points warrant special mention. First, there is no standard symbol in the SEM literature for mean structures. The symbol $\triangle$ is used in diagrams here mainly as a pedagogical device so that readers can quickly recognize the presence of a mean structure and determine which variables it includes. However, it is not absolutely necessary to explicitly represent mean structures in model diagrams. For example, some authors (e.g., Kaplan, 2000) present just the covariance structure in the diagram and report estimates about means in accompanying tables. Second, although it is theoretically possible to analyze means in a path analysis, this is rarely done in practice. It is more common in SEM to estimate means of latent variables represented in confirmatory factor analysis (CFA) measurement models or structural regression (SR) models. Third, special forms of maximum likelihood (ML) estimation for raw data files with missing observations, including the expectation-maximization (EM) algorithm, estimate both covariances and means; that is, they add a mean structure to the model even if the researcher is not interested in analyzing means. Depending on how these special methods are implemented in a particular SEM computer program, it may or may not be necessary to explicitly specify a mean structure even if the original model has only a covariance structure.

10.2 IDENTIFICATION OF MEAN STRUCTURES

The parameters of a model with a mean structure include the means of the exogenous variables (e.g., $\triangle \rightarrow X$ in Figure 10.1), the intercepts of the endogenous variables (e.g., $\triangle \rightarrow Y$), and the number of parameters in the covariance portion of the model counted in the usual way for that type of model (e.g., $X \rightarrow Y$ and the variances of X and D). A simple rule for counting the total number of observations available to estimate the parameters of a model with a mean structure is $v (v + 3)/2$, where v is the number of observed variables. The value of this expression gives the total number of variances, nonredundant covariances, and means of the observed variables. For example, if there are 5 observed variables, then there are $5(8)/2 = 20$ observations, which include 5 means and 15 variances and covariances (i.e., $5(6)/2$).

In order for a mean structure to be identified, the number of its parameters (i.e., exogenous variable means and endogenous variable intercepts) cannot exceed the total number of means of the observed variables. Also, the identification status of a mean structure must be considered separately from that of the covariance structure; that is, an overidentified covariance structure will not identify an underidentified mean structure. Likewise, an overidentified mean structure cannot remedy an underidentified covariance structure. If the mean structure is just-identified, it has just as many free parameters as observed means. Therefore, (1) the model-implied means (i.e., total effects of the constant) will exactly equal the corresponding observed means, and (2) the fit of the model with just the covariance structure will be identical to that of the model with both the covariance structure and the mean structure. For example, the mean structure of the model in Figure 10.1 has two parameters, $\triangle \rightarrow X$ and $\triangle \rightarrow Y$ (i.e., the mean of X and the intercept of Y, respectively). Because there are two observed means (M_X, M_Y), the mean structure here is just-identified. It was demonstrated earlier for this model that the total effect of the constant on X is 11.000 and on Y is 25.000. Each of these predicted means equals the corresponding observed mean. It is only when the mean structure is overidentified that the predicted means could differ from the observed means (i.e., one or more **mean residuals** may not equal zero).

10.3 ESTIMATION OF MEAN STRUCTURES

Many of the estimation methods described in earlier chapters for analyzing models with covariance structures only can be applied to models with both covariance and mean structures. This includes ML estimation, the most general method in SEM. However, not all standardized fit indexes for models with only covariance structures may be available for models with both covariance and mean structures or may be calculated for just the covariance part of the model. This is especially true for incremental fit indexes, such as the comparative fit index (CFI), measuring the relative improvement in the fit of the researcher's model over a null model. When only covariances are analyzed, the null model is typically the independence model, which assumes zero population covariances. However, the independence model is more difficult to define when both covariances and means are analyzed. For example, an independence model where all covariances and means are fixed to equal zero may be very unrealistic. An alternative independence model allows for the means of the observed variables to be freely estimated (i.e., they are not assumed to be zero). Check the documentation of your SEM computer program to determine how it defines the independence model, and provide this information in a written summary of the results when reporting values of incremental fit indexes when means are analyzed along with covariances.

10.4 STRUCTURED MEANS IN MEASUREMENT MODELS

A standard CFA model assumes that the means of all variables are zero. Presented in Figure 10.2 is a CFA model with a mean structure that relaxes this assumption for some variables. Its covariance structure assumes that indicators J1 to J5 measure a common factor. Its mean structure, represented by the direct effects that point from the constant to the indicators and the factor, includes means in the analysis along with covariances. Based on the principles just discussed, the unstandardized path coefficient for the regression of the exogenous factor on the constant should theoretically equal the mean of this factor. Also, because the indicators are endogenous, their means should be estimated by the total effect of the constant on each indicator. Estimation of the model in Figure 10.2 would thus seem to allow the researcher to simultaneously test two sets of hypotheses, one about measurement (i.e., a single-factor CFA model) and the other about means.

Unfortunately, the model of Figure 10.2 is not identified if it is esti-

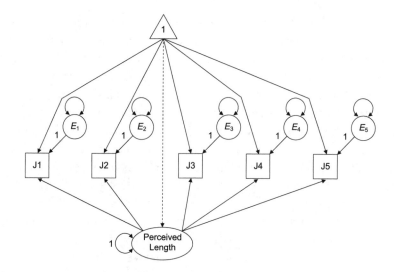

FIGURE 10.2. A single-factor confirmatory factor analysis measurement model with a mean structure.

mated with data from a single sample. This is because its mean structure is underidentified: there are five observations (the means of J1 to J5), but the mean structure has six parameters, including the mean of the factor and the intercepts of the five indicators. Perhaps the simplest way to deal with this problem is to exclude the factor from the mean structure, that is, to assume that its mean is zero. This assumption results in the elimination of one path from the model ($\triangle$ → Perceived Length, represented with a dashed line in Figure 10.2), which yields a just-identified mean structure.

The data for this example are from Bollen (1989), who asked five different judges (J1 to J5) to estimate, to the nearest tenth of an inch, the length of lines shown on 60 index cards with one line per card. Presented in Table 10.3 are the means and the covariance matrix for the five judges across the 60 cards. Note that each indicator in this analysis is a person (judge) and the sample size is the number of cards ($N = 60$). This is "backward" from the typical application in SEM, where covariances are computed by aggregating the data over cases instead of stimuli. There are $5(8)/2 = 20$ observations available to estimate the parameters of this model. Assuming that the variance of the factor is fixed to 1.0 to scale it and its mean is zero, the parameters include 5 factor loadings, 5 indicator intercepts, and 5 residual variances for a total of 15 (i.e., $df_M = 5$).

The model of Figure 10.2 without the path from the constant to the factor was fitted to the covariance matrix and means of Table 10.3 with the ML method of Mplus 3 (L. Muthén & B. Muthén, 1998–2004). The analysis converged to an admissible solution. Values of selected fit indexes are $\chi^2_M (5) = 3.984$, $p = .552$, NC = .797, CFI = 1.000, SRMR = .002, and RMSEA = 0 with the 90% confidence interval 0–.160. The independence model defined by Mplus assumes zero covariances among the indicators, but their means are freely estimated. The confidence interval based on the RMSEA is quite wide with a lower bound (0) that indicates excellent fit and an upper bound (.160) that indicates poor fit, but this is not surprising considering the small sample size ($N = 60$). Overall, the fit of the model in Figure 10.2 to the data seems acceptable.

Reported in the top part of Table 10.4 are ML parameter estimates generated by Mplus for the covariance structure of the model in Figure 10.2. Values of the unstandardized factor loadings in the table indicate increases in estimated lengths for each judge for every unit increase in perceived length. For example, the estimates of the third judge (J3) increase by 1.994 inches for every unit increase in the underlying perceived factor, which is almost twice the increase for the fifth judge (J5), 1.065 inches. The standardized factor loadings are all high and range from .968 to .992 across the five judges, which indicates convergent validity in factor measurement. Estimates for the mean structure are

TABLE 10.3. Input Data (Covariances and Means) for the Analysis of a Measurement Model with a Mean Structure for Perceived Line Length

Variable	1	2	3	4	5
1. Judge 1	2.19870				
2. Judge 2	1.72564	1.45873			
3. Judge 3	2.95467	2.34359	4.20910		
4. Judge 4	1.78994	1.42332	2.44670	1.50202	
5. Judge 5	1.57710	1.24435	2.17271	1.30718	1.20016
M	2.66076	2.23000	3.42667	2.09667	1.91833

Note. These data are from Bollen (1989, p. 316); $N = 60$. All judgments are in inches.

reported in the bottom part of Table 10.4. The intercepts of the indicators are actually model-implied means. This is because direct effects of the constant on the indicators (e.g., $\triangle \rightarrow J1$) are also total effects, and total effects of the constant on endogenous variables are means. Because the mean structure in Figure 10.2 is just-identified, the predicted mean will equal the observed mean for each judge. For example, the predicted mean for the first judge (J1) is 2.661 (Table 10.4), which equals the observed mean for this judge at three-decimal accuracy (Table 10.3).

By imposing equality constraints on the five intercepts (i.e., $\triangle \rightarrow J1 = \triangle \rightarrow J2 = \triangle \rightarrow J3 = \triangle \rightarrow J4 = \triangle \rightarrow J5$), one can test whether the means of the five judges are equal within sampling error. This restriction overidentifies the mean structure because now only one parameter must be estimated from five observed means. Values of selected fit indexes for the restricted model just described are $\chi_M^2 (9) = 89.900$, $p < .001$, NC = 9.989, CFI = .890, SRMR = 2.042, and RMSEA = .387 with the 90% confidence interval .317–.462; that is, in words, the fit of the restricted model is very poor, so we reject the hypothesis of equal mean estimated line lengths across the judges. See Arbuckle (1996) for an example of the analysis of a CFA model with a mean structure for a set of four quizzes in a university course where some scores are missing.

Factor means can be estimated if a CFA model is analyzed across multiple samples and constraints are imposed on certain parameter estimates. The most common strategy is to fix the factor means to zero in one of the samples. This constraint establishes that sample as a reference sample. The factor means in the other samples are freely estimated, and their values estimate the relative differences on the factor means compared with the reference sample. Additional constraints may also include cross-group equality constraints on the factor loadings and intercepts, which together test for invariance in measurement and in regressions of the indicators on the factors. This strategy is discussed in more detail in Chapter 11.

10.5 LATENT GROWTH MODELS

The term **latent growth model** (LGM) refers to a class of models for longitudinal data that can be analyzed in SEM or other statistical techniques, such as **hierarchical linear modeling** (HLM) (e.g., Raudenbush & Bryk, 2002). It may be the most common type of structural equation model with a mean structure evaluated in a single sample. The particular kind of LGM outlined below has been described by several different authors (e.g., T. E. Duncan, S. C. Duncan, Strycker, Li, & Alpert, 1999), is specified as an SR model with a mean structure, and can be analyzed with standard SEM software. The analysis of an LGM in SEM typically requires (1) a continuous dependent variable measured on at least three different occasions; (2) scores that have the same units across time, can be said to measure the same construct at each assessment, and are not standardized; and (3) data that are **time structured**, which means that cases are all tested at the same intervals. These intervals need not be equal. For example, a sample of children may be

TABLE 10.4. Maximum Likelihood Parameter Estimates for a Measurement Model with a Mean Structure for Perceived Line Length

Parameter	Unstandard-ized	SE	Standard-ized	Parameter	Unstandard-ized	SE	Standard-ized
			Covariance structure				
	Factor loadings				Variances		
Length → J1	1.458	.135	.992	E_1	.035	.010	.016
Length → J2	1.159	.113	.968	E_2	.091	.018	.064
Length → J3	1.994	.189	.980	E_3	.161	.034	.039
Length → J4	1.207	.112	.993	E_4	.020	.006	.014
Length → J5	1.065	.101	.980	E_5	.047	.010	.040
				Length	1.000[a]	—	1.000
			Mean structure				
	Intercepts				Means		
△ → J1	2.661	.190	0	△ → Length	0[a]	—	0
△ → J2	2.230	.155	0				
△ → J3	3.427	.263	0				
△ → J4	2.097	.157	0				
△ → J5	1.918	.140	0				

[a]Not tested for statistical significance; $p < .01$ for all other unstandardized estimates.

observed at 3, 6, 12, and 24 months of age. If some children are tested at, say, 4, 10, 15, and 30 months, their data cannot be analyzed together with those tested at the other intervals. (This is one advantage of HLM over SEM in the analysis of an LGM: it does not require time-structured data.)

The raw scores are *not* required to analyze an LGM. As with other applications of SEM, latent growth models can be analyzed with matrix summaries of the data. However, these matrix summaries must include the covariances (or correlations and standard deviations) and means of all variables, even of those that are not repeated measures variables. Willett and Sayer (1994) make the point, though, that inspection of the raw scores for each case—what they call the **empirical growth record**—can help to determine whether it may be necessary to include nonlinear growth terms in the model. This point is elaborated later.

Latent growth models can also be described as a special type of multilevel model for **hierarchical data**, in this case for panel data where individuals are observed over time and repeated measures are nested within each individual (Hser, Chou, Messer, & Anglin, 2001). Scores from the same case are probably not independent, and this lack of independence should be taken into account in the statistical analysis. Other kinds of hierarchical data structures arise when individuals are clustered into larger units, such as students within classrooms or siblings within families. Data within each level are probably not independent. For instance, students in the same classroom are probably all affected by the same teacher. Multilevel structural equation models other than latent growth models are considered in Chapter 13.

An Empirical Example

The data for this example are from S. C. Duncan and T. E. Duncan (1996), who conducted a longitudinal study of alcohol use among adolescents. A sample of 321 adolescents was surveyed annually over a 4-year period. Scores on the alcohol use variable ranged from 1 to 5, where a score of 1 indicates no use and higher scores indicate increasing frequencies of monthly use. The means, standard deviations, and correlations for annual reports of alcohol use are reported in Table 10.5. The year-to-year increases in mean levels of drinking are quite

TABLE 10.5. Input Data (Correlations, Standard Deviations, Means) for Latent Growth Models of Change in Alcohol Use over 4 Years

Variable	1	2	3	4	5	6
Alcohol use						
1. Year 1	1.000					
2. Year 2	.640	1.000				
3. Year 3	.586	.670	1.000			
4. Year 4	.454	.566	.621	1.000		
Predictors						
5. Gender	.001	.038	.118	.091	1.000	
6. Family Status	−.214	−.149	−.135	−.163	−.025	1.000
M	2.271	2.560	2.694	2.965	.573	.554
SD	1.002	.960	.912	.920	.504	.498

Note. These data are from S. C. Duncan and T. E. Duncan (1996); $N = 321$.

consistent (2.271, 2.560, 2.694, 2.965), which suggests a positive linear trend. Also reported in Table 10.5 are descriptive statistics for gender (coded 0 = male, 1 = female) and family status (coded 0 = single-parent family, 1 = two-parent family). The means of these variables are, respectively, the proportion of cases who are female (.573) or live with both parents (.554). These variables are analyzed later as potential predictors of change in alcohol use.

Modeling Change

Latent growth models are often analyzed in two steps. The first step involves the analysis of a change model that involves just the repeated measures variables. As the name suggests, a change model attempts to explain the covariances and means of these variables. Given an acceptable change model, the second step adds variables to the model that may predict change over time. This two-step approach makes it easier to identify potential sources of poor model fit compared with the analysis of a prediction model in a single step.

A basic model of change in alcohol use is presented in Figure 10.3. It has four essential characteristics:

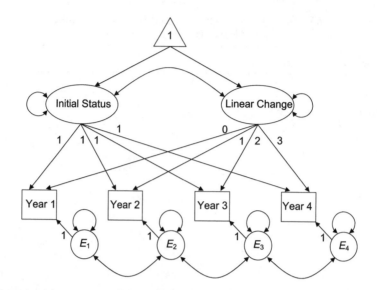

FIGURE 10.3. Latent growth model of change in level of alcohol use over 4 years.

First, each annual measurement is represented as an indicator of two latent growth factors, Initial Status (IS) and Linear Change (LC). The IS factor represents the baseline level of alcohol use. Because the IS factor is analogous to the intercept in a regression equation, the unstandardized loadings of all indicators on this factor are fixed to 1.0. In contrast, loadings on the LC factor are fixed to constants that correspond to the times of measurement, beginning with 0 for the first measurement and ending with 3 for the last. Because these constants (0, 1, 2, 3) are positive and evenly spaced, they specify a positive linear trend. Also, the specification that the loading of the Year 1 measurement on the LC factor equals 0 sets the initial level at this time. This means that the IS factor will be defined based on the Year 1 measurement. The initial level can be set to other times besides the first measurement. Suppose that the loadings for the LC factor were specified as (–1,0, 1,2). This set of loadings still defines a linear trend because the intervals are evenly spaced, but the initial level is now based on the second measurement, at Year 2. In general, the point in time at which the initial level is set is arbitrary as long as the loadings on the LC factor are consistently specified. However, where this initial level is set may affect the estimates of the factor covariance and means, which are discussed next. In general, it is probably simpler just to specify that the initial level corresponds to the first measurement.

Second, the IS and LC factors are specified to covary (IS ↻ LC). The estimate of this covariance indicates the degree to which initial levels of drinking predict rates of subsequent linear change, given the definition of the initial level. A positive estimated covariance would indicate that adolescents with higher initial levels of alcohol use at Year 1 show greater rates of linear increase over time, and a negative estimated covariance would indicate just the opposite.

Third, the LGM of Figure 10.3 has a mean structure in which the constant has direct effects on the exogenous IS and LC factors. This specification includes the means of these factors as free model parameters. The mean of the IS factor is the average initial level of reported alcohol use, adjusted for measurement error. This average is a characteristic of the whole sample. In contrast, the variance of the IS factor reflects the range of individual differences around the average initial level. Likewise, the mean of the LC factor reflects the average amount of year-to-year linear increase in average levels of drinking, also adjusted for measurement error. The variance of the LC factor provides information about the range of individual differences in the rate of linear annual increases in alcohol use over time.

The fourth key characteristic of the model in Figure 10.3 is that the measurement errors of adjacent years are assumed to covary (e.g., E_1 ↻ E_2). Other patterns are also possible, including no error covariances (i.e., the errors are independent over time) or the specification of additional error covariances (e.g., E_1 ↻ E_3). The capability to explicitly model measurement error is a potential advantage of SEM over other, more traditional methods for repeated measures data. For example, ANOVA assumes that the error variances of repeated measures variables are equal and independent. Data from repeated measures variables often violate both of these requirements. Another limitation is that the only way to analyze a continuous predictor of a repeated measures variable in ANOVA is to categorize it (e.g., split cases into two groups at the median), which implies the loss of numerical information (e.g., see MacCallum, Zhang, Preacher, & Rucker,

2002). Multiple regression can accommodate continuous or categorical predictors, but it shares with ANOVA the same restrictive assumptions about error variance. The technique of MANOVA (multivariate ANOVA) can also be applied to repeated measures data. Although assumptions about error variance are less restrictive in MANOVA (e.g., errors may covary; Cole, Maxwell, Avery, & Salas, 1993), MANOVA shares with ANOVA a crucial limitation: both techniques analyze changes only in observed group means and consequently treat differences among individual cases in their growth trajectories as error variance. In contrast, one of the aims of the analysis of an LGM in SEM is to explicitly estimate the range of individual differences in change over time (i.e., it is not treated as error variance).

It is no special problem to specify a linear trend if the measurement occasions are not evenly spaced. For example, Murphy, Chung, and Johnson (2002) measured levels of distress among parents at 4, 12, 24, and 60 months following the violent death of a child. Because the level of distress is expected to decline over time, the trend direction is negative. In latent growth models analyzed by Murphy et al., the loading for the initial assessment at 4 months on a linear change factor was fixed to 0 and the loading for the 12-months measurement (conducted 8 months later) was fixed to –1. Because the period of 8 months equals –1 in the slope metric, the loading of the 24-months measurement—which took place 20 months after the initial assessment—was fixed to –20/8, or –2.5. By the same logic, the loading of the 60-months measurement was fixed to –7 because it took place 56 months after the initial measurement, and –56/8 = –7. The set of loadings for the linear change factor analyzed by Murphy et al. (2002) is thus (0, –1, –2.5, –7).

It is also possible to estimate nonlinear trends in the analysis of an LGM. For example, a quadratic latent growth factor could be added to the model of Figure 10.3 by specifying that (1) the loadings of the repeated measures indicators on this factor equal the square of the corresponding loadings on the LC factor (i.e., 0, 1, 4, 9) and (2) the quadratic change factor is included in the mean structure and covaries with the IS and LC factors. However, the improvement in model fit due to adding a quadratic growth factor to the model should be appreciable; otherwise, the more parsimonious model (e.g., the one with just the IS and LC factors) would be preferred. Also, it is rarely necessary to estimate nonlinear trends higher than a quadratic one for most behavioral data.

The change model of Figure 10.3 has 12 parameters. These include 6 variances (of 2 factors and 4 measurement errors), 4 covariances (1 between the factors and 3 between measurement errors for adjacent years), and 2 factor means (i.e., the direct effects $\triangle \rightarrow \text{IS}$ and $\triangle \rightarrow \text{LC}$). With four observed variables (alcohol use over 4 years), there are $4(7)/2 = 14$ observations (10 variances and covariances, 4 means) available to estimate the model, so $df_M = 2$. The change model was fitted to the correlations, standard deviations, and means in Table 10.5 with the ML method of Mplus. The analysis converged to an admissible solution. Values of selected fit indexes are $\chi^2_M (2) = 4.877$, $p = .086$, NC = 2.439, CFI = .995, SRMR = .019, and RMSEA = .067 with the 90% confidence interval 0–.145. The last of these results is not favorable because the upper bound of the confidence interval based on RMSEA is so high (.145) that the hypothesis of close approximate fit in the population seems doubtful. In addition, inspection of the solution indicates that the estimated error covariances are generally about zero.

Based on these results, the change model was respecified so that all error covariances were trimmed (i.e., fixed to zero). Values of selected fit indexes for the respecified change model generally suggest better overall fit compared with the original model: $\chi^2_M (5) = 8.155$, $p = .148$, NC = 1.631, CFI = .994, SRMR = .033, and RMSEA = .044 with the 90% confidence interval 0–.097. The upper bound of the confidence interval based on the RMSEA (.097) is somewhat high, but absolute correlation residuals for the covariance structure of the respecified model were all less than about .05. Based on these results, the overall fit of the respecified change model is deemed to be at least acceptable. Thus, the final model of change in level of reported alcohol use over 4 years is identical to the original model in Figure 10.3 except there are no measurement error correlations.

The ML parameter estimates for the final change model are reported in Table 10.6. The direct effects of the constant on the latent growth factors are means. The estimated mean of the IS factor is 2.291, which is close to the observed average level of alcohol use at Year 1 (2.271; see Table 10.5). The two values are not identical because the

TABLE 10.6. Maximum Likelihood Parameter Estimates for the Final Latent Growth Model of Change in Alcohol Use over 4 Years

Parameter	Unstandardized	SE	Standardized
	Mean structure		
Latent growth factor means			
$\triangle \to$ IS	2.291	.054	0
$\triangle \to$ LC	.220	.018	0
	Covariance structure		
Variances and covariance			
Latent growth factors			
IS	.699	.077	1.000
LC	.038	.010	1.000
IS $\cup$ LC	−.080	.023	−.489
Measurement errors			
E_1	.342	.051	.328
E_2	.306	.033	.346
E_3	.273	.030	.339
E_4	.309	.046	.354

Note. $p < .01$ for all unstandardized estimates. Standardized estimates for measurement errors are proportions of unexplained variance. IS, Initial Status; LC, Linear Change.

former is adjusted for measurement error. The estimated mean of the LC factor is .220, which indicates the average annual increase in drinking, also adjusted for measurement error. The estimated variances of the LC and IS factors are, respectively, .699 and .038, and each is statistically significant at the .01 level. These results suggest that the adolescents are not homogeneous in either their initial levels of drinking at Year 1 or the slopes of subsequent linear increases in drinking. (The degree to which individual differences in these areas can be predicted by gender and family status is considered later.) The estimated covariance between the latent growth factors is −.080, and the corresponding estimated factor correlation is −.489. These results indicate that higher initial levels of alcohol use predict *lower* subsequent rates of linear annual increases (and vice versa). Other results reported in Table 10.6 concern measurement errors. In general, the final change model explains about 60% of the observed variance in alcohol use across the 4 years.

The indicator means are not model parameters. However, the unstandardized total effects of the constant on the indicators are predicted means that can be compared with the observed means. For example, application of the tracing rule shows that the total effect of the constant on the first measurement of alcohol use is the sum of the indirect effects through the IS factor ($\triangle \rightarrow$ IS, IS $\rightarrow$ Year 1) and through the LC factor ($\triangle \rightarrow$ LC, LC $\rightarrow$ Year 1); see Figure 10.3. Using results from Table 10.6, this total effect is estimated as follows:

$$\text{total effect of } \triangle \text{ on Year 1} = 2.291\ (1) + .220\ (0) = 2.291$$

The observed mean for Year 1 is 2.271 (see Table 10.5), so the mean residual is $2.271 - 2.291 = -.020$; that is, the predicted mean is quite close to the observed mean for Year 1. The other predicted means for alcohol use for Years 2, 3, and 4 are, respectively, 2.512, 2.732, and 2.953. (Readers should verify these results using the tracing rule.) Each of these predicted means is very similar to the corresponding observed means for Years 2, 3, and 4 (see Table 10.5). The final change model thus closely reproduces both the observed covariances and means.

Predicting Change

With an adequate model of change in levels of alcohol use now in hand, a model that predicts this change can be analyzed. Potential predictors of change are added to a basic change model by including them in the mean structure and by regressing the latent growth factors on the predictors. Consider the LGM for predicting change in alcohol use over a 4-year period that is presented in Figure 10.4. Note that the constant has direct effects on the predictors, gender and family status, which are presumed to covary. Each predictor is specified to have direct effects on both latent growth factors, IS and LC. This makes these factors endogenous, so now each has a disturbance. These disturbances are specified as correlated, which reflects the assumption that initial level and linear

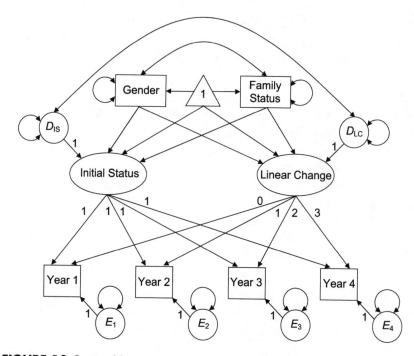

FIGURE 10.4. Final latent growth model of prediction of change in alcohol use over 4 years.

change in drinking share omitted causes besides gender and family status. The rest of the prediction model of Figure 10.4 is identical to the final change model analyzed earlier. The prediction model is also a MIMIC (multiple indicators and multiple causes) model because the factors have both effect and cause indicators.

With 6 observed variables, there are a total of 6(9)/2 = 27 observations available to estimate the 16 parameters of the prediction model in Figure 10.4. These include 8 variances (of 2 observed exogenous variables [the predictors], 2 factor disturbances, and 4 measurement errors), 2 covariances (1 between the predictors and another between the disturbances), 4 direct effects on the latent growth factors from the predictors (2 from each predictor), and 4 direct effects of the constant. The last 4 effects include the means of the predictors ($\triangle \rightarrow$ Gender, $\triangle \rightarrow$ Family Status) and the intercepts of the latent growth factors ($\triangle \rightarrow$ IS, $\triangle \rightarrow$ LC). The prediction model was fitted to the data summarized in Table 10.5 with

Mplus. Listed in Appendix 10.A is the Mplus syntax for this analysis. Note for this syntax that Mplus automatically estimates the variances, covariances, and means of observed exogenous variables as the sample values. Estimation in Mplus converged to an admissible solution, and values of selected fit indexes generally indicate adequate fit: $\chi^2_M (9) = 13.823$, $p = .129$, NC = 2.091, CFI = .992, SRMR = .027, and RMSEA = .041 with the 90% confidence interval 0–.081.

The ML parameter estimates for the prediction model are reported in Table 10.7. The results in the top part of the table concern the mean

TABLE 10.7. Maximum Likelihood Parameter Estimates for a Latent Growth Model of Prediction of Change in Alcohol Use over 4 Years

Parameter	Unstandardized	SE	Standardized	Parameter	Unstandardized	SE	Standardized
				Mean structure			
Predictor means				Latent growth factor intercepts			
$\triangle \rightarrow$ Gender	.573	.028	0	$\triangle \rightarrow$ IS	2.493	.100	0
$\triangle \rightarrow$ Family	.554	.028	0	$\triangle \rightarrow$ LC	.159	.034	0
				Covariance structure			
Direct effects				Disturbance variances and covariance			
Gender $\rightarrow$ IS	.011[a]	.105	.007	D_{IS}	.666	.074	.950
Family $\rightarrow$ IS	−.377	.106	−.224	D_{LC}	.037	.101	.961
Gender $\rightarrow$ LC	.065[a]	.035	.166	$D_{IS} \cup D_{LC}$	−.077	.022	−.469
Family $\rightarrow$ LC	.044[a]	.036	.122				
Predictor variances and covariance[b]				Measurement error variances			
Gender	.253	.020	1.000	E_1	.333	.050	.322
Family	.247	.020	1.000	E_2	.310	.033	.349
Gender $\cup$ Family	−.006[a]	.014	−.025	E_3	.273	.029	.339
				E_4	.312	.046	.357

Note. Standardized estimates for disturbances and measurement errors are proportions of unexplained variance. IS, Initial Status, LC; Linear Change.
[a]$p > .05$. For all other unstandardized estimates, $p < .01$.
[b]These results are just the observed values.

structure. The unstandardized direct effects of the constant on the predictors, gender (.573) and family status (.554), equal the observed means of each exogenous variable (see Table 10.5). In contrast, unstandardized direct effects of the constant on the endogenous latent growth factors, IS (2.493) and LC (.159), are intercepts. It is the total effects of the constant on IS and LC that are estimated factor means. They can be derived using the tracing rule as the sum of the direct effect of the constant (e.g., $\triangle \rightarrow$ IS) and the indirect effects through both predictors (e.g., $\triangle \rightarrow$ Gender $\rightarrow$ IS, $\triangle \rightarrow$ Family Status $\rightarrow$ IS). Using results from the top part of Table 10.7, the means of the latent growth factors are estimated as follows:

$$\text{IS factor mean} = 2.493 + .573\,(.011) - .554\,(.377) = 2.290$$
$$\text{LC factor mean} = .159 + .573\,(.065) + .554\,(.044) = .221$$

These values are very similar to those for the final change model (see Table 10.6), and they are interpreted the same way, too.

Parameter estimates reported in the lower part of Table 10.7 concern the covariance structure of the prediction model in Figure 10.4. The only unstandardized coefficient for a direct effect on the latent growth factors that is statistically significant at the .01 level is that for the path Family Status $\rightarrow$ IS. This unstandardized coefficient equals −.377, and the corresponding standardized coefficient equals −.224. Thus, adolescents with higher scores on the family status variable have lower initial levels of alcohol use, when we adjust for measurement error. Because this variable is coded 0 = single-parent family and 1 = two-parent family, we can say that adolescents who live with both parents have lower initials of drinking than their peers who live with only one parent. The unstandardized coefficient for the path Gender $\rightarrow$ LC (.065) is not statistically significant at the .05 level, but the standardized estimate for this path (.166) is nearly as large in absolute value as that for the path Family Status $\rightarrow$ IS; thus, it should not be ignored. Because gender is coded 0 = male and 1 = female, this result indicates that the rates of linear increase in alcohol use over time were generally greater for female than for male adolescents.

Standardized estimates for the disturbance variances of the latent growth factors expressed as proportions of unexplained variance indicate that the prediction model accounts for about 1 − .950 = .05, or 5% of the variance of the IS factor, and about 1 − .961 = .039, or 3.9% of the variance of the LC factor (see Table 10.7). The estimated disturbance correlation is negative (–.469), which indicates that higher initial levels of alcohol use are associated with lower rates of linear increases in alcohol use over time through their common omitted causes. This result parallels a similar one for the final change model described earlier (see Table 10.6).

The predicted means on the alcohol use indicators calculated by Mplus for Years 1, 2, 3, and 4 are, respectively, 2.291, 2.511, 2.732, and 2.953. These values are very similar to the corresponding observed means (see Table 10.5). Values of the predicted means just listed can also be calculated by hand with the tracing rule, but doing so is more difficult for the prediction model of Figure 10.4 than for the final change model. This is because the total effect of the constant on each indicator in the prediction model is made up of six different indirect effects through the predictors (gender, family status) and both latent growth factors. Fortunately, many SEM programs that analyze means can automatically calculate predicted indicator means.

10.6 EXTENSIONS

The basic framework for univariate growth curve modeling in a single sample just discussed can be extended in many ways. For example, the predictors in the empirical example (gender, family status) are **time-invariant predictors** in that they were measured only once. It is also possible to include in an LGM **time-varying predictors** that are themselves repeated measures variables, typically measured at the same intervals as the indicators of the latent growth factors (e.g., Kaplan, 2000, pp. 155–159). The predictors in the empirical example were each represented as error-free single indicators (e.g., see Figure 10.4). Given a priori estimates of the proportions of error variance for observed predictors in an LGM, one could use the method described in section 8.5 to take account of measurement error in single indicators. Another way to control for measurement error is to use multiple indicators of an exogenous factor specified to predict the latent growth factors; that is, the prediction part of an LGM can be fully latent (e.g., Chan, 1998).

It may also be possible within the limits of identification to specify that some loadings on a latent growth factor that does not represent initial status are free parameters. One strategy to do so in the empirical example would be to fix the loading of the Year 1 report of alcohol use on a second latent growth factor to zero to set this measurement as the initial level, fix the loading of the Year 2 report to 1.0 to scale the factor, and let the remaining two loadings be freely estimated. This tactic results in what could be seen as an empirical developmental function that optimally fits the change factor to the data in a particular sample. Ratios of freely estimated loadings on the change factor can also be formed to compare rates of development at different points in time. For instance, if the relative increases in the freely estimated loadings on the change factor are not constant over time, the overall pattern of change may be curvilinear rather than linear.

It is possible to analyze multivariate latent growth models of change across two or more domains for the same sample. For example, Curran, Harford, and B. Muthén (1996) analyzed data from an annual survey of young adults about their frequencies of heavy drinking and bar patronage over a 3-year period. Curran et al. evaluated models of **cross-domain change** in which the latent initial status and linear change factors for heavy drinking and bar patronage were allowed to covary across these domains. The results suggested that changes in heavy drinking over time were highly correlated with changes in bar patronage. Furthermore, initial levels in each of these domains were negatively associated with change in the other domain. For example, young adults who were initially heavier drinkers tended to visit bars less often over time, but the bar patronage of those with initially lower levels of drinking tended to increase.

Like just about any other kind of structural equation model, an LGM can also be analyzed across multiple samples. Next, Chapter 11 introduces principles of multiple-sample SEM, so only a brief example is described here. Willett and Sayer (1996) analyzed a cross-domain model of change in reading and arithmetic skills at three ages (7, 11, and 16 years) across samples of children who differed in health status (healthy, chronic asthma, seizure disorder). They found that healthy children and those with chronic asthma had generally similar growth curves for reading and arithmetic skills. However, children with seizure disorders showed generally declining trajectories over time, a result that could be due to side effects of anticonvulsant medication. Other results indicated that children with better reading skills at age 7 tended to progress more rapidly in mathematics but children who were initially stronger in arithmetic showed relatively lower rates of subsequent increase in their reading skills.

10.7 SUMMARY

Means are estimated in SEM by regressing exogenous or endogenous variables on a constant that equals 1.0. It is usually not necessary to manually create a constant because most full-featured SEM computer programs automatically do so when means are analyzed. The parameters of a mean structure include the means of the exogenous variables and the intercepts of the endogenous variables. Although means of endogenous variables are not generally considered model parameters, predicted means on these variables, calculated as total effects of the constant, can be compared with the observed values. In order to be identified, the number of parameters in a mean structure cannot exceed the number of observed means. The type of latent growth model for longitudinal data described in this chapter is a basically an SR model with a mean structure. Each repeated measures variable is specified as an indicator of at least two different factors—one representing the initial status and the other, the rate of change. These factors are usually assumed to covary, which allows for the possibility that this rate of change is related to the initial status. Latent growth models should be evaluated in two steps: the first evaluates a change model that involves just the repeated measures variables; the second involves adding predictors to the model. This is done by regressing the latent growth factors on the predictors, and the results indicate the degree to which variability in the initial status or the rate of change can be explained by the predictors. There are many other statistical methods for longitudinal data, but few offer the flexibility of SEM.

10.8 RECOMMENDED READINGS

Duncan, T. E., Duncan, S. C., Strycker, L. A., Li, F., & Alpert, A. (1999). *An introduction to latent variable growth modeling: Concepts, issues, and applications*. Mahwah, NJ: Erlbaum.

Hser, Y.-I., Chou, C.-P., Messer, S. C., & Anglin, M. D. (2001). Analytic approaches for assessing long-term treatment effects: Examples of empirical applications and findings. *Evaluation Review, 25*, 233–262.

Appendix 10.A

Mplus Syntax

```
TITLE: Figure 10.4
DATA: File is Duncan.dat;
   Type is correlation means stdeviations;
   Nobservations = 321;
   Variable: Names are YEAR1 YEAR2 YEAR3 YEAR4 GENDER
      FAM_STAT;
MODEL: Initial Linear | YEAR1@0 YEAR2@1 YEAR3@2 YEAR4@3;
       Initial Linear ON GENDER FAM_STAT;
OUTPUT: sampstat residual standardized;
```

Multiple-Sample SEM

The ability to analyze a structural equation model across multiple samples extends even further the range of hypotheses that can be tested in SEM. Considered next is multiple-sample path analysis (PA), which involves the estimation of a structural model of observed variables across two or more samples. Much of the rest of this chapter concerns the analysis across multiple samples of models where some latent variables represent hypothetical constructs, such as confirmatory factor analysis (CFA) models. These models may or may not have mean structures in addition to their basic covariance structures. Also considered in this chapter is the specification and analysis of MIMIC (multiple indicators and multiple causes) models where the cause indicators are categorical variables that represent group membership as an alternative way to estimate group differences on latent variables.

11.1 RATIONALE OF MULTIPLE-SAMPLE SEM

The main question addressed in a multiple-sample SEM is this: do values of model parameters vary across groups? Another way of expressing this question is in terms of an interaction effect; that is, does group membership moderate the relations specified in the model? Perhaps the simplest way to address these questions is to estimate the same model within each of two or more different samples and then compare the unstandardized solutions across the samples. Recall that unstandardized instead of standardized estimates should generally be compared when the groups differ in their variabilities. For the same reason, covariance matrices (or the raw scores) for each group should be analyzed when the model has only a covariance structure, and covariance matrices and means (or the raw scores) should be analyzed when the model has both a covariance structure and a mean structure. If the unstandardized estimates for the same parameter are appreciably different, then the populations from which the groups were sampled may not be equal on that parameter.

More sophisticated comparisons are available by using an SEM computer program that performs a multiple-sample analysis which simultaneously estimates a model across all samples. Through the specification of **cross-group equality constraints**, group differences on any individual parameter or set of parameters can be tested. A cross-group equality constraint forces the computer to derive equal unstandardized estimates of that parameter within all samples. The fit of the constrained model can then be compared with that of the unrestricted model without the equality constraints with the chi-square difference (χ_D^2) statistic. If the fit of the constrained model is much worse than that of the unconstrained model, we can conclude that the parameters may not be equal in the populations from which the samples were drawn. (This assumes that the unconstrained model fits the data reasonably well.) However, do not forget that estimates constrained to be equal in the unstandardized solution will typically be unequal in the standardized solution if the groups have different variabilities. In general, standardized estimates should be directly compared only across different variables within each sample.

11.2 MULTIPLE-SAMPLE PATH ANALYSIS

The basic rationale of a multiple-sample PA is the same whether the model is recursive or nonrecursive. A multiple-sample PA is demonstrated for a recursive model of delinquency by Lynam et al. (1993). Within samples of African American ($n_1 = 214$) and white ($n_2 = 181$) male adolescents, Lynam and colleagues administered measures of family social class and adolescent motivation, verbal ability, scholastic achievement, and delinquency. These data for each sample are summarized in Table 11.1. Note that although means for each group are reported in the table, they are not analyzed here.

TABLE 11.1. Input Data (Correlations, Standard Deviations) for Analysis of a Path Model of Delinquency across Samples of African American and White Male Adolescents

						African American	
Variable	1	2	3	4	5	M	SD
1. Social Class	—	.08	.28	.05	–.11	31.96	10.58
2. Motivation	.25	—	.30	.21	–.17	–.01	1.35
3. Verbal Ability	.37	.40	—	.50	–.26	93.76	13.62
4. Achievement	.27	.28	.61	—	–.33	2.51	.79
5. Delinquency	–.11	–.20	–.31	–.21	—	1.40	1.63
White M	34.64	.05	104.18	2.88	1.22		
SD	11.53	1.32	16.32	.96	1.45		

Note. These data are from Lynam et al. (1993); n_1 = 214 African Americans (above the diagonal), n_2 = 181 whites (below the diagonal). Means are reported but not analyzed.

Lynam et al. (1993) conceptualized social class, verbal ability, and motivation as exogenous variables that directly affect delinquency. They also hypothesized that scholastic achievement is directly affected by the same three variables and that achievement in turn affects delinquency. For example, adolescents with poor verbal ability may be more likely to drop out of school, which may contribute to delinquency because of reduced employment prospects or more unsupervised time on the streets. (The rationale for this directionality specification was discussed in section 5.2.) The path model specified by Lynam et al. is presented in Figure 11.1. Because this path model is just-identified, it would fit perfectly fit the data in each group if analyzed without constraints. With the imposition of cross-group equality constraints on the model's seven direct effects, however, this may no longer be true. In this analysis, the total number of observations is the sum across both groups; with 5 observed variables, there are 5(6)/2 = 15 observations in each group and 30 altogether. The total number of parameters of this just-identified model evaluated across both groups is similarly calculated (15 × 2 = 30), but 7—the path coefficients—are constrained to be equal. Thus, the total number of free parameters is actually 23, so df_M = 7.

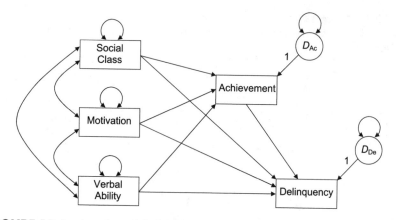

FIGURE 11.1. A path model of delinquency evaluated across samples of African American and white male adolescents.

The model of Figure 11.1 was simultaneously fitted to two covariance matrices each assembled from the correlations and standard deviations for the African American and white samples in Table 11.1 with EQS 6 (Bentler, 2003). The analysis with maximum likelihood (ML) estimation converged to an admissible solution. Values of selected fit indexes for the model with the unstandardized direct effects constrained to be equal across the groups are $\chi^2_M (7) = 11.676$, $p = .112$, NC $= 1.668$, CFI $= .983$, SRMR $= .041$, and RMSEA $= .041$ with the 90% confidence interval 0–.081. These results do not seem to suggest poor model fit. However, the absolute correlation residuals for the association between achievement and delinquency are about .10 in both the African American and white samples, so the model with equality-constrained direct effects does not seem to explain this correlation very well in either group.

Presented in Table 11.2 are the ML parameter estimates for the constrained path model. To save space, the variances and covariances of the observed exogenous variables are not reported because these values are just the observed ones in each sample (see Table 11.1). Reported in the top part of Table 11.2 are estimates for parameters that were not constrained to be equal across the groups. These estimates are for the disturbance variances, and they indicate that the model of Figure 11.1 has somewhat greater predictive power for white than for Afri-

TABLE 11.2. Maximum Likelihood Parameter Estimates and Modification Indexes for Analysis of a Path Model of Delinquency across Samples of African American and White Adolescents

Parameter	African American Unstandard-ized	SE	Standard-ized	White Unstandard-ized	SE	Standard-ized	Modification index $\chi^2(1)$
	Unconstrained estimates						
Disturbance variances							
D_{Ac}	.465**	.045	.702	.583**	.061	.674	—
D_{De}	2.354**	.228	.921	1.915**	.202	.873	—
	Equality-constrained estimates						
Direct effects							
Soc Cls → Ach	−.002	.003	−.031	−.002	.003	−.030	3.803[a]
Motiv → Ach	.037	.029	.062	.037	.029	.053	.182
Verbal → Ach	.032	.003	.532	.032	.003	.558	1.985
Soc Cls → Del	−.002	.007	−.013	−.002	.007	−.015	.882
Motiv → Del	−.101	.059	−.085	−.101	.059	−.090	.144
Verbal → Ach	−.017**	.006	−.144	−.017**	.006	−.186	.324
Ach → Del	−.255*	.102	−.130	−.255*	.102	−.160	5.453*

Note. Standardized estimates for disturbances are proportions of unexplained variance.
[a]$p = .051$; *$p < .05$; **$p < .01$.

can American male adolescents. For example, the proportions of explained variance for the endogenous achievement and delinquency variables in the African American sample are, respectively, .298 and .079, and the corresponding values in the white sample are, respectively, .326 and .127. Reported in the bottom part of Table 11.2 are results for the equality-constrained direct effects on achievement and delinquency. As expected, only the unstandardized path coefficients are equal across the groups. For example, the unstandardized coefficient for the path Verbal Ability → Achievement for both samples is .032. The standardized estimates for the same path are different in each sample, though: it is .532 in the African American sample and .558 in the white sample. The standardized estimates for the equality-constrained direct effects are unequal because the samples are not equally variable on these variables (see Table 11.1).

Reported in the bottom part of Table 11.2 are values of modification indexes (i.e., univariate Lagrange Multipliers) for each equality-constrained direct effect. One of these indexes, $\chi^2(1) = 5.453$ for the path Achievement $\rightarrow$ Delinquency, is statistically significant at the .05 level; another index, $\chi^2(1) = 3.803$ for the path Social Class $\rightarrow$ Achievement, is close ($p = .051$). To investigate group differences further, the path model of Figure 11.1 was reanalyzed without equality constraints on these two direct effects. Values of selected indexes for this respecified model suggested reasonable overall model fit: $\chi^2_M(5) = 2.254$, $p = .813$, NC = .451, CFI = 1.000, SRMR = .018, RMSEA = 0 with the 90% confidence interval 0–.043, and all absolute correlation residuals were less than .05 in both samples. In the African American sample, the unstandardized coefficient for the direct effect of achievement on delinquency is –.493 ($p < .01$). In the white sample, however, the unstandardized coefficient for the same direct effect is only –.087 ($p > .05$). Also, the signs of the unstandardized path coefficients for the direct effect of social class on achievement were different across the samples (African American, .005; white, –.105), but neither coefficient is statistically significant at the .05 level. Lynam and colleagues (1993) interpreted similar results in their analyses as indicating that school may have a larger role in the development of delinquency for African American than for white male adolescents.

Although only coefficients for the direct effects were constrained in this example, it is theoretically possible to impose additional constraints on other parameters. For example, constraining the disturbance variances to be equal provides a test of whether the model has comparable explanatory power across the groups; equality constraints on the variances of the observed exogenous variables provide tests of group differences in variabilities. Some of these constraints may be implausible, though, such as the expectation of equal group variances on the observed exogenous variables. Unless specific hypotheses demand otherwise, it is usually only the coefficients for the direct effects that are constrained to be equal across the groups in multiple-sample PA.

11.3 MULTIPLE-SAMPLE CFA

How to analyze a CFA measurement model across two or more samples is discussed next.

Measurement Models without Mean Structures

Considered first is the evaluation of a CFA measurement model without a mean structure (i.e., means are not analyzed) across multiple samples. The main question of a multiple-sample CFA concerns **measurement invariance**, which is whether a set of indicators assesses the same constructs in different groups. A related concept in the psychometric literature is that of **construct bias**, which implies that a test measures something different in one group than in another. If so, then group membership moderates the relation between the indicators and factors specified in the measurement model. The evaluation of measurement invariance with CFA typically involves the comparison of the relative fits with the χ_D^2 statistic of two-factor models, one with cross-group equality constraints imposed on some of its parameters and the other without constraints. A common practice is to constrain the unstandardized factor loadings to be equal across the samples. If the fit of a CFA model with equality-constrained loadings is not appreciably worse than that of the unconstrained model, then the indicators may measure the factors in comparable ways in each group. This assumes that the unconstrained model fits reasonably well across all samples; otherwise, it makes little sense to test additional constraints. This is the same principle for using the χ_D^2 statistic to compare two hierarchical models in a single sample: the least restrictive model should have reasonably good fit (see section 6.3).

If the fit of the constrained model is considerably worse, however, then individual unstandardized factor loadings should be compared across the samples to determine the extent of **partial measurement invariance**; that is, some factor loadings may vary appreciably across groups, but the values of others do not. Although it is theoretically possible to do so, cross-group equality constraints are usually not also imposed on estimates of variances or covariances. This is because groups may be expected to differ in their variabilities on either the common factors (i.e., those that represent constructs) or unique factors (i.e., the measurement errors) even if the indicators measure the common factors in comparable ways for all groups (MacCallum & Tucker, 1991).

As in a single-sample CFA, the factors must be assigned a scale in order for the model to be identified, but there are some special considerations in a multiple-sample CFA. It is generally inappropriate to scale the factors by standardizing them—that is, by fixing their variances to 1.0 by imposing a unit variance identification (UVI) constraint—in all samples. This specification assumes that the groups are equally variable on the factors. If group variances on the underlying factors are really different, then this method may lead to inaccurate results. A better way to scale the factors in a multiple-sample CFA is to fix the unstandardized loading of one indicator per factor to 1.0 by imposing a unit loading identification (ULI) constraint—that is, analyzing unstandardized factors. However, note that the loadings of the *same* indicator should be fixed to 1.0 in each sample (i.e., each factor should have the same reference variable across all groups).

Although the method just described allows the variances of the factors to be freely estimated in each sample, there are two potential complications. First, loadings fixed to 1.0 in all samples cannot be tested for group differences because they are constants, not variables. The second complication follows from the first: because fixed loadings are excluded from tests of measurement invariance, it must be assumed a priori that the associated indicator assesses the factor equally well in all groups. This means that if the researcher decides to fix the loading of an indicator that is not invariant across the groups, then the subsequent results may be inaccurate. One way to deal with this dilemma is to reanalyze the model after fixing the loading of other indicators to 1.0. If the unstandardized factor loadings that were originally fixed are comparable in new analyses in which they are free parameters, then that indicator may be measurement invariant. See Reise et al. (1993) for additional information about scaling factors in multiple-sample CFA.

Measurement Models with Mean Structures

It is also possible to analyze a CFA measurement model with a mean structure across multiple samples. This allows hypotheses about both measurement invariance and group mean differences on latent variables to be tested. The input data for this kind of analysis are presented as a covariance matrix and as means (or the raw data) for each group. Recall that a mean structure usually includes direct effects of a constant that equals 1.0 for every case (designated in diagrams in this book with the symbol $\triangle$) on the indicators or factors. Because the indicators in a CFA model are endogenous, direct effects of the constant on them are intercepts (but the total effects are means). In contrast, direct effects of the constant on the factors, which are exogenous, are means. However, also recall that it may be impossible to estimate both indicator intercepts and factor means when a CFA model with a mean structure is analyzed in a single sample. This is because the full mean structure may not be identified in this kind of analysis (section 10.4).

A two-part strategy by Sörbom (1974) to identify mean structures of CFA models analyzed across multiple samples involves the estimation of *relative* differences in factor means instead of absolute differences. The first part of this strategy is to fix the means of all factors to zero in one group, which is the same as constraining the direct effect of the constant on the factors to zero in that group. These constraints establish that group as a reference sample. The factor means are then freely estimated in the other groups, and their values are *relative* differences on the factor means. If this value is −5.00, for example, then the factor mean of the group in which this result was freely estimated is 5 points lower than that of the reference sample. When there are only two samples, it is arbitrary which group is selected as the reference sample. The choice is more critical with three or more samples because all factor mean differences are estimated relative to the same reference sample. For instance, given two treatment groups and a control group, it makes sense to specify the control group as the reference sample. Given this specification, all relative factor mean differences between each treatment condition and the control condition are estimated.

The second part of Sörbom's (1974) strategy concerns the covariance structure, which in this case is a measurement model. Specifically, in order to reasonably estimate relative group differences on either means or intercepts among the latent variables, it must be assumed that the factors are defined the same way for all samples. Scaling the factors by fixing the loading of the same indicators to 1.0 in each sample is one way to address this issue. Another is to constrain the factor loadings and intercepts of the indicators to be equal across the groups. The first of these equality constraints provides a test of measurement invariance. Factor measurement should be at least partially invariant across the groups. (Again, the unrestricted model should fit the data reasonably well before testing for measurement invariance.) At the least this means that the indicators should have the same basic factor structure and reasonably similar unstandardized factor loadings and intercepts across the groups in order to estimate relative factor mean or intercept differences. If the hypothesis of invariance does not hold for a couple of indicators, then their factor loadings or intercepts can be estimated separately within each group (i.e., release the equality constraints on those loadings). This controls for unequal direct effects of the factors on those indicators. Otherwise, it makes little sense to estimate relative factor mean or intercept differences if the indicators do not seem to measure the same basic constructs in each group. The second set of equality constraints just mentioned provides a test of whether the intercepts from the regressions of the indicators on the factors are comparable across the groups. Although not all of these equality constraints may be consistent with the data, they at least identify the mean structure of the CFA model and provide a starting point for the analysis. See R. Williams and Thomson (1986) for more information.

An Example

Sabatelli and Bartle-Haring (2003) administered to each spouse in a total of 103 married couples three indicators of family-of-origin experiences and two indicators of marital adjustment. The former were retrospective measures of the perceived quality of each spouse's relationship with his or her own father and mother and of the relationship between the parents while growing up. The latter were ratings of problems and intimacy in the marital relationship. Higher scores on all variables indicated more positive reports of family-of-origin experiences or marital adjustment. Reported in Table 11.3 are descriptive statistics for these variables for the samples of husbands and wives.

Two sets of hypotheses are tested in this analysis: Do the five indicators just described measure two factors (family-of-origin experiences and marital adjustment) in the same way for both husbands and wives? If so, are the means for husbands and wives different on the factors?

TABLE 11.3. Input Data (Correlations, Standard Deviations, Means) for Analysis of a Confirmatory Factor Analysis Model with Structured Means across Samples of Husbands and Wives

						Husbands	
Variable	1	2	3	4	5	M	SD
Marital adjustment indicators							
1. Problems	—	.658	.288	.171	.264	155.547	31.168
2. Intimacy	.740	—	.398	.295	.305	137.971	20.094
Family-of-origin experiences indicators							
3. Father	.265	.422	—	.480	.554	82.764	11.229
4. Mother	.305	.401	.791	—	.422	85.494	11.743
5. Father–Mother	.315	.351	.662	.587	—	81.003	13.220
Wives M	161.779	138.382	86.229	86.392	85.046		
SD	32.936	22.749	13.390	13.679	14.382		

Note. These data are from S. Bartle-Haring (personal communication, June 3, 2003); n_1 = 103 husbands (above the diagonal), n_1 = 103 wives (below the diagonal).

Analysis of the measurement model with a mean structure presented in Figure 11.2 across samples of husbands and wives will address both sets of hypotheses. The covariance structure of this model is a standard CFA model with two factors and five indicators. The mean structure includes direct effects of the constant on all five indicators and both factors. The direct effects on the factors are means and on the indicators are intercepts.

The model of Figure 11.2 is analyzed here in two steps. In the first step, the measurement model without the mean structure—a standard two-factor CFA model—is simultaneously estimated across samples of husbands and wives. The point of this analysis is to evaluate the degree of measurement invariance—that is, to determine whether the five indicators seem to measure the same two factors in both samples. Given reasonable evidence for at least partial measurement invariance, the mean structure will be added to the CFA model in the second step. In order to identify the mean structure, both direct effects of the constant on the factors are fixed to zero in the sample of husbands. This

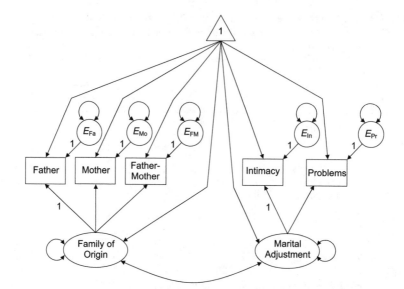

FIGURE 11.2. A measurement model of family-of-origin experiences and marital adjustment with a mean structure evaluated across samples of husbands and wives.

specification makes this group the reference sample. In contrast, these two direct effects are freely estimated in the sample of wives. Each of the unstandardized coefficients for these paths is the estimated mean difference between husbands and wives on that factor.

Evaluation of Measurement Invariance

In the first step, just the covariance structure of the model in Figure 11.2 was analyzed in a multiple-sample CFA. This standard two-factor CFA model was simultaneously fitted to two covariance matrices each assembled from the correlations and standard deviations for husbands and wives in Table 11.3 with LISREL 8 (Jöreskog & Sörbom, 2003). With five observed variables in each of two samples, there are a total of $5(6)/2 \times 2 = 30$ observations available for the analysis. The initial analysis assumed invariance across all model parameters; that is, cross-group equality constraints were imposed on the estimates of 7 variances (of 2 factors and 5 measurement errors), 1 factor covariance, and 3 factor loadings (see Figure 11.2). This specification reflects measurement invariance in the strictest sense. Because only one estimate of each parameter just mentioned was required when equality was assumed for husbands and wives, a total of 11 parameters were estimated with the 30 observations across both samples (i.e., df_M = 19).

Estimation with the ML method in LISREL of the initial CFA model converged to an admissible solution. Values of selected fit indexes are $\chi^2_M(19)$ = 23.190, p = .229, NC = 1.221, CFI = .990, and RMSEA = .038 with the 90% confidence interval 0–.098. (LISREL does not calculate the SRMR for a multiple-sample analysis.) The upper bound of the confidence interval based on RMSEA (.098) is not consistent with the hypothesis of approximate model fit in the population. Also, several absolute correlation residuals were greater than .10 in both samples. Based on these results, the initial CFA model that assumes equal estimates for all model parameters across samples of husbands and wives was rejected.

For the second CFA model, the factor variances and covariance were freely estimated in each sample (i.e., the cross-group equality constraints on these parameters were dropped). The analysis of this second CFA model converged to an admissible solution, and values of selected fit indexes are $\chi^2_M(16)$ = 16.127, p = .444, NC = 1.008, CFI = 1.000, and RMSEA = 0 with the 90% confidence interval 0–.087. The value for the upper bound of the confidence interval based on RMSEA (.087) is still not ideal. The only statistically significant modification index ($\chi^2(1)$ = 7.959, p < .01) within both samples was for the error covariance between the father and mother indicators of the family-of-origin experiences factor. Because it seems reasonable that reports about the quality of relationships with one's own parents may have common omitted causes, the second CFA model was respecified so that these error covariances were freely estimated in each sample. Values of selected fit indexes for this third CFA model were more favorable: $\chi^2_M(14)$ = 7.097, p = .931, NC = .507, CFI = 1.000, and RMSEA = 0 with the 90% confidence interval 0–.020, and all absolute correlation residuals within each sample were < .10.

Based on these results, the third CFA model was retained as the final measurement model. To summarize, this model assumes that all factor loadings and measurement errors are equal for husbands and wives, which satisfies a relatively strict form of measurement invariance. In contrast, the factor variances and covariance and the error covariance between the father and mother indicators are not assumed to be equal for husbands and wives (i.e., they were freely estimated in each sample). Overall, it seems that the five indicators represented in Figure 11.2 measure the same two factors in similar ways for both husbands and wives.

Estimation of Relative Factor Mean Differences

In the second step, the mean structure illustrated in Figure 11.2 was added to the final CFA measurement model from the first step. The husbands are the reference sample, so the direct effects of the constant on both factors (i.e., the factor means) were constrained to equal zero for this group. In contrast, these two parameters were freely estimated in the sample of wives, and their unstandardized values estimate relative mean differences between wives and husbands on each factor. The direct effects of the constant on the indicators (i.e., intercepts) were constrained to be equal for husbands and wives. This set of cross-group equality constraints (5 in total) tests the hypothesis of equal intercepts for regressions of the indicators on the factors. With five indicators in each sample, the total number of observations is $5(8)/2 \times 2 = 40$. The total number of free parameters is 23. This includes 13 parameters constrained to be equal for husbands and wives (5 indicator intercepts, 5 measurement errors, and 3 factor loadings), 4 parameters freely estimated within each sample (3 factor variances and covariance and 1 error covariance) for a total of 8 altogether, and 2 factor means estimated only for wives. Thus, $df_M = 40 - 23 = 17$.

The measurement model with structured means just described was simultaneously fitted in LISREL to the covariance matrices and means based on the data summarized in Table 11.3 for husbands and wives. The LISREL SIMPLIS syntax for this analysis is presented in Appendix 11.A. Estimation in LISREL converged to an admissible solution. Values of selected fit indexes suggest reasonable overall model fit: $\chi_M^2 (17) = 13.599$, $p = .695$, NC = .800, CFI = 1.000, and RMSEA = 0 with the 90% confidence interval 0–.070, and all absolute correlation residuals were < .10 in both samples. The ML parameter estimates for the covariance structure (i.e., the two-factor CFA model) are reported in Table 11.4. The standardized estimates reported in Table 11.4 are from the **within-groups completely standardized solution** (i.e., the

TABLE 11.4. Maximum Likelihood Parameter Estimates for the Covariance Structure of a Confirmatory Factor Analysis Model with Structured Means Analyzed across Samples of Husbands and Wives

Parameter	Husbands			Wives		
	Unstandard-ized	SE	Standard-ized	Unstandard-ized	SE	Standard-ized
			Unconstrained estimates			
Factor variances and covariance						
FOE	85.654	20.474	1.000	139.199	29.405	1.000
Mar Adj	459.104	106.660	1.000	595.682	149.121	1.000
FOE ∪ Mar Adj	95.052	28.249	.479	140.477	40.883	.488
Measurement error covariance						
E_{Fa} ∪ E_{Mo}	-8.925^a	14.293	-.067	20.782^a	14.442	.116
			Equality-constrained estimates			
Factor loadings						
FOE → Father	1.000	—	.828	1.000	—	.883
FOE → Mother	.859	.078	.668	.859	.078	.753
FOE → Fa–Mo	.932	.139	.663	.932	.139	.749
Mar Adj→Probs	1.000	—	.688	1.000	—	.734
Mar Adj→Intim	.917	.142	.979	.917	.142	.984
Measurement error variances						
E_{Fa}	39.421	15.789	.315	39.421	15.789	.221
E_{Mo}	78.371	15.438	.554	78.371	15.438	.433
E_{FM}	94.944	16.096	.560	94.944	16.096	.440
E_{Pr}	510.317	89.025	.526	510.317	89.025	.461
E_{In}	16.755^a	61.706	.042	16.755^a	61.706	.032

Note. FOE, family-of-origin experiences. Standardized estimates for measurement errors are proportions of unexplained variance.

$^a p > .05$. For all other unstandardized estimates, $p < .01$.

observed and latent variables are standardized based on the standard deviations within each sample).[1] They are directly comparable only across different variables within each sample. Results for the mean structure are reported in Table 11.5. Each set of results (covariance structure, mean structure) is described next.

Reported in the top part of Table 11.4 are estimates for parameters of the measurement model freely estimated in both samples. Wives may be somewhat more variable on both factors than husbands. For example, the estimated variance of the marital adjustment factor is 595.682 among wives but is 459.104 among husbands. Although the estimated factor covariance is also somewhat greater for wives than husbands (140.477 vs. 95.052, respectively), the estimated factor correlation in both samples is about .50. These correlations are consistent with discriminant validity in factor measurement in both samples because their values are not too high. Although neither estimated error covariance between the father and mother indicators of the family-of-origin experiences factor is statistically significant at the .05 level for husbands or wives, their values have opposite signs, negative for husbands (−8.925) but positive for wives (20.782). Reported in the bottom part of Table 11.4 are estimates for parameters of the measurement model constrained to have equal unstandardized values in both samples. Because the group sizes are the same (n = 103), the estimated standard errors of these estimates are also equal for husbands and wives. The pattern of standardized factor loadings is generally similar within each sample and consistent with convergent validity in factor measurement. Standardized measurement error variances expressed as proportions of unexplained variance indicate somewhat greater explanatory power for wives than for husbands. For example, the proportion of unexplained variance in the problems indicator of the marital adjustment factor is .461 for wives but is .526 for husbands.

Presented in the top part of Table 11.5 are the unstandardized estimates of the direct effects of the constant on the factors calculated for

---

[1]LISREL also optionally calculates a **common metric standardized solution** where the latent variables are automatically scaled so that the weighted average of their covariance matrices across the samples is a correlation matrix. These standardized estimates may be more directly comparable across the groups than are the within-groups standardized estimates, but the unstandardized estimates are still preferred for this purpose.

TABLE 11.5. Maximum Likelihood Parameter Estimates for the Mean Structure of a Confirmatory Factor Analysis Model with Structured Means Analyzed across Samples of Husbands and Wives

	Husbands		Wives	
Parameter	Unstandardized	SE	Unstandardized	SE
		Estimated for wives only		
Factor means				
△ → FOE	0	—	3.196[a]	1.643
△ → Mar Adj	0	—	.665[a]	3.275
		Equality-constrained estimates		
Indicator intercepts				
△ → Father	83.079	1.055	83.079	1.055
△ → Mother	84.493	1.009	84.493	1.009
△ → Fa–Mo	81.535	1.153	81.535	1.153
△ → Probs	158.330	2.664	158.330	2.664
△ → Intim	137.871	1.987	137.871	1.987

Note. FOE, family-of-origin experiences. All standardized estimates are zero.
[a]$p > .05$. For all other unstandardized estimates, $p < .05$.

wives only. They are interpreted as estimated factor mean differences between husbands and wives adjusted for measurement error. The result for the family-of-origin factor is 3.196, indicating that the mean score for wives on this factor is predicted to be 3.196 points higher than that for husbands. That is, wives generally report more positive family-of-origin experiences than their husbands. The estimated standard error for this factor mean difference is 1.643. In a large sample and if we assume normality and homogeneity of variance, the ratio 3.196/1.643 = 1.946 is interpreted as a z test of whether the estimated factor mean difference differs statistically from zero. (An overall sample size of $N = 206$ for this analysis is reasonably large.) Because the positive two-tailed critical value of z at the .05 level is 1.96, the estimated mean difference between wives and husbands of 3.196 points on the family-of-origin experiences factor falls just sort of statistical significance at the .05 level. By the same logic, the estimated group mean difference of .665 points on the marital adjustment factor is also not statistically significant at the .05 level because $z = .665/3.275 = .203 < 1.96$ (see Table 11.5). Thus, the relative overall standings of husbands and wives on the marital adjustment factor may be similar.

Reported in the bottom part of Table 11.5 are the estimates of intercepts for the regressions of the indicators on the factors when equal values are assumed for husbands and wives. The predicted indicator means are not model parameters, but they are calculated as the total unstandardized effects of the constant on the indicators. These total effects are not equal for husbands and wives because the indirect effects of the constant on the indicators through the factors equal zero for the husbands only. (This is because the direct effects of the constant on the factors are fixed to zero for the husbands.) The predicted indicator means automatically calculated by LISREL are listed in the same order as these indicators appear in Table 11.3 as follows:

Husbands: 158.330, 137.871, 83.079, 84.493, 81.535
Wives: 158.996, 138.482, 86.276, 87.238, 84.514

Each predicted mean is generally similar to the corresponding observed mean in both samples (see Table 11.3).

For additional examples of the analysis of measurement models with mean structures across multiple groups, see McArdle, Johnson, Hishinuma, Miyamoto, and Andrade (2001), who evaluated measurement invariance and estimated relative factor mean differences for self-reports of depression across samples of Hawaiian and non-Hawaiian high school students, and Byrne (2001, chap. 9), who evaluated the invariance of the mean structure for a four-factor model of academic self-concept across samples of students tracked as low ability versus high ability.

11.4 EXTENSIONS

The multiple-sample analysis of a structural regression (SR) model with both exogenous and endogenous factors and a mean structure that is not a latent growth model (LGM) follows the same basic rationale as for a CFA model with a mean structure. For example, factor measurement should be specified the same way for all groups, and for the group selected as the reference sample, all direct effects of the constant on the factors are fixed to zero in order to identify the mean structure. A notable difference is that direct effects of the constant on endogenous factors are interpreted as relative group differences in the intercepts for the regression of those factors on other variables in the model specified as direct causes. Also, measurement invariance (full or partial) is required before testing equality of paths in the structural model. Because of different identification requirements for an LGM, it is generally possible to estimate the means or intercepts of latent growth factors in a single sample (Chapter 10). This implies that latent growth factor means or intercepts can be estimated separately for each group when an LGM is simultaneously analyzed across multiple samples. These capabilities provide great flexibility in hypothesis testing with longitudinal data (e.g., T. E. Duncan et al., 1999).

11.5 MIMIC MODELS AS AN ALTERNATIVE TO MULTIPLE-SAMPLE ANALYSIS

An alternative way to estimate group differences on latent variables is through the specification of a MIMIC model where factors with effect indicators are regressed on one or more dichotomous cause indicators that represent group membership, such as one coded 0 = treatment and 1 = control. In this approach, the total sample is not partitioned into subsamples as is the case in a multiple-sample SEM (although subsamples are still required in the study design). Thus, there are no special identification requirements beyond the usual ones for single-sample analyses for the types of MIMIC models described here.

Consider the model presented in Figure 11.3. It is specified as a MIMIC alternative to the model of Figure 11.2, which was analyzed earlier across separate samples of husbands and wives. The single cause indicator in the MIMIC model of Figure 11.3 is a dichotomy that represents the spouse coded as 0 = husband and 1 = wife. That is, this variable is a dummy code that represents the comparison of husbands with wives. It is specified to have direct effects on a family-of-origin experiences factor with three effect indicators and a marital adjustment factor with two effect indicators. These are the same factors and indicators as

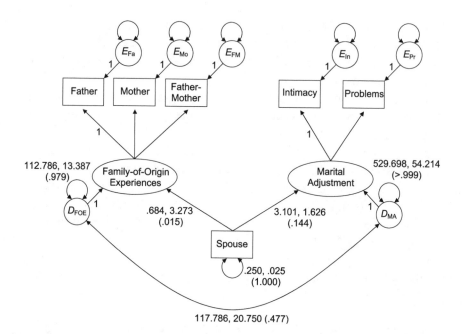

FIGURE 11.3. A MIMIC (multiple indicators and multiple causes) model of family-of-origin experiences and marital adjustment evaluated in a single sample with the spouse as a cause indicator. Parameter estimates are reported as unstandardized, standard error (standardized). Standardized estimates for disturbance variances are proportions of unexplained variance.

represented in Figure 11.2, but the factors are endogenous in the MIMIC model of Figure 11.3 and thus have disturbances. Note that these disturbances are specified as correlated, which reflects the assumption that the factors have common omitted causes besides the difference between husbands and wives. Also note that the MIMIC model of Figure 11.3 does not have a mean structure (i.e., it has only a covariance structure). This implies that all means are assumed to be zero (i.e., they are not analyzed). However, the path coefficients for the direct effects of the spouse variable will provide information about the degree to which the difference between husbands and wives predicts the factors.

Reported in Table 11.6 are the correlations, standard deviations, and means for the family-of-origin indicators and the marital adjustment indicators for the total sample of $N = 206$ cases (103 couples) in the Sabatelli and Bartle-Haring (2003) data set. These values were derived by combining the separate-group statistics from Table 11.3

using a method devised by Robinson (1950). Also reported in Table 11.6 are the point-biserial correlations (r_{pb}) between the spouse variable and each of the indicators calculated from the group means and standard deviations (e.g., Kline, 2004, chap. 4). With 6 observed variables altogether—including 5 effect indicators and 1 cause indicator (spouse)—there are 6(7)/2 = 21 observations available for analysis.

The MIMIC model of Figure 11.3 was fitted to the covariance matrix assembled from the correlations and standard deviations in Table 11.6 with the ML method of LISREL. The factor loadings and measurement error variances were specified as fixed and equal to the corresponding values reported in the bottom part of Table 11.4, which assume equality of husbands and wives across these parameters. Note that the MIMIC model of Figure 11.3 does not assume correlated errors between the father and mother indicators of the family-of-origin experiences factor. This is because this correlation was estimated earlier to be negative for husbands but positive for wives (see Table 11.4). In the total sample, this error correlation may be about zero. With these speci-

TABLE 11.6. Input Data (Correlations, Standard Deviations) for Analysis of a MIMIC (Multiple Indicators and Multiple Causes) Model of Family-of-Origin Experiences and Marital Adjustment

Variables	1	2	3	4	5	6
Marital adjustment indicators						
1. Problems	1.000					
2. Intimacy	.700	1.000				
Family-of-origin experiences indicators						
3. Father	.253	.409	1.000			
4. Mother	.247	.355	.659	1.000		
5. Father–Mother	.301	.330	.622	.513	1.000	
Predictor						
6. Spouse	.097	.010	.139	.035	.145	1.000
M	158.663	138.177	84.497	85.943	83.025	.500
SD	32.064	21.463	12.357	12.748	13.813	.500

Note. These data are derived from those summarized in Table 11.3; $N = 206$. Means are reported but not analyzed. Spouse is coded 0 = husband, 1 = wife.

fications, the MIMIC model has 6 free parameters, including 3 variances (of the spouse variable and 2 factor disturbances), 1 covariance between the factor disturbances, and the 2 direct effects of the dichotomous spouse variable on the factors, so $df_M = 21 - 6 = 15$.

The analysis of the MIMIC model with ML estimation in LISREL converged to an admissible solution. Overall model fit seems adequate based on values of selected fit indexes: $\chi_M^2 (15) = 14.188$, $p = .511$, NC = .946, CFI = 1.000, and RMSEA = 0 with the 90% confidence interval 0–.061. Estimates for the six free model parameters are presented in Figure 11.3 in the proper places. The estimated variance of the cause indicator (spouse) is just the observed value (see Table 11.6). The unstandardized coefficients (and standard errors) for the direct effects of the spouse cause indicator on the family-of-origin experiences factor and on the marital adjustment factor are, respectively, .684 (3.273) and 3.101 (1.626). Because spouse is coded 0 = husband and 1 = wife, these positive values indicate a higher predicted overall standing on both factors for wives than husbands. The coefficient for the path Spouse → Marital Adjustment is clearly not statistically significant at the .05 level ($z = .684/3.273 = .209$, $p = .834$), but the coefficient for the path Spouse → Family-of-Origin Experiences is nearly so ($z = 3.101/1.626 = 1.91$, $p = .056$). The standardized coefficient for the former path is quite small (.015), but it is somewhat larger for the latter path (.144). These results estimated in the total sample for the MIMIC model are similar to those for the measurement model with structured means analyzed earlier across both samples: wives report somewhat better family-of-origin experiences than their husbands do, but not clearly better marital adjustment.

See Kaplan (2000, chap. 4) for additional examples of the analysis of MIMIC models to estimate group differences on latent variables. See also Kano (2001), who describes the specification of MIMIC models for experimental designs that are SEM analogs of techniques such as multivariate analysis of variance or covariance (MANOVA, MANCOVA) except that groups are compared across latent variables instead of just observed variables.

11.6 SUMMARY

When we are analyzing structural equation models across multiple samples, it is common to impose cross-group equality constraints on certain unstandardized parameter estimates. In a multiple-sample path analysis, usually just the direct effects are constrained to be equal. If the relative fit of the constrained path model is much worse than that of the unconstrained path model (and the unconstrained path model fits the data reasonably well), we may conclude that the population direct effects are unequal. In multiple-sample CFA, cross-group equality constraints are often imposed to test the hypothesis of measurement invariance. There are degrees of measurement invariance, but a common tactic is to constrain just the unstandardized factor loadings to be equal across the groups. If the fit of the measurement model with constrained factor loadings is much worse than that of the unconstrained model, then we may conclude that the indicators measure the factors in different ways across the groups.

In order to estimate group mean differences on factors, the hypothesis of at least partial measurement invariance should be tenable. One way to identify the mean structure when CFA or SR models include means is to select one sample as the reference sample, constrain the factor means or intercepts to zero in this group, but freely estimate these parameters in all other groups. The results estimate the mean difference between each of these groups and the reference sample on the factor mean or intercept. An alternative way to estimate group differences on latent variables is to analyze a MIMIC model with data from the total sample. The factors in the MIMIC model are regressed on at least one cause indicator that represents membership in one group or another. An advantage of this approach is that there are no special identification requirements beyond those for a single-sample analysis.

This chapter concludes our in-depth tour of more advanced methods in SEM. Next, Chapter 12 reviews ways to fool yourself with SEM—and how to avoid doing so.

11.7 RECOMMENDED READINGS

Kano, Y. (2001). Structural equation modeling with experimental data. In R. Cudeck, S. Du Toit, & D. Sörbom (Eds.), *Structural equation modeling: Present and future* (pp. 381-402). Lincolnwood, IL: Scientific Software International.

Kaplan, D. (2000). *Structural equation modeling.* Thousand Oaks, CA: Sage. (Chap. 4)

LISREL SIMPLIS Syntax

```
Figure 11.2
Group 1: Husbands
Observed Variables: PROBS INTIM FATHER MOTHER FA_MO
Latent Variables: Mar_Adj FO_Exp
Correlation Matrix from file Sabatelli.dat
Standard Deviations from File Sabatelli.dat
Means from File Sabatelli.dat
Sample Size: 103
Equations
FATHER = CONST + 1*FO_Exp
MOTHER = CONST + FO_Exp
FA_MO = CONST + FO_Exp
PROBS = CONST + 1*Mar_Adj
INTIM = CONST + Mar_Adj
Set the Error Covariance of FATHER and MOTHER free
Group 2: Wives
Correlation Matrix from File Sabatelli.dat
Standard Deviations from File Sabatelli.dat
Means from File Sabatelli.dat
Equations
FO_Exp = CONST
Mar_Adj = CONST
Set the Covariance of FO_Exp and Mar_Adj free
Set the Variance of FO_Exp Free
Set the Variance of Mar_Adj free
Set the Error Covariance of FATHER and MOTHER free
LISREL Output: ND = 3 SC RS
End of Problem
```

12

How to Fool Yourself with SEM

The technique of SEM is a marvelously flexible analytical tool. But as with any complex statistical procedure, its use must be guided by reason. Although many ways to mislead yourself with SEM were mentioned in previous chapters, they are all discussed together here. Potential pitfalls are considered under four categories: specification, data, analysis and respecification, and interpretation. These categories are not mutually exclusive, but they correspond to the usual sequence in which researchers should address these issues. Readers are encouraged to use the points presented in this chapter as a checklist to guide the conduct of their own analyses.

Here they are: 44 ways to take leave of your senses in SEM. This list is not exhaustive, but it contains many of the more common mistakes. I wish to thank members of SEMNET for their comments on an earlier version of this list.

12.1 TRIPPING AT THE STARTING LINE: SPECIFICATION

Despite all the statistical machinations of SEM, specification is the most important part of the process. Occasionally, though, researchers spend the least amount of time on it. Listed below are several ways not to do your homework in this crucial area:

1. *Specify the model after the data are collected rather than before.* This case concerns the specification of a model for an archival data set. Potential problems caused by placing the data cart before the theory

horse are described under points that follow, but they include the realization that key variables are omitted or that the model is not identified. With the data already collected, it may be too late to do anything about the former. Also, the addition of exogenous variables is one way to remedy an identification problem, especially for a nonrecursive structural model.

2. *Omit causes that are correlated with other variables in a structural model.* If an omitted cause is uncorrelated with variables already in the structural model, then estimates of the direct effects are not biased because of this omission. It is rare, however, that the types of causal variables studied by behavioral scientists are independent. Depending on the pattern of correlations between an omitted variable and those in the model, estimates of causal effects can be too high or too low.

3. *Fail to have sufficient numbers of indicators of latent variables.* Measurement models with more than one factor typically require only two indicators per factor for identification. However, having only two indicators per factor may lead to problems. Such models may be more likely to be empirically underidentified than models with at least three indicators per factor. Other problems, such as nonconvergence of iterative estimation, are more likely to occur for models with only two indicators per factor, especially in small samples. It may be difficult to estimate measurement error correlations for factors with only two indicators, which can result in a specification error. Parts of the model where some factors have only two indicators are not "self-sufficient" in terms of identification, which means that they have to "borrow" covariance information from other parts of the model. This may result in propagation of a specification error from one part of the model to another. Suppose that the measurement error correlation for a factor with just two indicators is really substantial but it cannot be estimated because of identification. This specification error may propagate to estimation of the factor loadings for this pair of indicators (B. Muthén, personal communication, November 25, 2003). Kenny's (1979) rule of thumb about the number of indicators is apropos: "Two *might* be fine, three is better, four is best, and anything more is gravy" (p. 143; emphasis in original).

4. *Use psychometrically inadequate measures.* The analysis of variables with a lot of measurement error in the scores (e.g., unreliability) can lead to inaccurate results. The general effect of measurement error

is to underestimate causal effects, but—depending on the intercorrelations—estimates can also be too high. Although measurement error is taken into account in the analysis of a measurement model or structural regression model, estimates about latent variables are more precise when the indicators are psychometrically sound.

5. *Fail to give careful consideration to the question of directionality.* Directionality is a critical feature not only of structural models but also of measurement models. In the former, specifications of direct and indirect effects are explicit statements about the expected sequence of causality. Assumptions about directionality in measurement models are expressed by the specification of observed variables as either effect indicators or cause indicators of latent variables. If solid reasons cannot be provided for the specification of directionality, then either use another type of statistical procedure (e.g., multiple regression) or test alternative models with different causal sequences. However, some of the latter may be equivalent models that generate the same predicted correlations or covariances, which means there is no way to statistically distinguish them. This is why Meehl and Walker (2002) describe path analysis and related techniques as being good for estimating effects when the underlying causal mechanism is known but as less helpful in trying to discover the nature of that mechanism when it is not known.

6. *Specify feedback effects in structural models (e.g., $Y_1 \rightleftarrows Y_2$) as a way to mask uncertainty about directionality.* Not only do feedback relations have their own assumptions (e.g., equilibrium), but their presence also makes a structural model nonrecursive, which introduces potential problems (e.g., identification) in analyzing the model. A related mistake is to fail to rationally evaluate the equilibrium assumption for a feedback loop.

7. *Overfit the model (i.e., forget the goal of parsimony).* Any model, even theoretically nonsensical ones, will perfectly fit the data if they are specified to be as complex as possible (i.e., $df_M = 0$). Models just as complex as the data test no particular hypothesis, however. It is only more parsimonious models, in which some effects are intentionally constrained to zero, that allow tests of specific ideas. The goal of model parsimony is also important in respecification. Here one must be careful not to modify the model solely for the sake of improving fit.

8. *Add disturbance or measurement error correlations without substantive reason.* This is a variation on the previous point. When there is

justification (e.g., repeated measurement, use of a common measurement method), specification of these types of unanalyzed associations may be appropriate. Otherwise, they can be a way to improve fit simply by making a model more complex. This is especially true if the researcher initially specifies uncorrelated residuals because of the assumption of conditional independence of the indicators for a latent variable model. If the model in fact does not adequately explain the observed associations among the indicators, adding measurement error correlations without a substantive reason can be a way to mask this fact. However, in other disciplines such as econometrics the specification of correlated residuals is more routine (i.e., it is a standard assumption; W. Wothke, personal communication, November 24, 2003).

9. *Specify that indicators load on more than one factor without a substantive reason.* This is a second variation on point 7. This specification may be appropriate if you really believe that an indicator measures more than one construct. Just like unanalyzed associations between residual terms, however, adding factor loadings makes a measurement model less parsimonious.

12.2 IMPROPER CARE AND FEEDING: DATA

The potential missteps presented in this section involve leaping before you look, that is, not carefully screening the data before analyzing them:

10. *Don't check the accuracy of data input or coding.* Data entry mistakes are so easy to make, whether in recording the raw data or typing the values of a correlation or covariance matrix. Even machine-based data entry is not error free (e.g., smudges on forms can "fool" an electronic scanner). Mistaken specification of codes in statistical programs is also common (e.g., "9" for missing data instead of "–9").

11. *Ignore whether the pattern of missing data loss is random or systematic.* This point assumes that there are more just than a few missing scores. Some statistical methods for dealing with incomplete data sets, such as listwise deletion, assume that the data loss mechanism is random. However, there may be few instances in the social sciences when

this assumption is reasonable. Other methods, such as regression-based imputation, work better (i.e., bias is minimized) when there are variables that predict whether scores on other variables are missing or not (A. Acock, personal communication, November 24, 2003). If these predictor variables are unknown or unmeasured, however, then such methods may not be very effective. Multiple imputation methods may be most valuable in data sets such as those for survey results where many variables predict a data loss pattern (J.-P. Laurenceau, personal communication, November 24, 2003).

12. *Fail to examine distributional characteristics.* The most widely used estimation method in SEM—maximum likelihood (ML)—assumes normal distributions for continuous endogenous variables. Although values of parameter estimates are relatively robust against nonnormality, statistical tests tend to be positively biased (i.e., Type I error rate is inflated). If the distributions of continuous endogenous variables are severely nonnormal, then use an estimation method that does not assume normality or use corrected statistics (e.g., robust standard errors) when normal theory methods such as ML estimation are used. If the distributions are nonnormal because the indicators are discrete with a small number of categories, then use an appropriate estimation method for this type of data.

13. *Don't screen for outliers.* Even a few extreme scores in a relatively small sample can distort the results. If it is unclear whether outlier cases are from a different population, the analysis can be run with and without these cases in the sample. This strategy makes clear the effect of outliers on the results.

14. *Assume that all relations are linear without checking.* A standard assumption in SEM is that variable relations are linear. Curvilinear or interactive relations can be represented with product terms (more about this point in Chapter 13), but such variables must be created by the researcher and then included in the model. Simple visual scanning of scatterplots can detect bivariate relations that are obviously curvilinear, but there is no comparably easy visual check for interaction effects.

15. *Ignore lack of independence among the observations.* This problem may arise in two contexts. First, the observations are from a repeated measures variable or a hierarchical data set where the variables may not be repeated measures variables; the ability to specify a

model for the error covariances addresses this first context. The second context refers to nested data structures in which individuals are clustered within larger units, such as employees for the same manager. Scores within the same larger unit are probably not independent. The analysis of nested data with statistical techniques that assume independence may not yield accurate results. This problem is addressed in SEM through the specification of a multilevel model (described in Chapter 13).

12.3 CHECKING CRITICAL JUDGMENT AT THE DOOR: ANALYSIS AND RESPECIFICATION

The potential pitfalls described next concern the analysis and interpretation stages. However, problems at earlier stages may make these problems more likely to happen:

16. *Respecify a model based entirely on statistical criteria.* A specification search guided entirely by statistical criteria such as modification indexes may be unlikely to lead to the correct model. Use your knowledge of relevant theory and research results to inform the use of such statistics.

17. *Fail to check the accuracy of computer syntax.* Just as with data entry, it is easy to make an error in computer syntax that misspecifies the model or data. Although SEM computer programs have become easier to use, they still cannot generally detect a mistake that is a logical rather than a syntax error. The former does not cause the analysis to fail but instead results in an unintended specification (e.g., $Y_1 \rightarrow Y_2$ is specified when $Y_2 \rightarrow Y_1$ was intended). Carefully check to see that the model that was analyzed was actually the one that you attempted to specify.

18. *Fail to carefully inspect the solution for admissibility.* The presence of a Heywood case or other kinds of illogical results indicates a problem in the analysis; that is, the solution should not be trusted. For the same reason, avoid making interpretations about otherwise sensible-looking results in an inadmissible solution.

19. *Report only standardized estimates.* This mistake concerns the possible fooling of others; that is, always report the unstandardized estimates in a primary analysis. (Some exceptions to this practice were

made for a few analyses described in earlier chapters in order to save space, but these analyses were secondary and conducted for pedagogical reasons.) Otherwise, it may be difficult to compare the results to those from later studies where either the same or a similar model is estimated in different samples.

20. *Analyze a correlation matrix when it is clearly inappropriate.* These situations include the analysis of a model across independent samples with different variabilities, longitudinal data characterized by changes in variances over time, or a type of SEM that requires the analysis of means (e.g., a latent growth model, LGM), which needs the input of not only means but covariances, too.

21. *Estimate a covariance structure with a correlation matrix without using appropriate methods.* Standard ML estimation assumes the analysis of unstandardized variables and may yield incorrect results when a model is fitted to a correlation matrix. Appropriate procedures such as the method of constrained estimation should be used to analyze a correlation matrix in situations where it is not inappropriate to do (see the previous point).

22. *Fail to check for constraint interaction when testing for equality of loadings across different factors or of direct effects on different endogenous variables.* If the results of the chi-square difference test for the equality-constrained parameters depend on how the factors are scaled (i.e., unstandardized vs. standardized), there is constraint interaction. In this case, it may make sense to analyze the correlation matrix using the method of constrained estimation, assuming it is appropriate to analyze standardized variables.

23. *Analyze variables so highly correlated that a solution is unstable.* If very high correlations (e.g., $r > .85$) do not cause an SEM computer program to "crash" or yield a nonadmissible solution, then extreme multicollinearity may cause the results to be statistically unstable.

24. *Estimate a complex model with a small sample.* This is a related problem. As the ratio of cases to the number of parameters is smaller, the statistical stability of the estimates becomes more doubtful. Cases-to-parameter ratios less than 10:1 may be cause for concern, as are sample sizes less than 100. (These recommendations assume maximum likelihood estimation. Recall that some special methods, such as asymptotic distribution free estimation methods that make no distributional assumptions, may require very large samples.)

25. *Set scales for latent variables inappropriately.* In multiple-sample SEM, the tactic of standardizing factors by fixing their variances to 1.0 is incorrect if groups differ in their variabilities. Fixing the loadings of an indicator to 1.0 (i.e., the factor is unstandardized) is preferable, but note that (a) the same loading must be fixed for all groups and (b) indicators with fixed loadings are assumed to be invariant across all samples. In single-sample analyses, fixing to 1.0 the variances of factors measured over time is also inappropriate if factor variability is expected to change (see point 20).

26. *Ignore the problem of start values, or provide grossly inaccurate ones.* Iterative estimation may fail to converge because of poor initial estimates, which is more likely with complex models or nonrecursive models. Although many SEM computer programs can automatically generate their own start values, these values do not always lead to converged admissible solutions. When this happens, the researcher should try to generate his or her own initial estimates.

27. *When identification status is uncertain, fail to conduct tests of solution uniqueness.* The identification of only some types of models can be clearly determined without resorting to algebraic manipulation of their equations. If it is unknown whether a model is theoretically identified but an SEM computer program yields a converged admissible solution, then the researcher should conduct empirical tests of the solution's uniqueness. These tests do not prove that a solution is truly unique, but if they lead to the derivation of a different solution, then the model is probably not identified.

28. *Fail to recognize empirical underidentification.* Estimation of models that are identified can nevertheless fail because of data-related problems, including multicollinearity or estimates of key parameters that are close to zero or equal to one another. Modification of a model when the data are the problem may lead to a specification error.

29. *Fail to separately evaluate the measurement and structural portions of a structural regression model.* Two-step (or four-step) estimation of structural regression models can help determine whether the source of poor fit of the whole model lies in the measurement component or in the structural component. These sources of poor fit are confounded in one-step estimation.

30. *Estimate relative group mean or intercept differences on latent variables without establishing at least partial measurement invariance of*

the indicators. If the observed variables do not at least have the same basic factor structure across all groups, it makes little sense to evaluate relative group mean contrasts on or differences in regression slopes or intercepts among the latent variables.

31. *Analyze parcels of categorical items as continuous indicators without checking to see whether items in each parcel are unidimensional.* If a set of items assigned to the same parcel do not measure one common domain, analysis of the total score across the items may not be very meaningful.

12.4 THE GARDEN PATH: INTERPRETATION

Potential mistakes described in this section concern the (mis)interpretation of the output of an SEM computer program. Some of these may be consequences of mistakes listed in earlier sections of this chapter:

32. *Look only at indexes of overall model fit; ignore other types of information about fit.* This refers to "fit index tunnel vision," a disorder that is fortunately curable by looking through the entire output. It is possible that the fit of some portion of the model is poor despite seemingly impressive values of its average correspondence to the data. Inspection of the correlation residuals can help to spot particular observed associations that are poorly explained by the model. A related mistake is selective reporting of fit indexes—specifically, reporting values of only those fit indexes that favor the researcher's model when results on other indexes are clearly less favorable.

33. *Interpret good fit as meaning that the model is "proved."* Good model fit could reflect any of the following (not all mutually exclusive) possibilities: (a) the model accurately reflects reality; (b) the model is an equivalent version of one that corresponds to reality but itself is incorrect; (c) the model fits the data from a nonrepresentative sample but has poor fit in the population; or (d) the model has so many parameters that it cannot have poor fit even if it is blatantly wrong. In a single study, it is usually impossible to determine which of these scenarios explains the good fit of the researcher's model. Thus, SEM is more useful for rejecting a false model than for somehow "proving" whether a given model is in fact true.

34. *Interpret good fit as meaning that the endogenous variables are strongly predicted.* If the exogenous variables account for a small proportion of the variances of the endogenous variables and a model accurately reflects this lack of predictive validity, then the overall fit of the model may be good. Indexes of overall fit indicate whether the model can reproduce the observed correlations or covariances, not whether substantial proportions of the variance of the endogenous variables are explained.

35. *Rely solely on statistical criteria in model evaluation.* Other important considerations include model generality, parsimony, and theoretical plausibility. As noted by Robert and Pashler (2000), good statistical fit of an individual model indicates little about (a) theory flexibility (e.g., what it cannot explain), (b) variability of the data (e.g., whether the data can rule out what the theory cannot explain), and (c) the likelihoods of other outcomes. Robert and Pashler suggest that a better way to evaluate a model is to determine (a) how well the theory constrains possible outcomes (i.e., whether it can accurately predict), (b) how closely the actual outcome agrees with those constraints, and (c) if plausible alternative outcomes would have been inconsistent with the theory (Sikström, 2001; see also Kaplan, 2000, chap. 9).

36. *Rely too much on statistical tests.* This entry covers several kinds of errors. One is to interpret statistical significance as evidence for effect size (especially in large samples) or for importance (i.e., substantive significance). Another is to place too much emphasis on statistical tests of individual parameters that may not be of central interest in hypothesis testing (e.g., whether the variance of an exogenous variable that is not a latent growth factor differs statistically from zero when this is expected). A third is to forget that statistical tests tend to result in rejection of the null hypothesis too often when nonnormal data are analyzed by methods that assume normality. See point 16 for related misuses of statistical tests in SEM.

37. *Interpret the standardized solution in inappropriate ways.* This is a relatively common mistake in multiple-sample SEM—specifically, to compare standardized estimates across groups that differ in their variabilities. In general, standardized solutions are fine for comparisons within each group (e.g., the relative magnitudes of direct effects on Y), but only unstandardized solutions are usually appropriate for cross-group comparisons. A related error is to interpret group differences in

the standardized estimates of equality-constrained parameters: the unstandardized estimates of such parameters are forced to be equal, but their standardized counterparts are typically unequal if the groups have different variabilities.

38. *Fail to consider equivalent models.* Essentially all structural equation models have equivalent versions that generate the same predicted correlations or covariances. For latent variable models, there may be infinitely many equivalent models. Researchers should offer reasons why their models are to be preferred over some obvious equivalent versions of them.

39. *Fail to consider (nonequivalent) alternative models.* When there are competing theories about the same phenomenon, it may be possible to specify alternative models that reflect them. Not all of these alternatives may be equivalent versions of one another. If the overall fits of some of these alternative models are comparable, then the researcher must explain why a particular model is to be preferred.

40. *Reify the factors.* Believe that constructs represented in your model *must* correspond to things in the real world. Perhaps they do, but do not assume it.

41. *Believe that naming a factor means that it is understood or correctly named (i.e., commit the "naming fallacy").* Factor names are conveniences, not explanations. For example, it would be silly to specify a factor with the effect indicators gender, race, and education and then name the factor "background" or with some similar term. Even apart from the naming fallacy, gender and race are unrelated in representative samples, so one could not claim that these variables somehow measure the same underlying construct (L. M. Wolfle, personal communication, November 25, 2003).

42. *Believe that a strong analytical method like SEM can compensate for poor study design or slipshod ideas.* No statistical procedure can make up for inherent logical or design flaws. For example, expressing poorly thought out hypotheses with a path diagram does not give them more credibility. The specification of direct and indirect effects in a structural model cannot be viewed as a replacement for a longitudinal design. As mentioned earlier, the inclusion of a measurement error term for an observed variable that is psychometrically deficient cannot somehow transform it into a good measure.

43. *As the researcher, fail to report enough information so that your*

readers can reproduce your results. There are still too many reports in the literature where SEM was used in which the authors do not give sufficient information for readers to re-create the original analyses or evaluate models not considered by the authors. At minimum, authors should generally report all relevant correlations, standard deviations, and means. Also describe the specification of the model(s) in enough detail so that a reader can reproduce the analysis.

44. *Interpret estimates of relatively large direct effects from a structural model as "proof" of causality.* As discussed earlier, it would be almost beyond belief that all of the conditions required for the inference of causality from covariances have been met in a single study. In general, it is better to view structural models as being "as if" models of causality that may or may not correspond to causal sequences in the real world.

12.5 SUMMARY

Many of the ways to mislead oneself just listed are not unique to SEM but apply to essentially any analytical method that (1) requires certain assumptions about the integrity of the data and the researcher's hypotheses and (2) exacts a price of complexity for its potential advantages. That it is possible to misuse or misinterpret the results of a statistical tool like SEM, however, may not be so much a criticism of the procedure itself but of its user, who has the responsibility to learn both the strengths and limitations of SEM and to provide a complete and accurate account of its application.

12.6 RECOMMENDED READINGS

Blalock, H. M. (1991). Are there really any constructive alternatives to causal modeling? *Sociological Methodology, 21,* 325–335.

Freedman, D. A. (1991). Statistical models and shoe leather. *Sociological Methodology, 21,* 291–313.

Mason, W. M. (1991). Freedman is right as far as he goes, but there is more, and it's worse: Statisticians could help. *Sociological Methodology, 21,* 337–351.

13

Other Horizons

And so this journey of learning about the principles and practice of SEM draws to a close. The conclusion of any voyage, however, leaves the traveler at the threshold of other potential journeys. Because the SEM family is a large and growing one, there is no shortage of other horizons to explore. Only two such possibilities are described in this chapter—the estimation of interaction or curvilinear effects of latent variables and the analysis of multilevel structural equation models. It is beyond the scope of this presentation to describe these topics in any substantial detail. Instead, the main goal here is to make readers aware of these facets of SEM and to provide references for further study. See Marcoulides and Schumacker (2001) and Marcoulides and Moustaki (2002) for more information about these and other advanced methods in SEM and related techniques for latent variable modeling.

13.1 INTERACTION AND CURVILINEAR EFFECTS

There are two general ways to estimate interaction effects in SEM. The first is to analyze a model across multiple samples. If unstandardized estimates of effects of interest in the model differ appreciably across the samples, then we conclude that group membership moderates those effects (Chapter 11). The second way is to analyze a model in a single sample with product terms specified by the researcher. This same strategy can be used to estimate curvilinear relations (trends). Note that product terms that correspond to trends are often referred to as power terms or polynomials.[1]

Interaction or curvilinear effects of observed variables are represented by product terms that are entered along with the original variables in a statistical model. Presented next are two examples using the method of multiple regression. This same basic method not only underlies the estimation of interaction and trend effects in the analysis of variance (ANOVA), it can also be used to represent these kinds of effects in path models (e.g., Baron & Kenny, 1986; Lance, 1988). Consider data set (a) in Table 13.1. The relation between X and Y is obviously curvilinear. Specifically, it is quadratic because scores on Y decline and then rise as scores on X increase. Regressing Y on X for these scores yields a standardized regression coefficient (i.e., Pearson r) of $-.047$ and an unstandardized regression coefficient of $-.023$. These results reflect only the linear aspect of their relation, which is slight for these data. To also represent the quadratic trend, all that is needed is to create the power term X^2 and then regress Y on both X and X^2. The presence of X^2 in the equation adds one bend to the regression line, and its regression coefficient indicates the degree of the quadratic aspect of X's relation to Y. The multiple regression with both X and X^2 in the equation for data set (a) in Table 13.1 is .927, and the unstandardized regression coefficients for these predictors are, respectively, -2.714 and .083. Even higher-order curvilinear relations can be represented with the appropriate power term. For example, the term X^3 represents the cubic relation of X to Y, X^4 represents the quartic relation, and so on. However, it is rarely necessary to estimate curvilinear effects beyond a quadratic one in behavioral data.

Now consider data set (b) in Table 13.1. If the X and W are the only predictors in a standard regression analysis, their multiple correlation with Y is .183 and the unstandardized regression coefficients for X and W are, respectively, .112 and $-.064$. These results estimate the linear relations of each predictor with the criterion only, but inspection of the raw scores in this data set indicates a more complex pattern. For example, the relation of X to Y is linear and positive for cases with

[1]These two approaches can be combined. For example, it is theoretically possible to analyze a model with product terms across multiple samples.

TABLE 13.1. Data Sets for a Quadratic Effect and an Interaction Effect

| | (a) Quadratic effect | | | (b) Interaction effect | | | |
| | Predictors | | Criterion | Predictors | | | Criterion |
Case	X	X^2	Y	X	W	XW	Y
A	7	49	14	2	10	20	5
B	10	100	11	6	12	72	9
C	13	169	9	8	13	104	11
D	15	225	9	11	10	110	11
E	17	289	5	4	24	96	11
F	19	361	8	7	19	133	10
G	23	529	11	8	18	144	7
H	25	625	14	11	25	275	5

lower scores on W (≤ 16) but is linear and negative at higher levels of W. Although it is not as apparent, there is a similar change in the direction of the relation of W to Y: positive at higher levels of X; negative at lower levels of X. Thus, W moderates the relation of X to Y, just as X moderates the relation of W of Y. The product term XW represents the interaction effect in the regression analysis with X, W, and XW as predictors. The multiple correlation from the analysis just described for data set (b) in Table 13.1 is .910, and the unstandardized regression coefficients for X, W, and XW are, respectively, 1.768, .734, and –.108. The use of regression techniques to estimate interaction effects is sometimes called **moderated multiple regression**.

Although it exceeds the scope of this section to cover this topic in detail, the basic method just described can also be used to estimate higher-order interactions. For example, the product term XW represents the linear × linear interaction of X and W for data set (b) in Table 13.1. Such an interaction means that the linear relation of X to Y changes uniformly (i.e., linearly) across the levels of W. In contrast, the product term XW^2 represents a linear × quadratic interaction, which means that the linear relation of X to Y changes faster at higher (or lower) levels of W. Because the estimation of higher-order interactive (and curvilinear) effects may require the analysis of numerous product variables, very large samples may be necessary. See J. Cohen, P. Cohen, West, and Aiken (2003) for more information.

In the **indicant product approach** in SEM, product terms are specified as indicators of latent variables that represent interaction or curvilinear effects of latent variables. Consider the standard structural regression (SR) model in Figure 13.1(a). The path $A \rightarrow Y$ represents the linear effect of the factor on the observed endogenous variable. (The rationale outlined here also applies to the use of multiple indica-

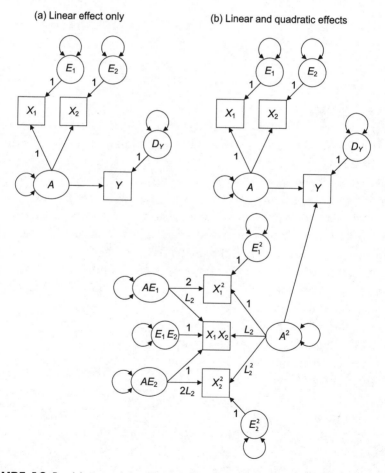

FIGURE 13.1. (a) A model with a linear effect of factor A only. (b) The corresponding model with linear and quadratic effects of A.

tors to measure an endogenous construct.) The measurement model for A can be represented with the following structural equations:

$$X_1 = A + E_1 \qquad\qquad (13.1)$$
$$X_2 = L_2 A + E_2$$

where the loading of X_1 is fixed to 1.0 to scale the factor and the loading of X_2 is a free parameter represented by L_2. The only other parameters of this measurement model are the variances of A and the error terms, E_1 and E_2.

Suppose that a researcher wished to estimate the quadratic effect of factor A on Y. This calls for adding to the model of Figure 13.1(a) the latent product variable A^2 that represents this effect, which is estimated by the coefficient for the path $A^2 \rightarrow Y$. Like its linear counterpart, A^2 is a latent variable measured indirectly only through its indicators. The indicators of A^2 are the product terms X_1^2, X_2^2, and $X_1 X_2$. (Note that the latter does not here represent an interaction effect because its components, X_1 and X_2, are specified to measure the same factor.) By squaring or taking the product of the corresponding expressions in Equation 13.1, the equations for the measurement model for A^2 with product indicators are

$$X_1^2 = A^2 + 2AE_1 + E_1^2 \qquad\qquad (13.2)$$
$$X_2^2 = L_2^2 A^2 + 2L_2 AE_2 + E_2^2$$
$$X_1 X_2 = L_2 A^2 + L_2 AE_1 + AE_1 + E_1 E_2$$

These equations (13.2) show that the measurement model for product indicators involves not just the latent product factor A^2 but also five additional latent product terms, AE_1, AE_2, E_1^2, E_2^2, and $E_1 E_2$. (The latter three are error terms for the product indicators.) Note that all of the factor loadings of the measurement model for the product indicators are either constants or functions of L_2, the loading of X_2 on A (Equation 13.1). Other parameters of this measurement model include the variances of A^2 and those of the five other latent product terms. Presented in Figure 13.1(b) is the SR model that includes the measurement models for A and A^2 (i.e., Equations 13.1 and 13.2) and the structural model for causal effects on Y. Among estimates for this SR model, of greatest interest here may be the two path coefficients that estimate the linear and quadratic direct effects (respectively, $A \rightarrow Y$ and $A^2 \rightarrow Y$).

Kenny and Judd (1984) were among the first to describe a method for estimating structural equation models with product indicators like the one of Figure 13.1(b). Assuming normal distributions and means that equal zero for the nonproduct variables (e.g., X_1, X_2, A, E_1, and E_2 in Figure 13.1), Kenny and Judd showed that the parameters of the measurement model for the product indicators (e.g., Equation 13.2) are functions of the parameters of the measurement model for the original indicators (e.g., Equation 13.1). For example, the variance of the latent quadratic factor A^2 equals two times the squared variance of the latent linear factor A, and the variance of the latent product term AE_1 equals the product of the variances of A and E_1. With these and other nonlinear constraints imposed on parameters for the measurement model of the product indicators, it is possible to estimate the effects of interest, such as the coefficients for the paths $A \rightarrow Y$ and $A^2 \rightarrow Y$ in Figure 13.1(b). Two drawbacks to this method are that not all SEM computer programs support nonlinear constraints and that correctly programming all such constraints can be tedious and error-prone (e.g., Jöreskog & Yang, 1996).

Ping (1996) described a two-step estimation method that does not require nonlinear constraints, which means that it can be used with just about any SEM computer program. It requires essentially the same basic statistical assumptions as the Kenny–Judd method. In the first step of Ping's method, the model is analyzed without the product indicators; that is, only the main effects in the structural model are estimated. One records parameter estimates from this analysis and calculates the values of parameters of the measurement model for the product indicators implied by the Kenny–Judd model. These values can be calculated either by hand or by using a set of templates for Microsoft Excel created by R. A. Ping that can be freely downloaded over the Internet.[2] These calculated values are then specified as fixed parameters in the second step where all variables, product and nonproduct, are analyzed. Included in the results of this analysis are estimates of interaction or curvilinear effects of latent variables. Applied to the figure, one would first analyze the model of

[2]http://home.att.net/~rpingjr/

Figure 13.1(a) to obtain estimates for all parameters of this standard SR model. Using these values to calculate estimates for the measurement model of the product indicators, one then specifies the calculated estimates as fixed parameters in the analysis of a simplified version of the model in Figure 13.1(b). The path coefficients for the linear and quadratic effects of factor A on Y are obtained from this second analysis.

Some technical problems may crop up with either the Kenny–Judd or the Ping methods for analyzing models with product indicators (Rigdon, Schumacker, & Wothke, 1998). One of these is multicollinearity. This is because correlations between product terms and their constituent variables can be relatively high. However, there are some ways to address this problem. One is to center the original indicators before calculating product terms based on them. **Centering** means that the average of a variable is adjusted to zero (i.e., the mean is subtracted from every score), and it tends to reduce correlations between product terms and constituent variables. Because means of zero are assumed in the Kenny–Judd and Ping methods, centering may also be part of the general analysis. Iterative estimation may be more likely to fail for models with many product variables. Ping (1995) suggests various "shortcuts" that involve analyzing fewer product variables if unidimensional measurement can be assumed for the original indicators. The assumption of normal distributions for the original indicators is crucial. If this assumption is not tenable, then parameter estimates implied by the Kenny–Judd method (which also determine estimates in Ping's method) may not be accurate. However, distributions of product indicators may be severely nonnormal even if those of the original indicators are generally normal. This means that normal-theory estimation methods such as maximum likelihood (ML) may not yield accurate results. There are methods for analyzing nonnormal data (Chapter 7), but they can be difficult to apply to models with product indicators (see Jöreskog & Yang, 1996).

A recent book edited by Schumacker and Marcoulides (1998) is a good resource for learning more about the estimation of interaction or curvilinear effects of latent variables in SEM. Several chapters in this volume list examples of syntax for EQS, LISREL, Mx, and the CALIS procedure of SAS/STAT that apply the Kenny–Judd, Ping, or related methods in actual or simulated data sets. Alternative conceptual models for estimating interaction or curvilinear effects of latent variables without product indicators are also described in this volume.

13.2 MULTILEVEL STRUCTURAL EQUATION MODELS

Multilevel models are also known as **random coefficient models** or **covariance components models**. These terms refer to classes of statistical models for hierarchical data where individuals are clustered into larger units, such as siblings within families or workers within departments. These larger units may themselves be classified under even higher-order variables, such as families within neighborhoods or departments within companies. Within each level, scores may not be independent. For example, siblings may all be affected by family characteristics, such as whether both parents are in the home, and family characteristics may be affected by neighborhood variables, such as crime rates or community socioeconomic status (SES). Repeated measures data sets are also hierarchical in the sense that multiple scores are clustered under each case, and these scores may not be independent.

Traditional statistical methods generally deal with a single unit of analysis only. They also typically assume independence of the observations. Applied to clustered data, traditional methods may require either aggregation or disaggregation of the scores in a way that ignores potentially important information. Suppose that math skills are measured in a large sample of students at Grade 6 and then again at Grade 8. The gender, minority group status, and participation in a federally funded school lunch program of each student is recorded. The three variables just mentioned and math skills measured at Grade 6 are the within-groups predictors of math skills at Grade 8. The students attend different schools, and each school is measured in terms of the quality of its programs, community SES, the proportion of minority students, and whether the school is a middle school with Grades 6–8 only or not. These four variables and Grade 6 math skills are the between-groups predictors of Grade 8 math skills. (Both math skills variables are here defined as the school average score.)

At the case (student) level, standard multiple regression could be applied to predict Grade 8 math skills from the four within-groups predictors, but these results would ignore the five between-groups (school-level) predictors and the possibility that scores within each school are not independent. However, analysis of the between-groups predictors with standard multiple regression would require the analysis of means on these variables aggregated over the case-level variables, which loses information. What is needed for this example is **two-level regression**, which analyzes two separate regression equations. The level-1 equation is for the regression of individual eighth-grade math test scores on the four other student variables, and the level-2 equation is for the regression of school average eighth-grade math test scores on the five other school variables. Unlike standard (single-level) regression, which assumes independence over all N scores, in two-level regression independence is assumed only over the schools. The level-1 equation would be fitted to a pooled within-groups covariance matrix, and the level-2 equation would be fitted to a between-groups covariance matrix. (Both matrices concern just the relevant variables for each analysis.) Through the simultaneous analysis of both equations in a two-level regression, the effects of level-1 (student) and level-2 (school) variables on Grade 8 math skills can be accurately estimated. In contrast, the use of single-level regression to analyze clustered data may not yield accurate results because of violation of the assumption of independence over all cases (e.g., Osborne, 2000).

Now suppose that Grade 6 math skills are believed to mediate the effects of other level-1 and level-2 predictors on Grade 8 math skills. Mediator (indirect) effects can be estimated in a **two-level path analysis** of the models presented in Figure 13.2. The model of Figure 13.2(a) is the level-1 path model, and it specifies that Grade 8 math skills within schools are directly affected by the four student variables of gender, minority group status, lunch program participation, and Grade 6 math skills. The model of Figure 13.2(b) is the level-2 (between-groups) path model. The exogenous variables in this model are school quality, the proportion of minority students, community SES, and whether the school is a middle school or not. Note that Grade 6 math skills in both models of Figure 13.2 are specified as being a mediator variable. Each model in Figure 13.2 can be analyzed simultaneously or separately with a computer program for SEM that supports multilevel analyses (more about this point momentarily).

In a multilevel path analysis, Heck (2001) estimated the models of Figure 13.2 with data from a large sample of Grade 8 students ($N = 9,410$)

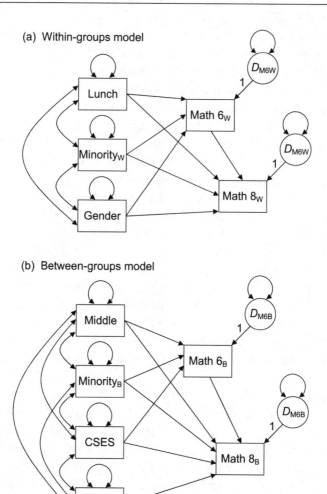

(a) Within-groups model

(b) Between-groups model

FIGURE 13.2. Example of a two-level path model of math achievement. The subscripts W and B indicate, respectively, within-groups and between-groups variables; CSES, community socioeconomic status.

who attended 51 different schools. At both the within- and between-groups levels, the single best predictor of eighth-grade math test scores was sixth-grade math test scores. For example, the standardized path coefficient for this direct effect in the within-groups model was .85 and in the between-groups model was .87. At the within-groups level, the predictive power of other student characteristics, such as gender and minority group status, was relatively small. At the between-groups level, the effect of community SES on Grade 8 math skills was entirely indirect through its effect on Grade 6 math skills; the standardized estimate of this indirect effect was .42. The effect of the proportion of minority students in each school was also primarily indirect. The standardized estimate of this indirect effect was −.14, about one-third the magnitude of the standardized indirect effect of community SES. School quality had only a slight positive standardized direct effect on Grade 8 math skills (.03).

A drawback of either single-level path analysis (Chapters 5 and 6) or multilevel path analysis is the inability to take direct account of measurement error or to represent the measurement of constructs with multiple indicators. Fortunately, there are also multilevel versions of confirmatory factor analysis (CFA) models and SR models. Just like their single-level counterparts (Chapters 7–8), these multilevel latent variable models adjust for measurement error and generally assume multiple-indicator measurement. These models can also optionally include a mean structure. A latent growth model (LGM; Chapter 10) is a special kind of two-level model in that repeated measures are clustered within individuals. A multiple-sample SEM (Chapter 11) can also be viewed as a restricted kind of multilevel model that lacks a distinct model at the group level. That is, all variables except group membership are within-groups variables.

Most examples of the analysis of multilevel models in the SEM literature are two-level models where level 1 concerns case variables and level 2 concerns group variables. For example, Kaplan (2000, chap. 7) describes the analysis of a two-level CFA model of student perceptions of school climate where the within-school model had three factors (teacher quality, negative school climate, and level of misbehavior) and the between-school model had a single general climate factor. T. E. Duncan et al. (1997) analyzed a multilevel LGM where adolescent gender and age predicted within-family variation in levels of substance use over a 4-year period and where family status variables, such as SES, predicted between-family variation. Rosser, Johnsrud, and Heck (2003) estimated a multilevel SR model of the effectiveness of academic administrators with predictor variables from both the individual and institutional levels. The former included academic rank (e.g., associate professor vs. full professor) and organizational role (e.g., departmental vs. faculty), and the latter included the size and types of the academic unit (e.g., professional school vs. liberal arts college). It is theoretically possible to analyze models with three or more levels of variables (e.g., teachers within schools within districts), but the need for ever-larger samples as additional levels are added beyond two makes these types of models relatively rare.

Until recently, it was rather difficult to analyze multilevel structural equation models. This is primarily because most SEM computer programs were intended for single-level analyses only. They could be applied to multilevel analyses, but the programming in order to do so tended to be complicated (e.g., T. E. Duncan et al., 1997, pp. 310–318). However, more recent versions of some traditional programs for SEM, such as EQS and LISREL, have featured specific syntax for multilevel analyses. The Mplus program is very flexible in that it can analyze multilevel models with either continuous or categorical latent variables. These computer programs may use special forms of ML estimation for multilevel data that adjust for unequal group sizes. Nevertheless, it can still be challenging to correctly specify and analyze a multilevel model with numerous within-groups and between-groups predictors even with a computer program that directly supports this type of analysis. Also, methods for multilevel SEM are still evolving. This means that there are fewer guidelines for interpreting and reporting the results of a multilevel SEM compared to a single-level SEM. This situation will probably change in the near future, however. For now, it would be well worth the effort for researchers who are familiar with the basics of SEM and who also analyze hierarchically structured data to learn more about multilevel SEM and related statistical techniques.

13.3 SUMMARY

So concludes this journey of discovery about SEM. As on any guided tour, you may have found some places along the way more interesting than others. Also, you may decide to revisit certain sites by using some of the related techniques in your own work. Overall, I hope the reading of this book has given you new ways of looking at your data and testing a broader range of hypotheses. Use SEM to address new questions or to provide new perspectives on older ones, but use it guided by your good sense and knowledge of your research area. Use it also as a means to reform methods of data analysis in the behavioral sciences by focusing on models instead of specific effects analyzed with traditional statistical significance tests. Go do me proud again!

13.4 RECOMMENDED READINGS

Heck, R. H. (2001). Multilevel modeling with SEM. In G. A. Marcoulides & R. E. Schumacker (Eds.), *New developments and techniques in structural equation modeling* (pp. 89–127). Mahwah, NJ: Erlbaum.
Schumacker, R. E., & Marcoulides, G. A. (Eds.). (1998). *Interaction and nonlinear effects in structural equation modeling*. Mahwah, NJ: Erlbaum.

References

Allison, P. D. (2001). *Missing data*. Thousand Oaks, CA: Sage.

Allison, P. D. (2003). Missing data techniques for structural equation modeling. *Journal of Abnormal Psychology, 112*, 545–557.

Anderson, D. R., Burnham, K. P., & Thompson, W. L. (2000). Null hypothesis testing: Problems, prevalence, and an alternative. *Journal of Wildlife Management, 64*, 912–923.

Anderson, J. C., & Gerbing, D. W. (1988). Structural equation modeling in practice: A review and recommended two-step approach. *Psychological Bulletin, 103*, 411–423.

Arbuckle, J. L. (1996). Full information estimation in the presence of incomplete data. In G. A. Marcoulides & R. E. Schumacker (Eds.), *Advanced structural equation modeling* (pp. 243–277). Mahwah, NJ: Erlbaum.

Arbuckle, J. L. (2003). Amos 5 [Computer software]. Chicago: SmallWaters.

Bandalos, D. L. (2002). The effects of item parceling on goodness-of-fit and parameter estimate bias in structural equation modeling. *Structural Equation Modeling, 9*, 78–102.

Bandalos, D. L., & Finney, S. J. (2001). Item parceling issues in structural equation modeling. In G. A. Marcoulides & R. E. Schumacker (Eds.), *New developments and techniques in structural equation modeling* (pp. 269–296). Mahwah, NJ: Erlbaum.

Baron, R. M., & Kenny, D. A. (1986). The moderator–mediator variable distinction in social psychological research: Conceptual, strategic, and statistical considerations. *Journal of Personality and Social Psychology, 51*, 1173–1182.

Bartholomew, D. J. (2002). Old and new approaches to latent variable modeling. In G. A. Marcoulides & I. Moustaki (Eds.), *Latent variable and latent structure models* (pp. 1–13). Mahwah, NJ: Erlbaum.

Beaubien, J. M. (2000). [Review of the book *Principles and practice of structural equation modeling*]. *Personnel Psychology, 53*, 793–795.

Beckie, T. M., Beckstead, J. W., & Webb, M. S. (2001). Modeling women's quality of life after cardiac events. *Western Journal of Nursing Research, 23*, 179–194.

Bedeian, A. G., Day, D. V., & Kelloway, E. K. (1997). Correcting for measurement error attenuation in structural equation models: Some important reminders. *Educational and Psychological Measurement, 57,* 785–799.

Bentler, P. M. (1980). Multivariate analysis with latent variables: Causal modeling. *Annual Review of Psychology, 31,* 419–456.

Bentler, P. M. (1990). Comparative fit indexes in structural models. *Psychological Bulletin, 107,* 238–246.

Bentler, P. M. (1995). *EQS structural equations program manual.* Encino, CA: Multivariate Software.

Bentler, P. M. (2000). Rites, wrongs, and gold in model testing. *Structural Equation Modeling, 7,* 82–91.

Bentler, P. M. (2003). EQS 6.1 for Windows [Computer software]. Encino, CA: Multivariate Software.

Bentler, P. M., & Bonett, D. G. (1980). Significance tests and goodness of fit in the analysis of covariance structures. *Psychological Bulletin, 88,* 588–606.

Bentler, P. M., & Dijkstra, T. (1985). Efficient estimation via linearization in structural models. In P. R. Krishnaiah (Ed.), *Multivariate analysis VI* (pp. 9–42). Amsterdam: North-Holland.

Bentler, P. M., & Raykov, T. (2000). On measures of explained variance in nonrecursive structural equation models. *Journal of Applied Psychology, 85,* 125–131.

Bernstein, I. H., & Teng, G. (1989). Factoring items and factoring scales are different: Spurious evidence for multidimensionality due to item categorization. *Psychological Bulletin, 105,* 467–477.

Berry, W. D. (1984). *Nonrecursive causal models.* Beverly Hills, CA: Sage.

Blalock, H. M. (1991). Are there really any constructive alternatives to causal modeling? *Sociological Methodology, 21,* 325–335.

Block, J. (1995). On the relation between IQ, impulsivity, and delinquency: Remarks on the Lynam, Moffitt, and Stouthamer-Loeber (1993) interpretation. *Journal of Abnormal Psychology, 104,* 395–398.

Bollen, K. A. (1989). *Structural equations with latent variables.* New York: Wiley.

Bollen, K. A. (1996). A limited information estimator for LISREL models with or without heteroscedastic errors. In G. A. Marcoulides & R. E. Schumacker (Eds.), *Advanced structural equation modeling* (pp. 227–241). Mahwah, NJ: Erlbaum.

Bollen, K. A. (2000). Modeling strategies: In search of the holy grail. *Structural Equation Modeling, 7,* 74–81.

Bollen, K. A. (2001). Two-stage least squares and latent variable models: Simultaneous estimation and robustness to misspecifications. In R. Cudeck, S. Du Toit, & D. Sörbom (Eds.), *Structural equation modeling: Present and future* (pp. 119–138). Lincolnwood, IL: Scientific Software International.

Bollen, K. A., & Lennox, R. (1991). Conventional wisdom on measurement: A structural equation perspective. *Psychological Bulletin, 110,* 305–314.

Bollen, K. A., & Paxton, P. (1998). Detection and determinants of bias in subjective measures. *American Sociological Review, 63,* 465–478.

Bollen, K. A., & Stine, R. A. (1993). Bootstrapping goodness-of-fit measures in structural equation models. In K. A. Bollen & J. S. Long (Eds.), *Testing structural equation models* (pp. 111–135). Newbury Park, CA: Sage.

Boomsma, A. (2000). Reporting analyses of covariance structures. *Structural Equation Modeling, 7,* 461–483.

Bozdogan, H. (1987). Model selection and Akaike's information criteria (AIC): The general theory and its analytical extensions. *Psychometrika, 52,* 345–370.

Breckler, S. J. (1990). Applications of covariance structure modeling in psychology: Cause for concern? *Psychological Bulletin, 107,* 260–273.

Brito, C., & Pearl, J. (2003). A new identification condition for recursive models with correlated errors. *Structural Equation Modeling, 9,* 459–474.

Browne, M. W. (1982). Covariance structures. In D. M. Hawkins (Ed.), *Topics in applied multivariate analysis* (pp. 72–141). Cambridge, England: Cambridge University Press.

Browne, M. W. (1984). Asymptotic distribution free methods in analysis of covariance structures. *British Journal of Mathematical and Statistical Psychology, 37,* 62–83.

Browne, M. W., & Cudeck, R. (1993). Alternative ways of assessing model fit. In K. A. Bollen & J. S. Long (Eds.), *Testing structural equation models* (pp. 136–162). Newbury Park, CA: Sage.

Bryant, F. B. (2000). Assessing the validity of measurement. In L. G. Grimm & P. R. Yarnold (Eds.), *Reading and understanding more multivariate statistics* (pp. 99–146). Washington, DC: American Psychological Association.

Burt, R. S. (1976). Interpretational confounding of unobserved variables in structural equation models. *Sociological Methods and Research, 5,* 3–52.

Byrne, B. M. (2001). *Structural equation modeling with Amos: Basic concepts, applications, and programming.* Mahwah, NJ: Erlbaum.

Calsyn, R. J., & Kenny, D. A. (1977). Self-concept of ability and perceived evaluation of others: Cause or effect of academic achievement? *Journal of Educational Psychology, 69,* 136–145.

Cameron, L. C., Ittenbach, R. F., McGrew, K. S., Harrison, P. L., Taylor, L. R., & Hwang, Y. R. (1997). Confirmatory factor analysis of the K-ABC with gifted referrals. *Educational and Psychological Measurement, 57,* 823–840.

Campbell, D. T., & Fiske, D. W. (1959). Convergent and discriminant validation by the multitrait–multimethod matrix. *Psychological Bulletin, 56,* 81–105.

Cattell, R. B. (1978). *The scientific use of factor analysis in behavioral and life sciences.* New York: Plenum Press.

Chan, D. (1998). The conceptualization and analysis of change over time: An integrative approach incorporating longitudinal mean and covariance structures analysis (LMACS) and multiple indicator latent growth modeling (MLGM). *Organizational Research Methods, 1,* 421–483.

Chen, F., Bollen, K. A., Paxton, P., Curran, P. J., & Kirby, J. B. (2001). Improper solutions in structural equation models: Causes, consequences, and strategies. *Sociological Methods and Research, 29,* 468–508.

Cheung, D. (2000). Evidence of a single second-order factor in student ratings of teaching effectiveness. *Structural Equation Modeling, 7,* 442–460.

Chou, C.-P., & Bentler, P. M. (1995). Estimates and tests in structural equation modeling. In R. H. Hoyle (Ed.), *Structural equation modeling* (pp. 37–55). Thousand Oaks, CA: Sage.

Cohen, J. (1988). *Statistical power analysis for the behavioral sciences* (2nd ed.). New York: Academic Press.

Cohen, J., & Cohen, P. (1983). *Applied multiple regression/correlation for the behavioral sciences* (2nd ed.). Hillsdale, NJ: Erlbaum.

Cohen, J., Cohen, P., West, S. G., & Aiken, L. S. (2003). *Applied multiple regression/correlation analysis for the behavioral sciences* (3rd ed.). Mahwah, NJ: Erlbaum.

Cole, D. A., & Maxwell, S. E. (2003). Testing mediational models with longitudinal data: Questions and tips. *Journal of Abnormal Psychology, 112,* 558–577.

Cole, D. A., Maxwell, S. E., Avery, R., & Salas, E. (1993). Multivariate group comparisons of variable systems: MANOVA and structural equation modeling. *Psychological Bulletin, 114,* 174–184.

Cooperman, J. M. (1996). *Maternal aggression and withdrawal in childhood: Continuity and intergenerational risk transmission.* Unpublished master's thesis, Concordia University, Montréal, Québec, Canada.

Cudeck, R. (1989). Analysis of correlation matrices using covariance structure models. *Psychological Bulletin, 105,* 317–327.

Curran, P. J., Harford, T. C., & Muthén, B. O. (1996). The relation between heavy alcohol use and bar patronage: A latent growth model. *Journal of Studies on Alcohol, 57*(4), 410–418.

Curran, P. J., West, S. G., & Finch, J. F. (1997). The robustness of test statistics to nonnormality and specification error in confirmatory factor analysis. *Psychological Methods, 1,* 16–29.

DeCarlo, L. T. (1997). On the meaning and use of kurtosis. *Psychological Methods, 2,* 292–307.

Diaconis, P., & Efron, B. (1983). Computer-intensive methods in statistics. *Scientific American, 248*(5), 116–130.

Diamantopoulos, A., & Winklhofer, H. M. (2001). Index construction with formative indicators: An alternative to scale development. *Journal of Marketing Research, 38,* 269–277.

Dilalla, L. F. (2000). Structural equation modeling: Uses and issues. In H. E. A. Tinsley & S. D. Brown (Eds.), *Handbook of applied multivariate statistics and mathematical modeling* (pp. 440–464). New York: Academic Press.

DiStefano, C. (2002). The impact of categorization with confirmatory factor analysis. *Structural Equation Modeling, 9,* 327–346.

Duncan. S. C., & Duncan, T. E. (1996). A multivariate latent growth curve analysis of adolescent substance use. *Structural Equation Modeling, 3,* 323–347.

Duncan, T. E., Duncan, S. C., Alpert, A., Hops, H., Stoolmiller, M., & Muthén, B. (1997). Latent variable modeling of longitudinal and multilevel substance abuse data. *Multivariate Behavioral Research, 32,* 275–318.

Duncan, T. E., Duncan, S. C., Strycker, L. A., Li, F., & Alpert, A. (1999). *An introduction to latent variable growth curve modeling: Concepts, issues, and applications.* Mahwah, NJ: Erlbaum.

Eaves, R. C. (1995). *The Visual Similes Test II—Affective and Cognitive forms.* Opelika, AL: Small World.

Efron, B., & Tibshirani, R. J. (1993). *An introduction to the bootstrap.* New York: Chapman & Hall.

Eliason, S. R. (1993). *Maximum likelihood estimation.* Newbury Park, CA: Sage.

Fabrigar, L. R., Wegener, D. T., McCallum, R. C., & Strahan, E. J. (1999). Evaluating the use of exploratory factor analysis in psychological research. *Psychological Methods, 4,* 272–299.

Finkel, S. E. (1995). *Causal analysis with panel data.* Thousand Oaks, CA: Sage.

Fraser, C. (1990). COSAN [Computer software]. Armidale, New South Wales, Australia: University of New England.

Frederich, J., Buday, E., & Kerr, D. (2000). Statistical training in psychology: A national survey and commentary on undergraduate programs. *Teaching of Psychology, 27,* 248–257.

Freedman, D. A. (1991). Statistical models and shoe leather. *Sociological Methodology, 21,* 291–313.

Glaser, D. (2000). [Review of the book *Principles and practice of structural equation modeling*]. *Structural Equation Modeling, 7,* 489–495.

Glaser, D. (2002). Structural equation modeling texts: A primer for the beginner. *Journal of Clinical Child Psychology, 31,* 573–578.

Gonzalez, R., & Griffin, D. (2001). Testing parameters in structural equation modeling: Every "one" matters. *Psychological Methods, 6,* 258–269.

Graham, J. M., Guthrie, A. C., & Thompson, B. (2003). Consequences of not interpreting structure coefficients in published CFA research: A reminder. *Structural Equation Modeling, 10,* 142–153.

Hagenaars, J. A., & McCutcheon, A. L. (Eds.). (2002). *Applied latent class analysis.* Cambridge, MA: Cambridge University Press.

Hancock, G. R., & Freeman, M. J. (2001). Power and sample size for the root mean square error of approximation of not close fit in structural equation modeling. *Educational and Psychological Measurement, 61,* 741–758.

Hayduk, L. A. (1996). *LISREL issues, debates, and strategies.* Baltimore: Johns Hopkins University Press.

Hayduk, L. A., & Glaser, D. N. (2000). Jiving the four-step, waltzing around factor analysis, and other serious fun. *Structural Equation Modeling, 7,* 1–35.

Heck, R. H. (2001). Multilevel modeling with SEM. In G. A. Marcoulides & R. E. Schumacker (Eds.), *New developments and techniques in structural equation modeling* (pp. 89–127). Mahwah, NJ: Erlbaum.

Heise, D. R. (1975). *Causal analysis.* New York: Wiley.

Herschberger, S. L. (1994). The specification of equivalent models before the collection of data. In A. von Eye & C. C. Clogg (Eds.), *Latent variables analysis* (pp. 68–105). Thousand Oaks, CA: Sage.

Herschberger, S. L. (2003). The growth of structural equation modeling: 1994–2001. *Structural Equation Modeling, 19,* 35–46.

Herting, J. R., & Costner, H. J. (2000). Another perspective on "the proper number of factors" and the appropriate number of steps. *Structural Equation Modeling, 7,* 92–110.

Hoyle, R. H. (2000). Confirmatory factor analysis. In H. E. A. Tinsley & S. D. Brown (Eds.), *Handbook of applied multivariate statistics and mathematical modeling* (pp. 465–497). New York: Academic Press.

Hoyle, R. H., & Panter, A. T. (1995). Writing about structural equation models. In R. H. Hoyle (Ed.), *Structural equation modeling* (pp. 158–176). Thousand Oaks, CA: Sage.

Hser, Y.-I., Chou, C.-P., Messer, S. C., & Anglin, M. D. (2001). Analytic approaches for assessing long-term treatment effects: Examples of empirical applications and findings. *Evaluation Review, 25*(2), 233–262.

Hu, L.-T., & Bentler, P. M. (1999). Cutoff criteria for fit indices in covariance structure analysis: Conventional criteria versus new alternatives. *Structural Equation Modeling, 6,* 1–55.

Hurley, A. E., Scandura, T. A., Schriesheim, C. A., Brannick, M. T., Seers, A., Vandenberg, R. J., & Williams, L. J. (1997). Exploratory and confirmatory factor analysis: Guidelines, issues, and alternatives. *Journal of Organizational Behavior, 18,* 667–683.

Jackson, D. L. (2003). Revisiting sample size and number of parameter estimates: Some support for the N:q hypothesis. *Structural Equation Modeling, 10,* 128–141.

James, L. R., Mulaik, S. A., & Brett, J. M. (1982). *Causal analysis: Assumptions, models, and data.* Beverly Hills, CA: Sage.

James, L. R., & Singh, B. K. (1978). An introduction to the logic, assumptions, and basic analytic procedures of two-stage least squares. *Psychological Bulletin, 85,* 1104–1122.

Jöreskog, K. G. (1993). Testing structural equation models. In K. A. Bollen & J. S. Lang (Eds.), *Testing structural equation models* (pp. 294–316). Newbury Park, CA: Sage.

Jöreskog, K. G., & Sörbom, D. (1981). *LISREL V: Analysis of linear structural relationships by the method of maximum likelihood.* Chicago: National Education Resources.

Jöreskog, K. G., & Sörbom, D. (2003). LISREL 8.54 for Windows [Computer software]. Lincolnwood, IL: Scientific Software International.

Jöreskog, K. G., & Yang, F. (1996). Nonlinear structural equation models: The Kenny–Judd model with interaction effects. In G. A. Marcoulides & R. E. Schumacker (Eds.), *Advanced structural equation modeling* (pp. 57–88). Mahwah, NJ: Erlbaum.

Kano, Y. (2001). Structural equation modeling with experimental data. In R. Cudeck, S. Du Toit, & D. Sörbom (Eds.), *Structural equation modeling: Present and future* (pp. 381–402). Lincolnwood, IL: Scientific Software International.

Kaplan, D. (2000). *Structural equation modeling.* Thousand Oaks, CA: Sage.

Kaplan, D., Harik, P., & Hotchkiss, L. (2001). Cross-sectional estimation of dynamic structural equation models in disequilibrium. In R. Cudeck, S. Du Toit, & D. Sörbom (Eds.), *Structural equation modeling: Present and future* (pp. 315–339). Lincolnwood, IL: Scientific Software International.

Kaplan, D., & Wenger, R. N. (1993). Asymptotic independence and separability in covariance structure models: Implications for specification error, power, and model modification. *Multivariate Behavioral Research, 28,* 483–498.

Kaufman, A. S., & Kaufman, N. L. (1983). *K-ABC administration and scoring manual.* Circle Pines, MN: American Guidance Service.

Kenny, D. A. (1979). *Correlation and causality.* New York: Wiley.

Kenny, D. A. (2002). Instrumental variable estimation. Retrieved March 15, 2003, from http://users.erols.com/dakenny/iv.htm

Kenny, D. A., & Judd, C. M. (1984). Estimating the nonlinear and interactive effects of latent variables. *Psychological Bulletin, 96,* 201–210.

Kenny, D. A., & Kashy, D. A. (1992). Analysis of the multitrait–multimethod matrix by confirmatory factor analysis. *Psychological Bulletin, 112,* 165–172.

Kenny, D. A., Kashy, D. A., & Bolger, N. (1998). Data analysis in social psychology. In D. Gilbert, S. Fiske, & G. Lindzey (Eds.), *The handbook of social psychology* (4th ed., Vol. 1, pp. 233–265). Boston: McGraw-Hill.

Kenny, D. A., & McCoach, D. B. (2003). Effects of number of variables on measures of fit in structural equation modeling. *Structural Equation Modeling, 10,* 333–351.

Klem, L. (1995). Path analysis. In L. G. Grimm & P. R. Yarnold (Eds.), *Reading and understanding multivariate statistics* (pp. 65–98). Washington, DC: American Psychological Association.

Klem, L. (2000). Structural equation modeling. In L. G. Grimm & P. R. Yarnold (Eds.), *Reading and understanding more multivariate statistics* (pp. 227–259). Washington, DC: American Psychological Association.

Kline, R. B. (1998). *Principles and practice of structural equation modeling* (1st ed.). New York: Guilford Press.

Kline, R. B. (2004). *Beyond significance testing: Reforming data analysis methods in behavioral research.* Washington, DC: American Psychological Association.

Kline, R. B. (in press). Reverse-arrow dynamics: Formative measurement models and feedback loops. In G. R. Hancock & R. O. Mueller (Eds.), *A second course in structural equation modeling.* Greenwich, CT: Information Age.

Koestler, A. (1989). *The act of creation.* New York: Penguin Books. (Original work published 1964)

Kühnel, S. (2001). The didactical power of structural equation modeling. In R. Cudeck, S. Du Toit, & D. Sörbom (Eds.), *Structural equation modeling: Present and future* (pp. 79–96). Lincolnwood, IL: Scientific Software International.

Lance, C. E. (1988). Residual centering, exploratory and confirmatory moderator analysis, and decomposition of effects in path models containing interaction effects. *Applied Psychological Measurement, 12,* 163–175.

Lance, C. E., Noble, C. L., & Scullen, S. E. (2002). A critique of the correlated trait–correlated method and correlated uniqueness model for multitrait–multimethod data. *Psychological Methods, 7,* 228–244.

Lee, S., & Herschberger, S. L. (1990). A simple rule for generating equivalent models in covariance structure modeling. *Multivariate Behavioral Research, 25*, 313–334.

Little, R. J. A., & Rubin, D. B. (2002). *Statistical analysis with missing data* (2nd ed.). New York: Wiley.

Little, T. D., Cunningham, W. A., Shahar, G., & Widaman, K. F. (2002). To parcel or not to parcel: Exploring the question, weighing the merits. *Structural Equation Modeling, 9*, 151–173.

Loehlin, J. C. (1998). *Latent variable models* (3rd ed.). Mahwah, NJ: Erlbaum.

Lynam, D. R., Moffitt, T., & Stouthamer-Loeber, M. (1993). Explaining the relation between IQ and delinquency: Class, race, test motivation, or self-control? *Journal of Abnormal Psychology, 102*, 187–196.

Maasen, G. H., & Bakker, A. B. (2001). Suppressor variables in path models: Definitions and interpretations. *Sociological Methods and Research, 30*, 241–270.

MacCallum, R. C. (1986). Specification searches in covariance structure modeling. *Psychological Bulletin, 100*, 107–120.

MacCallum, R. C. (1995). Model specification: Procedures, strategies, and related issues. In R. H. Hoyle (Ed.), *Structural equation modeling* (pp. 16–36). Thousand Oaks, CA: Sage.

MacCallum, R. C., & Austin, J. T. (2000). Applications of structural equation modeling in psychological research. *Annual Review of Psychology, 51*, 201–236.

MacCallum, R. C., & Browne, M. W. (1993). The use of causal indicators in covariance structure models: Some practical issues. *Psychological Bulletin, 114*, 533–541.

MacCallum, R. C., Browne, M. W., & Sugawara, H. M. (1996). Power analysis and determination of sample size for covariance structure modeling. *Psychological Methods, 1*, 130–149.

MacCallum, R. C., & Tucker, L. R. (1991). Representing sources of error in common factor analysis: Implications for theory and practice. *Psychological Bulletin, 109*, 501–511.

MacCallum, R. C., Wegener, D. T., Uchino, B. N., & Fabrigar, L. R. (1993). The problem of equivalent models in applications of covariance structure analysis. *Psychological Bulletin, 114*, 185–199.

MacCallum, R. C., Zhang, S., Preacher, K. J., & Rucker, D. O. (2002). On the practice of dichotomization of quantitative variables. *Psychological Methods, 7*, 19–40.

Marcoulides, G. A., & Drezner, Z. (2001). Specification searches in structural equation modeling with a genetic algorithm. In G. A. Marcoulides & R. E. Schumacker (Eds.), *New developments and techniques in structural equation modeling* (pp. 247–268). Mahwah, NJ: Erlbaum.

Marcoulides, G. A., & Drezner, Z. (2003). Model specification searches using ant colony optimization algorithms. *Structural Equation Modeling, 10*, 154–164.

Marcoulides, G. A., & Moustaki, I. (2002). *Latent variable and latent structure models.* Mahwah, NJ: Erlbaum.

Marcoulides, G. A., & Schumacker, R. E. (Eds.). (2001). *New developments and techniques in structural equation modeling.* Mahwah, NJ: Erlbaum.

Marsh, H. W., & Bailey, M. (1991). Confirmatory factor analysis of multitrait–multimethod data: A comparison of alternative models. *Applied Psychological Measurement, 15,* 47–70.

Marsh, H. W., Balla, J. R., & Hau, K.-T. (1996). An evaluation of incremental fit indices: A clarification of mathematical and empirical properties. In G. A. Marcoulides & R. E. Schumacker (Eds.), *Advanced structural equation modeling* (pp. 315–353). Mahwah, NJ: Erlbaum.

Marsh, H. W., & Grayson, D. (1995). Latent variable models of multitrait–multimethod data. In R. H. Hoyle (Ed.), *Structural equation modeling* (pp. 177–198). Thousand Oaks, CA: Sage.

Marsh, H. W., & Hau, K.-T. (1999). Confirmatory factor analysis: Strategies for small sample sizes. In R. H. Hoyle (Ed.), *Statistical strategies for small sample research* (pp. 252–284). Thousand Oaks, CA: Sage.

Maruyama, G. M. (1998). *Basics of structural equation modeling.* Thousand Oaks, CA: Sage.

Mason, W. M. (1991). Freedman is right as far as he goes, but there is more, and it's worse: Statisticians could help. *Sociological Methodology, 21,* 337–351.

McArdle, J. J., Johnson, R. C., Hishinuma, E. S., Miyamoto, R. H., & Andrade, N. N. (2001). Structural equation modeling of group differences in CES-D ratings of native Hawaiian and non-Hawaiian high school students. *Journal of Adolescent Research, 16,* 108–149.

McArdle, J. J., & McDonald, R. P. (1984). Some algebraic properties of the reticular action model for moment structures. *British Journal of Mathematical and Statistical Psychology, 37,* 234–251.

McDonald, R. P., & Ho, M.-H. R. (2002). Principles and practice in reporting structural equation analyses. *Psychological Methods, 7,* 64–82.

McDonald, R. P., & Marsh, H. W. (1990). Choosing a multivariate model: Noncentrality and goodness of fit. *Psychological Bulletin, 107,* 247–255.

Millman, E. J. (1998). [Review of the book *Principles and practice of structural equation modeling*]. *Readings: A Journal of Reviews and Commentary in Mental Health, 13,* 23.

Meehl, P. E., & Walker, N. G. (2002). The path analysis controversy: A new statistical approach to strong appraisal of verisimilitude. *Psychological Methods, 7,* 283–300.

Mulaik, S. A. (2000). Objectivity and other metaphors of structural equation modeling. In R. Cudeck, S. Du Toit, & D. Sörbom (Eds.), *Structural equation modeling: Present and future* (pp. 59–78). Lincolnwood, IL: Scientific Software International.

Mulaik, S. A., James, L. R., Van Alstine, J., Bennett, N., Lind, S., & Stillwell, C. D. (1989). Evaluation of goodness-of-fit indices for structural equation models. *Psychological Bulletin, 105,* 430–455.

Mulaik, S. A., & Millsap, R. E. (2000). Doing the four-step right. *Structural Equation Modeling, 7,* 36–73.

Murphy, S. A., Chung, I.-J., & Johnson, L.C. (2002). Patterns of mental distress following the violent death of a child and predictors of change over time. *Research in Nursing and Health, 25,* 425–437.

Muthén, B. (1984). A general structural equation model with dichotomous, ordered categorical, and continuous latent variable indicators. *Psychometrika, 49,* 115–132.

Muthén, B. (1993). Goodness of fit with categorical and other non-normal variables. In K. A. Bollen & J. S. Long (Eds.), *Testing structural equation models* (pp. 205–234). Newbury Park, CA: Sage.

Muthén, B. (2001). Latent variable mixture modeling. In G. A. Marcoulides & R. E. Schumacker (Eds.), *New developments and techniques in structural equation modeling* (pp. 1–33). Mahwah, NJ: Erlbaum.

Muthén, L. & Muthén, B. (1998–2004). MPlus (Version 3) [Computer software]. Los Angeles: Muthén & Muthén.

Neale, M. C., Boker, S. M., Xie, G., & Maes, H. H. (2002). *Mx: Statistical modeling* (6th ed.). Richmond: Virginia Commonwealth University, Virginia Institute for Psychiatric & Behavioral Genetics.

Neuman, G. A., Bolin, A. U., & Briggs, T. E. (2000). Identifying general factors of intelligence: A confirmatory factor analysis of the Ball Aptitude Battery. *Educational and Psychological Measurement, 60,* 697–712.

Nevitt, J., & Hancock, G. R. (2001). Performance of bootstrapping approaches to model test statistics and parameter standard error estimation in structural equation modeling. *Structural Equation Modeling, 8,* 353–377.

Nunnally, J. C., & Bernstein, I. H. (1994). *Psychometric theory* (3rd ed.). New York: McGraw-Hill.

Osborne, J. W. (2000). Advantages of hierarchical linear modeling. *Practical Assessment, Research & Evaluation, 7,* Article 1. Retrieved December 3, 2002, from http://pareonline.net/getvn.asp?v=7&n=1

Peters, C. L. O., & Enders, C. (2002). A primer for the estimation of structural equation models in the presence of missing data. *Journal of Targeting, Measurement and Analysis for Marketing, 11,* 81–95.

Ping, R. A. (1995). A parsimonious estimating technique for interaction and quadratic latent variables. *Journal of Marketing Research, 32,* 336–347.

Ping, R. A. (1996). Interaction and quadratic effect estimation: A two-step technique using structural equation analysis. *Psychological Bulletin, 119,* 166–175.

Raftery, A. E. (1993). Bayesian model selection in structural equation models. In K. A. Bollen & J. S. Long (Eds.), *Testing structural equation models* (pp. 163–180). Newbury Park, CA: Sage.

Raudenbush, S. W., & Bryk, A.S. (2002). *Hierarchical linear models* (2nd ed.). Thousand Oaks, CA: Sage.

Raykov, T., & Marcoulides, G. A. (2000). *A first course in structural equation modeling.* Mahwah, NJ: Erlbaum.

Raykov, T., & Marcoulides, G. A. (2001). Can there be infinitely many models equivalent to a given covariance structure? *Structural Equation Modeling, 8,* 142–149.

Reichardt, C. S. (2002). The priority of just-identified, recursive models. *Psychological Methods, 7*, 307–315.

Reise, S. P., Widaman, K. F., & Pugh, R. H. (1993). Confirmatory factor analysis and item response theory: Two approaches for exploring measurement invariance. *Psychological Bulletin, 114*, 552–566.

Rigdon, E. E., Schumacker, R. E., & Wothke, W. (1998). A comparative review of interaction and nonlinear modeling. In R. E. Schumacker & G. A. Marcoulides (Eds.), *Interaction and nonlinear effects in structural equation modeling* (pp. 1–16). Mahwah, NJ: Erlbaum.

Robert, S., & Pashler, H. (2000). How persuasive is a good fit?: A comment on theory testing in psychology. *Psychological Review, 107*, 358–367.

Robinson, W. S. (1950). Ecological correlations and the behavior of individuals. *American Sociological Review, 15*, 351–357.

Rodgers, J. L. (1999). The bootstrap, the jackknife, and the randomization test: A sampling taxonomy. *Multivariate Behavioral Research, 34*, 441–456.

Romney, D. M., Jenkins, C. D., & Bynner, J. M. (1992). A structural analysis of health-related quality of life dimensions. *Human Relations, 45*, 165–176.

Rosser, V. J., Johnsrud, L. K., & Heck, R. H. (2003). Academic deans and directors: Assessing their effectiveness from individual and institutional perspectives. *Journal of Higher Education, 74*, 1–25.

Rossi, J. S. (1997). A case study in the failure of psychology as a cumulative science: The spontaneous recovery of verbal learning. In L. L. Harlow, S. A. Mulaik, & J. H. Steiger (Eds.), *What if there were no significance tests?* (pp. 175–197). Mahwah, NJ: Erlbaum.

Roth, D. L., Wiebe, D. J., Fillingim, R. B., & Shay, K. A. (1989). Life events, fitness, hardiness, and health: A simultaneous analysis of proposed stress-resistance effects. *Journal of Personality and Social Psychology, 57*, 136–142.

Roth, P. L. (1994). Missing data: A conceptual review for applied psychologists. *Personnel Psychology, 47*, 537–560.

Sabatelli, R. M., & Bartle-Haring, S. (2003). Family-of-origin experiences and adjustment in married couples. *Journal of Marriage and Family, 65*, 159–169.

Santor, D. (1999). [Review of the books *Using LISREL for structural equation modeling* and *Principles and practice of structural equation modeling.*] *Canadian Psychology, 40*, 381–383.

Saris, W. E., & Alberts, C. (2003). Different explanations for correlated disturbance terms in MTMM studies. *Structural Equation Modeling, 10*, 193–213.

Saris, W. E., & Satorra, A. (1993). Power evaluations in structural equation models. In K. A. Bollen & J. S. Long (Eds.), *Testing structural equation models* (pp. 181–204). Newbury Park, CA: Sage.

SAS Institute Inc. (2000). The SAS System for Windows (Release 8.01) [Computer software]. Cary, NC: Author.

Satorra, A., & Bentler, P. M. (1994). Corrections to test statistics and standard errors on covariance structure analysis. In A. von Eye & C. C. Clogg (Eds.), *Latent variables analysis* (pp. 399–419). Thousand Oaks, CA: Sage.

Schmidt, F. L. (1996). Statistical significance testing and cumulative knowledge in psychology: Implications for the training of researchers. *Psychological Methods, 1,* 115–129.

Schmidt, F. L., & Hunter, J. E. (1997). Eight common but false objections to the discontinuation of significance testing in the analysis of research data. In L. L. Harlow, S. A. Mulaik, & J. H. Steiger (Eds.), *What if there were no significance tests?* (pp. 37–64). Mahwah, NJ: Erlbaum.

Schumacker, R. E., & Lomax, R. G. (1996). *A beginner's guide to structural equation modeling.* Mahwah, NJ: Erlbaum.

Schumacker, R. E., & Marcoulides, G. A. (Eds.). (1998). *Interaction and nonlinear effects in structural equation modeling.* Mahwah, NJ: Erlbaum.

Shahar, G., Chinman, M., Sells, D., & Davidson, L. (2003). An action model of socially disruptive behaviors committed by persons with severe mental illness: The role of self-reported childhood abuse and suspiciousness–hostility. *Psychiatry, 66,* 42–52.

Shen, B.-J., & Takeuchi, D. T. (2001). A structural model of acculturation and mental health status among Chinese Americans. *American Journal of Community Psychology, 29,* 387–418.

Shrout, P. E., & Bolger, N. (2002). Mediation in experimental and nonexperimental studies: New procedures and recommendations. *Psychological Methods, 7,* 422–445.

Sikström, S. (2001). Forgetting curves: Implications for connectionist models. *Cognitive Psychology, 45,* 95–152.

Silvia, E. S. M., & MacCallum, R. C. (1988). Some factors affecting the success of specification searches in covariance structure modeling. *Multivariate Behavioral Research, 23,* 297–326.

Smith, R. L., Ager, J. W., & Williams, D. L. (1992). Suppressor variables in multiple regression/correlation. *Educational and Psychological Measurement, 52,* 17–29.

Snyder, P., & Lawson, S. (1993). Evaluating results using corrected and uncorrected effect size estimates. *Journal of Experimental Education, 61,* 334–349.

Sobel, M. E. (1986). Some new results on indirect effects and their standard errors in covariance structure models. In N. B. Tuma (Ed.), *Sociological methodology* (pp. 159–186). San Francisco: Jossey-Bass.

Sörbom, D. (1974). A general method for studying differences in factor means and structure between groups. *British Journal of Mathematical and Statistical Psychology, 27,* 229–239.

Spearman, C. (1904). General intelligence, objectively determined and measured. *American Journal of Psychology, 15,* 201–293.

StatSoft Inc. (2003). STATISTICA (Version 6.1) [Computer software]. Tulsa, OK: Author.

Steiger, J. H. (1990). Structural model evaluation and modification: An interval estimation approach. *Multivariate Behavioral Research, 25,* 173–180.

Steiger, J. H. (2001). Driving fast in reverse: The relationship between software development, theory, and education in structural equation modeling. *Journal of the American Statistical Association, 96,* 331–338.

Steiger, J. H. (2002). When constraints interact: A caution about reference variables, identification constraints, and scale dependencies in structural equation modeling. *Psychological Methods, 7,* 210–227.

Steiger, J. H., & Fouladi, R. T. (1997). Noncentrality interval estimation and the evaluation of statistical models. In L. L. Harlow, S. A. Mulaik, & J. H. Steiger (Eds.), *What if there were no significance tests?* (pp. 221–257). Mahwah, NJ: Erlbaum.

Stevens, J. (2002). *Applied multivariate statistics for the social sciences* (4th ed.). Hillsdale, NJ: Erlbaum.

Stewart, E. A., Simons, R. L., Conger, R. D., & Scarmella, L. V. (2002). Beyond the interactional relationship between delinquency and parenting practices: The contributions of legal sanctions. *Journal of Research in Crime and Delinquency, 39,* 36–59.

Strube, M. J. (2000). Reliability and generalizability theory. In L. G. Grimm & P. R. Yarnold (Eds.), *Reading and understanding more multivariate statistics* (pp. 23–66). Washington, DC: American Psychological Association.

Systat Software Inc. (2002). SYSTAT (Version 10.2) [Computer software]. Richmond, CA: Author.

Thompson, B. (1992). Two and one-half decades of leadership in measurement and evaluation. *Journal of Counseling and Development, 70,* 434–438.

Thompson, B. (Ed.). (2003). *Score reliability: Contemporary thinking on reliability issues.* Thousand Oaks, CA: Sage.

Tomarken, A. J., & Waller, N. G. (2003). Potential problems with "well-fitting" models. *Journal of Abnormal Psychology, 112,* 578–598.

van Prooijen, J.-W., & van der Kloot, W. A. (2001). Confirmatory analysis of exploratively obtained factor structures. *Educational and Psychological Measurement, 61,* 777–792.

Vriens, M., & Melton, E. (2002). Managing missing data. *Marketing Research, 14,* 12–17.

Wagner, R. K., Torgeson, J. K., & Rashotte, C. A. (1994). Development of reading-related phonological processing abilities: New evidence of a bidirectional causality from a latent variable longitudinal study. *Developmental Psychology, 30,* 73–87.

West, S. G. (2001). New approaches to missing data in psychological research [Special section]. *Psychological Methods, 6(4).*

Widaman, K. F., & Thompson, J. S. (2003). On specifying the null model for incremental fit indexes in structural equation modeling. *Psychological Methods, 8,* 16–37.

Wilkinson, L., & the Task Force on Statistical Inference. (1999). Statistical methods in psychology journals: Guidelines and explanations. *American Psychologist, 54,* 594–604.

Willett, J. B., & Sayer, A. G. (1994). Using covariance structure analysis to detect correlates and predictors of individual change over time. *Psychological Bulletin, 116,* 363–381.

Willett, J. B., & Sayer, A. G. (1996). Cross-domain analyses of change over time:

Combining growth modeling and covariance structure analysis. In G. A. Marcoulides & R. E. Schumacker (Eds.), *Advanced structural equation modeling* (pp. 125–157). Mahwah, NJ: Erlbaum.

Williams, R., & Thomson, E. (1986). Normalization issues in latent variable modeling. *Sociological Methods and Research, 15,* 24–43.

Williams, T. O., Jr., Eaves, R. C., & Cox, C. (2002). Confirmatory factor analysis of an instrument designed to measure affective and cognitive arousal. *Educational and Psychological Measurement, 62,* 264–283.

Winer, B. J., Brown, D. R., & Michels, K. M. (1991). *Statistical principles in experimental design* (3rd ed.) Boston: McGraw-Hill.

Wolfle, L. M. (2003). The introduction of path analysis to the social sciences, and some emergent themes: An annotated bibliography. *Structural Equation Modeling, 10,* 1–34.

Worland, J., Weeks, G. G., Janes, C. L., & Strock, B. D. (1984). Intelligence, classroom behavior, and academic achievement in children at high and low risk for psychopathology: A structural equation analysis. *Journal of Abnormal Child Psychology, 12,* 437–454.

Wothke, W. (1996). Models for multitrait–multimethod matrix analysis. In G. A. Marcoulides & R. E. Schumacker (Eds.), *Advanced structural equation modeling* (pp. 5–56). Mahwah, NJ: Erlbaum.

Wright, S. (1921). Correlation and causation. *Journal of Agricultural Research, 20,* 557–585.

Wright, S. (1934). The method of path coefficients. *Annals of Mathematical Statistics, 5,* 161–215.

Yung, Y.-F., & Bentler, P. M. (1996). Bootstrapping techniques in analysis of mean and covariance structures. In G. A. Marcoulides & R. E. Schumacker (Eds.), *Advanced structural equation modeling* (pp. 195–226). Mahwah, NJ: Erlbaum.

Author Index

352

Subject Index

Italicized page numbers indicate tables and figures.

356